敦煌文化·译丛（汉英对照）

Dunhuang Culture in Translation: A Series

主　编　姜秋霞

副主编　[美]安瑞　柳菁

艺苑瑰宝
莫高窟壁画与彩塑

Art Treasures: Murals and Painted Sculptures in Mogao Caves

赵声良　著　姜焕文　译

甘肃教育出版社

图书在版编目（CIP）数据

艺苑瑰宝：莫高窟壁画与彩塑 =Art Treasures: Murals and Painted Sculptures in Mogao Caves：汉英对照 / 赵声良著；姜焕文译. -- 兰州：甘肃教育出版社，2021.11
（敦煌文化·译丛 / 姜秋霞主编）
ISBN 978-7-5423-5147-0

Ⅰ.①艺… Ⅱ.①赵… ②姜… Ⅲ.①敦煌壁画－介绍－汉、英②敦煌石窟－彩塑－介绍－汉、英 Ⅳ.①K879.41②K879.3

中国版本图书馆CIP数据核字(2021)第135838号

艺苑瑰宝——莫高窟壁画与彩塑
Art Treasures: Murals and Painted Sculptures in Mogao Caves

赵声良 著　　姜焕文 译

责任编辑　李慧娟
封面设计　石　璞
内文设计　方　圆
图片支持　敦煌研究院

出　　版　甘肃教育出版社
社　　址　兰州市读者大道568号　　730030
网　　址　www.gseph.cn　　E-mail　gseph@duzhe.cn
电　　话　0931-8436105（编辑部）　　0931-8773056（发行部）
传　　真　0931-8773056
淘宝官方旗舰店　http://shop111038270.taobao.com

发　　行　甘肃教育出版社　　印　刷　山东新华印务有限公司
开　　本　787毫米×1092毫米　1/16　　印　张　26.25　　字　数　396千
版　　次　2021年11月第1版
印　　次　2021年11月第1次印刷
书　　号　ISBN 978-7-5423-5147-0　　定　价　98.00元

图书若有破损、缺页可随时与印厂联系：0531-82079130
本书所有内容经作者同意授权，并许可使用。
未经同意，不得以任何形式复制转载。

"丝绸之路·敦煌文化翻译"工程
编委会

主　　任：王嘉毅
副 主 任：王刚毅　郭锦诗　姜秋霞　杨　平
顾　　问：黄友义　郑炳林

主　　编：姜秋霞
副 主 编：Andrea M. Harwell（美）
编　　委：（按姓氏音序排序）
　　　　　白玉春　崇天霖　贾　慧　姜焕文
　　　　　柳　菁　刘晓霞　马凌飞　辛红娟
　　　　　徐　珂　曾丽馨　赵粉琴

"丝绸之路·敦煌文化翻译"工程是甘肃文化翻译中心在甘肃省委宣传部的领导下所实施的文化翻译工程，旨在助力共建"一带一路"，弘扬丝路文化和敦煌文化，推进敦煌文化国际交流与传播，推动中国文化"走出去"。

"敦煌文化·译丛"为"丝绸之路·敦煌文化翻译"工程系列成果之一。

三危山 (赵声良 摄)
The Sanwei Mountain (photo: Zhao Shengliang)

"敦煌文化·译丛"简介

近年来,在"中华文化走出去""讲好中国故事"与共建"一带一路"的大背景下,充分展示了中华民族文化自信的敦煌文化,以其丰富的内涵和独特的魅力吸引着全世界的目光。越来越多的海内外人士渴望掀起敦煌文化神秘的面纱,走近敦煌,从而走进敦煌。"敦煌文化·译丛"的编纂,以"敦煌文化走出去"为目标,以"讲好敦煌故事"为原则,对外传播敦煌文化,交流敦煌学思想,传承敦煌精神。

一、丛书内容

"敦煌文化·译丛"在传播内容上重视知识的可接受度,甄选了既有学术价值,又便于普及的敦煌学著作和敦煌文化读物进行翻译。所选书籍均为敦煌学著名专家所著,集学术性与科普性于一体,且呈现出一定的系统性,主题逐步涵盖敦煌文化完整版图,着力打造出相对全面的敦煌文化外宣丛书体系。本系列译丛采用中外语言对照的编纂方式,传播敦煌文化,交流敦煌学研究思想等。

"敦煌文化·译丛"以开放的模式分期分批编辑出版。第一辑包含《丝路明珠:敦煌》《艺苑瑰宝:莫高窟壁画与彩塑》《箫管霓裳:敦煌乐舞》及《遗响千年:敦煌的影响》四部作品的汉英对照读本。

《丝路明珠:敦煌》(郑炳林、李军著)以敦煌的历史、地位和周边名胜古迹为主题,分别讲述了从新石器时代、两汉、魏晋南北朝到西夏、元、明、清各个不同朝代历史背景下敦煌的发展和变迁;论述了丝绸之路开通后,敦煌作为中西交通线路上的重要枢纽、中西贸易的中转站和中央王朝经营西域的军事重镇的历史地位;介绍了包括莫高窟、榆林窟等佛教石窟,玉门关、阳关等城池关隘,及鸣沙山、月牙泉等自然景观在内的敦煌周边历史文化名胜和古迹。全书脉络清晰,语言生动,集资料性、故事性和知识性于一体,既突出了敦煌的地域文化特点,又展现了敦煌厚重的历史内涵,使这颗沉睡在茫茫大漠之中的璀璨明珠在世人面前焕发出夺目的光华。

《艺苑瑰宝:莫高窟壁画与彩塑》(赵声良著)概括介绍了敦煌彩塑和壁画的基本风貌,包括塑像、佛像画、飞天、故事画、经变画、山水画、装饰画等单元,并阐述了包含其中的文化价值、历史价值、艺术价值,展示出千年中国美术的脉络。这本书还对古代印度、中亚艺术与中国艺术的交流与融合作了分析,全书浸透着作者全方位学术研究的成果,以及自豪自信的文化情怀。文笔流畅,深入浅出,图文并茂,雅俗共赏,把博大精深的敦煌艺术成功地传达给了读者。

《箫管霓裳:敦煌乐舞》(王克芬、柴剑虹著)以敦煌莫高窟为主题,分别介绍了敦煌乐舞的人文背景及源流、经变画中的天宫乐舞、世俗画里的歌舞、特色鲜明的民族舞蹈、生动活泼的童子舞姿、敦煌乐舞的文化特征等内容。作者用凝练、简洁、流畅的笔触,以敦煌莫高窟壁画、彩塑为着眼点,文解图义,栩栩如生地展示了敦煌莫高窟壁画中丰富多彩的佛国乐舞形象。全书凝练紧凑,主题鲜明,语言流畅,专业性与普及性兼顾,为中外读者了解与欣赏敦煌乐舞打开了一扇大门。

《遗响千年:敦煌的影响》(刘进宝著)以敦煌文献的整理刊布与敦煌艺术探索和文艺创作为主题,分别介绍了敦煌学的产生背景、敦煌文献在各国的研究概况、中外文化艺术名人与敦煌的故事、敦煌艺术光辉照耀下的文学艺术创作成果、敦煌文物的保护及研究等内容。作者用通俗易懂、生动活泼的语言,将专业性与普及性融为一体,让读者与敦煌渐行渐近,相知相亲,向世人展现了敦煌文化在中国和世界所产生的深远影响。全书图文并茂、材料翔实、叙述生动,吸引中外读者走进敦煌辉煌灿烂的文化圣殿与艺术宝库。

这四部作品涵盖了敦煌文化中的重要板块,系统阐释了敦煌文化的历史发展、艺术价值与人文精神。一方面,从本体视角出发介绍敦煌的历史地理知识;另一方面,从认识视角出发展示敦煌文化艺术中最为人感知的两张名片——壁画雕塑与音乐舞蹈；最终，从价值视角出发凸显敦煌文化及敦煌学在全世界产生的影响。本系列译丛将促进敦煌艺术之美的国际化交流，补充与敦煌乐舞相关的深度双语语料，拓展敦煌历史地理相关的系统语言资料，为"敦煌在中国、敦煌学在世界"这一国际化命题提供了必要参考。

二、译介特点

"敦煌文化·译丛"以"传播敦煌文化，交流敦煌学思想"为主旨，采用"中英对照"的形式讲述敦煌故事、阐释敦煌精神。在译介方式上，运用多元的翻译策略和方法，进行文本对比与转换。在原文阐释上，一方面通过系统查阅历史文献、背景资料、中外敦煌学研究成果等，深刻理解原文语义；另一方面通过译者与原作者的对话与沟通，精准把握敦煌文化的精髓要义。在外文表达上，注重信息的有效表达，通过"中西合璧"的模式展开翻译，由中外译者通力合作，以"读者接受"为主导，运用适切的话语方式，综合的翻译方法，进行语言转换。译文尽可能贴近英语读者的表达习惯、思维模式、语言风格和理解能力，使所译作品不仅在文字上实现了"走出去"，同时使其文化内涵真正能够"走进去"，力图实现文化的深度传播。

"敦煌文化·译丛"的总体翻译原则：在充分理解和尊重原文的基础上，对于汉英语言文化中存在对应概念和表达的内容，尽量忠实于原文的内容和风格，力求准确再现原文的语言和文化信息。在遵循翻译基本原理的前提下，根据汉英两种语言和文化之间的差异，综合运用"归化""异化""融合化"等翻译策略，对原文部分内容进行适度的增减编改，灵活采用节译、概译、编译和解释性翻译等方法进行语言文本的转换。

"敦煌文化·译丛"的基本翻译方法：

1. 对于原文中文化概念和术语的翻译，一般采用我国官方出版物和官方网站中已有的外文表达。

2. 对于中国的历史朝代，在外文文本中补充了公元纪年法中的年份信息。但对于个别年代信息有争议的历史朝代，则不再标注年份。

3. 对于历史官衔名称，以"传播历史文化，兼顾读者理解"为目的，采用

"音译+名词""音译+释义"等方法，一方面保留原有的文化特质，另一方面使读者易于接受；对于官衔、官职修饰词语过多的情况，则采用意译或概译的方法进行语义对应；对于官职官衔名在不同历史时期，虽名称未变，但语义内涵发生变化的，根据其语境中相应的含义进行转换。

4. 对于原文中出现的书籍名称，首先遵循"名从历史""名从主人"的原则，沿用已有的译名。如果已有译名为汉语拼音，则在保留原有名称的基础上，增补英文译名；无英译文的书籍名称，则采用常规翻译方法进行文本对应。

5. 对于原文中的引文（如诗词、古籍文献），根据引文的作用进行有选择性的转换。若引文为核心论点，或用于描写相应的文化内容，且上下文未对引文内容进行解释或重述，则全文翻译；若引文仅用于衬托或强化相应的文化内容，且相关内容已在上下文说明或提及，则进行概译或省译。

6. 对于一些描写壁画形象的直白语言，为提升其艺术美感，采用"优化"的策略和"解释性翻译"的方法，进行语篇结构的扩充对应。

7. 对于宗教文化概念，首先采用已有的英文表达；对于有固定梵语表达的佛教概念，则采用"回译法"进行转换；没有约定俗成表达的宗教概念、中国本土宗教概念及其他宗教与中国文化相融合后产生的概念，则根据情况采用音译、直译或意译进行文本对应。

8. 对于需要补充文化背景信息的内容，一般采用"译者注"的方式进行补充说明，以便更有效地提高阅读理解力。包括但不限于下列情况：一是对于一些在历史演变过程中语义发生变化的文化名称，采用"译者注"的方式加以说明，如"刺史"这一官职名称，分别译为Inspector / Governor / Prefect，并通过"译者注"说明同一名称在不同历史时期因其职责发生变化采用不同译文的背景信息。二是对于一些特殊地名，为避免产生阅读障碍，在翻译的同时加"译者注"进行说明，如不以行政区划命名的大地区概念（中原、西域等），翻译的同时，通过"译者注"明确其内涵和范围；含有古代行政区划"州""郡""府""县""道"等的地名，在翻译行政区划词的同时适当增加"译者注"解释其含义；由于历史原因更改地名的，亦通过"译者注"加以阐明。三是当同音异义词音译后在译文中无法分辨时，也采用"译者注"的方式加以区分。

9. 本译丛遵循一致性原则,运用统一的翻译策略和方法,但同时也存在一些体现译者个体风格的差异化表达。

三、几点说明

1. 中文文本之外附加的内容,如附录等,经与中文作者沟通,不再收录。

2. 中文文本中个别问题需要进行勘误时,英译文转换正确的语义内容,同时增加必要的说明。

3. 本译丛在翻译过程中参考了大量国内外相关著作、辞典、图册、音像资料、网络资料及数据库等,具体参考目录将在每本书后单另列出。

最后需要说明的是,敦煌文化翻译是一项十分具有挑战性的工作,难点很多,难度很大。因此,作为"丝绸之路·敦煌文化翻译"工程的第一辑译丛,在翻译中难免存在许多不足之处,甚至可能有误译和错译之处。我们真诚期待广大读者、专家学者批评指正!

致 谢

"敦煌文化·译丛"在策划、翻译、出版过程中得到甘肃省委宣传部、中国外文局、兰州大学敦煌学研究所等单位的大力支持;在翻译过程中得到了著作者的翻译授权和学术指导;同时得到了甘肃省人民政府新闻办、兰州城市学院等单位的支持,在此一并感谢。

"敦煌文化·译丛"编委会

An Introduction to *Dunhuang Culture in Translation: A Series*

In recent years, Dunhuang culture—an emblem of the pride of Chinese civilization—has increasingly attracted the world's attention with its profound significance and unique charms. This has taken place against the backdrop of "Chinese culture going global," "telling China's story to the world," and the joint pursuit of the Belt and Road Initiative. Ever-increasing numbers of people both internationally and domestically want Dunhuang's veil of mystery to be lifted. Through reading this series, people can become more familiar with Dunhuang, paving the way to really "get into" Dunhuang. Thus, along the principles of "Dunhuang culture going forth into the world," as well as "telling Dunhuang's story," the *Dunhuang Culture in Translation* series has been compiled with the goal of communicating the concepts of Dunhuang culture, carrying on the spirit of Dunhuang, and promoting Dunhuang to an international audience.

Series Content

The *Dunhuang Culture in Translation: A Series* emphasizes appropriateness for its readers, selecting works in the field of Dunhuang studies which embody academic value and also can be made accessible to a general audience. All the books in this series were written by well-known experts in the field of Dunhuang studies, blending academic knowledge with popular science and presenting information in a systematic way, and using a compilation method in both Chinese and English. The topics cover the essential part of Dunhuang culture, resulting in a relatively comprehensive framework for disseminating this subject to the world. The translated volumes in this series use a Chinese-English format to promote Dunhuang culture and academic exchanges of Dunhuang studies.

Dunhuang Culture in Translation is a multi-volumed, inclusive series published in sets. The first set in the series includes four bilingual volumes: *Dunhuang: Pearl of the Silk Road*; *Art Treasures: Murals and Painted Sculptures in Mogao Caves*; *Raiment of Rainbows and Feathers: Music and Dance from the Dunhuang Murals*; and *Dunhuang: Its Everlasting Impact.*

Dunhuang: Pearl of the Silk Road (by Zheng Binglin and Li Jun) takes as its subject matter the history of Dunhuang as well as its surrounding attractions. It traces Dunhuang's development and changes against the historical background of different periods, from the Neolithic Age, the Han Dynasty, Wei, Jin, Northern and Southern dynasties to the Western Xia, Yuan, Ming, and Qing dynasties. This volume explores the opening of the Silk Road and Dunhuang's historical status as an important crossroads for Sino-Western exchanges, the part it played as an important hub for Sino-Western trade, and its role as a military center for the Central Plains' operations in the Western Regions. It introduces the Buddhist rock-cut cave temples of the Mogao Caves and the Yulin Caves, historical and cultural sites such as the Yangguan and Yumen passes, and surrounding natural scenic spots including the Mingsha Mountain and the Crescent Moon Spring. The whole book is presented with clear ideas and vivid language, integrating factual data, literary narrative, and scholarly expertise. It not only highlights the regional cultural characteristics of Dunhuang, but also reveals its profound historical connotations as well, making this bright pearl, sleeping in the vast desert, glow with its brilliance for the world to see.

Art Treasures: Murals and Painted Sculptures in Mogao Caves (by Zhao Shengliang) outlines the basic features of Dunhuang sculptures and murals, including polychromed statues, Buddhist iconography, apsaras, narrative paintings, sutra illustrations, landscape paintings, decorative motifs, and other elements, expounding their cultural, historical, and artistic value in addition to tracing the course of Chinese art for thousands of years. This volume, steeped in Dr. Zhao's comprehensive academic research and brimming with pride in Chinese culture, also analyzes the exchange and synthesis of visual arts from ancient India, Central Asia, and China. The writing is fluent and easy to understand, with copious illustrations accompanying the text. Sharing an appreciation of both the sophisticated and the popular, it successfully conveys Dunhuang's broad and profound art to its readers.

Raiment of Rainbows and Feathers: Music and Dance from the Dunhuang Murals (by Wang Kefen and Chai Jianhong) takes the Mogao Caves as its subject, introducing the cultural background and origins of Dunhuang music and dance, images of palace entertainment depicted in sutra illustrations, singing and dancing as found in secular paintings, distinctive ethnic dances, the lively lotus child dance, and more. The authors use concise and natural language to discuss the murals and the painted sculptures of the Mogao Caves, explaining the meaning of the images and vividly revealing the rich Buddhist and Chinese music and dance images found in Dunhuang wall paintings. Compact and concise, the book's themes are clear and the language is articulate, with an emphasis on balancing professional scholarship with accessibility to the public, opening the door for readers at home and abroad to understand and appreciate the performing arts of Dunhuang.

Dunhuang: Its Everlasting Impact (by Liu Jinbao) takes the compilation and classification of Dunhuang manuscripts, the exploration of Dunhuang art, and Dunhuang literary creation as its themes. It introduces the background of Dunhuang studies as a field, the research overview of Dunhuang manuscripts in various countries, the famous names behind Dunhuang studies both in China and around the world, and the literary and creative achievements in Dunhuang art, as well as the research, and conservation of Dunhuang relics. The author uses easy-to-understand, lively and dynamic language to integrate scholarship with mass-market appeal, allowing readers to "get closer" to Dunhuang, showing the profound influence of Dunhuang culture in China and internationally. The book's pictures and texts, informative materials, and vivid narrative style encourage both Chinese and English-speaking audiences to truly enter the brilliant cultural temples and treasure houses of Dunhuang.

The four works in this set form a system of their own, covering important areas of the Dunhuang cultural sphere, and systematically explaining the historical development, artistic value, and humanistic spirit of Dunhuang culture. On the one hand, the main objective of the books sets out to introduce the history and geography of Dunhuang, while on the other hand, it explores two of the most well-known aspects of Dunhuang arts: the visual arts and the performing arts. Finally, judging from its value, the set highlights the influence of Dunhuang culture and Dunhuang studies around the world. This collection of translations aims to promote international understanding of the aesthetics of Dunhuang art, supplement in-depth bilingual works related to Dunhuang music and dance, expand systematic language materials related to Dunhuang history and geography, and provide a must-have language reference for researchers of Dunhuang studies both in China and overseas.

Special Features of the Translation

Dunhuang Culture in Translation is organized around the themes of promoting Dunhuang culture and transmitting Dunhuang thought, telling the stories of Dunhuang, and expounding the spirit of Dunhuang in a Chinese-English format. In terms of translation methods, this series uses multiple strategies and methods to compare and translate texts. In terms of the interpretation of the original text, on the one hand, we can deeply understand the semantics of the original text through systematic review of historical documents, background materials, and research results in Dunhuang studies in China as well as internationally; on the other hand, we can accurately grasp the essence of Dunhuang culture through dialogue and communication between the translators and the original authors. In terms of foreign language expression, special attention has been paid to the effective expression of information. The translation has been done according to a Sino-Western model. The Chinese and English language translators have closely cooperated with one other, with reader accessibility as their primary consideration, using appropriate discourse modes and comprehensive translation methods to exchange languages. The translation is as close as possible to the idiomatic expression, modes of thought, language style, and reading comprehension of English-language readers, so that the translated text of the works not only achieves a "going out" in a literary sense, but simultaneously also allows the cultural connotations to truly "go in" and achieve a deep transmission into the readers' conceptualization.

The overarching translation principles of the *Dunhuang Culture in Translation: A Series* are as follows: on the basis of understanding and respecting the original text, for those expressions which have a corresponding concept and expression in English language and culture, the translation strives to accurately reproduce the original language and cultural information, faithful to the content and style of the original Chinese text. Moreover, on the premise of following standard principles of translation, according to differences between Chinese and English languages and cultures we have comprehensively employed translation strategies such as domestication, foreignization, and fusion to appropriately add, delete, edit, and modify the original content. We have adopted a flexible mixture of approaches such as abridged translation, generalized translation, compilation, and interpretative translation for language and text conversion.

The basic translation methods for the *Dunhuang Culture in Translation: A Series* are as follows:

1. For the translation of cultural concepts and terminology in the original text, foreign language expressions found in official publications and official websites of China have generally been used.

2. For historical dynasties, information for the dates using AD and BC has been added to the foreign language text. However, for historical dynasties with dates in dispute, the year is not noted.

3. For the translations of historical titles of official rank, our purpose is to enhance exchanges of history and culture, taking into account the readers' understanding. Thus, we have employed methods such as "*pinyin* transliteration + nouns," and "*pinyin* transliteration + gloss," on the one hand, retaining the original cultural characteristics of the titles, and, on the other hand, allowing readers to easily accept the title names. For official titles with multiple versions or modifiers, free translation or generalized translation methods have been used for semantic correspondence; for official titles from different historical periods, when the name has remained unchanged, but the semantic connotation has changed, the meaning has been conveyed according to the appropriate context.

4. For the titles of Chinese books, the principles of "using historical names" and "using names created by the original parties" have been followed. If an existing title is in *pinyin*, the English translation has been added on the basis of keeping the original name; if there is no English translation of the name of the classic text, conventional translation methods have been applied.

5. For citations or quotations in the original text (such as poems, classics), selective conversion has been carried out according to the function of the citation. If a quotation or citation functions as a core idea or is used to describe corresponding cultural content, and the context does not explain or restate the citation content, the full text is translated; if the quotation is only used to highlight or strengthen the corresponding cultural content, and the relevant content has been explained or mentioned in the context, general translation or deletion has been applied.

6. For certain basic, straightforward language describing mural imagery, in order to enhance their artistic beauty, "optimization" strategies and interpretative translation methods have been applied to expand the text.

7. For religious and cultural concepts, we have first adopted existing English terms and expressions where they exist; for Buddhist concepts with fixed, conventional Sanskrit names, we have used the back translation method to convert the terms from Chinese back into their original Sanskrit again. Religious concepts that are not expressed by conventional usage or fixed terms, native Chinese religious concepts, and concepts arising from the fusion of other religions and Chinese culture have been rendered by transliteration, literal translation or free translation based on the situation or context.

8. For the content that needs to be supplemented with cultural background information, we have generally used footnotes as supplementary explanations, in order to more effectively improve the readers' comprehension. This includes but is not limited to the following situations: First, for some cultural names whose semantics have changed in the course of historical evolution, we have used footnotes to explain them. For example, the official title of "*cishi*" is translated variously as Inspector, Governor, or Prefect, and a footnote is used to explain that the title for this post was modified over time due to changes in the position's responsibilities in

different historical periods. Second, for special place names, footnotes have been added to avoid confusion. For example, the concept of large geographical regions such as the Central Plains, the Western Regions, and so forth, was provided with footnotes to clarify their meaning and scope. Footnotes have been provided for place names with ancient administrative divisions such as "*zhou*" "*jun*" "*fu*" "*xian*" "*dao*" etc., where necessary or appropriate. Changes in place names due to historical reasons have also been clarified through the addition of footnotes. Third, when homophones cannot be distinguished in the translation after transliteration, footnotes or annotations have also been used to distinguish them.

9. This translation series follows the principle of consistency and uses unified translation strategies and methods, but some terms and expressions may vary and reflect the individual style of the translators.

Special Points for the Readers' Consideration

1. Appendices, indices, and glossaries in the original Chinese versions are not included in the volumes of this set, which is permitted by the original authors.

2. Where individual issues in the Chinese text have required correction, the information in the English translation has been presented in the corrected, revised form, and explanations have been added where necessary.

3. This translation series relies on a large number of Chinese and English language reference works, dictionaries, atlases, audiovisual materials, internet resources, and databases during the translation process. A specific bibliography is listed separately at the back of each volume.

One final thing to be said is that Dunhuang culture translation is a very demanding task, with many difficulties and great challenges. Therefore, as the first series in the Silk Road Dunhuang Culture Translation Project, there are inevitably many shortcomings in the translation, and there may even be mistranslations and errors. We sincerely encourage criticism and correction from readers, experts, and scholars in the field.

Introduction

Acknowledgements

The *Dunhuang Culture in Translation : A Series* received strong support from the Publicity Department of the Gansu Provincial Party Committee, China Foreign Languages Publishing Administration, Institute of Dunhuang Studies of Lanzhou University, and other governmental offices in the planning, translation, and publication process of this series. Throughout the translation process, permission, authorization, and guidance were granted by the authors of each volume. The Information Office of the People's Government of Gansu Province, Lanzhou City University as well as other governmental offices and leaders all gave their encouragement and support to this project. We extend our heartfelt thanks and gratitude to them all.

Editorial Committee of *Dunhuang Culture in Translation: A Series*

目　录

序言一	001
序言二	008
序言三	023
前言	001
充满人间气息的佛像	001
早期彩塑——外来风格与中原风格并存	004
隋代——风格的转变期	019
唐代——走向世俗化	026
佛像画的世界	043
说法图	045
菩萨	061
天王、力士（药叉）	074
美丽的天使——飞天艺术	079
飞天是什么	081
北朝的飞天	087
隋代的飞天	100
唐代前期的飞天	106
唐代后期的飞天	116

Contents

Foreword I

Foreword II

Foreword III

Introduction

Images of the Buddha Filled with the Spirit of the Mortal World

Early Painted Sculptures: Foreign Patterns Juxtaposed with Styles from the Central Plains

The Sui Period: Transformation of Styles

The Tang Period: Towards Secularization

The World of Painted Buddhist Iconography

Dharma-Preaching Scenes

Bodhisattvas

Heavenly Kings and *Lokapalas*

Angels of Beauty: the Art of *Apsaras*

What are *Apsaras*?

Apsaras of the Northern Dynasties

Apsaras of the Sui Dynasty

Apsaras of the Early Tang

Apsaras of the Late Tang

目 录

佛教故事画 **125**
佛传故事画 128
充满牺牲精神的本生故事 140
具有忠孝思想的佛教故事 152
佛教史迹故事画 161
附属于经变画中的故事 169
故事画的艺术成就 178

佛国之境(经变画) **181**
涅槃经变 184
维摩诘经变 193
弥勒经变 204
阿弥陀经变、无量寿经变、观无量寿经变 211
药师经变 223
法华经变 229
报恩经变及其他经变画 241
经变画的艺术成就 251

青山绿水看唐风 **255**
北朝至隋代的山水画 258
雍容华美之风——唐代前期壁画中的山水 278
恬静淡泊之景——唐代后期壁画中的山水 301
屏风画中的山水 310
五台山图 317

装饰的艺术 **323**

敦煌壁画的风格与成就 **337**

参考文献(原文) **351**

参考文献(译文) **352**

Contents

Buddhist Narrative Paintings

Narratives of the Buddha's Life

Jataka Tales Imbued with the Spirit of Sacrifice

Buddhist Narratives Marked by Loyalty and Filial Piety

Narratives of Buddhist Legends and Transmission

Tales Affiliated with Sutra Illustrations

Artistic Achievements in Buddhist Narrative Paintings

Realms of the Buddhist World: Sutra Illustrations

Nirvana Sutra Illustrations

Vimalakirti Nirdesa Illustrations

Maitreya Triple Sutra Illustrations

Amitabha Sutra, Sukhavativyuha Sutra, and *Amitayurdhyana Sutra* Illustrations

Bhaisajyaguru Sutra Illustrations

Lotus Sutra Illustrations

Sutra of Requiting Kindness Received Illustrations and Others

Artistic Achievements in Sutra Illustrations

Blue–Green Landscape: Styles of the Tang Dynasty

Landscapes from the Northern Dynasties to the Sui Dynasty

Pursuit of Grace and Beauty: Landscapes in Early Tang Murals

Peaceful and Simple Scenery: Landscapes in Late Tang Murals

Landscapes in Screen Paintings

The *Map of Mount Wutai*

The Art of Ornamentation

Style and Artistic Achievements of the Dunhuang Murals

Works Cited

Translation References

菩萨 莫高窟第57窟南壁 初唐
Bodhisattva, Mogao Cave 57, Early Tang

序言一

1975年,中国与英国签订了教育交流协议,恢复了中断将近10年的留学生互换项目。我作为首批留学生之一,同14位同学到英国学习。与此同时,英国学生也到中国留学。很多年以后,我遇到其中一位当年曾经在北京大学留学的英国学者,那时她已经是大英图书馆的东亚部负责人。她告诉我正在做的一件事情就是和中国文物局合作,把大英图书馆收藏的来自敦煌的历史资料复制给中方,以此加深两国专家围绕敦煌学的研究活动。可见因为历史上的多种原因,大量敦煌资料流散在海外,这对中国是一种损失,但是也催化了国外对敦煌的关注。

然而,敦煌学不局限于仅仅流散在海外的史料研究,真正的研究中心永远在敦煌,永远在中国。比如石窟代表的敦煌文化就是搬不走的,敦煌背后的历史和哲学思想是搬不走的。近些年,中国学者对敦煌的研究成绩斐然,加之敦煌文化的博大精深,非常有必要通过翻译,把中国学者的研究成果,把敦煌文化的精华,大张旗鼓地传播出去。特别是"一带一路"倡议不仅强化了中国与沿线国家的经济活动,也拉近了文化上的联系。民心相通首先要以文明互鉴为依托,以文化传播为纽带,达到美美与共。敦煌文化重要,对外传播更为重要。然而,集历史、艺术、宗教为一体的敦煌学覆盖历史时段长,涉及艺术门类全,代表的宗教影响深,反映的社会发展广,要翻译成外文实在太难了。

令人欣喜的是,以甘肃文化翻译中心姜秋霞教授领衔的团队卧薪尝胆、呕心沥血达六年,终于把首批共四部中英文对照版的"敦煌文化·译丛"呈现给国内外的读者。这四部图书分别是《丝路明珠:敦煌》《艺苑瑰宝:莫高窟壁画与彩塑》《箫管霓裳:敦煌乐舞》和《遗响千年:敦煌的影响》。这套图书的出版标志着我国首次有计划、成规模地、系统地把敦煌文化最新的研究成果用英文对外介绍。四本书用当代的语言把一个中国故事的过去与现在讲述给国际受众。这个翻译出版项目成就有多大,其艰难历程就有多长。翻译难,中译外更难,敦煌文化的翻译难上加难。这六年来,姜教授的团队经历了多少艰辛,比如为寻找一个准确的词汇花费多少心血,为精准传达一个观点熬去多少时光,读者只需翻阅一下这四本书,就会一目了然。

既然难度这么大,为什么还要翻译?姜教授说:"翻译,不仅仅是语言的转换,更是对文化的阐释。翻译敦煌文化,不是简单的话码转换,也不是单纯的信息传递,更重要的是解释和阐释敦煌文化和历史遗存蕴含的哲学思想、人文精神、价值理念、道德规范;弘扬和传承蕴含其中的中华民族的文化精神、文化胸怀和文化自信。"通过她的话我感到,敦煌文化翻译反映了译者的一种家国情怀、对外传播的理想抱负和迎难而上的治学精神。没有坚定的信念、远大的抱负和刻苦的工作干劲,译者早已在翻译任务的困难面前望而却步。所以,在向译者团队表示祝贺的同时,我更想向他们表示崇高的敬意。

一套丛书有那么大的意义吗?文明互鉴需要文化信息的交流,做好对外交流就是要拿出外国人读得懂、看得明白的作品来。展示文化自信,需要拿出难啃的硬骨头成果来。这套丛书就是文化自信的产物,敦煌文化对外传播的最新之作。

然而,"敦煌文化·译丛"的意义不仅仅在作品上。丛书的翻译还是翻译团队不断成熟的一个过程。"敦煌文化·译丛"是"丝绸之路·敦煌文化翻译工程"的第一期项目。启动后译者发现翻译的难度极大,文化概念的翻译难度尤其大。于是翻译团队又启动了"敦煌文化中英对照术语库"的编制工作,并在《敦煌文化关键词》完成后,再开始推进"敦煌文化·译丛"的工作。"敦煌文化·译丛"第一辑四部图书以及衍生作品的问世见证了一支年轻的翻译队伍从无到有、从小到大、从弱到强的发展壮大。而作为设在兰州城市学院的一个团队,译者们作为教师也在培育着更加年轻的译者。他们的精神和经验必然让他们带出一支对外传播的人才队伍。

"敦煌文化·译丛"的意义还在于填补了"一带一路"建设的一个空白。敦煌,曾经是古代丝绸之路的重镇,如今是"一带一路"建设的重要支点。丛书给敦煌乃至甘肃省的对外文化交流提供了精品之作,增添了灿烂的文化光彩。讲好中国故事,传播中国声音不是一句口号,需要一部部的作品来支撑和实现。"敦煌文化·译丛"不仅展示了一段辉煌的历史,更彰显了中国文化自信和文化繁荣在新时代的成果。四部作品宣扬的不仅仅是中国历史上的文化积累,它们所介绍的四个方面更是代表中国在文明互鉴过程中的四颗璀璨明星,反射中国文化发展的过去,照亮中国文化传承的当今,预示中国文化生生不息的未来。

也正因为如此,我们期待"丝绸之路·敦煌文化翻译工程"的下一个项目。

中国外文局原副局长
中国翻译协会常务副会长　黄友义

2020年10月

Foreword I

In 1975, China and the United Kingdom signed an educational exchange agreement, resuming the exchange program for foreign students which had been suspended for nearly 10 years. I went to the UK to study with 14 classmates as part of the first group of these students. At the same time, British students also came to study in China. Some years later, I ran into one of the British scholars who had studied at Peking University when I was studying in the UK. At the time we met, she was already head of the Department of Oriental at the British Library. She told me that she was working on a joint project with the State Bureau of Cultural Relics, replicating historical documents and materials from Dunhuang held in the British Library, in order to facilitate Dunhuang research by experts from our two nations. Due to various historical reasons, a large amount of Dunhuang materials were scattered in various places overseas. This may have been a loss for China, but it also catalyzed foreigners' attention on Dunhuang.

However, Dunhuang studies is not limited merely to the study of historical materials scattered around the world. The real center of research has always been in Dunhuang and in China. For example, Dunhuang culture, as represented by its cave temples, is irremovable. Likewise, the history and philosophical thought behind Dunhuang is also deeply rooted here. In recent years, Chinese scholars have made outstanding achievements in the study of Dunhuang, and, coupled with the profundity of Dunhuang culture, it has become truly necessary to make these research findings—along with the essence of Dunhuang culture—widely known through their translation. In particular, the Belt and Road Initiative has not only strengthened the economic activity between China and the countries along the route, but has also brought closer cultural ties between them. People-to-people exchange must first rely on cultural communication and mutual learning among civilizations so as to uphold the beauty and diversity of civilizations in the world. Dunhuang culture is important, but communication with the international community is even more significant. However, Dunhuang studies, which integrates history, art, and religion, covers a long historical period of time, involves a full range of arts, represents deep religious influences, and reflects a wide range of social developments. It is thus an extremely challenging task to translate the achievements of Dunhuang studies into another language.

It is now gratifying to see that the team led by Professor Jiang Qiuxia of the Gansu Cultural Translation and Interpreting Center has, after six years of hard work, completed the first four volumes of the Chinese-English bilingual *Dunhuang Culture in Translation* series, now being presented to readers at home and abroad. The titles of these four books are *Dunhuang: Pearl of the Silk Road*; *Art Treasures: Murals and Painted Sculptures in Mogao Caves*; *Raiment of Rainbows and Feathers: Music and Dance from Dunhuang Murals*; and *Dunhuang: Its Everlasting Impact*. The publication of this set of books marks the first time that China has introduced the latest Dunhuang culture research in English and Chinese at the same time, and on a planned, large-scale, and systematic basis. The four books use contemporary language to convey the past and present of a Chinese story to an international audience. This translation and publishing project has been a great achievement, and the process has been long and arduous. Translation in general is not an easy job and it is even more difficult to translate Chinese into another language; the difficulty in translating Dunhuang culture lies even beyond all this. For the past six years, Professor Jiang's team has gone through many hardships, for example, expending great effort researching and finding the exact vocabulary and terminology, and considerable time spent on accurately and faithfully conveying each author's point of view. Readers only need to browse through these four books and the difficulties they had to overcome will be made immediately evident.

Since it is so difficult, then why translate? As Professor Jiang said, "Translation is not merely the conversion of language, but also the interpretation of culture. Translating Dunhuang culture is not a simple code conversion, nor is it purely the transmission of information. More importantly, translation reveals and interprets the philosophical thought, humanistic spirit, and values contained in Dunhuang culture and historical relics, which is imbued with the cultural spirit, mind, and confidence of the Chinese nation." Her words convince me that Dunhuang culture translation reflects the translators' deep love for their country and their ideals and determination for communicating with the world at large, as well as their devoted academic scholarship in the face of challenges. Unless translators have firm beliefs, lofty commitment, and a strong work ethic, they may easily pull back from the difficulties of translation work. While congratulating the team of translators, I would also like to express my highest respect for them.

Why does a series of books hold that much significance? Mutual learning between civilizations requires the interchange of cultural information, and doing a good job in communication involves producing works that people from other countries can readily understand. Conveying cultural confidece requires extremely hard and sophisticated work. This book series, the latest achievement in the introduction of Dunhuang culture, is a product of that cultural confidece.

The significance of *Dunhuang Culture in Translation* however is not only in the finished works. The translation of the series also represents a process of continuous maturity of the translation team. *Dunhuang Culture in Translation* marks the first phase of a much larger program—the Silk Road Dunhuang Culture Translation Project. After its launch, the translators found that the work was extremely challenging, especially the translation of cultural concepts. Thus, the translation team began by compiling the Dunhuang Culture Chinese-English Terminology Database, and after the completion of the bilingual *Key Concepts in Dunhuang Culture*, it began to focus on the work of the *Dunhuang Culture in Translation* series. The publication of these four books and their related works of the first series of *Dunhuang Culture in Translation* witnessed the development and growth of a team of young translators starting from scratch, growing from small to large, and from weak to strong. Based at Lanzhou City University, members of this translation team are also teachers who are bringing up even younger translators. Their spirit and experience will inevitably guide them in fostering the next generation of talent for presenting information and culture to the international community.

What is significant is that the *Dunhuang Culture in Translation* series has filled a gap in the promotion of the Belt and Road Initiative. Dunhuang was once an important town on the ancient Silk Road and now holds an important position in promoting the Belt and Road Initiative. This book series provides excellent works for not only Dunhuang but also Gansu Province to conduct exchanges with the world, adding a superb new dimension in cultural communication. Telling China's story and getting China's voice heard is not just a slogan: it needs a series of solid works to help make it happen. *Dunhuang Culture in Translation* not only reveals a glorious history, but also demonstrates the achievements of Chinese cultural confidece and cultural prosperity in our present era. These four works make known not only the formation of culture in Chinese history, but the four facets they introduce also represent four bright stars of China in the process of mutual learning between civilizations. Reflecting the past of China's cultural development and illuminating the heritage of Chinese civilization, they herald the limitless future of Chinese culture.

It is precisely because of this that we now look forward to the next installment in the Silk Road Dunhuang Culture Translation Project.

Huang Youyi

Former Deputy Director-General of China Foreign Languages Publishing Administration

Vice President of Translators Association of China

October 2020

序言二

敦煌文化是丝绸之路文明的精髓,是中外文化交流背景之下形成的哲学思想、人文精神、价值理念、道德规范等,而丝绸之路是连接古代中国与中亚、南亚、东欧的经济文化的交通要道,因其贩运的商品主要是丝绸,所以称之为丝绸之路。同时还因其贩运的物品和使用的货币而被称作为玉石之路、白银之路、香药之路、茶马之路等。

丝绸之路还是一条中外文化交流的重要通道,西方的先进科学技术和文化都是通过这条通道传入中国的,同时中国的先进文化和科学技术也是通过这条国际通道传播到世界各国,中西文化经过这条道路互相碰撞、交融和接纳,促进了汉唐帝国和学术文化的发展。通过这条道路,印度的佛教、欧洲的景教、中亚的祆教和摩尼教进入中国,并在中国迅速传播开来,由于佛教寺院的建造和石窟的开凿,佛教造像的兴盛,犍陀罗佛教艺术流传中国,影响了中国佛教艺术及中国道教艺术的发展。

因景教艺术传入,中亚艺术风格传入中国,并影响了中古时期中国社会生活的方方面面。通过这条道路,产生于印度的天竺乐和中亚的康国乐、安国乐和新疆地区龟兹乐、疏勒乐、高昌乐等的音乐舞蹈相继传入并迅速传播开来,由外来音乐舞蹈和中国古代清乐融合而产生的西凉乐,成为中古中国乐舞的重要组成部分,推进了中国文化艺术的发展。

通过这条道路,中亚西域的物种、医技医籍、饮食、服饰、生活习惯等都进入中国,影响中国古代社会生活的各个方面。汉唐文化就是在对外来文化包容接纳的基础之上产生的。中国古代儒家典籍和道教以及先进的科学技术也是通过这条道路传播到中亚和东欧地区,推动了世界文化和科学技术的发展。古代中国通过这条道路了解世界,而世界也通过这条道路接纳中国。

敦煌文化形成之地的敦煌是丝绸之路东段和中段的交汇之地，也是丝绸之路的必经之地。敦煌最早见载于中国历史典籍《山海经》，《山海经》北山经记载敦薨之山出敦薨之水，敦薨之水西流注入泑泽，是为河源。

敦薨就是敦煌，是历史典籍对敦煌的最早记载。后来张骞出使西域，被匈奴扣押在河西及蒙古高原十余年，对这里的地理地貌非常熟悉，后来又到中亚从大月氏人那里收集到他们在敦煌一带生活的信息，敦煌一词很可能首先是从张骞开始使用，实际上就是敦薨的音译。

根据《汉书》的记载，实际上在汉朝设置敦煌郡之前的元鼎四年，敦煌一词已经开始使用。而敦煌地区的三危山就见载于《尚书·禹贡篇》，记载导黑水经过三危山流入南海，三危山就是敦煌的三危山，而黑水经我们根据《太平广记》和敦煌文书《瓜沙两郡史事编年并序》研究，就是流经敦煌的疏勒河，疏勒河在汉唐间曾称之为冥水，疏勒河上的沼泽湖泊也叫作乌泽，沿着疏勒河修建的军事屏障称之为昆仑障，都与黑有密切关系。

敦煌也是古代中国领导人行经之地，根据《穆天子传》的记载穆天子即位十五年，曾巡游至泑泽，即今天的罗布泊，前往罗布泊必须经过敦煌，因此周穆王十五年就曾来到敦煌。如果这个记载不误的话，公元前962年中国领导人已经来到了敦煌，到了新疆的罗布泊地区或者更远的哈密或者帕米尔高原一带。敦煌的龙勒山就因周时有龙马朝出咸阳，暮至寿昌，遗其衔勒，故名龙勒山。就是说周穆王时中原王朝已经同西域地区进行玉石贸易和马种交换。

汉武帝击败匈奴取得河西地区，置敦煌等河西四郡而拥有二关，玉门关、阳关是汉唐通西域的主要关隘，敦煌是汉唐中央政府经营西域的军事基地，同时也是来往商贾的都会城市。阳关是出敦煌到西域的和亲通使关隘，而与阳关对应的玉门关是出敦煌经营西域的军事关隘，俗称阴关或者凶关，与玉石贸易没有任何关系。

出敦煌西行分别有三条道路，南道至鄯善，中道到高昌，北道经伊吾，总汇敦煌。这三条道路都必须穿越戈壁沙漠地带，"上无飞鸟，下无走兽，复无水草"；"行旅负水担粮，履践沙石，往来困弊"；"西路险恶，人行迷误，沙河阻道，鬼魅热风，遇无免者"。这种情况说明没有充分的准备绝不敢贸然进入沙碛西行。

这样一来，经过沙碛考验的人们才能顺利来到敦煌，他们的精神和灵魂都经过严酷的自然环境的洗礼，有了一个质的升华。汉代李广利征大宛两次都是从敦煌出兵，两汉敦煌太守都参与经营西域，吐蕃占领敦煌之前的唐代，沙州刺史或者敦煌太守，经常参与经营西域的事务。

汉唐的敦煌是一个都会城市，国际化程度非常高。从两汉时期敦煌就居住着很多西域质子和西域商贾，特别是粟特人经常见载于出土文献和典籍中，到唐代更是这样，敦煌的胡人在唐朝中央军队中任职的很多，有的晋升为中央禁军的首领，像曹怀直，祖上帮助唐朝建功立业，被赐姓为曹，历代担任禁军要职。

特别是唐中宗神龙年间石城镇康艳典后裔部落随戍守播仙镇的凉州兵迁居敦煌，唐朝政府为安置这些粟特人在敦煌城周围专门设置了从化乡，从化乡最少有两个里四个村落，粟特人控制敦煌的市场贸易，出任市壁师并管理敦煌市场贸易。直到吐蕃时期敦煌粟特人康秀华仍然担任部落使，而安景旻出任敦煌都督。

张氏归义军时期，安景旻出任归义军节度使副使，而康秀华出任瓜州刺史左威卫将军，到张承奉时期，粟特人安怀恩出任押衙。914年粟特人曹议金出任归义军节度使，敦煌成了粟特人领导下的归义军政权。除了粟特人，敦煌外来居民很多，有达怛人、回鹘人、突厥人、吐蕃人、波斯人、印度人、鄯善人、于阗人等，他们开店经营商品，经营酒店出卖食品，很多行市的头目都是这些胡人担任，特别是前往各地的商业贸易团体的头目都是由粟特胡人担任，胡商是敦煌市场贸易的主体，因此敦煌市场贸易的商人具有很高程度的国际性。

敦煌市场的商品也具有很高的国际性，敦煌地不产珍，献无奇玩，是一个贫乏的地方。由于敦煌地处交通要道，敦煌市场上商品非常丰富，有西域地区贩运而来的西州布、安西氎，有龟兹出产的胡粉，有中亚来的金青和水银，吐蕃地区的颜料石青、石绿和毛织品，波斯等地出产的胡锦和珠宝，伊州出产的铁器，于阗出产的玉石，东罗马的银器，西域印度的药材和香料，高丽出产的高丽锦，达怛和吐蕃出产的畜牧产品和兵器等，商品来自相邻各个地区或者中亚、南亚和东亚及中国内地各个地方。

作为交换的等价物是银币。金银器皿作为流通货币在晚唐五代的敦煌贸易市场比较常见,有罗马银盏、银盘子、金花银瓶子、银碗等;这些银器标明重量,用于支付物价,其性质显然是货币,不是作为一般意义上的器皿,表明银碗是作为货币流通于敦煌等地的贸易市场中;在对外贸易中还使用丝绸支付物价;在对内或小宗贸易上多用实物特别是粮食支付物价,作为交换的等价物进行交换。因此货币也具有国际性。

敦煌是佛教最早进入的地区。敦煌文献是关于中国佛教最为详细和真实的记载。敦煌汉简中就已经记载了寺院,寺院内的一切均有助于重构中国寺院的面貌。敦煌文献中还保存有最早的汉文景教经典、摩尼教经典,虽然敦煌文献中没有祆教经典,但是作为官府主办祆教祭祀仪式足以看出祆教的影响力。在敦煌佛教、道教、祆教、景教、摩尼教以及儒教之间的和谐共处超过相互排斥和争斗。特别是西域地区的胡腾舞、胡旋舞在敦煌地区非常流行,敦煌人在重大节日都要踏苏幕遮,出现于龟兹的舞蹈成为敦煌的流行舞。这种局面的基础就是敦煌多民族和平共处,互相包容,互相借鉴,共同发展。敦煌作为丝绸之路上的明珠,他的魅力就在于此。

丝绸之路也可称之为科技之路。西域地区的科学技术如医学、医方、天文历法等都是通过这条道路传入中国,中国的科学技术也是通过这条道路传向西域地区。敦煌文献的记载就是很好的见证。我们要交代的是敦煌出产瓜得名称瓜州,传说狐狸吃瓜首尾俱入瓜中,表明敦煌出产的瓜很大。回鹘瓜和大食瓜,名见于敦煌文献中,回鹘瓜,又叫瓢桃,这些地方在晚唐五代时期属于回鹘统治地区,所谓伊州回鹘、西州回鹘,大概称之为回鹘瓜就是出产于回鹘地区。

大食瓜,就是出产在大食地区的瓜,这种瓜是什么瓜呢,我们认为是西瓜,西瓜原产地南非,后来传播到埃及,又从埃及传到中亚,金代陕西同州有个官员出使西域,从中亚引进并在中原地区大量传播开来,当时人对这种瓜没有统一的名称,所以按照以地命名的习惯,称之为西瓜,原意可能是西域的瓜、西方的瓜等。今天陕西大荔的瓜还是很有名的,个大皮厚瓤甜。

医学技术的交流通过丝绸之路也很明显,汉唐时期虽然中医学很发达,但有些医术还没有西域波斯、印度先进,比如眼科中的白内障手术,就是从西域传入，唐史将其作为特殊案例记载。敦煌当地医学家的造诣是学兼中西。

敦煌是丝绸之路上的一颗明珠，敦煌文化是丝绸之路文明精髓所在，而丝绸之路是中西交通文化交流永恒的通途。第一，政治稳定是丝绸之路顺畅的基本要素，这包括历史上中央政权和丝绸之路沿线民族和国家的稳定。先秦时期，由于中原地区文化经济的发展，与周边地区形成很大的社会差异，这种差异导致一种稳定的向心力，加上周边民族对中原政府还不能构成威胁，中原政权虽然没有鼓励也并没阻止中外交往，中西交往属于一种原始状态进行，很多西域地区的特产通过丝绸之路流入中原地区，而中国的产品也经过这条通道进入西域。关于穆天子与西王母的会面，《山海经》关于河源和丝绸之路沿线的地理地貌的记载就是这一背景下的产物。

汉武帝凭借强大的军事实力打败匈奴，重新开启丝绸之路，开始了利用军事政治力量维系丝绸之路安全的时期，汉唐时期都是由国家经营沿线交通设施配置、道路维护和安全保障等，丝绸之路的兴衰几乎与国家政权稳定一致。宋代以后陆路衰落与海路有很大关系，但是沿线政治环境的变化因素起了极大的作用。

第二，经济利益的互惠是丝绸之路发展的基础，维系丝绸之路经久不衰的经济因素是利益的互惠。丝绸之路贸易有几个层面：首先是贡赐贸易，这是一种严重的不对等贸易，中央政府承受非常大的经济压力，贡赐之间的比例1∶10到1∶40左右，这种贸易是国家政治利益为主的贸易活动。其次是一般性贸易，基本上是由地方政府控制的经济贸易，由政府管理的贸易使团进行的贸易活动，这种贸易活动的利润都在100%以上，使用等价物以金银丝绸为主，多数进行以物易物贸易，中国的丝绸外销和西域的香料宝物内售，有相当一部分的商人是西域胡人，在中国内地经营。胡商在中国进行的对外贸易和对内贸易，促进了汉唐社会经济繁荣发展，同时由于经济贸易的带动，沿线各地的经济也发展起来。特别是丝绸之路沿线物产并不丰富但地位十分重要的地区，财富经丝绸之路贸易在这些地区得到重新分配。经济上互惠是丝绸之路保持畅通的经济因素。

第三，丝绸之路文化研究是重新发展丝绸之路经济带的先决条件。今天我们研究丝绸之路经济带，更应当重视丝绸之路文化的研究。古代丝绸之路将古代沿线不同地区不同文化连接起来，这些文化通过文物文献等形式在丝绸之路沿线各个地区保存了下来，研究这些文物文献对揭示这一地区古代文明十分重要，研究该地区历史上对丝绸之路经营的经验和教训对今天有十分重要的借鉴作用，只有将其远古文明研究清楚，才有利于丝绸之路的发展。丝绸之路沿线的敦煌、高昌、哈密、库车、于阗等都是丝绸之路上的明珠，因此研究这些地区的历史文化就是丝绸之路的个案研究，是一项十分有意义的工作。

甘肃文化翻译中心组织翻译的"敦煌文化·译丛"，就是响应习近平总书记敦煌讲话精神，弘扬传承敦煌文化，提高文化自信的一个有力举措。

兰州大学敦煌学研究所所长　郑炳林

2020 年 10 月

Foreword II

Dunhuang Culture is the essence of Silk Road civilization, with philosophical ideas formed in the context of cultural exchange between China and the outside world. It also represents the spirit of humanism, the concept of values, and the code of ethics. The Silk Road was the major economic and cultural link connecting ancient China, the Central Asia, South Asia and Eastern Europe. The Silk Road is so-called because silk was the main commodity transported along the route. But the Silk Road was also known as the Jade Road, the Silver Road, the Spice Road, and the Tea and Horse Road, among others, because such goods and currencies were also transported and used along the route.

The Silk Road was also an important route for cultural exchange between China and the outside world. This international thoroughfare was the means by which the West's advanced science, technology, and culture reached China, and by which China's advanced culture, science, and technology spread to other nations of the world. Through the Silk Road, Chinese and Western cultures met, mingled, and accepted each other, bringing about developments of the Han and Tang empires as well as academic cultures that have influenced the world. It was via this route that India's Buddhism, Europe's Nestorianism, and Central Asia's Zoroastrianism and Manichaeism entered China and spread quickly. Buddhist temple construction and cave excavation, the rise of Buddhist iconography, and the spread of Gandharan Buddhist art into China all contributed to the proliferation of magnificent Chinese Buddhist art, facilitating the development of the Taoist art.

The presence of Nestorian art and Central Asian art styles in China influenced medieval Chinese society and lifestyles in a multitude of ways. The music and dance originated from Indian music, Central Asia music and music of Xinjiang region entered through the Silk Road and quickly spread. The mingling of foreign music and dance and ancient Chinese *Qingyue* music produced Xiliang music, which became an essential element of medieval Chinese music and dance, and furthered the development of Chinese culture and art.

Through the Silk Road, plant species, medical technology, diet, dress, and everyday habits all entered China, influencing the lifestyle of ancient Chinese society in various ways. The culture of the Han and Tang dynasties emerged on the basis of these outside influences. Ancient Chinese Confucian texts, Taoism and advanced science and technology also passed along the Silk Road on their way to Central Asia and Eastern Europe, promoting the development of culture, science, and technology throughout the world. Through the Silk Road, ancient China was able to understand the world, and the world was able to accept China.

Dunhuang, where Dunhuang culture emerged, is located at the crossroads of the eastern and central sections of the Silk Road; travelers had to pass through Dunhuang on their way. Among Chinese historical texts, Dunhuang was first mentioned in the *Classic of Mountains and Seas*, from which the *North Mountain Classic* records that the Dunhong river flowed down Dunhong Mountain, and then westward into Lop Nur, where it formed the source of the Yellow River.

Dunhong was thus the name for Dunhuang, and was the earliest reference to the site. Later, Zhang Qian had his mission to the Western Regions, but was detained by the Xiongnu for more than ten years in the west of the Hexi Corridor and on the Mongolian plateau, becoming very familiar with the geography and landforms of the area. Then he traveled to the Central Asia to gather information from the Greater Yuezhi people about their life in the Dunhuang area. It is very likely that the name Dunhuang originated with Zhang Qian; he actually transcribed "Dunhong" as Dunhuang.

According to the *Book of Han*, in the fourth year of the Yuanding Era, before the establishment of Dunhuang Prefecture in the Han dynasty, the name Dunhuang was in fact already in use. Moreover, the Sanwei Mountain, recorded in the *Book of Yugong*, through which the Heishui River flowed into the South China Sea was the one situated in Dunhuang, while according to our research into the *Extensive Records of the Taiping Era* and the Dunhuang document *Chronology and Preface of the History of Guazhou and Shazhou*, the Heishui River was the Shule River which flows through Dunhuang. In the Han and Tang dynasties, the Shule River was known as the Mingshui River ("Dark Water"). The marshy lakes on the Shule River were also called the Black Marsh. The military barriers built along the Shule River were called the Kunlun Barrier. All three have implications of "darkness" or "blackness."

In ancient China, Dunhuang was also a place which emperors and high-rank officials passed during their travel to the west. In his 15th year of regin, King Mu, once travelled to present-day Lop Nur according to the *Tale of King Mu*. To reach Lop Nur, one must pass through Dunhuang; that is to say, King Mu had been to Dunhuang. If this account is to be believed, then Chinese leaders had already been to Dunhuang by 962 BC, as well as to present-day Xinjiang's Lop Nur region, or even further to Hami or the Pamir Plateau. Dunhuang's Longle Mountain (*longle* meaning headstall of dragon horse) was so-named because during the Zhou Dynasty, a powerful steed known as "dragon horse" left its headstall there during its trip from Xianyang in the morning to Shouchang (part of Dunhuang) in the evening. That is to say, by the time of King Mu, the Kingdoms in the Central Plains had already exchanged jade and horse breeds with the Western Regions.

Emperor Wu of the Han Dynasty defeated the Xiongnu to gain control of the Hexi Corridor. He set up Dunhuang and three other prefectures on the western side with the Yumen Pass ("Jade Gate") and the Yangguan Pass, which were the main border controls in the western part of the Han and Tang dynasties. Dunhuang was a military base for the central governments of the Han and Tang dynasties, as well as a leading mercantile city. Yangguan Pass was for peace-making envoys from Dunhuang heading west, while Yumen Pass was a protected pass for merchants heading west. It was commonly known as the Yinguan Pass, and actually had nothing to do with the jade trade.

There were three routes heading west from Dunhuang: the southern road to

Shanshan; the central road to Gaochang; and the northern road going via Yiwu. These three routes all crossed the Gobi and desert. These western routes were treacherous: there were no birds above, no animals on the ground, and no succulent plants. Carrying water and grain, walking over sand and rocks, going to and fro, people got lost, and rivers of sand blocked the way while otherworldly hot winds inevitably blew. This indicated that travelers did not dare go to the western side of the moraine without adequate preparation.

Only people who knew the lay of the land were able to get to Dunhuang. Their spirits were baptized by the character-building harshness of such an environment. In the Han Dynasty, Li Guangli conquered Dayuan twice from his base in Dunhuang. The Dunhuang governors of the Eastern and Western Han dynasties were involved in the administration of the Western Regions; likewise, in the Tang dynasty before the occupation of Dunhuang by the Tubo, the Shazhou inspectors or governors were also often involved in running affairs in the Western Regions.

Dunhuang was a burgeoning international metropolis during the Han and Tang dynasties. From the time of the Eastern and Western Han dynasties, Dunhuang was home to descendants of hostages and merchants from the Western Regions. The Sogdians in particular are often mentioned in excavated documents and texts, even more so in those from the Tang Dynasty. Foreigners served in the Tang Imperial Army in large numbers. Some were even promoted to leadership roles, such as Cao Huaizhi, whose ancestors helped build the Tang Dynasty. They were granted the surname Cao, and successive generations of the family served important roles in the Imperial Army.

In particular, during the Shenlong Era of the Emperor Zhongzong in the Tang Dynasty, the descendants of Kang Yandian from the Shicheng Town moved to Dunhuang with the Liangzhou soldiers who guarded the Boxian town; the Tang government set up the Conghua township to house the Sogdians. Conghua was at least two *li* large and contained four villages. The Sogdians controlled and managed Dunhuang's market trade. When the Tubo took over Dunhuang, the Sogdian Kang Xiuhua served as a tribal commissioner, while An Jingmin was appointed governor.

During the *Guiyijun* period under the Zhang clan, An Jingmin served as deputy military commissioner of the *Guiyijun* Force, while Kang Xiuhua served as general of the prefect of Guazhou. In the Zhang Chengfeng period, the Sogdian An Huai'en was appointed to a position equal to the military commissioner. In 914, the Sogdian Cao Yijin was appointed as the *Guiyijun*'s military commissioner, and the Dunhuang *Guiyijun* Force came under Sogdian leadership. Apart from the Sogdians, there were considerable numbers of other foreign residents in Dunhuang, including Tartars, Uyghurs, Turkic people, Tubo people, Persians, Indians, Shanshan people and Khotanese. They set up shops and restaurants, with many business leaders of foreign origin. In particular, commercial and trade groups that traveled to various places were led by Sogdians. Foreign traders made up the majority of Dunhuang market traders. For this reason, Dunhuang's business community was strongly multinational.

The goods for sale in Dunhuang's markets also had a strongly international flavor. Dunhuang itself produced little, with no treasures or exotic goods to offer. But because of the city's location on a major transportation route, its markets offered a rich array of goods. There were textiles from the Western Regions, fine muslin from Anxi, *Hu* powder from Kucha (Qiuci), lapis lazuli and mercury from Central Asia, blue and green mineral pigments as well as woolen fabrics from Tubo, Persian brocade and jewelry, ironware from Yizhou, Khotanese jade, silverware from Byzantium, medicines and spices from western India, brocade from Korea, and livestock products and weapons from Tartary and Tubo. Merchandise arrived here from neighboring regions in Central, South, and East Asia as well as the interior of China.

Silver coins were the currency for trade. Gold and silverware were also used as common circulating currencies in the markets of Dunhuang in the Late Tang era. There were Roman silver chalices, silver plates, gold and silver bottles, silver bowls, and so on. The silverware with marked weight was used when paying for goods, so that its value was as a currency rather than as a functional utensil or vessel in the general sense, revealing that silverware was used as a currency in the markets of Dunhuang and other places. Silk was also used for payment in foreign trade, while in domestic or small-scale trade, goods—especially food or grain—were often paid in-kind. Goods were exchanged for equivalent value, so the currencies themselves were multinational.

Dunhuang was Buddhism's original point of entry into China. The Dunhuang manuscripts themselves offer the most detailed and accurate records of Chinese Buddhism and the monastery is mentioned in Han bamboo slips from Dunhuang. These records are helpful in reconstructing the architecture and appearance of ancient Chinese temples. Among the Dunhuang texts are also the earliest extant Nestorian and Manichaean scriptures in Chinese. Although the Dunhuang manuscripts do not include Zoroastrian classics, the influence of Zoroastrianism can be seen in the fact that Zoroastrian rituals enjoyed official sponsorship. In Dunhuang, the peaceful co-existence of Buddhism, Taoism, Zoroastrianism, Nestorianism, Manichaeism, and Confucianism overcame any mutual exclusion or contention. This is especially true of the *Huteng* dance from the Western Regions, which was extremely popular in Dunhuang. It was enjoyed on important festival days. This dance, which first appeared in Qiuci, became Dunhuang's favorite dance. The basis of this situation was the peaceful co-existence of the many ethnic groups in Dunhuang, as well as their mutual inclusiveness, mutual learning, and common development. Dunhuang was the pearl of the Silk Road, and therein lies its charm.

The Silk Road can also be called the Technology Road. Science and technology from the Western Regions, such as medicine, pharmacology, and the astronomical calendar, entered China via this route; Chinese science and technology, in turn, also flowed westward along the same route. The Dunhuang manuscripts provide historical evidence of this. Dunhuang produced so many melons that it was named Guazhou (land of melons). Legend had it that a fox could eat a Dunhuang melon with its head and tail in it, such was the size of the melons. Uyghur melons and Dashi melons are even mentioned in Dunhuang historical records, where Uyghur melons were also known as "*rangtao.*" In the Late Tang period and Five Dynasties, the area was held by Uyghurs. Among the so-called Yizhou and Xizhou Uyghurs, Uyghur melons, as they were probably called, were those produced in Uyghur areas.

Dashi melons were those from Arabia. What type of melons were these? It is believed that they were watermelons, which were originally from South Africa, and later reached Egypt, and from there it was made into Central Asia. In the Jin Dynasty, an official from Tongzhou of Shaanxi travelled west as an envoy, and introduced watermelon, after which it became widespread. The people of the time did not have a uniform name for watermelons, so according to naming conventions, it became the *xigua*. This probably just meant "melon from the Western Regions" or "melon from the West." Today, the melons from the Dali county of Shaanxi are also very well-known, with a thick rind and sweet taste.

The exchange of medical technology along the Silk Road was evident. While traditional Chinese medicine was highly developed by the time of the Han and Tang dynasties, many medical skills were absent. Persia and India, however, was at the forefront in certain skills such as cataract surgery, and this was introduced via the West, with Tang dynasty historical records giving it a special mention. Dunhuang's local medical specialists were accomplished in both Chinese and Western methods.

Dunhuang was the Pearl of the Silk Road, the essence of Silk Road civilization, and an eternal thoroughfare for communication and cultural exchange between China and the West. First, political stability was a basic element for the smooth operation of the route. This included the stability of central political power throughout its history, as well as that of ethnic groups and nations along the route. In the pre-Qin period, owing to cultural and economic development of the Central Plains, great social differences took shape as compared with the surrounding areas. These differences led to a stable centripetal force, with the surrounding ethnic groups not having sufficient strength to threaten the government of the Central Plains. Although the Central Plains government did not encourage Chinese exchanges with foreigners, it is not known to have prevented them, either. Exchanges between China and the West were rudimentary. Many specialty goods from the Western Regions passed into the Central Plains via the Silk Road, and Chinese products also headed west via the same road. According to legend, King Mu and the Queen Mother of the West met in the area extending from the Shule River to Lop Nur; the *Classic of Mountains and Seas* which details the geography and landforms along the Yellow River and the Silk Road is a product of this background.

Emperor Wu of the Han Dynasty defeated the Xiongnu with his powerful military, opened up the Silk Road again, and started using the strength of his military government to sustain a period of peace along the Road. During the Han and Tang dynasties, the state operated transport facilities along the route, maintained roads, and guaranteed safety. The rise and fall of the Silk Road occurred almost in line with the stability of state power. After the Song Dynasty, the decline in overland routes was correlated to the rise of the maritime trade routes, but changes in the political environment along the Silk Road also played a major role.

Second, mutual economic benefit was the basis of development along the Silk Road. The reciprocity of benefits was the factor that sustained the Silk Road economically. There were several dimensions of trade on the Silk Road: foremost was tribute trade, which had serious disparities. The central government withstood enormous economic pressure, with the ratio between tributes roughly somewhere between 1 : 10 to 1 : 40. This kind of trade asserted national political interest above all else. This was followed by general trade, which was basically controlled by regional authorities with government-managed trade envoys conducting trade. Profits from this trading activity exceeded 100%. Gold, silver, and silk were the primary mediums of exchange used, with many traders also engaged in bartering. Quite a few of the merchants engaged in China's silk exports and the sale of the Western Regions' treasured spices within China were foreigners from the West. China's foreign-led exports and domestic trade boosted the economic fortunes of Han and Tang society. Driven by trade, places all along the Silk Road also received an economic boost. For Silk Road areas that were not very productive but were nonetheless in important locations, wealth was distributed thanks to trade along the route. Economic reciprocity was the key factor that kept the Silk Road running smoothly.

Third, research into Silk Road culture is a prerequisite for an economic revival along this route. Today, when we research the Silk Road economic belt, we should pay more attention to the culture that developed there. The ancient Silk Road brought together disparate regions and cultures along the route. These cultures have been preserved in forms of artifacts and other material in different regions along the Silk Road. Researching these artifacts is extremely important if we want to learn more of the ancient civilizations of this area. Researching the historical experiences and lessons from the Silk Road trade is a vital reference point for today. Only careful study of its ancient civilizations will benefit future Silk Road development. Places such as Dunhuang, Gaochang, Hami, Kucha, and Khotan are all "pearls of the Silk Road." For that reason, research into the historical culture of these regions amounts to a special case study. It is an immensely significant work.

The *Dunhuang Culture in Translation* series, organized by the Gansu Cultural Translation and Interpreting Center, is a powerful initiative with which to respond to the spirit of General Secretary Xi Jinping's Dunhuang speech, promoting Dunhuang culture and enhancing cultural confidece.

Zheng Binglin

Head of Institute of Dunhuang Studies of Lanzhou University

October 2020

序言三
翻译,让敦煌文化走向世界

敦煌文化是中华文明几千年不断融会贯通的典范,是中国文化精神的重要代表。曾经,敦煌文化经历"敦煌在中国,敦煌学在国外"的历史。诚然,自20世纪初,敦煌藏经洞的发现、敦煌部分文献流失海外,引发世界各国敦煌学者对敦煌文化的关注,在国外产生了众多敦煌学研究成果。但敦煌文化的"根"在中国,对敦煌文化的认识与理解,源于中国。敦煌学的国际化发展,则需要通过文化的传播与学术的交流形成共识、共知与共享。翻译,无疑是使敦煌文化走向世界、敦煌精神被全人类共享的重要途径。

一、翻译是敦煌文化对外传播的"言说者"

文化对外传播、交流与沟通的重要途径是翻译。翻译敦煌文化,就是对外"言说"敦煌文化,传播敦煌文化的各个方面、各种内容。敦煌文化是包括宗教、艺术、科技、文学、医药、农业、建筑、民俗等内容的综合文化体系。翻译敦煌文化,就是对外讲述敦煌开放交流的文明历史,展示敦煌在中西互学互鉴中形成的艺术,介绍敦煌的科技医药,以及讲述融合发展的宗教文化思想等。通过系统翻译,让世界认识敦煌文化,了解全面的敦煌文化、真正的敦煌文化。

翻译敦煌文化,就是言说和表达最具代表性的、最能体现敦煌文化之源流的优秀文化。就其文化内容而言,一方面转换语言为载体的文化内容,如敦煌文献、敦煌学研究成果、敦煌学术思想等;另一方面转换艺术为载体的文化信息。敦煌文化,就其文化载体而言,具有多元的符号形式。语言载体包含写经、变文、宝卷、简牍等文学与非文学形态;艺术载体包含石窟建筑、雕塑、壁画等。翻译敦煌文化,即对敦煌文化各种载体所蕴含的历史、宗教、文学、艺术等文化内容,及其文化思想和文化精神进行语言转换,精确表达。以翻译言说敦煌文化,既要用语言讲述语言文化,还要用语言讲述非语言文化。一般而言,翻译是语言文本的转换。但在敦煌文化翻译中,除了常规的语际翻译,还存在符际转换方式,即对艺术文化的翻译,运用语言进行"互文性"表达。通过语际与符际双重转换,构建敦煌文化对外传播的系统体系。作为敦煌文化对外传播言说者的翻译,需要注重"言说"的方式,构建有效的话语体系。翻译,在传播文化中,表达文化,沟通文化,协调不同语言之间的文化理解。话语方式、话语风格决定文化元素的显现方式,决定文化内容的接受度,从而决定文化传播的效果和效力,是实现文化传播与交流的基础。翻译敦煌文化,要协调"异化""归化"转换策略,在尊重文化、名从历史的基础上,运用恰当适切的对外言说话语方式,针对文化内容、受众接受等用国际化语言表达方式,准确言说和表达敦煌文化,构建敦煌文化对外传播的完整叙事。

以翻译言说文化,不仅使敦煌文化充分"走出去",更使敦煌精神深入"走进去",有效实现敦煌文化的国际性传播与世界认同。

二、翻译是敦煌文化学术交流的"互动者"

翻译敦煌文化,就是搭建中外敦煌学术交流的互动平台,开展中外敦煌学研究的学术对话。20世纪初以来,国内外学者对敦煌文化的研究,产生了众多研究成果,建树颇丰。通过对中外敦煌学研究成果的互译,对话学术,交流思想,从而深化对敦煌文化的认识。诚然,博大精深的敦煌文化及其精神价值,依旧存在有待认识与研究的极大空间,但交流已有的学术思想,无疑对进一步研究敦煌文化、认识敦煌文化具有重要的意义。互译,为搭建互动机制、建构交互认知,提供必要的路径。

一是开展敦煌文献的互译,通过对各国拥有的敦煌文献进行翻译转换,补充因文献缺省造成的"认识差",化解研究上的局限。敦煌莫高窟藏经洞发现的文献(包括写本、简牍),涉及佛教经典、道教经典、儒家典籍以及(敦煌)佛教文学、俗文学等文化内容,语言包含除汉文之外的藏文、回鹘文、于阗文、龟兹文、突厥文、粟特文和梵文等。敦煌文献是丝绸之路上中西文明交流的历史书写,是研究敦煌文化,以及其中蕴含的中国文化思想的重要文献资料。但敦煌文献因特殊的历史遭遇,一大部分遗书被劫掠至海外(如英国近万卷,法国五千余卷),有关同一文化内容的文献资料散藏于中、英、法、日、俄等不同的国家,造成各国对敦煌文化认识的支离破碎,导致敦煌学研究的片面性。通过文献资料的译入、译出,可以搭建国内、国外敦煌学的多维研究平台、系统认识平台,将历史片段缀合起来,将同一文化现象进行综合研究,从而形成世界范围内的"系统敦煌学"。

二是进行敦煌学研究成果的互译,通过互译,使学术思想产生碰撞、比较,从而打开各自封闭的敦煌学,经由"他者"的敦煌学术参照系,关照自身的研究,丰富自身的认识;在与"他者"的交流中、在思想碰撞中深化对敦煌文化的理解。

敦煌文化是在中西方文化交融中形成和发展的,具有综合的文化内容体系、多元的文化思想,以及多样的历史发展形态。它是一个内在结构相互作用的文化体系,存在各系统成分之间的内在关系,如敦煌艺术研究与宗教文化研究的互补,中西方文化交流与文化融合过程的历史关系,文化演变与朝代结构的互动等。对敦煌文化的认识,需要系统地研究,才能构成认识的互补体系;只有互为补充的认识,才能不断完善对敦煌文化认识体系的构建。不同国家、不同时代,基于各自专业领域的研究,难免存在"认识差"。通过中外敦煌学研究思想的双向翻译,进行学术交流与对话,在互动中学习,在交流中互鉴,不仅能够产生新思路和新成果,而且能够使各国学者更深刻地理解敦煌文化,一方面可以减少因文化差异造成的认识误差,减少误读与误解;另一方面通过不同时代、不同文化背景、不同信仰体系的学者对历史文明的学术对话,协调敦煌学研究中的审美心理和文化价值"差",以便达成共识,形成对敦煌历史文化概念的共同解读,从而提升敦煌文化的交流深度,实现敦煌文化的高层次对话与互动传播。

三、翻译是敦煌文化精神的诠释者和世界传承者

翻译,不仅仅是语言的转换,更是对文化的阐释。翻译敦煌文化,不是简

单的语码转换,也不是单纯的信息传递,更重要的是揭示和阐释敦煌文化和历史遗存所蕴含的哲学思想、人文精神、价值理念、道德规范;弘扬和传承蕴含其中的中华民族的文化精神、文化胸怀和文化自信。敦煌文化是中西文化交流融合的典范,敦煌石窟建筑、壁画,以中原文化为基础,充分吸收了中亚、西亚佛教艺术思想内容,体现了多元文化交融互鉴的内在精神,是中华文明开放体系的重要代表。在综合、系统的翻译过程中,深刻阐释其文明历程、文化精髓,阐释敦煌文化文明交流融合的思想方法,诠释中华文明海纳百川、兼容并蓄、博采众长的文化精髓,挖掘世界文明共同的存在根源,以及人类共同的理想目标。

翻译是一种诠释,具有文化"阐释力"。翻译敦煌文化,就是在研究敦煌文化的前提下,诠释敦煌文化的深刻含义。翻译敦煌文化,是译者与敦煌文化思想、文化精神的交流和互动,是现代视域与历史精髓的互文。作为敦煌文化"诠释者"的翻译,是某种意义上的敦煌文化研究,是敦煌学的一种组成部分。但诠释不是自创性解读,正如孔子所言,文化的传承,要遵循"述而不作,信而好古"。真正的敦煌文化翻译,就是在精准理解与充分诠释的基础上向世界传播敦煌文化思想,传承敦煌文化精神。

敦煌文化是在中西文明的相遇、相识、相融中形成和发展的,是各种文明交流融汇的结晶,蕴含开放包容、互学互鉴的文化精神。翻译是文化的交流、思想的对话,其本身就是敦煌文化精神的"外显"形式。敦煌学研究成果的翻译,是学术思想的互学与互鉴,尤其建立在中外学者"中西合璧"方式上的合译,更是在互动的理解过程中实践敦煌精神,是传承与弘扬敦煌文化的又一种深化、物化、具象化的方式。敦煌文化翻译,以其特有的文化交流与对话方式,向世界讲述敦煌故事,传播敦煌思想,弘扬敦煌精神,让敦煌文化在交流中成为世界的文化,敦煌学研究成为"世界的敦煌学",敦煌精神成为人类的思想精神。

兰州城市学院副校长 教授 姜秋霞
甘肃文化翻译中心 主任
2020 年 10 月

Foreword III

Translation Connects Dunhuang Culture with the World

Dunhuang culture is a model of the continuous amalgamation of Chinese civilization over a span of thousands of years, and an important representation of the essence of Chinese culture. There was a time when Dunhuang culture experienced a historical reality of "Dunhuang itself is in China, yet Dunhuang studies is in the West." Of course, the discovery of the Dunhuang manuscripts at the beginning of the 20th century—with many of them taken overseas—brought the attention of scholars from all over the world to Dunhuang culture, and produced a large corpus of research from Dunhuang studies abroad. But Dunhuang culture is rooted in China, and the knowledge and understanding of Dunhuang culture originated in China. The international development of Dunhuang studies requires consensus, common knowledge, and sharing through cultural dissemination and academic exchange. Thus, translation is undoubtedly an important way to bring Dunhuang culture out to the world and for the spirit of Dunhuang to be shared by all humankind.

1. Translation is the voice of Dunhuang culture for the world community

Translation is an important method of cultural dissemination and communication. To translate Dunhuang culture is to introduce Dunhuang to the outside world, in other words, to share all aspects and content of Dunhuang culture. Dunhuang culture is a comprehensive cultural system that integrates religion, art, technology, literature, medicine, agriculture, architecture, and folk customs. Translating Dunhuang culture informs the public about the history of Dunhuang's civilization and its open exchanges, reveals the art of Dunhuang as a reflection of the mutual learning between China and the West, introduces Dunhuang's science, technology, and medicine, and explains the integration and development of its religious culture. Thus, systematic translation allows the world to not only know about Dunhuang, but also understand the true, comprehensive culture of Dunhuang.

Translating Dunhuang culture is to relate and express that which is most quintessential, reflecting the pinnacle of culture emanating from its source in Dunhuang itself. As far as cultural content is concerned, on the one hand, Dunhuang translation converts language—that of the Dunhuang manuscripts, Dunhuang studies, and Dunhuang academic theories—as a carrier of cultural content; on the other hand, it converts art as a carrier of cultural information. Dunhuang culture is embodied in multiple symbolic and semiotic forms. Language carriers include literary and non-literary forms such as scripture, *bianwen* (transformation texts), *baojuan* (prosimetric narratives), and bamboo slip archives; artistic carriers include rock-cut architecture, sculpture, and murals. Translating Dunhuang culture entails language conversion and the precise expression of its historical, religious, literary, artistic, and other cultural content contained in various carriers, as well as its cultural values and cultural spirit. The expression of Dunhuang culture through translation requires the use of both linguistic and non-linguistic conversion. Generally speaking, translation is the conversion of language text. However, in Dunhuang culture translation, in addition to the conventional interlingual translation, there is also an intersemiotic transformation method, which is to say that translation of art and culture uses language to express intertextuality. Through this interlingual and intersemiotic conversion, a systematic method for the communication of Dunhuang culture can be constructed. When we translate as the "voice" of Dunhuang culture, it is necessary to pay attention to the manner of "speaking," in order to construct an effective discourse system. Translation, in disseminating, expressing, and communicating culture, must coordinate cultural understanding between different languages. The style and mode of discourse—the foundation for achieving cultural dissemination and communication—determine how cultural elements appear, determine the acceptability of cultural content, and thus determine the effect as well as effectiveness of cultural transmission. When translating Dunhuang culture, it is necessary to closely coordinate both foreignization and domestication conversion strategies, and, on the basis of respecting culture and history, use appropriate foreign language expressions as well as international expressions for cultural content and audience acceptance. To accurately express Dunhuang culture, a complete narrative must be constructed for communicating Dunhuang culture to the world outside China.

Speaking through the language of translation not only enables Dunhuang culture to fully "go forth" into the world, but also enables the essence of Dunhuang to "go in" deeply as well, effectively realizing the international spread and world recognition of Dunhuang culture.

2. Translation is the liaison for Dunhuang cultural and academic exchange

Translating Dunhuang culture creates an interactive platform for academic exchange between China and the rest of the international community, facilitating academic dialogue between Chinese and overseas Dunhuang scholars. Since the beginning of the 20th century, academics both within China and abroad have produced much research on Dunhuang culture, making considerable achievements in the field. The understanding of Dunhuang culture can be deepened through the mutual translation of research findings in Dunhuang studies both within China and overseas, as well as through academic dialogue and the exchanging of ideas. It is true that there is still a great deal to be learned about Dunhuang with its extensive, profound culture and spiritual value, but the exchange of existing academic theories is undoubtedly of great significance for the further research and understanding of Dunhuang. Mutual translation provides a necessary pathway for constructing an interactive mechanism for the field and for the interchange of expertise.

The first task is to carry out the mutual translation of Dunhuang documents. The translation and conversion of Dunhuang documents owned by various countries can help supplement the deficiencies in understanding caused by dispersed and fragmented manuscripts, and thus resolving the limitations of research. The documents, manuscripts, and bamboo slip found in the Dunhuang Mogao Caves include Buddhist, Taoist, and Confucian classics, Buddhist scriptures unique to Dunhuang, popular literature, and other cultural content. In addition to Chinese, the languages include Tibetan, Uyghur, Khotanese, Kuchean, Turkic, Sogdian, Sanskrit, and more. The Dunhuang manuscripts constitute historical written records of the cultural exchanges between China and the West along the Silk Road. They are important documents for studying Dunhuang culture and the Chinese cultural thought contained therein. However, due to the special history of the Dunhuang documents, a large part of the manuscripts was unlawfully removed overseas, including nearly 10,000 manuscripts now located in the United Kingdom, and more than 5,000 in France. As a result, various countries have a fragmented interpretation of Dunhuang culture, leading to one-sidedness in research. Through the translation of documents and materials, a multi-dimensional research platform and a systematic understanding for Dunhuang studies at home and abroad can be developed, with historical manuscript fragments recombined to allow comprehensive research on the same cultural phenomena, thereby forming a worldwide system for Dunhuang studies.

The second task is to carry out the mutual translation of research findings in Dunhuang studies. Through mutual translation, academic theories can interact and undergo comparison, thereby broadening researchers' own closed-off Dunhuang research. Through "other" Dunhuang research and reference, scholars can reflect on their own research, enrich their own expertise, exchange ideas with the "other," and deepen the understanding of Dunhuang culture through the interaction of different theories.

Dunhuang culture was formed and developed as a fusion of Chinese and Western cultures. It comprises a comprehensive system of cultural content, ideology, and historical development. It is a cultural system with interactive structures, and there are internal relationships between the components of the system, as well. For example, Dunhuang art research and religious cultural studies complement one another; there has been a historical connection between the exchange of Chinese and Western cultures and the process of cultural diffusion; and there has been an interrelationship between cultural evolution and dynastic structures. The understanding of Dunhuang culture requires systematic research in order to form an interrelated branch of knowledge; only when mutual understanding is complementary, can the knowledge of Dunhuang culture be continuously improved. Differences in interpretation have been inevitable amongst different countries and throughout different eras, based on research in their respective professional fields. The Sino-Western translation of Chinese and international Dunhuang research findings and theories, academic exchange and dialogue, and interchange of ideas can not only generate new ideas and new results, but can also enable scholars from all over the world to have a deeper understanding of Dunhuang culture. On the one hand, this can reduce errors from misreading as well as misunderstandings caused by cultural differences. On the other hand, academic dialogue between scholars from different eras, cultural backgrounds, and religious viewpoints on historical civilizations can redress the gaps in Dunhuang research regarding its artistic and cultural value. This will better form a consensus and a common interpretation of Dunhuang historical and cultural concepts, thereby enhancing the depth of Dunhuang cultural exchange as well as enabling high-level dialogue and interactive communication on Dunhuang culture.

3. Translation is the interpreter and world inheritor of the spirit of Dunhuang culture.

Translation is not merely the conversion of language, but also the interpretation of culture. Translating Dunhuang culture is not simple code conversion, nor is it purely the transmission of information. More importantly, translation reveals and interprets the philosophical thought, humanistic spirit, and values contained in Dunhuang culture and historical relics, which is imbued with the cultural spirit, mind, and confidence of the Chinese nation. Dunhuang culture stands as a model of Chinese and Western cultural exchange and diffusion. Dunhuang cave temple architecture and murals are based on the Central Plains culture, which also absorbed the content of Central and Western Asian Buddhist art aesthetics and ideals, reflecting the inherent spirit of multicultural synthesis and mutual learning. Dunhuang is an important representation of the openness and inclusiveness of Chinese civilization. Comprehensive, systematic translation can profoundly explain Dunhuang's historical development and its cultural essence, reveal the thinking behind Dunhuang cultural exchange and integration, interpret the cultural essence of Chinese civilization, explore the common roots of world civilizations, and even tap into the common ideals of the human race.

Translation is a type of interpretation, with cultural interpretative power. Translating Dunhuang culture is to interpret the profound meaning of Dunhuang culture under the auspices of researching it. The translation of Dunhuang culture is the exchange and interaction between the translator and Dunhuang cultural ideology and spirit, as well as the intertextuality of modern vision and historical essence. To engage in translation as the "interpreter" of Dunhuang culture is indeed the study of Dunhuang culture in a certain sense, and is a component of Dunhuang studies in and of itself. However, interpretation is never self-generated. As Confucius said, the inheritance of culture must follow the principle of "transmitting but not innovating, loving antiquity and having faith in it." Dunhuang culture translation means sharing and inheriting the essence of Dunhuang culture on the basis of accurate understanding and full interpretation.

We can conclude that Dunhuang culture has formed and developed from the encounter, acquaintance, and fusion of Chinese and Western civilizations. It is the crystallization of the exchange and synthesis of various civilizations, and contains a cultural spirit of openness, inclusiveness, and mutual learning. Translation is cultural exchange, a dialogue of ideas, and itself is the "external" form of Dunhuang's cultural essence. The translation of Dunhuang studies involves the interchange and mutual appraisal of academic ideas. In particular, co-translations based on the Sino-Western cooperation by Chinese and foreign scholars put the spirit of Dunhuang culture into action. Through the process of interactive understanding, the inheritance and promotion of Dunhuang culture is further deepened and substantiated. Dunhuang culture translation brings the story of Dunhuang to the world, shares Dunhuang thought, and promotes the essence of Dunhuang via its unique cultural exchange and methods of communication. Thus Dunhuang culture becomes the world's culture in the exchange, Dunhuang studies becomes the world's Dunhuang studies, and the spirit of Dunhuang culture becomes humankind's ideological spirit.

Jiang Qiuxia

Professor and Vice President of Lanzhou City University

Head of Gansu Cultural Translation and Interpreting Center

October 2020

持璎珞的飞天　莫高窟第158窟西壁　中唐
Apsara Carrying Necklace of Jade and Pearls, West Wall of Mogao Cave 158, Middle Tang

Art Treasures: Murals and Painted Sculptures in Mogao Caves

前 言

Introduction

莫高窟位于敦煌市东南25公里处宕泉河畔,宕泉河水源于敦煌南部数百公里处祁连山的支脉,自南向北流下。宕泉河在下游把敦煌的地势分成了两部分,东面是三危山(图1、图2),山石坚硬,西侧是由沙漠形成的鸣沙山,山势平缓,常有流沙。据说在前秦建元二年(366年),一个叫乐僔的和尚从中原云游至此,当他面对三危山参禅入定之时,忽见对面的三危山上出现了万道金光,在金光中仿佛有千佛化现而出。乐僔感到十分神奇,

The Mogao Caves lie 25 kilometers southeast of Dunhuang City, on the bank of the Dangquan River, which originates in one of the ranges of the Qilian Mountains, hundreds of kilometers to the south. The river heads north, its lower reaches dividing the terrain into two: in the eastern section lies the Sanwei Mountain (Figs.1, 2), hard and rocky, while the western section is home to the Mingsha Mountain, with gently sloping geographical features and numerous sand dunes. It is said that in the 2nd year of the Jianyuan Era of the Former Qin (336), a monk from the Central Plains[1] of China named Le Zun visited there. While sitting in deep meditation, facing the Sanwei

---

[1] The Central Plains (*Zhongyuan*) refers to both a geographical area of China as well as the historical center of its political power and culture. The area in present-day Henan Province was originally China's cradle of civilization, particularly the regions in the Yellow River Valley. Later the term "Central Plains" was used to signify this area, and also included parts of the nearby provinces of Shandong, Shanxi, Hebei and Shaanxi. Generally speaking, it can be interpreted as "interior China" or "inland China" and the succession of imperial dynasties located there.

图1 三危山
Fig.1 The Sanwei Mountain

他想一定是自己虔诚的修行得到的感应,便决定在此住下修行。于是,他在宕泉河西岸的岩壁上开凿了一个石窟,用于坐禅修行。不久,一个叫法良的和尚从东方来到这里,在乐僔的禅窟旁又开凿了一个石窟。此后,这里石窟开凿得越来越多,有的是和尚们坐禅用的禅窟,更多的则是世俗的人用来礼拜的洞窟。到了唐代,石窟已达1000多

Mountain, Le Zun suddenly saw thousands upon thousands of beams of golden light shooting upwards from the mountain in front of him. It seemed to him that 1,000 images of the Buddha came into view from among those golden beams. Feeling it was a miracle, Le Zun thought that he had received a sign from the Buddha as a result of his devout spiritual cultivation. Thus he decided to settle there and continue his spiritual journey. He cut a cave in the rock on the western bank of the Dangquan River for the purpose of Buddhist meditation and practice. Not long after, another monk named Fa Liang arrived from the east and dug a second meditation cave next to Le Zun's. Later on, more and more caves were constructed in the rocky cliff. Many of these caves were used by monks for Buddhist

图 2　三危山

Fig.2　The Sanwei Mountain

座。这一片石窟后被称为"莫高窟",也叫千佛洞(图 3、图 4)。

莫高窟开窟的故事,来自唐代碑文的记录。虽说其中不免带有传说的成分,但从历史上考察,敦煌在魏晋南北朝时期已经是佛教兴盛之地,石窟和寺院的营建,完全是合乎史实的。

敦煌早在公元前 111 年的西汉时代就已设郡,这加强了与中央政

meditation, but even more were used by the laity for their worship. The number of caves rose to over 1,000 by the beginning of the Tang Dynasty (618–907). This complex of caves was later called the Mogao Caves; it was also known as the Thousand Buddha Caves (Figs. 3, 4).

Stone inscriptions dating to the Tang Dynasty record stories of the Mogao Caves. While it is likely that there are elements of legend in these records, a historical examination reveals that cave-cutting and temple-construction are consistent with the history of the region, as Buddhism was already well-established in Dunhuang during the period of the Wei, Jin, and the Northern and Southern Dynasties (386–589).

As early as 111 BC, during the Western Han

图3 莫高窟外景
Fig.3 Panoramic Exterior View of Mogao Caves

府的联系。在此后西汉至东汉中原与西域的多次征战中,敦煌成为强大的后方基地,具有十分重要的战略地位。张骞通西域以后,丝绸之路不断地繁荣,敦煌以其得天独厚的条件,源源不断地接受着来自西域和内地的不同风格文

Dynasty (206 BC–AD 25), Dunhuang was established as a prefecture, indicating its strong connections with the central government. After that, from the Western Han Dynasty to the Eastern Han Dynasty (25–220), Dunhuang enjoyed an important strategic position as a solid rear base throughout many military campaigns against the Western Regions①. The Silk Road grew increasingly prosperous after Zhang Qian's diplomatic mission to the Western Regions. Dunhuang, with its special advantages in location, was successively influenced by different forms of art

---

① The Western Regions (*Xiyu*) was a historical name used by China to refer to areas west of the Yumen Pass. Although the specific areas changed over time, it primarily referred to Central Asia, but could also include the Tarim Basin in present-day Xinjiang, as well as other regions to the west of China, including India. The Western Regions were an important part of the Silk Road and also played an important role in the transmission of Buddhism into China.

Art Treasures: Murals and Painted Sculptures in Mogao Caves

化艺术的影响，最终形成了敦煌石窟这一独特的文化现象。

石窟这种形式最早源于古代印度。至今印度还保存着著名的阿旃陀石窟、埃罗拉石窟等多处石窟寺。佛教产生以后，作为

and culture coming from either the Western Regions or the interior areas of China. Finally, the Dunhuang caves, a unique cultural phenomenon, came into being.

The earliest Buddhist rock-cut caves began in ancient India. Today, several cave temples such as the renowned Ajanta Caves and the Ellora Caves are still preserved there. After the emergence of Buddhism, monks were supposed to

图4 莫高窟九层楼外景
Fig.4 Nine-Storey Tower, Mogao Caves

日常工作，僧侣们要进行修行、说法及参加各种佛教仪式，于是针对不同的需要，就产生了相应的寺院和石窟等建筑。寺院是用砖石或木材建造的房屋建筑，而石窟则是开凿在山崖中的洞窟。本来，寺院与石窟有着同样的功能，为什么有了寺院后还要建造石窟呢？这恐怕有两个原因：一是寺院多建造在城市里，虽然有利于传播佛教教义，但僧侣们要修行，需要一个更为安静的环境。在幽静的山上或森林中，最适合修行，在山里凿窟而居的修行方式便成了佛教徒修行的重要方法。二是土木结构的寺院常常会因火灾而化为灰烬，地处闹市，也会因政治变动或战争而受灾。所以，选择在山中凿窟以代替寺院，其中也有避灾远祸的用意。因此，除了敦煌之外，在中国内地不少地方也开凿了石窟，如位于山西省大同市附近的云冈石窟，河南省洛阳市附近的龙门石窟，河北省邯郸市附近的响堂山石

undertake, as their daily practice, meditation, Dharma preaching, and other types of Buddhist rites. As a result, temples and caves were constructed according to different needs. Temples were buildings made of brick, stone, or wood, while caves were spaces cut into mountain cliffs. Both functioned similarly, but why were caves constructed when there were already temples? There may be two reasons. First, temples were mainly built in urban areas with concentrated populations, which was helpful for the spread of Buddhism. However, monks needed to undertake spiritual cultivation, and a more peaceful environment was necessary. Quiet mountains or woods were the best places for such purposes, so digging caves in the mountains and staying inside became an important way to achieve that practice. Secondly, temples, made of earth and wood and built in the center of urbanized areas, were often destroyed by fire, or damaged by political turbulence and warfare. Thus, caves were cut into mountains as a way to avoid the disaster and destruction suffered by temples. As a result, caves were also constructed in many other locations, in addition to those in Dunhuang. The Yungang Caves near Datong in Shanxi Province, the Longmen Caves near Luoyang in Henan Province, the Xiangtangshan Caves near Handan in Hebei Province, and the Maijishan Caves near Tianshui in Gansu Province are examples. All of these caves shared one common feature: while locales with beautiful scenery were chosen as their sites, they were

窟，甘肃省天水市附近的麦积山石窟，等等。这些石窟都有一个特点，虽然总是选择风景优美的地方，但离一个城市的距离少则十来公里，多则二十多公里，在古代是人们步行可以到达的距离，这样就可以维持正常的生活供给。同时，也让信众们去参拜时不至于太辛苦。现在敦煌市到莫高窟的公路有25公里长，而古代从市镇穿越沙漠到达石窟的路途只有十多公里。

敦煌石窟从建筑形制来看，大体上有三种形式：

1. 禅窟，是僧人们坐禅修行的洞窟（图5）。

2. 中心柱窟，它源于印度的支提窟，也称塔庙窟（图6）。支提的意思是塔。塔本是存放佛舍利（舍利，指佛的遗骨）的地方。在佛像产生之前，塔作为佛的象征物而被崇拜。所以，在寺院和石窟中建塔，人们绕塔礼拜。敦煌的塔庙窟平面为长方形，在洞窟的后部有一个方形的柱子，直通窟顶，称为塔柱，象征着佛塔，供人礼拜。

3. 殿堂窟（图7），是敦煌石

always located 10 to 20 kilometers away from a town, which was the distance people could cover on foot in ancient times. Thus, on the one hand, daily necessities could be readily provided for them, and on the other hand, the distance into town was not too burdensome for lay followers. Today, the Mogao Caves are located 25 kilometers from Dunhuang City, but in the past, a journey on foot through the desert was only 10 kilometers or a bit more.

The Dunhuang caves, observed from their types, can more or less be classified into three categories:

1. Meditation caves: caves that were used by monks for sitting in meditation and undertaking spiritual cultivation (Fig.5).

2. Central pillar caves: a type derived from the Indian caitya caves, also called stupa temple caves (Fig.6). Caitya translates as "stupa", which originally was a place for keeping śarīra, meaning Buddhist relics such as the bones of the Buddha. Stupas were taken as symbols of the Buddha before iconography of Buddhism was developed, so they were built into temples and caves for people to circumambulate in worship. The stupa temple caves in Dunhuang are in the shape of a rectangle, and in the back half of the cave there is a square pillar, rising and connecting to the ceiling. This pillar, venerated by believers, is called a stupa pillar, as it is regarded as representing a Buddhist stupa.

3. Hall caves: the greatest number of

艺苑瑰宝
莫高窟壁画与彩塑

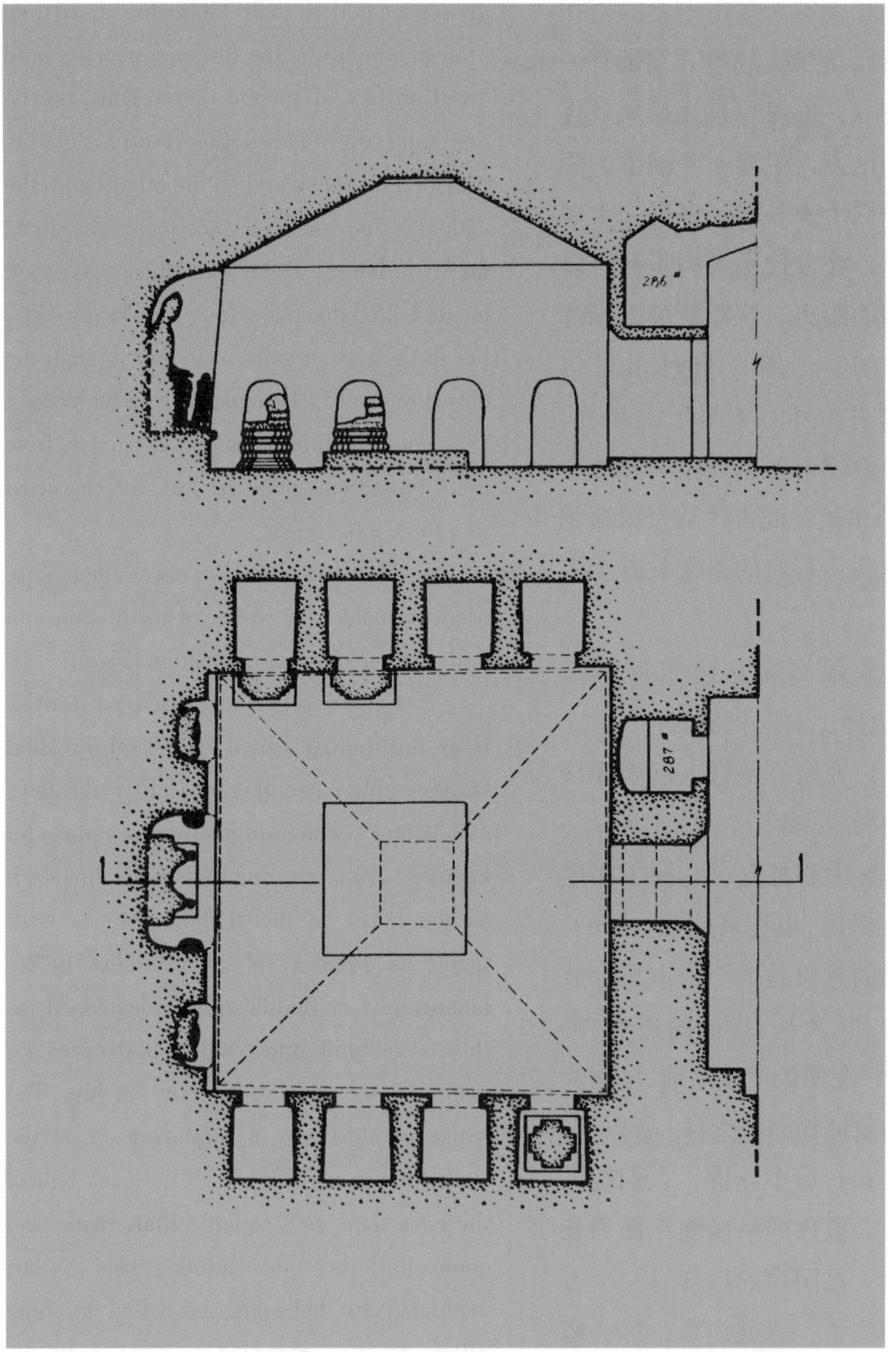

图5 禅窟 莫高窟第285窟平剖面图
Fig.5 Diagram of a Meditation Cave, Mogao Cave 285

Art Treasures: Murals and Painted Sculptures in Mogao Caves

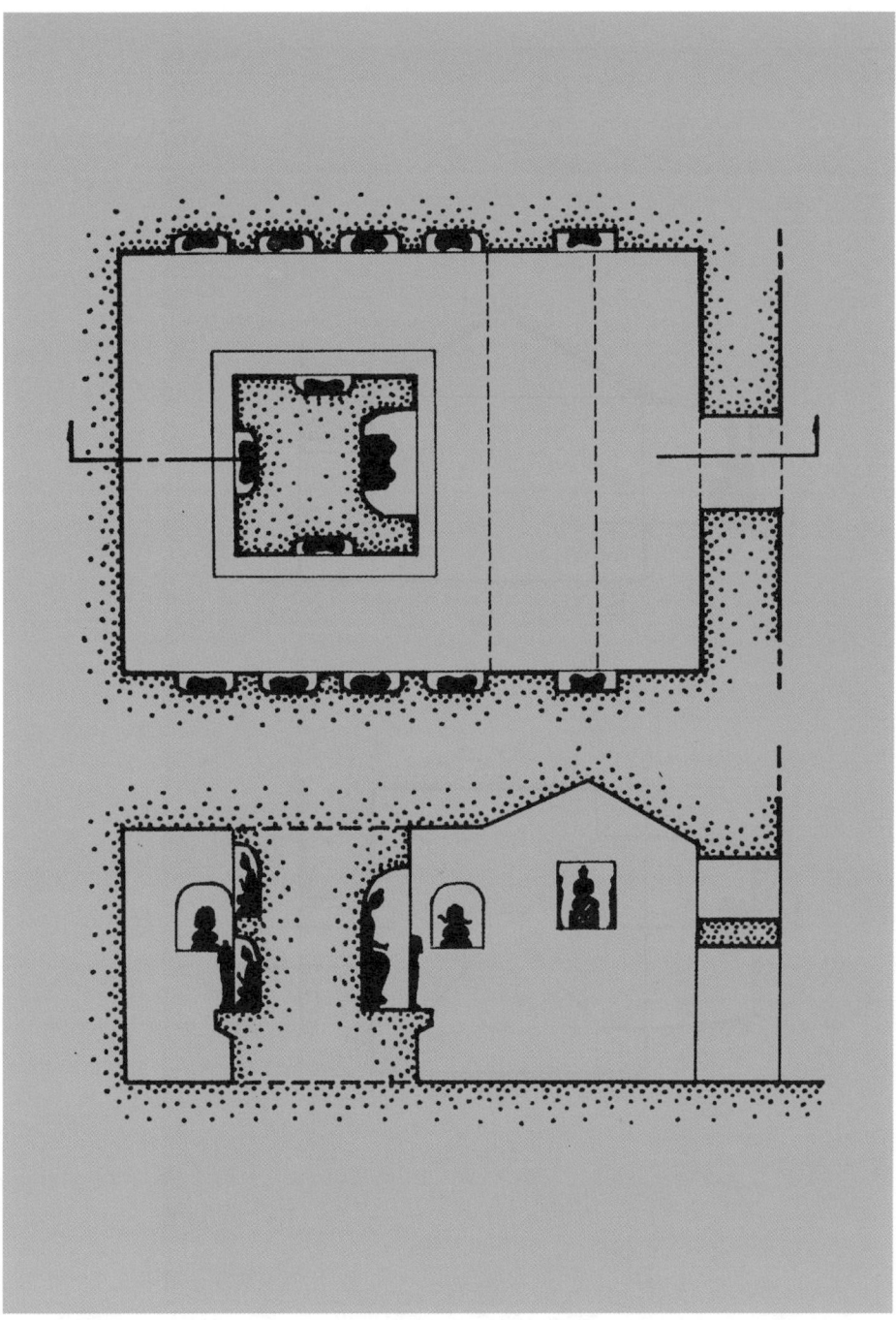

图 6 中心柱窟 莫高窟第 254 窟平剖面图
Fig.6 Diagram of a Central Pillar Cave, Mogao Cave 254

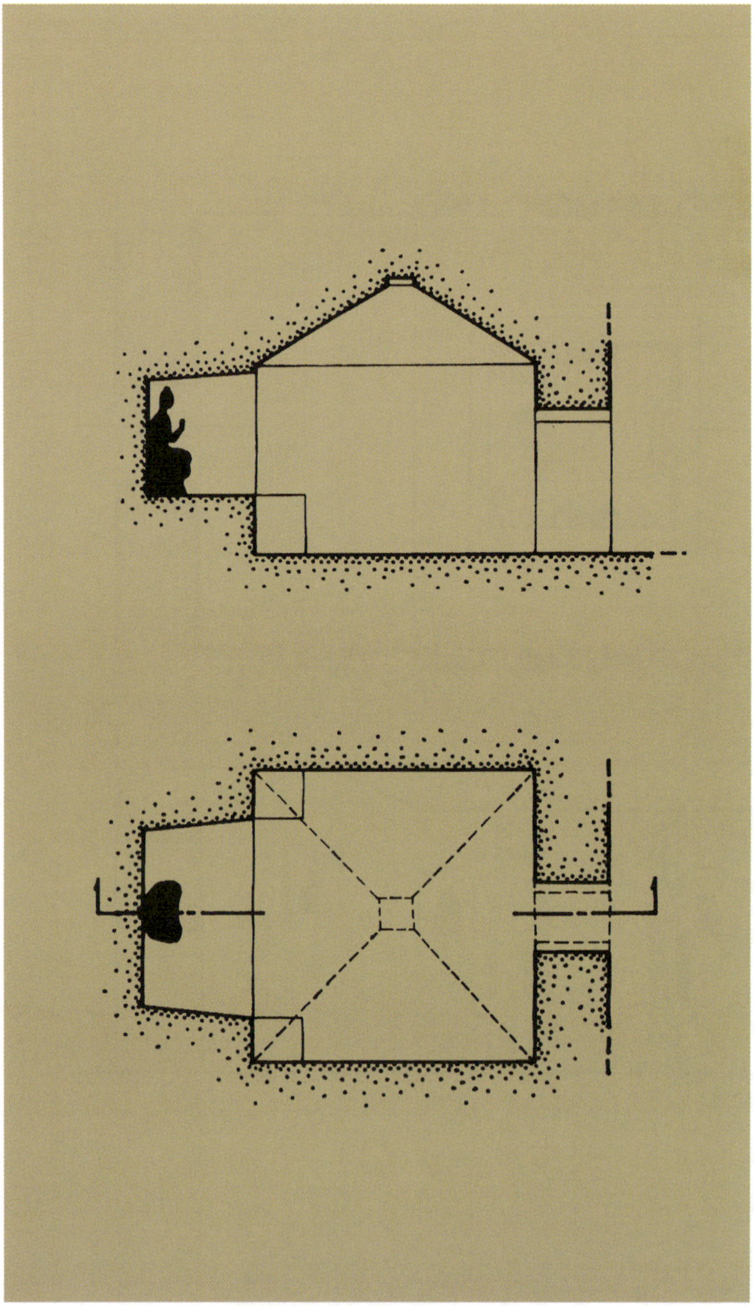

图7 殿堂窟 莫高窟第 217 窟平剖面图
Fig.7 Diagram of a Hall Cave, Mogao Cave 217

窟中为数最多的洞窟，通常平面为方形，在石窟正面开一大龛。这种洞窟的空间较大，如殿堂一样，所以称为殿堂窟。因窟顶为覆斗顶形，也叫覆斗顶窟。唐代后期还出现了一种不开龛的殿堂窟，只在窟中央设佛坛，佛坛上有众多佛像。

除了以上三种洞窟形制外，还有大像窟和涅槃窟等特别的窟型。不管是什么形制的洞窟，窟内都要塑佛像供人礼拜，窟顶和四壁都画满了壁画。壁画的内容主要是依据佛经画出佛像或者佛教故事，表现佛国世界，配合塑像，使窟内形成一个完整的佛教世界。在佛教崇拜的时代，艺术家们倾注了极大的热情来描绘佛教的各种内容，留下了无比精美的艺术作品。虽经千百年自然和人为的破坏，但莫高窟至今仍保存着2000多身彩塑和4.5万平方米的壁画。这些壁画和彩塑包含着宗教、历史、文化等多元的内容，是我们了解公元4世纪至14世纪中

Dunhuang caves are hall caves (Fig.7). Such a cave is generally square in shape, with a huge altar niche in the main wall. It is comparatively spacious like a hall, hence the name. The ceiling of a hall cave is in the shape of a pyramid with top removed, so it is known as a truncated pyramid ceiling cave. During the Late Tang, there was a variant of the hall cave, with no niche, and only a platform in the center, on which several statues of the Buddha were normally placed.

In addition to the three types mentioned above, there are also some special ones such as great Buddha caves and Nirvana caves. All of the caves, no matter what type they belong to, hold sculptures of the Buddha for believers to worship and venerate. Furthermore, all the cave walls and ceilings are covered with murals containing images of the Buddha or Buddhist stories as their main subject, painted according to Buddhist scriptures. These murals, accompanying the sculptures, portray an integrated Buddhist world within the cave temples. The artists, in the name of Buddhist worship, exerted great passion, enthusiasm, and creativity to present an incredible variety of Buddhist beliefs and doctrines, leaving the world with unparalleled works of fine art of great beauty. The Mogao Caves have undergone centuries of human-caused as well as natural damage, yet within, more than 2,000 painted sculptures and 45,000 m² of wall paintings remain. Important elements of religion, history, and culture are all contained in these relics,

艺苑瑰宝
莫高窟壁画与彩塑

国传统文化以及中外文化交流的重要资料。同时,作为艺术品,它反映了中古时代我国绘画和雕塑艺术的重要成果,是中国和世界人类文化艺术的瑰宝。这些精美绝伦的艺术,对于我们今天的艺术创作和欣赏均具有十分重要的意义。

which have proved to be invaluable records on both traditional Chinese culture as well as cultural exchange between China and other countries from the 4th to the 14th centuries. Meanwhile, as works of art, the Mogao Caves represent great achievements in the fields of painting and sculpture during China's medieval period. They are treasures of the art and culture of China as well as the entire world. These works of art, exquisite beyond compare, are of great significance for present-day art creation and appreciation.

艺苑瑰宝：莫高窟壁画与彩塑
Art Treasures: Murals and Painted Sculptures in Mogao Caves

充满人间气息的佛像

Images of the Buddha Filled with the Spirit of the Mortal World

中国古代雕塑作品保存至今者，有相当大一部分都与佛教相关。这些佛教雕塑构成了中国雕塑史的主旋律。莫高窟中的雕塑作品以其时代的完整性和系统性，反映着近千年中国雕塑发展的历史，为重新认识中国美术史提供了大量珍贵的资料。

佛教传入中国后，由于各地寺院石窟的繁荣，佛像的制作就成为一种广泛的社会需要，从而大大地刺激了雕塑艺术的发展。所以佛教也被称作"像教"，说明"像"在佛教中占有重要的地位。可以想象：宗教的发展，形成了对佛教雕塑、绘画的一股强大的社会需求，使当时的中国投入了比以往任何时代都要多得多的美术工匠。秦汉以来，中国雕塑曾经取得辉煌的成就，也形成了中国雕塑的传统。但是由于佛教来自外国，佛教的塑像作为一种崇拜物也是从外国传来的，所以，最初的佛像雕塑往往是取法于印度和西域传来的佛像样式，外来的造型观

A fairly large proportion of ancient Chinese sculptures that have been preserved until present day are related to Buddhism. Indeed, it is Buddhist statuary that constitutes the main thread of the history of Chinese sculpture. The works of art found in the Mogao Caves, chronologically complete and systematic, mirror this development for nearly 1,000 years, providing a large number of invaluable materials for the contemporary study of Chinese art history.

After Buddhism's dissemination into China, temple and cave construction flourished everywhere, and creation of Buddhist icons became a profound religious need that dramatically stimulated the development of the art of sculpture. Buddhism is called a "religion of icons" because of this, meaning that its iconography plays a vital role in the faith. It can be imagined that this expansion of religion brought about so strong a social demand for Buddhist paintings and sculptures that more artisans were employed in China than ever before. Since the Qin and the Han dynasties, China attained splendid achievements in the plastic arts and had established its own standards for sculpture as well. However, since Buddhism was transmitted from abroad, it necessarily followed that Buddhist statues, as objects for worship, were also from foreign countries. The earliest Chinese sculptures of the Buddha adopted their features from India and the Western

念及手法成为新的时尚。于是,包括犍陀罗风格、马图拉风格以及龟兹风格等由西域而传入的雕塑便大量地出现在敦煌和中国北方的石窟与寺院中。随着佛教在中国的进一步发展,随着佛教与中国的儒家、道家思想的斗争与融合,外来的审美意识也与汉民族传统的审美观念之间不断地产生冲突与融合,中国传统的审美趣味便逐渐渗透进了佛教雕塑中,经过不断地交融、改革,终于在南北朝后期到隋唐时代,逐步确立了中国式的佛教雕塑。也正是在与外来艺术的冲击与融合中,中国的雕塑艺术得以迅速发展。

莫高窟中保存的十六国至元代各朝代的彩塑达2000多身,较为完整地反映了近千年间佛教雕塑艺术在中国发展的历程,可以说是一部形象的雕塑史。

Regions, and as a result, modeling concepts and techniques from abroad became a new fashion. A huge number of sculptures appeared in the temples and caves in Dunhuang as well as Northern China, with styles introduced from the Western Regions, including Gandhara, Mathura, Qiuci (Kucha), and others. Nevertheless, while Buddhism, as it further expanded into China, both clashed and blended with Confucian and Daoist ideas, foreign aesthetics also conflicted with and integrated into the conventional aesthetic conceptions of the ethnic Han. Finally, traditional Chinese aesthetic tastes gradually permeated Buddhist sculpture. A Chinese style was progressively established after undergoing continuous synthesis and adaptation, over a process of many years spanning the period from the late Northern and Southern Dynasties to the Sui and Tang dynasties. It was precisely these conflicts and fusion with foreign art that hastened the growth of Chinese sculpture.

There are presently over 2,000 extant painted sculptures in the Mogao Caves, dating from the era of the Sixteen Kingdoms to the Yuan Dynasty (1279-1368). They demonstrate, in a relatively integrated way, the development of the art of Buddhist sculpture in China over the course of nearly 1,000 years. It can be said that these works display a vivid history of Chinese sculpture.

艺苑瑰宝
莫高窟壁画与彩塑

早期彩塑——外来风格与中原风格并存
Early Painted Sculptures: Foreign Patterns Juxtaposed with Styles from the Central Plains

佛像是一个洞窟的主体,是人们崇拜的对象。莫高窟早期洞窟中的彩塑具有浓厚的外来艺术风格。一方面佛教是从印度经西域传来的,对于当时的人们来说,印度和西域的样式具有一定的权威性;另一方面,中国的雕塑家们还没有一套表现佛像的技法,还需要学习和采用外来的雕塑手法。

在北凉第275窟内,有一尊高达3米的交脚弥勒菩萨像,头戴三面宝冠,面相庄严,鼻梁较高而直,双目有神,上身半裸,身着短裙,交脚坐于双狮座上(图8)。早期的交脚菩萨像一般被认为是弥勒菩萨,弥勒菩萨先是在兜率天宫修行。兜率天是佛教所说的欲界六天中的第四天。佛

The image of the Buddha was both the subject of a cave and an object for worship as well. Sculptures in the earlier grottoes of the Mogao Caves are characterized by strong influences from foreign styles. On the one hand, Buddhism was transmitted to China from India by way of the Western Regions, and models from India and the Western Regions were to some extent authentic and authoritative in the views of people at that time; while on the other hand, mature skills or techniques for making statues of the Buddha had not yet been developed by Chinese sculptors, and thus they needed to learn from foreign artists, adopting their methods.

In Cave 275 from the Northern Liang, there is a three-meter statue of Maitreya Bodhisattva in cross-ankled pose. The figure wears a three-sided jewel-encrusted crown, looking dignified, with a straight, high-bridged nose and luminous eyes. He is partially clothed on his upper torso and dressed in a short *dhoti*, sitting with ankles crossed in a seat composed of double lions (Fig.8). Early bodhisattva images in cross-ankled pose were generally considered to be Maitreya, who cultivated himself spiritually in Tuṣita Heaven. According to Buddhist scriptures, Tuṣita Heaven is what Buddhism refers to as the fourth of the six heavens of the sensuous realm (Kāmadhātu).

经上说弥勒菩萨在未成佛之前就是居住在兜率天宫,宣说佛说。后来,释迦牟尼涅槃后,弥勒菩萨从天宫下凡人间而成佛。所以弥勒佛称为未来佛。在释迦牟尼涅槃之后,就会接替释迦牟尼成为未来佛。早期的佛教强调"禅观",僧人们修禅时,观弥勒菩萨像,观兜率天,念弥勒佛名的善果,可往生兜率天及来世值遇弥勒。所以这一时期的弥勒菩萨像盛行。弥勒造像最早出现于公元2世纪至4世纪,盛行于印度北部的犍陀罗地区。犍陀罗雕刻中的弥勒身披璎珞、天衣,戴项饰、臂钏或冠饰等,作菩萨打扮;造像特征是长卷发垂肩,头上结髻及左手持瓶(图9)。第275窟这尊交脚弥勒塑像上可以看出较浓厚的犍陀罗艺术特征。如交脚坐式、三面冠、三角靠背以及双狮座均可以从犍陀罗艺术中找到例子。

第275窟南北两壁上部各开三龛,其中内侧二龛为

Maitreya resides in Tuṣita Heaven preaching the Dharma, in preparation for his rebirth as a Buddha. At some point after the nirvana of the Sakyamuni Buddha, Maitreya will descend into the human world and become a Buddha. Therefore, he is called the Buddha of the Future, since he is believed to become the next Buddha in Sakyamuni's place. Early Buddhism laid stress upon "Zen View". When monks sat in meditation, they were instructed to visualize the image of Maitreya and Tuṣita Heaven, and chant Maitreya's name, with the miraculous result that the observer could ascend to Tuṣita Heaven and meet Maitreya in his next life. As a result, the image of Maitreya Bodhisattva was in vogue during this period. The earliest Maitreya statue appeared from around the 2nd to the 4th centuries, prevailing in the area of Gandhara in Northern India. In Gandharan sculptures, Maitreya is identifiable as a bodhisattva by his necklace of jewels, and celestial clothing, in addition to other ornaments on his neck, arms, and head. His image was characterized by long, wavy hair reaching the shoulders, hair piled in a topknot on the head, and a bottle in his left hand (Fig.9). Features of Gandharan art are evident on the statue of Maitreya in Cave 275. For example, the cross-ankled pose, three-sided jeweled crown, triangular seatback, and throne with double lions are all characteristic of the Gandharan style.

Also in Cave 275, there are three niches on

图 8 交脚弥勒菩萨 莫高窟第 275 窟 北凉
Fig.8 Cross-Ankled Maitreya Bodhisattva, Mogao Cave 275, Northern Liang

阙形龛，也塑交脚菩萨，表现弥勒菩萨高居兜率天宫。这些小型的弥勒菩萨头戴宝冠，宝冠上饰有化佛，上身半裸，腰束羊肠裙，项饰璎珞，身披天衣，双脚足踝部相交。阙形龛仿照汉式城阙形式，是敦煌石窟中特有的龛形。按古代的礼制，阙为帝王的建筑特征，在此用来表示弥勒所居的兜率天宫，表明了中国人对佛教的理解。

北魏以后，彩塑的数量增加了。中心柱正面主尊佛像多为交脚坐式和倚坐式佛像，其余三面多为结跏趺坐的形式。结跏趺坐是佛教修行最常见的坐式，形式为双膝弯曲，盘腿而坐，双足的足心向上，双手相叠放于两足上。其中又分为降魔坐和吉祥坐两种。降魔坐为：先以右足压左股上，后以左足压右股上；二足掌仰于二股上，手也是左

each of the north and south walls. On both walls, the inner two are *que*-style niches, with sculptures of the Buddha in cross-ankled pose, representing Maitreya sitting high above in Tuṣita Heaven. These smaller-sized sculptures of Maitreya wear jeweled crowns, ornamented with images of the Buddha. Partially clothed on their upper torso, they are dressed in flowing, pleated *dhotis* and cloaked in celestial clothing with necklaces of jade and pearls, ankles crossed. *Que*-style niches are stylistic replicas of cities and imperial palaces of the Han Dynasty (206 BC–AD 220), something unique to the Dunhuang caves. According to ancient rites, an imperial palace was the architectural symbol of the emperor, and therefore the sinicized depiction of Tuṣita Heaven, Maitreya's dwelling, reveals how Chinese people interpreted Buddhism.

The number of painted sculptures increased after the Northern Wei (386–534). The principal statues of the Buddha on the front side of central pillars usually sit in *pralambapādāsana* (sometimes called "European pose" in English), with both legs pendant and feet flat on the floor, or sit in cross-ankled pose. Those on the other three sides are usually seated in *padmasana*, known as lotus pose. Lotus pose, the most common posture for meditation, involves bending the knees and sitting with both legs crossed, with each foot resting on the opposite thigh and the soles facing upwards; the hands with upturned open palms rest on the feet. It is further classified into two types; one is called

7

艺苑瑰宝
莫高窟壁画与彩塑

图9 犍陀罗雕刻菩萨像 2世纪
Fig.9 Bodhisattva in Gandharan Style, 2nd Century

手居上。吉祥坐为：先以左足压右股，后以右足压左股。这些彩塑的造型特点是比例适中，袈裟厚重，衣纹写实。第254窟、259窟等窟的彩塑是北魏时期的代表。

第259窟是北魏石窟中彩塑较多的一窟，除正壁开一龛塑有二佛并坐像外，在南北两壁各开有列龛，分别塑佛像与胁侍菩萨像，现存全窟塑像还有19身。正壁龛内塑释迦牟尼、多宝佛并坐说法像。二佛高1.40米，高螺髻、波状发型，前额宽广，鼻梁高耸，眼睛较大，两眉之间有毫相，偏袒右肩。（图10）

释迦牟尼和多宝佛并坐说法像，是根据《法华经·见宝塔品》的内容塑造的。经中说在释迦牟尼讲《法华经》之时，多宝佛便从地下涌出七宝塔升虚在半空中。释迦牟尼以右指开启塔门，多宝

demon-subjugating pose, while the other is called auspicious pose. In demon-subjugating pose, the right foot is put on the left thigh and the left foot on the right thigh, and the soles of both feet face upwards, while the left hand rests on top of the right hand with both palms facing upwards. In auspicious pose, the left foot is put on the right thigh and the right foot on the left thigh. These sculptures are characterized by moderate proportions, thick and heavy *kasayas*, and realistic fabric texture. The painted sculptures in Caves 254 and 259, among others, are representative works of the Northern Wei.

Cave 259 holds relatively a larger number of painted sculptures among the grottoes constructed during the Northern Wei. In addition to the two Buddha sculptures sitting side by side in the niche in the main wall, two rows of niches are cut separately into both the north and south walls. These niches contain statues of the Buddha and his attendant bodhisattvas. The entire cave contains 19 extant sculptures in total. The two Buddha sculptures in the niche in the main wall are of Sakyamuni and Prabhutaratna, seated side by side preaching the Dharma. The two sculptures are both 1.4 meters high, each with wavy hair and an *ushnisha*, or cranial protuberance, on the top of the head. They have broad foreheads, high-bridged noses, and large eyes with whorls of hair between the eyebrows. The right shoulder is bare and exposed on each (Fig.10).

Sakyamuni and Prabhutaratna seated side by side preaching the Dharma is based on the *Lotus Sutra (Saddharmapuṇḍarīka Sūtra)*. According to the *Lotus Sutra: Chapter on the Vision of the Jeweled*

于其中分半座请释迦牟尼入塔。多宝佛是过去佛,佛经以多宝佛证明了释迦牟尼的正确。随着《法华经》的流行,释迦牟尼、多宝二佛并坐像也多见于云冈石窟、炳灵寺石窟、麦积山石窟等。

南北壁分上下两层开龛,上层为阙形龛,内塑交脚弥勒菩萨。下层为圆券龛,内塑坐佛,佛两侧均有胁侍菩萨。北壁下层龛内的佛像塑造精美,保存也较好。如东侧的这尊佛像结跏趺坐,身着通肩袈裟,用阴刻线表现细腻的衣纹,线条自然流畅,表情恬静、淡泊,眼中似乎露出睿智的光芒。

Stupa, as Sakyamuni expounded the Dharma of the sutra, he caused a seven-jeweled stupa to push up from underground, rising high in the air. Sakyamuni then opened the stupa's door with his right finger, and the Prabhutaratna Buddha, who was within, moved aside, making room for Sakyamuni and inviting him in. Prabhutaratna is the Buddha of the Past. Thus, according to the sutra, Sakyamuni's teachings are correct, and Prabhutaratna's appearance verifies their truth. With the popularity of the *Lotus Sutra* in China, statues of Sakyamuni and Prabhutaratna seated side by side are frequently seen in the Yungang Caves, the Binglingsi Caves, the Maijishan Caves, and elsewhere.

The niches for this cave are arranged in a pattern of two rows, in each of the north and south walls. Those in the upper row are *que*-style niches, with Maitreya statues in cross-ankled pose. Those in the lower row are arched niches, with seated Buddhas inside, on both sides of whom are attendant bodhisattvas. The Buddha statues in the lower row of the north wall's niches are elegantly sculpted and well preserved. For example, the one on the right side of the wall[①] sits in lotus pose. He is dressed in a *kasayas* with both shoulders covered. The fine folds in his clothes are shown in engraved lines, natural and smooth. He looks tranquil and peaceful; his eyes seem to shine with wisdom. In the corners of his mouth, a gentle smile is detected, seeming to reveal an inner delight, possibly the very

---

① For the purposes of this book, "left" and "right" refer to the viewer's perspective facing the artwork, unless specified. The main niches and altars for shrines are usually located in either the center of the cave temple or on the west side, with the main statues facing the entrance on the east. Most of the largest murals are located on the north and south walls, flanking the shrines.

图 10 释迦多宝并坐像 莫高窟第 259 窟 北魏
Fig.10 Statues of Sakyamuni and Prabhutaratna Seated Side by Side, Mogao Cave 259, Northern Wei

嘴角微微显露出笑意,似乎有一种发自内心的喜悦。或许这正是佛教所追求的禅定的境界。下层中央佛龛内的佛像为倚坐佛,着袒右袈裟,衣纹简洁,头部微低,目光下视,面部表情呈现出恬静的愉悦,与东侧的佛像同时,成为北魏佛像"古典式微笑"的典型(图 11)。

北魏佛像还有一种苦

state of "Zen View" that Buddhists seek. The one in the middle of this same row sits in *pralambapādāsana*, or "European pose", wearing a *kasaya* with simple lines in the cloth, right shoulder uncovered. He lowers his head slightly, looking downward with an appearance of tranquility and bliss. Similar to the one on the right side, his look also conveys the typical "classic smile" of Buddha sculptures from the Northern Wei period (Fig.11).

The ascetic Buddha is another type of sculpture from the Northern Wei period, depicting how Sakyamuni practiced asceticism in the mountains before he became a Buddha. In Cave

修像，表现释迦牟尼在成佛之前于山中苦修的状况。第248窟中心柱西向面下层龛，在龛两侧以绘塑结合的形式分别表现树木，所以这样的龛又称"双树龛"。龛内就是释迦牟尼苦修像，佛像结跏趺坐，着宽松的双领下垂式袈裟，露出里面的僧祇支（指僧人所穿的类似于衬衣的一种内衣）。佛面庞清瘦，颧骨突出，透过袈裟衣纹，下面的肋骨也历历可见（图12）。苦修像最早也出现于犍陀罗雕刻中。犍陀罗雕刻中的苦修像往往上身为裸体，夸张地表现佛像清瘦如骷髅般的样子。但敦煌彩塑中的苦修像始终没有采用那种过分悽惨的形象，而是相对真实地表现释迦牟尼苦修的样子，更富有人性化的色彩。

北魏后期到西魏，

248, in the lower row of niches on the west side of the central pillar, trees are either painted or sculpted on both sides of each niche—known as double-tree niches. Inside the niche, a statue of Sakyamuni is depicted practicing asceticism. He sits in lotus pose, wearing a loose *kasaya* with the upper portion hanging open, exposing his *uttarasanga*, a kind of undergarment similar to a long shirt, worn by monks. He looks emaciated, with protruding cheekbones and ribs clearly visible through the lines in his *kasaya* (Fig.12). These early ascetic images are found among Gandharan sculptures as well. The torsos on the figures are normally unclothed from the waist up, revealing, in a more exaggerated way, the Buddha's skeletal appearance. The ascetic Buddha images among Dunhuang painted sculptures are not, however, figures of pure misery. They are, instead, a realistic portrayal, showing Sakyamuni practicing austerities, with very human features.

During the period from the late Northern Wei to the Western Wei (535—556), Emperor Xiaowen's reforms gave rise to the adoption of ethnic Han art styles; art forms from the south began to be in vogue in the north, as well. An artistic style characteristic of the Central Plains was developed, embodied by the Longmen Caves. Sculptures of the Buddha were tall and trim, with fine, delicate features, such that they were called "slim and smart figures" in Chinese. Owing to this influence, images of the Buddha in the Central Plains style also emerged among the painted sculptures in Dunhuang. The one seated in *pralambapādāsana* in the central pillar's front niche in Cave 432, for example, wears a *kasaya* in the style of a broad robe with hanging edges of fabric. The

图 11　佛像　莫高窟第 259 窟　北魏
Fig.11　Buddha Statue, Mogao Cave 259, Northern Wei

图 12 苦修像 莫高窟第 248 窟中心柱西向龛 北魏
Fig.12 Ascetic Buddha Statue, West-Facing Niche in Central Pillar, Mogao Cave 248, Northern Wei

由于孝文帝改革，吸收了汉民族艺术风格，来自南方的艺术形式也开始在北方流行，形成了以龙门石窟为代表的中原风格，佛像雕刻，身体瘦长，面目清秀，被称为"秀骨清像"。在中原艺术风格的影响下，敦煌彩塑也出现了中原风格的佛像。第432窟中心柱正面龛中央的倚坐佛像着褒衣博带式袈裟，衣纹形成有规律的曲线，垂下的衣角飘举流动（图13）。龛两侧的菩萨像上身半裸，下着长裙。左侧的菩萨身上的飘带沿双臂环绕而垂下，右侧的菩萨身上的飘带在腹前交叉而分开搭于双手腕上。在中心柱北向面的龛两侧胁侍菩萨则身体扁平，穿着宽松的大衣，飘带在腹前交叉于圆环内，更多地体现着中原传来的特征。除了第432窟外，同时期的第435窟、437窟等窟的菩萨也呈现着眉清目秀、神采飞扬、衣饰繁多、飘带较长的特征，体现着以龙门石窟为代表的新的中原风格。

北周以后，在第428窟、297窟等窟又出现了另一种新

lines in the clothing are wavy and the narrow, hanging edges of the clothing seem to be floating in air (Fig.13). The bodhisattvas on either side of the niche are partially-clothed on the upper torso while wearing long skirts or *dhotis*. The narrow shawl on the bodhisattva on the proper left side encircles his arms and hangs down, while the shawl on the bodhisattva on the proper right side is knotted at his abdomen and drapes over his two wrists. The attendant bodhisattvas on both sides of the niche in the central pillar's north side are sculpted with flat bodies. They wear loose upper garments with long sashes which cross through a ring at the abdomen, embodying more of the features coming from the Central Plains. In addition to those in Cave 432, the bodhisattvas in grottoes from the same period, such as Caves 435 and 437, are all characterized by delicate features, radiating expressions, rich flowing clothes, and long narrow sashes, which reflect the new style from the Central Plains as represented by the Longmen Caves.

Starting with the Northern Zhou (557-581), another new style appeared in cave temples including Caves 428, 397, and others. The Buddha images of this period were sculpted with relatively round faces, and smaller, tighter facial features. The upper body was larger and stronger, while the lower body was shorter and smaller. Figures of bodhisattvas appear to be small and agile. These features are consistent with sculptures

图 13　佛像　莫高窟第 432 窟中心柱正面一组　西魏
Fig.13　Buddha and Attendant Bodhisattvas, Main Niche in Central Pillar, Mogao Cave 432, Western Wei

的形式:佛像的面型较圆,五官细小而较集中,上身粗大,下半身短小。菩萨的形象也显得小巧而灵活。这些特点与西域的龟兹地区和阿富汗一带出土的塑像非常一致,表明敦煌再次吸取了西域风格。此时的佛像组合由北魏时期的一佛二菩萨变为一佛二弟子二菩萨,这样的格局一直延续到隋唐。二弟子像一身为年纪最大的

unearthed in places like Qiuci of the Western Regions and Afghanistan, showing that for a second time Dunhuang had absorbed the art styles of the Western Regions. During this time, one Buddha, two disciples, and two bodhisattvas were grouped together to replace the combination of one Buddha and two bodhisattvas that marked the Northern Wei period. This new style continued until the Sui and Tang dynasties. As to the two disciples depicted, one was the Buddha's

弟子迦叶,表现出饱经风霜的样子;另一身为年纪最小的弟子阿难,表现出年轻聪慧的神态。这一老一少富有个性的刻画也在北周形成了一定的模式。(图14)

敦煌早期彩塑反映了外来风格强劲的佛教雕塑渐渐地与中国本土风格融合的过

oldest disciple, Mahakasyapa, portrayed as a figure having experienced plenty of hardships, and the other was the Buddha's cousin Ananda, the youngest disciple, bearing an expression of youth and intelligence. This individualized portrayal of one elder and one youth became a prototype of the Northern Zhou (Fig.14).

The early painted sculptures in Dunhuang reflected the process of how

图14 佛像 莫高窟第297窟西壁龛 北周
Fig.14 Buddha Statue, Niche in West Wall of Mogao Cave 297, Northern Zhou

程。但在南北朝纷纭复杂的政治形势和文化的影响下，中原风格也呈现出多姿多彩的特点。从敦煌彩塑中也可看出，不论是来自西域、印度的风格，还是来自中原的风格，都不是一成不变的，从而形成了早期敦煌彩塑纷繁复杂的样式特征。

Buddhist sculpture, with strong exotic characteristics, was gradually integrated into the local Chinese style. However, under the complicated political and cultural currents of the Northern and Southern Dynasties, there were also manifold types and styles from the sculpture of the Central Plains. It can be seen from Dunhuang painted sculptures that no style remained immutable, whether it came from India and the Western Regions or from the Central Plains, thus a hallmark of the diverse and complex art patterns of early painted sculptures in Dunhuang has been formed.

隋代——风格的转变期
The Sui Period: Transformation of Styles

北朝晚期以来，中原特别是华北、山东等地区接受了印度笈多朝造像艺术的影响，形成身体敦厚如圆柱形、动态较少、体积感强的造像特征。从山东青州所发现的北齐到隋代的佛像雕刻中，我们可以看到这种富有时代气息的佛教造像风格。隋代以后，这样的风格开始传入敦煌，逐渐成为此时期佛教造像的主流，标志着一个新时代的开始。

隋朝的塑像有着承前启后的特征，与前相比已有很大的发展变化。首先是内容更加丰

Since the late Northern Dynasties[①], iconography in the Central Plains—especially in areas such as North China and the area east of the Taihang Mountains—was influenced by the artistic styles from the Gupta Dynasty of India. Statues were modeled with such features as stout, rounded bodies with less animation and more expression of space, which could be seen in the Buddha sculptures found in Qingzhou, Shandong Province, from the Northern Qi (550–577) to the Sui Dynasty (581–618). These statues are reflections of their day. After the Sui Dynasty, the art form spread into Dunhuang and gradually became the main trend of the age, marking the beginning of a new era.

Sui period statuary inherited the past while ushering in the future. Compared with those before, considerable progress and changes had occurred. To begin with, the content was greatly enriched. Earlier groupings of three statues were developing into new combinations with more than three figures, and more importance was attached to group compositions, signifying a powerful momentum as well as religious didacticism. A typical sample of this new pattern can be seen in Cave 427, in which there are as many as

---

① The Northern Dynasties, a geographical area of the Northern and Southern Dynasties, comprises five successive shorter dynasties, including the Northern Wei, the Eastern Wei, the Northern Qi, the Western Wei and the Northern Zhou.

富,塑像由一铺三身向一铺多身发展。其次是艺术上注重群体组合,从而体现出一种雄浑的气势与宗教精神。第427窟是此期的代表,全窟彩塑总数达28身之多。中心柱正面一铺三尊的中央佛像头微向下垂,面含微笑,仿佛在俯视着尘世的芸芸众生,庄严中透出慈祥的神情,左手平伸作与愿印,右手竖掌,手指向上,施无畏印。单纯而简练的袈裟,古朴而庄重的色调,衬托出佛陀的睿智。佛陀两侧站在莲花台上的胁侍菩萨,比佛像略低,她们面容端庄,嫣然微笑。与佛不同的是,她们的衣饰华丽:右侧的菩萨头戴花蔓冠,上身着菱形连珠纹短上衣,肩挎红色帔帛,浅绿色的飘带和金色的璎珞下垂,下身着菱形花纹锦裙,一手托莲蕾,一手自然下垂;左侧的菩萨头冠已失,上衣为菱格狮凤纹,华丽的璎珞和飘带下垂,菱花格锦裙垂于脚下,一手拈花,一手紧靠腿侧,具有少女般的矜持(图15)。南北两壁的塑像与

28 painted sculptures. On the front side of the central pillar there is a grouping of three statues. The Buddha in the middle slightly lowers his head with a gentle smile on his face. He seems to be looking over all the mortal beings of the mundane world. A sense of kindness can be detected from behind his tranquil expression. His left hand extends horizontally, in the *varada mudra* of supreme generosity, while his right hand extends vertically, fingers spreading upward, displaying the *abhaya mudra* of fearlessness. The *kasaya* he wears is uncomplicated and modest, and the color is sober and simple, showing a profound inner wisdom. The two attendant bodhisattvas on both sides of the Buddha's lotus throne stand a little shorter than he does. They both look dignified, smiling beautifully. What makes them different from the Buddha is that they are dressed and ornamented extravagantly. The one on the right wears a coronet of flowers and vines, and an upper garment with lozenge and linked-pearl motifs. She also wears an embroidered red shawl on her shoulders, a pale green sash, and a bejeweled golden necklace hanging down. She has a brocade skirt with lozenge motifs, one hand holding a lotus bud and the other hanging down naturally at her side. The coronet of the bodhisattva on the left is missing. She wears an upper garment of lozenge motifs with lions and phoenixes, her magnificent sashes and gorgeous necklace of jewels floating

Art Treasures: Murals and Painted Sculptures in Mogao Caves

图 15　佛三尊像　莫高窟第 427 窟中心柱正面　隋
Fig.15　Grouping of One Buddha and Two Attendant Bodhisattva Statues, Front Side of the Central Pillar, Mogao Cave 427, Sui Dynasty

中心柱正面塑像的姿势、神情基本一致。从身体简练的轮廓来看,我们可以感受到笈多时代马图拉以及南印度雕刻的某些特征。以超常的体量,对观众形成一种威压的气势,同时又能以慈祥而安静的神态,给信众以信赖

downward, her brocade skirt with lozenge lattices rippling down to her feet, one hand holding a flower and the other hanging close to her side, with the reserve of a young woman (Fig.15). The poses and the expressions of the sculptures on both the north and south walls are basically similar to those of the central pillar's front side. Certain features of sculptures from the Gupta period of Mathura and South India can be sensed from the simply contoured profiles of these figures. The sheer number of statues gives the viewer an overwhelming

21

感,从而产生巨大的宗教力量。这就是在中国的土地上形成的富有本土艺术精神的雕塑。

如果说第427窟主室的佛、菩萨形象具有含蓄、内敛的情感,那么,前室的天王、力士则要外露得多。门两侧是护法的金刚力士。左侧力士张口大呼,右拳回收,似要砸将出去。他的头部与下颌、脖子等转折处棱角分明,胸部、手臂隆起一块块强健的肌肉,表现出一个刚毅、勇猛的战士形象。右侧力士正紧握双拳,准备上阵厮杀。他牙关紧咬,双目圆睁,充满张力的肌肉表现出一种强烈的感情和正待暴发的力量。前室南北壁各有两身天王,这便是所谓的四大天王,在佛国世界里他们是守卫着东西南北四方之神。这些天王身着铠甲、战袍,手持法器,足踏恶鬼,同勇猛的金刚力士相

religious feeling and at the same time, with their expressions of benevolence and peace, a sense of trustworthiness is created as well. As a result, the great power of religion is conveyed. Such is the sculpture that developed in China, imbued with native Chinese aesthetics.

If we can say that the emotions of the Buddha and bodhisattvas in the main chamber of Cave 427 are subtle and restrained, then the Heavenly Kings and the other *lokapalas* in the antechamber are much more revealing. *Lokapalas* stand on both sides of the door. The one on the left shouts, with his mouth wide open. His right fist is drawn back, ready to strike a punch at any moment. Edges are clearly defined at all curved parts including his head, jaw, and neck. The large, bulging muscles on his chest and arms suggest that he is a brave, strong fighter. The one on the right clenches his two fists tightly and seems to be ready to dash onto the battlefield, teeth gritting together and eyes wide open. The terrific tension in his muscles demonstrates an intense passion and an uncontainable force. There are two Heavenly Kings, of the well-known "Four Great Heavenly Kings", one on each side of the north and south walls of the antechamber. In Buddhist cosmology these are supernatural beings who guard over the directions of north, south, east, and west. These Heavenly Kings wear armor and battle dress, hold Buddhist weapons in their hands, and crush demons underfoot. Compared with the fierce and brave *lokapalas*, they appear to be steady, with victorious smiles on their faces. They behave boldly and heroically, maintaining the magnanimous spirit of a

比,显得沉着,且面含胜利的笑意,动作豪迈而又不失将军气概。

隋代的彩塑大多注重体积感,面相丰圆,体现出一种质朴的精神。如第419窟、420窟的彩塑菩萨,身体不像北朝晚期彩塑那样富有动态,但却显得稳重而矜持,自有一种纯朴而优雅的风姿。如第420窟的西壁龛外南侧的两身菩萨亭亭玉立,一手上举,轻拂柳枝,一手提净瓶,面庞清秀、光润,神态拘谨而露出稚气(图16)。这一时期佛弟子迦叶与阿难的形象个性化特征更加明显。如第419窟西壁龛内北侧迦叶像,额头上皱纹密布,眼窝深陷,胸部的肋骨凸现,表现出一个饱经沧桑的老僧形象(图17)。而与之相对的南侧阿难像则是一幅单纯的少年形象。第412窟的一组13身塑像,把佛的十大弟子都塑出来了,气势宏大,造型朴拙,很能代表隋代精神。

general at the same time.

Most of the painted sculptures of the Sui period emphasize volume, with full, round faces, embodying a spirit of simplicity. The bodhisattvas in Caves 419 and 420 can be regarded as examples. Their figures are not as dynamic as those of the late Northern Dynasties. However, they appear to be steady and reserved, revealing themselves to be simple but graceful. The two bodhisattvas on the left side of the west wall's niche in Cave 420, for instance, are slim and calm, with one hand raised, gently holding a willow branch, the other carrying a ritual bottle vase. They have comely faces and smooth skin; they appear reserved yet childlike (Fig.16). In this period, the individuality of the two disciples, Mahakasyapa and Ananda, is delineated even more clearly. For example, on the statue of Mahakasyapa on the right side of the west wall's niche in Cave 419, his forehead is densely covered with wrinkles, with deep eye sockets and ribs protruding from his chest. This is the portrait of an old monk who has experienced many vicissitudes of life (Fig. 17). Ananda stands opposite him on the left side of the niche, depicted as a simple, naïve youth. In Cave 412 there are 13 statues, among which are sculpted the ten principal disciples, with grand momentum and simple features, accurately representing the spirit of the Sui Dynasty.

图 16 菩萨 莫高窟第 420 窟西壁龛外南侧 隋
Fig.16 Bodhisattva Statue, Left Side of Niche in West Wall, Mogao Cave 420, Sui Dynasty

图 17 迦叶 莫高窟第 419 窟西壁龛内北侧 隋
Fig.17 Statue of Mahakasyapa, Right Side of Niche in West Wall, Mogao Cave 419, Sui Dynasty

唐代——走向世俗化
The Tang Period: Towards Secularization

唐代,随着全社会经济文化的飞速发展,彩塑艺术也快速走向成熟。在莫高窟初唐第332窟、57窟等窟中的彩塑还保持着一定的隋代遗风。盛唐以后,以第328窟、320窟、45窟等窟为代表的彩塑代表着一种全新的雕塑风格,体现了唐代雕塑艺术发展的高潮。

初唐彩塑群像以第328窟的一铺9身塑像为代表(现存8身,其中一身已被美国人华尔纳于1924年盗走,现藏哈佛大学赛克勒博物馆)。佛端坐于中央,两侧是佛弟子阿难和迦叶。阿难号称多闻第一,是最年轻的弟子,艺术家塑出他天真而略带稚气的面孔,体态潇洒,具有一种年轻的活力。与他相对的迦叶号称头陀第一,是年纪最大的弟子,他紧锁双眉,老态龙钟,一副饱经沧桑的样子。这性格鲜明的一老一少,形成强烈的对

During the Tang Dynasty, society witnessed a great cultural and economic boom at all levels, and the art of painted sculptures was developing rapidly into maturity. Although some artistic features of the Sui period are still visible in Caves 332 and 57 of the Early Tang, a completely new style emerged in Mogao during the flourishing period of the High Tang, represented by Caves 328, 320, and 45—embodying the zenith of Tang sculptural art.

A typical grouping of painted sculptures from the Early Tang are found in Cave 328, where a collection of nine statues were modeled. Eight of them still stand today; one was unlawfully removed by an American Langdon Warner in 1924 and is now housed in the Sackler Museum at Harvard University. The Buddha sits upright in the middle, with disciples Mahakasyapa and Ananda standing at each side. Ananda was the Buddha's youngest disciple, famous for his erudition. The artist molded his childlike face with a hint of innocence, and his pose is elegant and unrestrained with the vigor of youth. On the opposite side is Mahakasyapa, the oldest disciple, who enjoys a reputation as the first mendicant Buddhist monk. His eyebrows are knit in a frown and he looks weighed down with age, with an appearance of having

比。弟子外侧的菩萨作游戏坐式,这种坐姿显得随意、自然,配合她们健美而灵活的身体,充满了青春的魅力。外侧的几身供养菩萨跪在莲花座上,身体小巧玲珑,别有风韵。这组彩塑,不论站式、坐式,都反映出艺术家对人体比例的熟练掌握和对人物神态刻画的细致入微。(图18)

盛唐第45窟保存着一铺完整的7身彩塑(图19),以佛为中心,两侧分

experienced the many changes of life. This pairing of old and young, with distinctive characteristics, forms a sharp contrast. The bodhisattvas beside them sit in *lalitāsana* pose (known as "royal ease" pose), one leg hanging down, one leg bent at the knee, looking free and natural. Echoed by their vigorous, graceful, and agile physical manner, they are full of the attractiveness of youth. Several attendant bodhisattvas on the outer side kneel down on lotuses, small and nimble with charmingly distinctive features. The composition of painted sculptures, whether standing or sitting, reveals the exquisite skill of the artisans in capturing both the physical proportions as well as the poses and detailed expressions of human figures. (Fig.18).

Cave 45 from the High Tang holds an entire

图18 佛像一铺 莫高窟第328窟龛内 初唐
Fig.18 Statue Arrangement of Buddha, Attendants, and Disciples, Central Niche of Mogao Cave 328, Early Tang

图 19　佛像一铺　莫高窟第 45 窟龛内　盛唐
Fig.19　Standing Statue Arrangement of Buddha, Attendants, and Disciples, Central Niche of Mogao Cave 45, High Tang

别是弟子、菩萨、天王，除佛外其余均取站立姿势。阿难双手抱于腹前，身披红色袈裟，内着僧祇支，衣纹的刻画简洁、单纯，胯部微微倾斜，神态安详，在恭谨中又透出青年的朝气。迦叶则老成持重，颇具长者风范，他一手平伸，一手上举，慈祥的眼神中充满睿智的光彩。菩萨上身璎珞垂胸，帔帛斜挎，下身着华丽的锦裙；头部微侧，眼睛半闭，身体微微弯曲作"S"形；一手下垂，一手平端，动

preserved group of seven painted statues, with the Buddha at the center and disciples, bodhisattvas, and Heavenly Kings standing on both sides (Fig.19). Ananda clasps his hands in front of his stomach, wearing an *uttarāsaṇga* and a red *kasaya*. The lines on his clothes are sharp and simple. His hips tilt forward slightly and he has a peaceful expression, showing the vitality of youth through a look of respectful obedience. Mahakasyapa looks experienced and circumspect, with the demeanor of an elder. One of his hands extends level and the other raises upward. His eyes shine with compassion and wisdom. The bodhisattvas' jeweled necklaces hang across their chests, their silk sashes draped over brocade *dhotis*, and their heads are angled with eyes half-closed. Their

作优美，神情娴雅；洁白莹润的肌肤下面，似乎能感觉出血液在里面流动。天王身披铠甲，一手叉腰，一手执兵器，足踏恶鬼，英姿飒爽，神情激昂

figures bend slightly in the classic *tribhanga* (S-shaped posture) pose, with one arm hanging down at the side and the other arm extending forward from the elbow, the hand palm up. They look graceful and with elegant expressions, and their blood seems palpable, flowing underneath their bright, smooth skin. The Heavenly Kings wear armor,

图20　菩萨和弟子、天王像　莫高窟第45窟　盛唐

Fig.20　Statues of Mahakasyapa, Bodhisattva, and Heavenly King, Mogao Cave 45, High Tang

（图20）。从这里可以看出，这一时期的彩塑写实性很强，艺术家们根据现实生活中的妇女、将军等形象来塑造菩萨、天王，于是这些神看起来显得格外可亲；同时，艺术家这种高度的写实技巧，又使这些塑像动态逼真、栩栩如生。而每一身彩塑的动作又各不相同：阿难双手抱在腹前，显得忠厚、谦恭；迦叶扬手似乎正在说什么；两身菩萨都一手伸出，一手下垂，显得漫不经心；天王则是表情激昂，肌肉绷紧。这一动一静、一松一紧，各具性格却又统一在佛的周围，产生了极强的艺术魅力。

另外，艺术家非常注意这些雕塑的群体性。这一组彩塑以佛为中心，左右对称排列；他们目光俯视。可以想象，古代的佛教信徒进入洞窟，面对佛像跪拜之时，由于处在较低的位置，就会看到每身塑像都在慈祥地看着自己。雕塑艺术是一种

each with one hand on the hip and the other holding a weapon, a demon crushed under one foot. They appear mighty in spirit with a heroic bearing (Fig.20). The strong realism of the painted sculptures from this period is evident. The artists modeled the images of bodhisattvas and Heavenly Kings based on real women and generals, such that these supernatural beings appear to be approachable. At the same time, the artisans' advanced techniques in realism enabled them to produce statues that are dynamic and lifelike. Each figure's movements is different from the others. Ananda, clasping his hands together in front of his abdomen, looks honest, modest, and courteous; Mahakasyapa raises his hand as if he is saying something. Both bodhisattvas extend one hand and drop the other, appearing relaxed; the Heavenly Kings are roused to action, muscles tightly stretched. The dynamic juxtaposed with the static, and the lax with the tense, each statue has its own personality, and all of them are unified around the Buddha, resulting in impressive artistic appeal.

Furthermore, the artists paid special attention to the group dynamics of painted sculptures. This grouping, with the Buddha as the central figure, are arranged symmetrically. Their eyes all look downward. It can be imagined that, in those days, when a Buddhist entered the cave and knelt down to worship the Buddha, he would be in a lower position and find each statue looking down at him benevolently. Sculpture is a kind of environmental art, and because it is three-dimensional, its surroundings are an

环境艺术，由于它是立体的，就必须考虑到它周围的环境。为了渲染宗教的气氛，石窟内的雕塑起到了极为重要的作用。

早期的菩萨形象，一般都表现得比较拘谨。而在唐代，往往表现得自由自在，或坐于莲花座上，一脚下垂，一足横支，作游戏坐式，神情恬淡自然（如第328窟、205窟的菩萨）；或立于莲花台上，身体略呈"S"形弯曲，双目微闭，仪态娴雅，体现出对佛理的觉悟甚高，"得大自在"的精神境界（如第45窟、320窟的菩萨）。唐代彩塑中的佛弟子阿难和迦叶以及天王力士的形象没有了隋以前那种夸张的成分，更注重写实性和人物内心的刻画。

直到隋代为止的敦煌彩塑大多具有高浮雕的特点，背面与墙壁连在一起，最佳观察点只是在正面。而进入唐代以后，彩塑逐渐发展为圆塑，即从不同的角度都可以看到完美的塑像。这一点

important aspect to be taken into account. The sculptures in the caves play a key role in heightening the religious atmosphere.

The demeanor of the early images of bodhisattvas was usually reserved. However, in the Tang period, they were depicted as free and casual. They either sit on lotus thrones, one leg hanging down and the other bent at the side, in *lalitāsana*, quiet and natural, such as the bodhisattvas in Caves 328 and 205; or, as with those in Caves 45 and 320, they stand on a lotus platform with a refined bearing, their curvaceous bodies in *tribhanga*, the S-shaped posture, eyes slightly closing, embodying a high degree of realization of the Buddhist truth—as well as an awareness of being spiritually "at ease and unfettered". There are no elements of exaggeration in the sculptures of the disciples, Ananda and Mahakasyapa, or in the images of the Heavenly Kings and other *lokapalas*, as there were during the Sui period. Rather, emphasis is placed on realistic presentation and on how to capture the inner world of mortal people.

Until the Sui Dynasty, most painted sculptures in Dunhuang were created in high relief, with backs joined to the wall. The ideal vantage point for observation was from the front only. Free-standing statuary in the round was developed during the Tang, resulting in perfect views of the image from different angles. This fundamentally marked the maturity of painted sculptures in Dunhuang. In Cave 205, there is a

图 21 菩萨 莫高窟第 205 窟中心佛坛上 盛唐
Fig.21 Bodhisattva Statue, Central Altar in Mogao Cave 205, High Tang

是敦煌彩塑成熟的重要标志。在第 205 窟佛坛南侧的一身菩萨像，双臂已损，其他部位保存完好，菩萨做游戏坐姿，比例协调，姿势自然，体魄健美（图 21）。不论从哪个方向看，都是那样完美，特别是上身肌体的表现，似乎可以感觉到富有弹性的肌肤，以及流动的血液。这样成功的表现，在第 328 窟、45 窟等窟的彩塑中也同样可以看到。艺术家不再借助于夸张变形和象征的手法，而是以写实主义的手法表现出人（神）的精神世界。在这些菩萨、天王、弟子等形象中，我们可以感觉到那个时代的仪态万千的贵族妇女、娇媚多姿的宫女、威风凛凛的将军、饱读经书的僧人等等的形象。晚唐第 17 窟的洪䛒像，则是石窟中为数极少的塑造现实人物的彩塑。这是一个坐禅僧人，艺术家特别注重面部表情的刻画，表现出一个智者的精神状态。袈裟笼罩住全身，流畅的衣纹表现完整的形体，又体现出生动之趣。

statue of a bodhisattva at the south side of the Buddhist altar. The arms are missing, but other parts of the body remain in relatively good condition. He sits in a relaxed, natural pose, with lifelike proportions, and a strong, graceful build (Fig.21). From whichever angle he is observed, the view is excellent, especially of the upper body, where the skin and musculature appear soft and supple, blood seeming to flow through the veins. Similar successful sculptural presentations can also be found in Caves 328, 45, and others. The artists no longer applied exaggerated distortions or symbolism, but instead, they depicted the spiritual world of mortals—and thus deities—in a realistic way. From these images of bodhisattvas, Heavenly Kings, disciples, and the like, we can see contemporary figures of dignified noblewomen in all their glory, sweet and enchanting young palace ladies, majestic-looking military generals, and scholarly, erudite monks of that time. Cave 17 of the Late Tang is among the very rare caves in which an actual historical figure is sculpted: the monk Hong Bian sitting in meditation. The artists laid special emphasis on his facial expressions, showing the spiritual state of a man of wisdom. He is completely cloaked in his *kasaya*, and the flowing and graceful lines of his clothes show not only his full physical features, but also his lively nature.

Because of the strong trend towards

艺苑瑰宝
莫高窟壁画与彩塑

唐代彩塑一方面由于写实性的加强而使佛教变得可亲可感，另一方面也通过一些大型彩塑来表现佛的宏大。第96窟、130窟分别造出高达35米和26米的大佛（图22），

realistic depiction, Tang painted sculptures made Buddhism intimate and tangible to people on the one hand; while on the other hand, it was an era when massive statues were sculpted to convey the grandeur of the Buddha. In Caves 96 and 130, Buddha statues were sculpted as tall as 35 and 26 meters

图22　大佛　莫高窟第130窟　盛唐
Fig.22　Great Buddha Statue, Mogao Cave 130, High Tang

第 148 窟和 158 窟分别造出了长达 16 米的卧佛；在榆林窟第 6 窟也造出了高达 23 米的佛像。巨型佛像通过其体量给人一种崇高感，这是宗教信仰的需要，也体现着唐人雄强自信的精神。虽说由于武则天等帝王们的倡导而使全国各地纷纷制作巨型佛像，但如果没有一套成熟的雕塑技法和雄厚的经济基础恐怕也很难进行。

从保存完好的第 130 窟大佛（南大像）和第 158 窟的卧佛

respectively (Fig.22), and in both Caves 148 and 158 lie reclining nirvana Buddha statues as long as 16 meters. There is also a 23-meter tall statue of the Buddha in Yulin Cave 6. These monumental works give a sense of the sublime through their sheer mass, which is necessary for a religious faith, but they also embody the Tang era's spirit of strength and self-confidence. Although the creation of giant Buddha sculptures was encouraged all over China by rulers like Empress Wu Zetian, it would have been an impossible feat had it not been for mature sculpting skills and sufficient financial support.

The great Buddha in Cave 130 (Southern

图 23　卧佛　莫高窟第 158 窟　中唐
Fig.23　Nirvana Buddha, Mogao Cave 158, Middle Tang

来看（图23），以巨大的体量表现大佛，却没有一点粗糙之感。浑圆的脸形，半闭的眼睛，由袈裟衣纹形成的一道道弧线，形成有规律的韵律，处处体现出柔和之感，而在整体上又表现着一种雄强的阳刚之风。刚与柔、阳与阴，在这里完美地融合在一起。这便是敦煌彩塑的魅力，也是中国雕塑艺术的特色所在。

盛唐后期的彩塑逐渐失去了前期那种雄强气势和生动的韵味，但在制作上更加精致，世俗化的倾向更加强烈，不论佛弟子还是天王、力士形象都富于人间性。神性消失了，在艺术家的努力下，佛教石窟与人们的距离缩短了，仿佛神与人沟通了。

第194窟是一个小型洞窟，正面开一个帐形龛，内塑一佛二弟子、二菩萨、二天王，龛外侧各塑力士一身。中央的佛双腿下垂，作善跏坐式，一手上举作说法相，一手放在膝盖上，表情平静，神态慈祥。这样稳重而庄严的坐姿也是当

Buddha Statue) and the reclining nirvana Buddha in Cave 158 are quite well-preserved (Fig.23). These images show that despite the colossal scale, there is nothing crude in the sculpting. The round faces, the half-closed eyes, the draped curves of the *kasaya*, the regular lines in the clothes, all show a sense of rhythm as well as delicacy. Regarded as a whole, a bearing of strength and masculinity is demonstrated. Hard and soft, *yin* and *yang*, are perfectly integrated here, which is exactly the allure of Dunhuang's painted sculptures, and precisely the artistic characteristics of Chinese sculpture in general.

Painted sculptures of the later High Tang gradually gave up their masculine strength and fascinating vividness of earlier days, but they were more delicately made and the tendency towards secularization intensified. Whether they were disciples, Heavenly Kings, or *lokapalas*, the sculptures appeared more human. Deification disappeared, and by effort of the artists, the distance between the Buddhist cave temples and human beings was shortened, as if celestial beings and humans could be linked.

Cave 194 is a smaller one, where a tent-style niche is cut into the main wall. Inside the niche stand one Buddha, two disciples, two bodhisattvas, and two Heavenly Kings. Outside the niche there is one *lokapala*—a Dharma guardian—on either side. The Buddha in the center sits in *pralambapādāsana*, legs pendant and both feet on the floor, one hand raised in *vitarka mudra* to teach the Dharma and the

时中原地区流行的样式。龙门石窟擂鼓台中洞、惠简洞,天龙山石窟第4窟等唐代洞窟中都有类似的倚坐佛像。龛北侧的弟子迦叶右袒袈裟,双手合十,表现出虔诚的神情。与他相对的弟子阿难,眯着眼睛,两手交叠在腹前,像一个无忧无虑的少年。北侧的菩萨站在莲花台上,斜挎帔帛,罗裙垂地,身体向后微微倾斜,妩媚多姿;她面容洁白莹润,带着微笑。南侧的菩萨头梳双环髻,面颊丰腴,双目低垂,嘴角露出隐隐笑意;身穿华丽的圆领无袖上衣,帔帛围绕,搭于左肘;体态丰腴,肌肤莹洁,身体自然舒展,衣纹飘柔,表现出纺织品的质感,反映了古代匠师高超的造像技巧。值得注意的是,此时菩萨的服饰不再强调印度传来的那些飘带与璎珞,而更多地表现当时中国妇女所穿的衣服,呈现出世俗化的倾向(图24)。

other placed on the knee. He bears a benevolent look of serenity. This type of sedate, tranquil seated pose was also prevalent in the sculptures of the Central Plains during this period. Images of the Buddha in other locations, such as Leigutai middle grotto and Huijian grotto of the Longmen Caves, as well as Cave 4 of the Tianlongshan Caves, are all sculpted in this type of seated pose. On the north side of the niche, the disciple Mahakasyapa wears a *kasaya* with his right shoulder bare and his palms folded devoutly, bearing an expression of piety. Opposite him, the disciple Ananda clasps his hands in front of his abdomen and narrows his eyes, revealing himself as a carefree young man. The bodhisattva on the north side stands on a lotus platform. She leans slightly back, a brocade sash crossing her body and silk *dhoti* dropping to the ground. She wears a gentle smile on her radiant and smooth face, looking gorgeous and colorful. The bodhisattva on the south side wears her hair combed into a chignon with two buns, cheeks full and round, eyes downcast, and a slight smile in the corners of her mouth. She is dressed in a floral-patterned sleeveless upper garment with a round neckline. Her narrow shawl enfolds her, draping over her left elbow. Her physical frame is robust and well-built, her skin is bright and smooth, and her whole body relaxed and comfortable. The lines on her clothes are soft and flowing, showing the texture of the fabric. All these reveal the exquisite skill of the ancient craftsmen in creating iconography. Worth mentioning here is that during

图24 菩萨 莫高窟第194窟龛内北侧 盛唐
Fig.24 Bodhisattva, Right Side of Niche, Mogao Cave 194, High Tang

北侧的天王，戴头盔,着铠甲,雄健威武。南侧的天王与之相对,发髻高耸，神情敦厚,面带爽朗的笑容。古代塑像中的天王,大多是横眉怒目、杀气腾腾的样子,而这一身却一改天王传统形象,显得极有人情味。龛外有两身力士，都是上身赤裸,一手挥拳，一手舒掌,好像准备厮杀的样子。艺术家着意刻画了天王那发达的肌肉、暴胀的筋脉以及圆瞪的双眼,他的全身无处不显示着一种强劲的力量。

第159窟正面也开帐形龛,原有一铺7身彩塑,中央的佛像已不存在，只剩下二弟子、二菩萨、二天王。这种格局与第194窟相似,菩萨的形象也很有特色:北侧的菩萨双目下视,上身袒裸,下着绣花锦裙，肌肤洁白，一

this time, the bodhisattvas' style of dress no longer emphasized narrow sashes and jeweled necklaces from India, but instead they wore the clothing of contemporary Chinese women, showing a marked tendency toward secularization (Fig.24).

The Heavenly King on the north side wears armor and a helmet, looking mighty and powerful. The one on the south side, standing opposite, looks sincere and earnest, with a topknot gathered high on his head and a broad smile. In ancient times most sculptures of the Heavenly Kings had fierce expressions with frowning brows and angry eyes, but this one is completely different from conventional ones—he exudes plenty of human kindness. The two *lokapalas* outside the niche are both shirtless, with each raising a fist while extending the palm of the other hand, as if they are ready to fight. With great attention to detail, the artisans depicted strong muscles, bulging veins, and staring eyes; every part of the body symbolizes strength and power.

There is another tent-style niche in the main wall of Cave 159. Originally seven painted sculptures stood there, but now the central Buddha statue is lost, leaving only the two disciples, two bodhisattvas, and two Heavenly Kings. The sculptures are arranged similarly to those in Cave 194; the features of the bodhisattvas are quite distinctive. The eyes of the one on the north side gaze downward. She is round and full, with bright, smooth skin, dressed in an embroidered brocade *dhoti*, with a bare upper torso. She raises one hand and drops the other naturally, looking dignified and poised. The bodhisattva on the south side has curved eyebrows and round cheeks,

艺苑瑰宝
莫高窟壁画与彩塑

图25　佛像　莫高窟第55窟佛坛正面佛像　宋
Fig.25　Seated Buddha Statue, Central Figure in Altar of Mogao Cave 55, Song Dynasty

手上举，一手自然垂下，身体丰盈，姿态落落大方；南侧的菩萨曲眉丰颊，发髻高耸，衣饰华丽，一手托物上举，一手下垂，轻握飘带，姿势优雅。外侧的两身天王挺胸怒目，直视前方，两手紧握，仿佛正要出击。天王与菩萨形成动静对比，又和谐统一。

五代、北宋彩塑所存甚少，第55窟保存一组彩塑，填补了这一时期彩塑的空白。这个洞窟是一个方形殿堂窟，中央设马蹄形佛坛，佛坛上塑三铺佛像，分西、南、北三面而坐，为三世佛，均为倚坐式（图25）。西壁正面的佛像右手扬起，左手放在膝上，神情静穆；左右两侧佛像也大体一致。正面佛像北侧存弟子迦叶像，一臂已残，他身体僵直，神态拘谨。南侧佛两旁存两身菩萨，北侧存一身菩萨，她们比例和谐，衣纹

hair worn high in a topknot. Her clothes have a flowered pattern. She raises one hand as if holding something, and drops the other hand at her side gently grasping the edges of her sashes, looking rather elegant. The two Heavenly Kings on the outer sides stand upright with glaring eyes looking straight ahead, hands clenched into fists, as if in combat. The Heavenly Kings and bodhisattvas form a contrast between motion and stillness, yet they are in complete harmony.

Few painted sculptures of the Five Dynasties (907-960) or the Northern Song (960-1127) are preserved today, but the group in Cave 55 helps fill in this gap. It is a square hall cave, with a horseshoe-shaped Buddha altar in the center, where three images of the Buddha are sculpted, all seated in *pralambapādāsana*, or "European pose", along the three sides: north, south, and west. They are the Trikāya Buddhas—the Buddhas of the Three Ages (Fig.25). The Buddha on the west side, in the central position, raises his right hand and places his left hand on his knee, looking solemn and respectful. The two Buddhas on the north and south sides adopt similar postures. The disciple Mahakasyapa, standing on the north side of the central Buddha, looks stiff and reserved; one of his arms is broken. On both sides of the Buddha on the south side of the altar are two bodhisattvas, while only one bodhisattva remains beside the Buddha statue on the north side. All these bodhisattvas are harmoniously proportioned, with gentle mannerisms and well-suited lines on their sculpted clothing. The Heavenly King in the southwest corner reveals

贴体，神态温和。西南角上的天王形象，体现出刚毅和威武的气质。南侧佛座边的天王造型较为新颖，他左手托着佛座，好像不堪重负又拼命用力的神态颇为生动。总的来说，这些彩塑都能准确把握人体比例，在形象刻画，衣纹、服饰的表现，以及总体精神上都努力追摹唐风，但体形过分僵硬，表情呆滞，缺乏唐朝那种鲜活的气息。

敦煌彩塑以木为骨架，以黏土塑制而成，最后还要上彩，以绘画补充泥塑的不足，是绘塑结合的艺术。千百年以前，中国的艺术家们就通过这些散发着泥土气息的彩塑，表现出如此精美而感人的艺术形象，直到今天仍然散发着独特的魅力。

a temperament of strength and courage, while the Heavenly King beside the Buddha's lotus throne on the south side is rather unusual. With his left hand, he props up the throne, the weight of which seems to be almost too much for him to bear, but he holds it with all his might. The Herculean effort is vivid. Generally speaking, the human body's proportions in these sculptures are presented accurately. In terms of figure portrayal, the zeitgeist of the Tang Dynasty is assiduously imitated in the lines of the clothing, dress style, and overall demeanor. However, due to the stiff shapes and lackluster facial expressions, these sculptures lack the liveliness of the Tang period.

For sculptures in Dunhuang, wood was used as the core or armature, and clay as the modeling material; they were then painted over with polychrome colors. The painting could correct any minor defects in the sculpting process. Thus, painted statuary was the combined art of sculpting and painting. Thousands of years ago, it was by using humble, ordinary clay that Chinese artists created these exquisite and impressive painted sculptures, which carry their unique artistic appeal to this day.

艺苑瑰宝：莫高窟壁画与彩塑
Art Treasures: Murals and Painted Sculptures in Mogao Caves

佛像画的世界

The World of Painted Buddhist Iconography

莫高窟壁画的内容主要包括六类：

1. 佛像画；

2. 佛教故事画（包括本生故事、因缘故事、佛传故事、佛教史迹故事）；

3. 中国传统神怪像；

4. 经变画；

5. 供养人画像；

6. 装饰图案画。

除了装饰图案以外，绘画都是以人物（包括佛、菩萨或世俗人物）为主体的。莫高窟500多座石窟中留下了无数的人物形象，可以说是中国人物画艺术的宝库。

本章将主要介绍莫高窟壁画中的佛像画。

The subjects of murals in the Mogao Caves mainly comprise six genres:

1. Painted icons of the Buddha.

2. Buddhist narrative literature (including *jataka* tales, *nidana* stories, narratives of the Buddha's life, legends and stories of Buddhist transmission).

3. Traditional Chinese deities and spirits.

4. Sutra illustrations (*jingbian*).

5. Portraits of donors.

6. Ornamental motifs.

The subjects of all murals, except for ornamental motifs, are figures, including the Buddha, bodhisattvas, and mortal humans. Huge numbers of human images are found in the 500 or more grottoes of the Mogao Caves, making them a treasure trove for the art of Chinese figure painting.

This chapter focuses on the painted images of the Buddha found in the Mogao Cave murals.

说法图
Dharma-Preaching Scenes

佛像包括佛与弟子、菩萨、天王等尊像,他们是洞窟的主体,是信徒崇拜的对象。一般来说,洞窟中把佛像等主要礼拜对象做成彩塑,安置在重要的位置。壁画相对而言是处于陪衬地位的,但是在一些洞窟中,彩塑较少或者没有塑像的情况下,以壁画绘制的佛像也同样是礼拜的对象。在壁画中往往首先要突出那些独立的或者成组的尊像画。早期壁画中流行说法图。说法图是表现佛说法的场面,通常画出一铺3身、5身或者更多的尊像,中央为如来佛,两侧为佛弟子、菩萨和天王等。北魏以后,说法图往往两侧有众多的菩萨、飞天等,一铺说法图可能有十几身尊像(图26)。

一般来说,在中心柱

Statues of the Buddha, bodhisattvas, disciples, and Heavenly Kings, among others, are all Buddhist icons. They are normally the subject of a cave temple as well as the object of Buddhist worship. Generally speaking, the major objects for worship in a cave, such as images of the Buddha, are made into painted statues and placed in the most prominent position, while murals serve as a background for them. However, in some of the caves where there are few or no painted sculptures, images of the Buddha painted as murals can likewise be objects for worship. Thus it is often the case that, among the murals, importance should first be attached to a single Buddha or a grouping of Buddhist images. In earlier murals, Dharma-preaching scenes are prevalent. Such paintings depict a Buddha expounding the Buddhist teachings, or the Dharma. The scene is usually composed of three, five, or more figures, with the Buddha at the center, and disciples, bodhisattvas, and Heavenly Kings on both sides. After the Northern Wei, Dharma-preaching scenes were typically composed of groupings of more than 10 figures, with several bodhisattvas, *apsaras*, and others on each side (Fig.26).

Generally speaking, in a central pillar cave, the niche in the front side of the pillar is usually the main niche, while on the walls of both the left and the right sides of the cave (the north and south

图 26 说法图 莫高窟第 248 窟北壁 北魏
Fig.26 Dharma-Preaching Scene, North Wall of Mogao Cave 248, Northern Wei

窟中，中心塔柱的正面龛是主龛，那么在洞窟的左右两侧壁往往要配合中央的彩塑画出大型的说法图，强化佛教的主题。如早期的第 251 窟、254 窟、257 窟等窟都是如此。在殿堂窟中，正面开龛造出佛与菩萨等像，两侧壁也画说法图，同样与正面的 sides, respectively), large paintings of Dharma-preaching scenes are made to match the painted sculptures in the center, reinforcing the Buddhist themes. Earlier grottoes such as Caves 251, 254, and 257 are examples of this pattern. In a hall cave, a niche is cut into the main wall and statues of the Buddha and bodhisattvas were sculpted inside. Dharma-preaching scenes also cover both the side walls. Similarly, these paintings, coordinating with the painted sculptures in the main niche, make up a combination of three groupings of Buddhas in the cave. This type of combination depicts the Trikāya Buddhas, that is, the Buddhas of the Past, Present, and Future.

In the paintings of Dharma-preaching scenes of

彩塑组成三组佛像的形式。这样的组合往往就是表现过去、现在、未来三世佛的形式。

北凉、北魏的说法图，佛像庄严沉静，菩萨身体往往呈"三道弯"形式，显得活泼多姿；色彩较浓厚，由于时代久远而变色，大部分身体部位的晕染都变黑，所以观众往往会感到奇怪。第263窟南壁的说法图，由于从表层壁画中剥出，画面色彩保存了当时的原作，使我们得知北魏时期真实的色

the Northern Liang and the Northern Wei, the Buddha is tranquil and serene, while the bodhisattvas are normally portrayed in the *tribhanga*, or S-shaped posture, looking lively and graceful. The pigments, though thick and applied heavily, have changed due to the passing of the years, causing most parts of the bodies to have darkened from oxidation, often astonishing visitors. The Dharma-preaching scene on the south wall of Cave 263 is preserved in its original colors and appearance because the surface murals were peeled off, enabling us to see the original true pigments and line drawings of the Northern Wei (Fig.27). It is a mural with three Dharma-preaching Buddhas. The one in the middle is a bit taller. The edge of his *kasaya* is tinted blue with azurite, forming a sharp contrast with red, the

图27 三佛说法图 莫高窟第263窟南壁 北魏
Fig.27 Three Buddhas Preaching the Dharma, South Wall of Mogao Cave 263, Northern Wei

彩和线描的情况(图27)。这是一幅三佛说法图,中央一尊佛像身体稍高,袈裟的边缘以石青色染出,与袈裟本来的红色形成强烈的对比。两侧的佛像都面朝中央,最外两侧还各有一身菩萨。菩萨对称地站在两旁,头部微低,面向佛像,一手扶着髋部,一手自然下垂,身体略呈"S"形弯曲,上身半裸,下着长裙,飘带自双肩下垂,在腹前交叠在一起。金色的项饰和臂钏,体现着华贵的气息,粉色的肌肤、明亮的石青色长裙与土红色背景形成对比,更体现出菩萨优雅的气质。在画面上部两侧,还各有一身飞天,身着红色长裙,向着中央飞来。整铺画面格调统一,色彩不多,却对比鲜明、华丽灿烂。

西魏第285窟(开凿于538~539年)的说法图,与北魏时期有了很大的区别,较为独特。由于受到中原艺术的影响,佛像和菩萨形象呈现出新的面貌。本窟在北壁画出了八铺说法图,在东壁画出三铺说法图。特别是东壁门两侧各有一铺说法图规模较大,人物也较多。如

original dominant color of the *kasaya* itself. The other two Buddhas on either side face the one in the middle. On the outermost sides are two bodhisattvas, standing symmetrically and facing the Buddha. They lower their heads slightly, each with one hand resting on the hip and the other dropping down naturally at the side. They are dressed in long *dhotis*, their upper bodies partially clothed with long, narrow sashes hanging down from their shoulders and knotted in front of their abdomens, and their curvaceously-shaped figures slightly bent. They wear golden ornaments including necklaces and armlets, creating an air of sumptuousness. Their pink skin and their bright *dhotis*, in azurite, contrast sharply with the background color of the red earth pigment, better revealing their elegant temperament. On each side of the upper part of the mural is an *apsara*, wearing a long red *dhoti* or skirt and flying towards the center. The result is a pleasant combination of just a few colors in perfect harmony, providing contrast and a magnificent effect.

The Dharma-preaching scenes in Cave 258 of the Western Wei (constructed from 538 to 539) are unique and quite different from those of the Northern Wei. Influenced by the art of the Central Plains, new features appear in the images of the Buddha and bodhisattvas. In this cave alone, eight preaching scenes are painted on the north wall and three on the east wall. What is special here is that on the east wall, respectively on each side of the entrance

图 28　说法图　莫高窟第 285 窟东壁门北　西魏
Fig.28　Dharma-Preaching Scene, Left Entrance in East Wall of Mogao Cave 285, Western Wei

北侧这一铺（图 28），中央是佛结跏趺坐于方形佛座上，面容清瘦，双手作说法印。身着红色通肩袈裟，但不像印度的通肩袈裟那样紧缠身体，而是领口较宽松，可以看出里面的僧祇支。袈裟从身上垂下，形成很多褶襞，有规律地在佛座下面展开。佛两侧上部各有两身弟子像，下部各有两身菩萨像。靠近佛像的两身菩萨身着

there is a larger picture with many more figures. An example is the one on the left side of the entrance, in which the Buddha sits in a lotus pose upon the square seat at the center (Fig.28). He looks thin, with both hands in the *vitarka mudra*. He wears a red *kasaya* different from those of the Indian style that wrapped tightly on the body. His is draped over both shoulders, with a loose collar, and the inner *uttarāsaṅga* exposed. The *kasaya* hangs upon the body, heavily pleated, rhythmically spreading down and out to the seat. On each side of the Buddha, there are two disciples in

49

汉式大衣，在衣服上又有飘带自双肩垂下，在腹前交叉，然后经双臂而向两侧展开。外侧的两身菩萨也有与前两身菩萨一致的飘带垂下，下着红色长裙，虽说是上身半裸，但宽大的飘带几乎把身体完全遮盖住了，已经没有北魏以前那种"裸"的意味。这也许就是中国式的审美思想在起作用吧。佛和菩萨的衣服及飘带下部都呈尖角形，这可能是画家想表现衣服飘举的感觉。魏晋时代中原的绘画讲究表现飘飘欲仙的情态，这正是受中原审美思想影响的产物。

唐代的说法图，人物大量增加，而画家更注重对不同人物个性的刻画，出现了很多杰出的作品。如第57窟南壁的说法图（图29），画中佛、菩萨、弟子等形象达十五六身，中央是佛结跏趺坐于莲花座上，佛两侧绘一老一少二弟子，年老的弟子手持净瓶，年轻的弟子托钵，侍奉于两侧。再往外是两身大菩萨，特别是左侧的

the upper section, and two bodhisattvas in the lower section. The two bodhisattvas closer to the Buddha are dressed in Han-style robes and long shawls with sash-like edges that hang down, criss-crossing at the stomach and draping across both arms. The two outer bodhisattvas also wear sashes hanging down like the inner two. They are dressed in long red *dhotis*. Although only partially clothed on the upper torso, they are almost completely covered by the wide sashes. No traces of nakedness from before the Northern Wei remain—possibly Chinese moral standards were exerting their influence here. There are clear, sharp corners along all the lower hems of the clothes and sashes worn by the Buddha and bodhisattvas. The artists likely wanted to create an effect of flowing garments. Paintings in the Central Plains during the Wei and the Jin dynasties attempted to convey a spirit of flowing and floating like celestial beings, and this type of effect is exactly an adoption of such aesthetic standards here.

During the Tang period, the number of characters greatly increased in Dharma-preaching scenes. The artists laid more emphases on the portrayal of personalities of different characters. More outstanding works were created, such as the one on the south wall of Cave 57 (Fig.29), for example. There are as many as 15 or 16 figures in it, including the Buddha, bodhisattvas, and disciples. The Buddha is at the center, sitting on a lotus throne in *padmasana*, or full lotus pose. The two disciples, one old and one young, are painted one on each side,

Art Treasures: Murals and Painted Sculptures in Mogao Caves

图 29　说法图　莫高窟第 57 窟南壁　初唐
Fig.29　Dharma-Preaching Scene, South Wall of Mogao Cave 57, Early Tang

图 30 菩萨 莫高窟第 57 窟南壁 初唐
Fig.30 Bodhisattva, South Wall of Mogao Cave 57, Early Tang

胁侍菩萨绘制得最为优美，她头戴化佛冠，上身半裸，肩披长巾，身佩璎珞，一手上举轻扶飘带，一手托供品，体态优美，身体略呈"S"形，目光下视，若有所思，肌肤细腻，体现出雍容高贵的美。从这身菩萨身上佩戴的璎珞、所穿华丽的衣裙上看，俨然是一位贵妇人的形象（图30）。胁侍菩萨身后的四身菩萨也面相俊美，画家特别注意刻画她们的眼神，有的矜持，有的娇媚，有的若不经意，有的如秋波暗送。所谓"传神阿睹"，就是指对眼睛的绘描，可以传达精神的内涵。

菩萨和弟子的面部主要采用中国传统的敷色方法，即在某些凸出部分如两颊、下颌等处以红色用水晕开，自成浓淡凹凸效果的晕染技法，达到不露笔痕保持颜面红润本色的审美要求。这是外来的"天竺遗法"在唐代技法中的新创造。以此表现年轻女性皮肤的细腻润泽，展示出一种理想化

attending upon him. The older is holding a ritual water vase and the younger an alms bowl. Standing on the outside of the composition are two large attendant bodhisattvas. The one on the left is especially well-portrayed. She wears a Buddhist crown, is partially clothed on the upper body, with a long shawl draped over the shoulders, a necklace of jade and pearls hanging down, one of her hands raised gently supporting the shawl, and the other holding offerings in the palms of her hands. Her body is painted in an S-shaped posture, showing perfect elegance. Her eyes gaze downward as if in deep reflection. Her skin is fine and smooth, conveying a graceful and poised beauty. Judging from the necklace of jewels she wears and the splendid shawl and *dhoti* she is dressed in, she resembles a dignified aristocrat (Fig.30). The four bodhisattvas standing behind her also look very attractive. The artists spared no effort in presenting their eyes, including timid eyes, sweet charming eyes, inattentive eyes, and bright happy eyes. The well-known "lifelike expression in the eyes" especially refers to such skills, which also convey spiritual connotations.

Traditional Chinese techniques of applying pigments were adopted in painting the faces of bodhisattvas and disciples. For certain protruding parts like the cheeks and the jaws, red pigment was diluted with water, and the effects of a halo were produced automatically, with colors thick or thin, parts concave or conve. This was called the *sfumato* technique. The result was that no sign of the paint brush was left, and yet the natural color of the face came through, which could meet the

的美,说明初唐时期在晕染技法上融合中西的技法已非常成熟。

胁侍菩萨的化佛冠与身上佩戴的璎珞之上都是沥粉堆金。沥粉堆金,是以胶和泥合成沥粉,表现人物的一些部分,待沥粉干透,再涂胶水于沥粉线纹上,贴以金箔,即成沥粉堆金。沥粉堆金的画法使平面的画上显出一定立体成分,强化了金色的效果,更增添了菩萨的雍容高贵。由于第 57 窟的菩萨描绘得十分优美,有人把此窟称为"美人窟"。

初唐第 322 窟北壁的说法图(图 31),中央是阿弥陀佛着田相袈裟,倚坐,两手作说法印,佛座下面是七宝水池。两旁二菩萨分别立于水中的大莲花上,右侧的菩萨头戴宝冠,目光下视,身体微微呈"S"形弯曲,一手上举,一手自然下垂,轻扶飘带。左侧的菩萨同

aesthetic standards of that time. This was partly due to the Indian heritage from abroad, but it was combined with the innovative techniques of the Tang Dynasty. In this way, the skin of young women was depicted as delicate and smooth, portraying a type of idealized beauty, which shows that in the early Tang, the *sfumato* technique had reached its maturity because of the integration of Eastern and Western methods.

Both the Buddhist crown and the jeweled necklace the attendant bodhisattva wears were painted by applying a gelatinous mortar mixture and then gilding, in a technique known as *lifen-duijin*. A pliable mixture of glue and gypsum powder was used to mold certain parts of the figures. After the mixture was applied and allowed to completely dry, fresh glue was spread over the lines and crevices, and then gold leaf was overlaid on the surface. It provided a three-dimensional effect on an otherwise flat surface, enhancing the gleam of gold, and increasing the grace and nobility of the bodhisattva. The bodhisattva in Cave 57 is so exquisitely portrayed that some people call this the "Cave of the Beauty".

The Dharma-preaching scene on the north wall of Cave 322 of the Early Tang is intricately composed (Fig.31). At the center is Amitabha, wearing a patchwork *kasaya*, sitting in lotus pose, two hands in *vitarka mudra* and a seven-treasure pool under his lotus throne. The two bodhisattvas, one on each side, stand on huge lotuses in the water. The one on the right wears a jewel-encrusted crown, looking downward, standing in the *tribhanga* S-shaped pose, with one hand raised, and the other extending naturally at her side, gently touching the

Art Treasures: Murals and Painted Sculptures in Mogao Caves

图 31　说法图　莫高窟第 322 窟北壁　初唐
Fig.31　Dharma-Preaching Scene, North Wall of Mogao Cave 322, Early Tang

样衣饰华丽,身体修长,面佛而立,飘带仿佛是从两手指间流过。纤长的手指,优雅的动作体现出女性的美。七宝水池中还有6身供养菩萨,有的跪在莲花上,双手捧莲花,做供养状;有的斜靠在莲花上,低头仿佛在观鱼,神态闲适;有的盘腿而坐,从容地听佛说法。图中还描绘了化生童子活泼可爱的形象。佛经中说,生于西方净土世界的人,"皆于七宝水池中化生,便自然长大,亦无乳养之者,皆食自然饮食"。图中透过莲花瓣可以看到化生童子盘腿坐在莲花中,周围碧绿的水池中,还画出游来游去的鸭子,富有情趣。图中两侧各有三身持节飞天乘云而下,天空中还飞舞着不鼓自鸣的筝、箜篌等天乐,充满了祥和的气氛。箜篌是一种弹拨乐器,有卧箜篌和竖箜篌之别。卧箜篌源于中国古代的琴瑟类乐器,但后来被琴、筝等乐器所取代。现在所说的箜篌通常是指竖箜

edges of her shawl. The one on the left is sumptuously dressed and richly ornamented. She stands tall and slender, facing the Buddha, with her shawl hanging down as if flowing through her long, slim, elegant fingers. All her motions, coordinating with her graceful presence, reflect a feminine beauty. There are six more bodhisattvas making offerings in the seven-treasure pool. Some are kneeling on lotuses in a state of devotion and worship, holding lotus flowers in both hands; some are leaning against lotuses, lowering their heads as if watching the fish, free and relaxed; and some are sitting cross-legged, calmly listening to the Buddha. The charming, lively figures of lotus children are also depicted in the painting. Buddhist scriptures claim that those who are reborn in the Western Paradise of the Pure Land "are all endowed with spontaneous rebirths from lotus flowers in the seven-treasure pool and grow up naturally; they need no breast milk, living on a diet of nature." In the painting, through the flower petals, a lotus child is seen sitting cross-legged in the center of the lotus. A pool of green water surrounds it and ducks are even painted swimming to and fro across the pool. Everything is full of delight. On either side of the painting there are three *apsaras*, each holding a flag made from a yak's tail and flying alongside a cloud. Heavenly music from a *zheng* (plucked zither), *konghou*, and other instruments waft through the air as well, all sounding automatically. The atmosphere is joyful and peaceful. A *konghou* is a stringed musical instrument which can be further classified into

篌，源于古代埃及，形状为一个近似三角形的两个边，其间有多根弦，通过弹拨不同的弦形成不同的音色。这类乐器在西方乐器中后来发展成了竖琴，在中国则称为箜篌。敦煌壁画中箜篌出现较早，在北魏就很流行了。

这铺说法图，人物虽多却不太拥挤，以较多的笔墨来描绘水池和树木，使人有一种身临其境之感。这一点正预示着唐代经变画境界的形成。画家开始描绘一种佛国世界的景象，而不单是一些佛和菩萨的形象。

千佛也是洞窟中大量出现的形象。大乘佛教中有"三世三千佛"之说，指过去世庄严劫千佛、现在世贤劫千佛、未来世星宿劫千佛。在壁画中千佛通常画成高10cm~20cm的小佛像，一个接一个排列起来，铺满墙壁。每个佛像身上袈裟的颜色都不相同，又按色彩的变化有规律地排列起来，从整体来看就成了一道道色彩

the horizontal *konghou* and vertical *konghou*. The horizontal *konghou* had its origins in ancient Chinese musical instruments such as the *qin* and *se*, but was later replaced by the *qin*, *zheng*, and the like. The present–day *konghou* is always vertical, originating in ancient Egypt. It is shaped roughly like two sides of a triangle, inside which are fixed strings. Different notes are produced by plucking different strings. This kind of musical instrument later developed into the harp in the west, while it is still called a *konghou* in China. The *konghou* appeared quite early in the Dunhuang murals. It was popular as early as the Northern Wei.

Although there are many figures in this composition, it does not seem crowded. The pool and trees are depicted with greater care, creating a sense of being personally at the scene, an indicator that sutra illustrations of the Tang period were starting to take shape. The artists had begun to provide the context of the Buddhist world instead of just the figures of the Buddha and bodhisattvas.

The thousand–Buddha motif is a type of Buddha images found in large numbers in the Dunhuang caves. According to Mahayana Buddhism, there are a thousand Buddhas for each of the three *kalpas*, or eons, referring to the thousand Buddhas of the 'glorious' past *kalpa*, the thousand Buddhas of the 'good' present *kalpa*, and the thousand Buddhas of the 'constellation' future *kalpa*. In the murals, images of the thousand Buddhas are generally drawn as small as 10–20 centimeters tall,

斑斓的装饰带,使洞窟华丽而庄严(图32)。北朝时期还有不少洞窟用影塑的形式来表现千佛,具有浮雕的效

arranged one by one in rows all across the wall. The color of the *kasaya* on each Buddha is different. The images are arranged in a repeating pattern according to the color variations. Viewed as a whole, these colorful decorative bands make the cave magnificent and awe-inspiring (Fig.32). During the Northern Dynasties there were many caves where the method of molded relief was used to

图32 千佛 莫高窟第263窟 北魏
Fig.32 Thousand Buddha Motif, Mogao Cave 263, Northern Wei

Art Treasures: Murals and Painted Sculptures in Mogao Caves

图 33　影塑千佛　莫高窟第 428 窟　北周
Fig.33　Molded Thousand Buddha Motif, Mogao Cave 428, Northern Zhou

果（图 33）。

　　佛教最初是反对偶像崇拜的，后来在宗教的发展中，为了适应崇拜者的需要而产生了佛像。在古代印度，佛和菩萨的形象往往是以当时的贵族形象为模特，按照当时的审美标准来塑造的。佛经中对佛像的特征做了很多说明，如"三十二相""八十种好"等等，体现着古代印度的美学思想。而在印度北部的犍陀罗地区，由于受到古希

represent the thousand Buddhas, creating an effect of *bas-relief* (Fig.33).

　　Originally, Buddhism was opposed to the use of human images or direct representations of the Buddha. Later, with the development of the religion, iconography was created to meet the needs of its followers. In ancient India, the Buddha and bodhisattva icons were modeled on figures of contemporary nobles, portrayed according to the aesthetic standards of the time. In Buddhist literature, accounts were created about the features of Buddhist iconography, such as "32 major representations", as well as "80 minor representations" of a Buddha, for example, all embodying the aesthetic ideals of

59

腊文化的影响,形成了与印度有所不同的审美标准。佛教传入中国后,最初是模仿印度和中亚传来的佛像形式;隋唐以后,逐渐形成了中国式的佛像。不仅面部形象中国化了,而且佛像的衣饰也变成了中国人的服饰,反映了外来的佛教艺术与中国本土艺术的融合。同时,在佛教艺术长期繁荣发展之中,中国的绘画艺术也受到强烈的刺激,从而得到飞速的发展。敦煌石窟北朝到隋唐的佛像艺术反映了中国绘画艺术发展的一个侧面。

ancient India. However, in the Gandhara region of northern India, due to influences from Hellenistic Greece, aesthetics were established quite differently from the initial Indian model. After Buddhism spread into China, the Buddha figures imitated the styles from India and Central Asia at first; the Chinese style did not take shape until after the Sui and Tang dynasties. After that, not only did the face of the Buddha resemble the features of Chinese people, the figures were also dressed in Chinese clothing. This trend illustrates the integration of foreign Buddhist art and native Chinese art. Throughout the process of expansion and flourishing of Buddhist art, strong influences were brought to the Chinese art of painting, resulting in its rapid development. Thus, Buddhist art in the Dunhuang caves from the Northern Dynasties to the Sui and Tang periods outline the development of Chinese painting.

菩萨
Bodhisattvas

佛两侧的菩萨通常称作胁侍菩萨。根据主尊佛的不同，胁侍菩萨也有所不同。如释迦牟尼佛的两侧，配以文殊菩萨和普贤菩萨。这主要来自《华严经》教义，所以称作"华严三圣"。阿弥陀佛的两侧配以观世音菩萨和大势至菩萨，来自《阿弥陀经》等净土经典思想，称作"西方三圣"，因为阿弥陀佛是西方净土世界的教主。东方药师佛的两侧则是日光菩萨和月光菩萨，称为"东方三圣"，这是源于《药师如来本愿功德经》等经典的思想。

在早期壁画中，佛与菩萨组成说法图，一组三身或有更

Bodhisattvas standing on both sides of the Buddha are known as attendant bodhisattvas. Subordinate attendant bodhisattvas can vary according to the main Buddha in the center of the grouping. For example, on either side of the Sakyamuni Buddha stand the bodhisattvas Manjusri (*wenshu*) and Samantabhadra (*puxian*). This specific arrangement comes from the doctrines of the *Flower Garland Sutra (Avatamsaka Sutra* or *Mahāvaipulya Buddhāvatamsaka Sutra;* Chinese: *Huayan Jing*), so this combination is known as the Three Sages of Huayan. The bodhisattvas Avalokitesvara (*guanyin*) and Mahasthamapraptapta (*daishizhi*) stand on the sides of the Amitabha Buddha. This arrangement comes from the tenets of the Pure Land as found in the *Amitabha Sutra*, and the combination is called the Three Western Saints, as Amitabha is the Buddha of Sukhāvatī, the Pure Land in the West. On the sides of Bhaisajyaguru of the East stand the bodhisattvas Suryaprabha and Candraprabha, whose names literally translate as "Sunlight" and "Moonlight", respectively. This combination is called the Eastern Trinity and is rooted in doctrines from the *Medicine Buddha Sutra* (*Bhaiṣajyaguru – vaiḍūrya – prabhā –rāja Sutra*).

In the early murals, the Buddha and bodhisattvas were grouped together in what was known as a Dharma-preaching scene. Often there were groupings of three, but more bodhisattvas could be found attending on both sides of the Buddha. After the Tang period more and

多身的菩萨侍立左右。唐代以后，单独画出菩萨的画面多了起来，通常在佛龛两侧或窟门两边画出文殊和普贤菩萨的赴会图（也有人称之为"文殊变""普贤变"）。与中央佛龛中的佛像相对应，扩展了说法图的意义。如第172窟的门两侧分别画出文殊和普贤赴会图。门北侧文殊菩萨骑狮子前行，旁有昆仑奴牵狮，后面跟着文殊的眷属及众多的菩萨天人。门南侧普贤菩萨乘白象，前后也有眷属及众多的天人簇拥着。引人注目的是在文殊变和普贤变的上部都画有山水图，如文殊变上部左侧是一组突兀高耸的山崖，接近江面的山峰壁立千仞，令人想起三峡的雄奇。山的颜色用青绿和赭红色相间染出，鲜明而又有光感；山崖后面，一条河

more murals were painted solely depicting bodhisattvas. Normally images of the bodhisattvas Manjusri and Samantabhadra attending the Buddha's Dharma preaching were painted on both sides of a Buddha niche, or on both sides of the entrance to a cave—these were also called Manjusri illustration paintings and Samantabhadra illustration paintings—which echoed the image of the Buddha in the central niche, reinforcing the sense of the Dharma-preaching scenes. For example, on either side of the entrance to Cave 172, there are paintings of Manjusri and Samantabhadra attending the Buddha's sermon. On the north side is Manjusri riding a lion, followed by his family and many other bodhisattvas and *devas* (celestial beings), with a Kunlun servant leading the lion at the side; while on the south side is Samantabhadra riding a white elephant, attended by his own retinue of family, bodhisattvas, and *devas*. What is attractive are the landscapes over both the Manjusri illustration and the Samantabhadra illustration. For example, on the left side above Manjusri is a group of towering cliffs. Near the surface of the river, mountain peaks shoot up hundreds and thousands of meters, reminding us of the breath-taking sight of the Three Gorges. The mountains are colored with alternating dark green and brownish-red, brilliant with the sense of light. From behind the cliffs, a winding river emerges, and the closer to the foreground, the clearer the waves appear, rising and falling. At last it converges into a huge swelling river. The middle section of the landscape is a vast plain, where gentle hills can be seen. Behind the hills there is another river, joining the one on the right. The right side of the landscape is a boundless flat

流蜿蜒流出，越往近处，水波的起伏越明显，最后汇成滔滔大河。中段是一片广袤的平原，其中可见平缓的山丘，山丘后面又有河流，与右侧的河水交汇在一起。右侧则是一望无垠的平川，一条河流曲曲折折，来自迷茫的远方，河边的树木愈远愈小，消失在天边。由远及近，这三条河汇于一处，形成壮阔的水面。这种辽阔的山水画无论是对透视关系处理，还是对光的明暗及色彩的表现，都达

land, where a river zigzags forward from the vast, hazy distance. The trees by the river, appearing smaller as they recede into the distance, gradually disappear beyond the horizon. From further away, the three rivers join together, forming a great body of water. Such an extensive landscape achieves a superb artistic level, whether in terms of perspective, or in terms of light and shading. In its composition, the landscape is not like those in later periods that seek unusual and obscured images as well as considerable amounts of mountain peaks, but rather it makes an effort to depict the bold, vast scenery of the north. The whole painting

图 34　文殊赴会图　莫高窟第 172 窟东壁　盛唐
Fig.34　Manjusri Attending a Dharma Preaching, East Wall of Mogao Cave 172, High Tang

到了很高的水平。它不像后代的山水画那样，追求构图的怪、奇、晦涩和重山叠岭，而是努力反映出北方雄浑、壮阔的风光。整幅画体现着阔大、爽朗、健康的精神（图34）。

第159窟西壁的文殊和普贤赴会图也绘制精美。龛北侧文殊菩萨坐于雄狮背上的宝座，神情安详，手执如意，前后有天龙八部等众神环绕。这些菩萨圣众表情各异，动态不一：如狮尾后部的天女探头外视，天真无邪；下面的菩萨凝神俯视，仿佛沉浸在遐想中；牵狮的昆仑奴双眼圆睁，正用力牵绳，动作神态极为真实。最动人的是狮前的三身伎

embodies a spirit of expansiveness and vigor (Fig.34).

The scenes of Manjusri and Samantabhadra attending the Buddha's sermon on the west wall of Cave 159 are also delicately painted. Manjusri on the north side of the niche looks calm and peaceful, sitting on his jeweled seat on his mount, the lion, *ruyi*① in hand, and surrounded by the Heavenly Kings of the Aṣṭasenā (Chinese: *tianlong babu*)②, the eight classes of supernatural beings. These bodhisattvas and celestial beings have different expressions and dynamics: the *deva* behind the lion stretches her neck to look out, appearing innocent; the bodhisattva below is gazing downward with fixed attention as if absorbed in his meditations; the Kunlun servant, who is leading the lion, opens his eyes wide, pulling the reins with all his might, exquisitely real in his movements and mannerisms. What is most impressive are the three musical performers in front of the lion: the one in the front is playing a bamboo flute, with her face turned sideways, eyes looking downward, her head moving gently as if swaying to the music; the one behind her keeps time with clappers, head raised slightly, looking cheerful and joyous; the third one is playing a *sheng*③ with concentration, her eyes fixed on the movements of her fingers, while standing barefoot upon the lotus platform, her toes lifted as if beating to the rhythm of the music (Fig.35).

---

① An S-shaped ornamental object, usually made of jade, formerly a symbol of good luck. *Ruyi* means "as ones wishes."

② The Aṣṭasenā: eight classes of supernatural, nonhuman beings with special powers to defend Buddhism and protect the Dharma. They include *devas*, *asuras*, *gandharvas*, *nagas*, *garudas*, *kinnaras*, *yaksa*, and *mahorāgas*.

③ a reed pipe, a wind musical instrument.

图35 文殊赴会图 莫高窟第159窟龛外北侧 中唐
Fig.35 Mañjuśrī Attending a Dharma Preaching, Right Side of Niche in Mogao Cave 159, Middle Tang

乐：前面的一身吹着横笛，侧着脸，目光下视，她的头仿佛随着乐曲在轻轻晃动；后面的一身打着拍板，头微微上仰，眉开眼笑，一副喜悦之情；另一身神情专注地吹笙，眼睛注视着手指的动作，赤脚站在莲花台上，翘起的脚趾似乎也在随着音乐的节奏打着拍子（图35）。

在文殊、普贤赴会图的下部往往以屏风画的形式画出五台山图。五台山在山西省，因为山有五顶称为五台。北魏以来人们发现五台山的形势与佛经中记载的文殊菩萨的道场——清凉山十分相似，便在五台山建立了供奉文殊菩萨的寺院，后来不断地出现了文殊菩萨在五台山显现的传说，促进了五台山佛教的繁荣。到了唐代，皇帝也多次派人到五台山送供，并有人画出《五台山图》在首都长安一带流传开来，甚至连边远地区的敦煌也出现了五台山图。莫高窟五代时期的第61窟，称作文殊堂，就是专门供奉

It is often the case that the lower registers of murals depicting Manjusri and Samantabhadra attending the Buddha's dharma sermons include scenes of Mount Wutai, pictured in the form of a screen painting. Mount Wutai is located in Shanxi Province. It is so named because it has five peaks[①]. Since the Northern Wei it had been understood that the terrain of Mount Wutai very much resembled that of the Qingliang Mountains, which, according to Buddhist literature, was the *bodhimaṇḍa*, or sacred abode, of Manjusri, where he performed his Buddhist rites. Thus, a special temple was constructed on Mount Wutai to worship him. Later, legends came one after another that Manjusri appeared in Mount Wutai, which helped Buddhism to flourish in that area. During the Tang Dynasty, quite often, the emperors sent offerings there as well, and the *Map of Mount Wutai* was drawn and distributed around the ancient capital city of Chang'an. The map was even copied in places as remote as Dunhuang. Cave 61, which was constructed in the Five Dynasties and is called the Hall of Manjusri, is a special cave for making offerings to him. There is a Buddhist altar at the center of the cave, but the sculpture of Manjusri riding his lion is now lost, leaving only the traces of the paws

---

① "Five-Terrace", the literal meaning of Wutai in Chinese. "Peak" is sometimes interpreted as synonym of terrace when describing mountains.

文殊菩萨的。洞窟中央设佛坛，原来塑有骑狮的文殊菩萨像，现在已失，仅有狮子的足迹和尾巴保存下来。在此窟的后壁，画出了长达13米多的巨幅《五台山图》(图36)。

除了文殊菩萨、普贤菩萨以外，观音菩萨也是最流行的壁画题材。南北朝时期在中国就出现了表现观音菩萨的浮雕，内容来源于《法华经·观世音菩萨普门品》。后来的民间信仰中，把这部分内容从《法华经》中抽出来，单独诵习，称为《观音经》。唐代壁画中出现了表现《观音经》的观音经变画，如第205窟南壁和第45窟南壁都画出了观音经变画，第45窟画得最完整，艺术水平也较高。中央是观音菩萨像，两侧分别画出观音菩萨救苦求难的场面。佛经中说，如若在海上遇风浪或海中的妖怪，只要口念观音名号，即可消灾免难。壁画中画出一条大帆船航行在大海中，船中有七八个旅客和五六个艄公，船周围的水中有不少怪鱼怪兽纷纷向这条船攻击，情况十分危急。船中之人都双手合十向观音菩萨祈祷。还有一个画面表

and tail of the lion. On the back wall of the cave, there is a huge painted *Map of Mount Wutai* over 13 meters long (Fig.36).

In addition to Manjusri and Samantabhadra, Avalokitesvara was also one of the most popular subjects for murals. As early as the Northern and Southern Dynasties, molded reliefs depicting Avalokitesvara appeared in China, the contents of which came from the *Lotus Sutra*, particularly the "Chapter on the Universal Gate of Bodhisattva Avalokitesvara". Later, owing to folk beliefs, this chapter was separated from the *Lotus Sutra* and chanted and recited independently, and was known simply as the *Avalokitesvara Sutra*. Among the murals of the Tang period, illustration paintings, or *jingbian*, were created of the *Avalokitesvara Sutra* to expound the creeds. For example, there are murals with *Avalokitesvara Sutra* illustrations on the south walls of Caves 205 and 45. Those in Cave 45 are rendered most fully, and a higher artistic level is achieved as well. At the center is Avalokitesvara; flanking both sides are scenes of Avalokitesvara saving people from suffering and distress. It is stated in Buddhist scriptures that when people meet with storms or monsters at sea, they can stave off disaster by reciting Avalokitesvara's name. In this painting, a huge ship is depicted sailing on the sea. In the ship are seven or eight passengers and

图 36 五台山图（局部） 莫高窟第 61 窟西壁 五代
Fig.36 Section of *Map of Mount Wutai*, West Wall of Mogao Cave 61, Five Dynasties

现商人们牵着毛驴行进在山中时,忽然山后出来几个手执刀杖的强盗,商人们心惊胆战,做出祈求的样子。这也是表现遇盗难而得观音菩萨救助的情况(图37)。这些生动的场面如果抛开其说教内容,正表现了古代的商人或旅行者的真实生活。

随着观音菩萨信仰的盛行,在敦煌壁画中还出现了千手千眼观音像、如意轮观音像、六臂观音像、十一面观音像、水月观音像等等(图38、图39)。其中水月观音像较有特色。据文献记载,唐代画家周昉最早创作了水月观音像,以水光月色表现出一种空灵的境界,把美丽的自然风景与观音像结合起来,深受人们欢迎。水月观音像反映了中国文人审美意识对佛教美术的影响。

five or six sailors. In the water all around, frightening fish and beasts attack the ship. The situation is dire indeed. People in the ship fold their hands and pray devoutly to Avalokitesvara. Another painting shows some merchants advancing through the mountains, leading their donkeys, when suddenly several robbers rush out from behind the hills, weapons in hand. The merchants are so terrified that they can only lift off a prayer. This mural also illustrates being saved by Avalokitesvara (Fig.37). These vivid scenes, apart from their didacticism, reveal the real life of ancient merchants and travelers.

As faith in Avalokitesvara became widespread, a variety of iconography emerged among the Dunhuang murals. These included the Thousand-Armed and Thousand-Eyed Avalokitesvara, Cintāmaṇicakra Avalokitesvara, Six-Armed Avalokitesvara, Eleven-faced Avalokitesvara, and Water-Moon Avalokitesvara (Figs.38, 39). Among these, Water-Moon Avalokitesvara carries the most distinctive features. According to historical records, Zhou Fang of the Tang Dynasty was the first artist who painted this image. He depicted an ethereal realm with the light of the water and the color of the moon, integrating the beautiful natural scenery with the figure of Avalokitesvara. The rendering was well received by his contemporaries, and reflected how the aesthetic concepts of Chinese intellectuals influenced Buddhist art.

Art Treasures: Murals and Painted Sculptures in Mogao Caves

图37 胡商遇盗 莫高窟第45窟南壁 盛唐
Fig.37 Hu Merchants Encountering Bandits, South Wall of Mogao Cave 45, High Tang

图38 六臂十一面观音 莫高窟第76窟 宋
Fig.38 Eleven-Headed Six-Armed Avalokitesvara, Mogao Cave 76, Song Dynasty

Art Treasures: Murals and Painted Sculptures in Mogao Caves

图39 千手千眼观音 莫高窟第3窟 元
Fig.39 Thousand-Armed Thousand-Eyed Avalokitesvara, Mogao Cave 3, Yuan Dynasty

天王、力士(药叉)
Heavenly Kings and *Lokapalas*

早期的洞窟中,常常在洞窟的四壁下部画出金刚力士的形象。金刚力士也称"药叉",是佛国世界中护法镇邪的神,其地位较低,所以画在四壁的下部。

第254窟在四壁下部和中心柱四面的下部都画出了一排金刚力士。他们的面貌奇特,动作各异,有的呈马面,有的长猫耳;有的憨厚朴实,有的似相互私语,有的则似相互斗殴,或伸臂露拳,或弓腿挺胸(图40)。这些金刚力士的一个共同特征是体格强健,个个都充满着勇武精神。画家还通过不同的颜色表现出鲜明、强烈而又多少有些怪异的特点。第249窟、288窟、290窟、428窟等北朝各期的洞窟中,都可

In the earlier-period caves, Dharma protectors were commonly painted at the lower parts of the four walls. In the Buddhist world, these guardians, also called *lokapalas*, were supernatural beings who defended Buddhist doctrine and fought against demons. The status of these guardians was relatively lower in the Buddhist pantheon, and thus they were placed in the lower sections of paintings.

In Cave 254, a row of *lokapalas* are successively drawn along the lower registers of the four walls and around the bottom of the central pillar. They are strangely shaped, with different dynamics: some have horse faces, some have cat ears; some appear simple and honest, some seem to be whispering to each other; others seem to be fighting with one another, stretching out their arms and clenching their fists, or bending their legs and throwing out their chests (Fig.40). *Lokapalas* share one feature in common. They are strong and filled with the spirit of power and courage. The artists, by using different colors, present their distinct, strong, and more or less bizarre characteristics. Such figures can be seen painted at the lower parts of the four walls in caves from different eras of the Northern Dynasties, and Caves 249, 288, 290, and 428 are examples. The paintings in Cave 288 are relatively clear and the *lokapalas* are minimally clothed, wearing only short trousers. Tension is fully revealed in their strong muscles. Although they open their eyes wide and look very

Art Treasures: Murals and Painted Sculptures in Mogao Caves

图 40　金刚力士　莫高窟第 254 窟　北魏
Fig.40　*Dharmapālas*(Dharma Protectors), Mogao Cave 254, Northern Wei

以看到在四壁下部画出的金刚力士。第 288 窟画面较清楚,我们可以看到金刚力士身体赤裸,仅穿犊鼻裤,强劲的身体充满了一种张力。虽然双眼圆睁,表现着愤怒之态,但由于身体浑圆,动作稚拙,显出憨态可掬的样子。隋代以后,由于壁画构成的格局发生了很大变化,金刚力士出现较少。

天王,是指镇守佛国四方的四大天王。最早出现于西魏第 285 窟,画在西壁佛龛外两侧(图 41),各有两身,头冠与菩萨的头冠一致,身着铠甲,在铠甲下面还露出与菩萨所穿一样的长裙。天王都手持武器,其中有一身天王右手托塔,可以判定是北方天王,其余

angry, their round figures and clumsy movements make them seem innocent. After the Sui Dynasty, fewer Dharma guardians appear in murals due to some remarkable structural changes in painting.

　　Heavenly Kings refer to the four great *lokapalas* who are responsible for guarding all the quarters of the Buddhist world. The earliest Heavenly Kings are found in Cave 285 of the Western Wei, painted on both sides of the niche in its west wall, two on each side (Fig.41). The crowns they wear are similar to those worn by bodhisattvas. They are dressed in armor, underneath which are long

图41 天王 莫高窟第285窟西壁 / 西魏
Fig.41 Heavenly Kings, West Wall of Mogao Cave 285, Western Wei

的三身天王所持长枪大体一样，还没有像后来的四大天王那样有着明显不同的手持物。但总的来说，天王形象在北朝出现较少。

唐代以后，在一些说法图和经变画中也出现了天王的形象，还出现了一些关于毗沙门天王（北方天王）的故事，也有不少单独表现毗沙门天王的画面。天王的形象也逐渐定形，通常穿着中式铠甲，表现出一位将军的形象。五代以后，天王信仰更加盛行，往往在大型洞窟窟顶的四个角画出四大天王。如第61窟、98窟、108窟、146窟就是其中的代表（图42）。第98窟窟顶四角的天王画面很大，西侧两身天王已变得模糊，东侧两身天王保存较好。窟顶东北角画出北方天王，他身着铠甲坐在座位上，左手托着宝塔，右手扶在右膝上，头上戴着金光闪闪的头冠，目光炯炯，英姿飒爽。两侧还有天王的眷属

dhotis, also similar to the clothing of bodhisattvas. All Heavenly Kings carry weapons in their hands, and one of them is holding a pagoda in his right palm, from which it can be judged that he is the Heavenly King of the North. The long spears the other three are holding are quite similar, not like the later Four Great Heavenly Kings who carry clearly distinct implements in their hands. Generally speaking, fewer images of Heavenly Kings appeared in the paintings of the Northern Dynasties.

Beginning with the Tang Dynasty, Heavenly Kings appeared in certain Dharma-preaching scenes as well as sutra illustrations. There were also tales of Vaiśravaṇa, the Heavenly King of the North, and quite a few pictures were even painted to show Vaiśravaṇa alone. Gradually the iconography of a Heavenly King was standardized, and they were depicted in Chinese armor of a military general. After the Five Dynasties, faith in Heavenly Kings became more popular, and the Four Great Heavenly Kings were often painted at the four ceiling corners of some of the larger caves. Caves 61, 98, 108, and 146 are typical examples of this (Fig.42). The Heavenly Kings at the four corners of the ceiling of Cave 98 are huge paintings. The images on the west side have become indistinct while those on the east side are better preserved. In the northeast corner of the ceiling is the Heavenly King of the North, Vaiśravaṇa. He is seated, wearing armor, and holding a pagoda in his left palm. His right hand rests on the right knee, eyes bright and crown shining with golden light. He appears to be a

图 42　天王　莫高窟第 108 窟窟顶东北角　五代
Fig.42　Heavenly King, Northeast Corner of Ceiling in Mogao Cave 108, Five Dynasties

和侍从。同窟东南角画出东方天王，也是头戴宝冠，身着铠甲，右手持宝杵，双目圆睁。天王两旁也有随从人员。两身天王旁边都有文字题记，东方天王旁边的题记是"谨请东方提头赖吒天王主领一切乾闼婆神，毗舍鬼并诸眷属来降此窟"。表明了天王的身份，也说明了在窟顶绘天王，具有镇窟的意义。

valiant and heroic man. To both sides of him are dependents and servants. In the southeast corner of the ceiling is the Heavenly King of the East. Again his crown is jewel-encrusted, and he wears armor, holding a treasure pestle in his right hand, with eyes wide. He also has his attendants. Next to both the Heavenly Kings there are inscriptions: beside the Heavenly King of the East is written, "The Heavenly King who guards the gate to the east is solemnly invited here to rule over all the *gandharvas* and hungry ghosts, and their dependents must surrender in this cave". This reveals the identity of the Heavenly Kings and also shows that the purpose of painting them on the ceiling of the cave is to protect the location.

艺苑瑰宝：莫高窟壁画与彩塑
Art Treasures: Murals and Painted Sculptures in Mogao Caves

美丽的天使——飞天艺术

Angels of Beauty: the Art of Apsaras

Art Treasures: Murals and Painted Sculptures in Mogao Caves

飞天是什么
What are *Apsaras*?

飞天作为佛教艺术中一种独特的形象，以她们轻快的动态、流畅的舞姿，吸引着广大的众生。尽管飞天在佛教艺术中出现较多，可我们在佛经中根本就没有找到"飞天"一词，更没有见到对飞天的相关记录。通常的看法认为，"飞天"是一种俗称，而不是佛教名词。

飞天通常是指佛教诸天。"天"是佛教中一个独特的概念，是指佛国世界里的天部诸神（如天龙八部众神）。在天龙八部中，乾闼婆与紧那罗是主管音乐舞蹈之神。这两类天神多表现为飞天的形象，所以有人认为飞天就是指乾闼婆与紧那罗。佛经中又记载，当佛说法的时候，常常有天人、天女或做散花，或做歌舞供养。

如《大庄严论经》中讲到尸毗王舍身救鸽之时：

Apsaras are a type of unique image among Buddhist art. They attract all living beings with their lively movements and graceful dance. However, the term "*apsara*" has never been found anywhere in Buddhist literature, nor are there records of their sightings, though their images are found in great numbers among Buddhist art. It is generally believed that "*apsara*" is not a Buddhist term but originally a secular definition.

The word *feitian* (the Chinese word for *apsara*) normally refers to Buddhist heavenly realms of existence. *Tian* is a unique term in Buddhism, and it includes all heavenly deities in Buddhist cosmology, for example, deities from the Aṣṭasenā, the eight classes of supernatural beings. In the Aṣṭasenā, *gandharvas* and *kinnaras* are heavenly deities in charge of music and dance, who are mostly presented as supernatural heavenly beings in the image of *apsaras*. As a result, it is believed by some that *apsaras* refer to the *gandharvas* and *kinnaras*. It is also recorded in Buddhist scriptures that when the Buddha was preaching the Dharma, there were often *devas* and heavenly maidens scattering blossoms or singing and dancing as a form of offering.

For example, in the tale of King Śibi

81

艺苑瑰宝

莫高窟壁画与彩塑

天人音乐等,一切皆作唱。……

虚空诸天女,散花满地中。……

《大般涅槃经》也有如下记载:

诸天龙八部,于虚空中,雨众妙花。……又散牛头栴檀等香,作天伎乐,歌唱赞叹……

《佛本行集经》中讲太子出家之时:

其虚空中,有一夜叉,名曰钵足,彼钵足等诸夜叉众,于虚空中,各以手承马之四足,安徐而行。……复共无数乾闼婆众、鸠般荼众、诸龙夜叉……在太子前,引导而行。……上虚空中,复有无量无边诸天百千亿众,欢喜踊跃,遍满其身,不能自胜,将天水陆所生之花散太子上。

sacrificing his own life to save a dove, recorded in *Ornament for the Mahayana Sutras*, it was said that:

All the celestial beings sang, and all music started to play...

In the air the heavenly maidens scattered blossoms over the ground...

And in the *Nirvana Sutra* (*Mahāparinirvāṇa Sutra*), it was also written:

In every part of the realm of the Aṣṭasenā, pretty blossoms floated in the air... and incense of ox-head sandalwood was also spread; music of heavenly singers and dancers rang out; voices of chanting and praising were heard...

The *Abhiniṣkramaṇa Sutra* (*The Dharmaguptaka Biography of the Buddha*) stated that when Prince Siddhartha renounced the world in search of enlightenment:

In the air, empty, a *yakṣa* named Bo Zu was supporting the Prince with other *yakṣa* in the vast emptiness, carrying the horse by holding its four hooves in hand, moving calmly and slowly... Also great numbers of *gandharvas, kumbhāṇḍas,* and *nagas*… were walking in front of the Prince, leading the way... High in the air were millions upon millions of *devas*, countless and boundless. They were ebullient and exhilarated, and could not help showering upon the Prince blossoms from heaven, from land and from sea.

从以上所举的佛经记述中,我们知道在有关佛的本生故事、佛传故事以及佛说法时的情景中,往往有诸天人、天女做歌舞供养。这些天人、天女如果飞行于天空,以绘画的形式表现出来,自然就是我们在敦煌壁画中所看到的飞天了。其中当然也包括了乾闼婆、紧那罗这两类歌舞之神。

早在佛教产生之前,古印度的神话传说中就已经有不少关于天人、天女的传说。印度最古老的历史与神话传说都记录在四部吠陀著作中,其中《梨俱吠陀》就有不少关于天地的开创、天上众神的故事。其后还有伟大的史诗《摩诃婆罗多》和《罗摩衍那》继承了不少神话传说故事。这些故事中关于天女(阿卜莎罗)的传说是十分流行的。《罗摩衍那》中记载创世之初的"搅海"的故事,就提到了由于搅海而出现了天女。在诗篇中,天女是水之妖精。传说中这些天女是公共的女人,反映

From the accounts in Buddhist literature cited above, it can be seen that in situations in *jataka* tales, narratives of the Buddha's life, and scenes of the Buddha preaching the Dharma, there are often *devas* and heavenly maidens, singing and dancing to make offerings. If these *devas* and heavenly maidens are flying in heaven realms and presented in paintings, it is certain that these are the *apsaras* that we see among the Dunhuang murals. Doubtlessly, *gandharvas* and *kinnaras*, the two types of gods in charge of music and dance, are included among them.

Long before the beginning of Buddhism, there had been a great many tales about *devas* and heavenly maidens among the myths and legends of ancient India. The earliest history, myths, and legends were all recorded in the four works of the Vedas, one of which was the *Rig-Veda*, in which plenty of genesis stories abound on the origin of heaven and earth, and about gods in heavenly realms. Great epics like the *Mahabharata* and the *Ramayana* came later, but borrowed heavily from the myths and legends. Among them, tales about one celestial maiden, "*Apsara*", were widely known. It was recorded in the *Ramayana* that in the beginning of the world there was the story of "the stirring of the sea", in which heavenly maidens were mentioned, saying that they came into view because the sea water was churned. In poetry, celestial maidens were presented as evil spirits of the sea. According to legends, these celestial females were communal wives. This reflected the vestiges of mixed marriages in primitive times. There were many

了原始时代男女杂婚的遗风。阿卜莎罗作为天上的美女，有着很多的爱情故事。所以，在后来的佛教艺术中，也自然地吸取了印度古代传说中的天女阿卜莎罗以及乾闼婆等形象。那些飞行于天空的飞天，多数是成双成对的形象，也许就是源于乾闼婆和阿卜莎罗传说的影响。

随着佛教传入中国，飞天这一形象也伴随着佛教艺术传入了中国。我们从中国西部新疆地区的石窟到敦煌、河西地区的石窟，一直到中原地区的石窟寺或者散见的佛教雕刻、壁画中都可以看到飞天的形象。

如前所述，中国人最初认识飞天，也只是像印度一样作为一种天人来看待。虽然"天人"在佛教中可以包括天龙八部等天部的诸神，但在实际的绘画或雕刻中，我们很难一一确认其形象，只好笼统地称为天人了。在魏晋南北朝以后，由于受到传统的神仙思想影响，"飞

legendary love stories of *Apsara*, the beauty of the heavens, and thus later Buddhist art naturally accepted images like the heavenly maiden, *Apsara*, as well as the *gandharvas* from ancient Indian legends. In addition, most of the *apsaras* that were flying in heaven were presented in pairs, which was probably influenced by the tales of the *gandharvas* and *Apsara*.

As Buddhism spread into China, images of *apsaras* were also brought into China along with Buddhist art. They are frequently seen in caves from Xinjiang, Dunhuang, regions west of the Yellow River, to the Central Plains in China, or seen scattered in Buddhist sculpture or murals elsewhere.

As is stated above, *apsaras* were considered to be a type of *deva* in India, and the earliest perception of them by Chinese people was quite the same. In Buddhism, *devas* could include all heavenly deities such as those in the Aṣṭasenā, yet in paintings or sculpture it was rather difficult to identify their images individually, so they could only be called *devas* collectively. After the Wei, Jin, and the Northern and Southern Dynasties, owing to the influences from traditional Chinese concepts of the immortal realm, *apsaras* were gradually integrated with Chinese supernatural beings—including the "flying immortals" in Daoism—and their images appeared to be floating and flying. As a result, the original features of *devas* as there were in Buddhism, such as the *nagas*, *gandharvas*, *kinnaras* (in the shape of a bird),

天"这一形象与中国式的神仙（包括道教的"飞仙"）逐渐结合,形象也显得飘逸起来。佛教中本来意义上的诸天形象,诸如龙神、乾闼婆、紧那罗（鸟形）、阿修罗、迦楼罗（本来是金翅鸟）等原来的形象特征都看不到了,而只是飞行在天空的人形。

飞天在中国,其数量及表现的普及程度已远甚于印度,而且在表现形式上与印度也大不相同,但在中国的佛教艺术中,依然可以找出印度的某些样式特征。毕竟飞天作为佛教艺术的一种形象,本来就是来自印度,它不可避免地带有印度的痕迹。如双飞天的形式,在印度是较为常见的,通常表现为在佛的两侧上部各有一身飞天相对而飞,表示在佛说法时,天人们散花供养的场面。还有一种双飞天,就是两身飞天紧靠在一起飞。在印度多为女男成对在一起。这两种形式的双飞天都传入了中国,但那种男女双飞的形式却有所改变,再也看不出男女的区别了,而是都表现出非男非

asuras, and *garudas* (originally a golden-winged bird) were indistinct, but instead, they were simply human figures flying in heaven.

There were far greater numbers and much wider dissemination of the *apsara* image in China than in India. Furthermore, the Chinese way of presenting them was also quite different from that of India. However, certain Indian styles and features were maintained in the Buddhist arts in China. After all, as a type of image found in Buddhist art, *apsaras* came from India, and therefore, it was inevitable that traces of Indian art would remain. For example, *apsara* pairs were commonly seen in India. They were generally painted above the Buddha, one on each side, flying towards each other. This type of painting displayed scenes of the Buddha preaching the Dharma, while *devas* scattered blossoms as offerings. Another type of *apsara* pair was painted in a combination of two *apsaras* flying close together, side by side. In India, *apsara* pairs usually consisted of one male and one female. Both types of pairs spread into China, but the pattern of one male and one female flying together was more or less changed. Differences between males and females were no longer seen, and they were shown in an androgynous, genderless state. The changes in the way *apsara* pairs were rendered in China revealed the precise differences in aesthetic values between China and India. In

女的形态。从双飞天形式在中国的变迁，可以看出中印两国审美精神的差异。印度所欣赏的那种带有深厚性爱特征，表现形式上又注重肉体感观之美的双飞天在中国几乎消失殆尽，而代之以中国自魏晋以来对神仙境界的追求，在形式上则追求一种流动飘逸之美。中国画的流畅舒展的线条美在飞天身上表现得淋漓尽致，这正是中国艺术所追求的美之所在。

India, in the portrayal of *apsara* pairs, features such as sexuality and eroticism, shown by strengthening the sense of bodily beauty, were appreciated, while in China almost all such features disappeared. Instead, they were replaced by a type of beauty characterized by floating and flying, for Chinese art continuously pursued a state of immortality from the Wei and Jin dynasties onward. The beauty of the smooth, pleasing lines of Chinese painting was fully expressed in the *apsaras*, and this was exactly what Chinese art was seeking.

北朝的飞天

Apsaras of the Northern Dynasties

北凉、北魏时代的飞天形体较短,受西域风格影响,身体呈"V"字形,转折强烈,由于身体强壮,有一种沉重之感。飞天多画在佛龛内或说法图中,佛的两侧上部往往相对画出两身或四身飞天。如第254窟中心柱正面佛龛上部两侧各有两身飞天(图43),他们上身半裸,斜披天衣,上着长裙,但露出赤脚,飘带绕着双臂飘下,在飘带的末端形成尖角。身体转折较大,差不多形成90度直角,显得力量有余,柔软不足。第257窟北壁说法图虽已残损大部,但在左上部的一组飞天却完整地保留下来(图44)。这组飞天共8身,有的迎风而舞,有的双手合十,有的面向后倒着飞行,姿态各不相同,飘带和衣裙随风而飞舞,

The figures of *apsaras* from the Northern Liang and Northern Wei were relatively short in stature. Influenced by styles from the Western Regions, *apsaras* were shaped like a V, with a sharp bending of the body. A sense of heaviness was palpable because of their strong physiques. *Apsaras* were commonly painted inside niches or in scenes of Dharma preaching, often in compositions with two or four figures depicted in opposite positions at the upper section, on both sides of the Buddha. For example, in Cave 254, two *apsaras* are drawn respectively on each side of the lintel of the Buddha niche in the central pillar's front side (Fig.43). Their upper bodies are partially clothed, with their celestial clothing draping casually. They wear long *dhotis*, but their feet are exposed and bare. Their long, narrow sashes flow downward, winding around their arms and forming sharp angles at the ends. Their bodies are so sharply bent that they are almost shaped into right angles. The images show a state of sufficient strength, but insufficient softness. Most of the Dharma-preaching scenes on the north wall of Cave 257 are damaged or lost, but the group of *apsaras* on the upper left side is preserved intact (Fig.44). The group is made up of eight *apsaras*, some dancing in the wind, some folding their palms devoutly, and some flying but looking back. They each have different poses with ribbon-like sashes

艺苑瑰宝
莫高窟壁画与彩塑

图 43　飞天　莫高窟第 254 窟中心柱正面　北魏
Fig.43　*Apsaras*, Front Side of Central Pillar, Mogao Cave 254, Northern Wei

形成一种满壁风动的效果。

第 248 窟的飞天较多地画在人字披东西两面的仿木结构的橡间,采用了中原式画法,注重线条,没有西域式那种厚重的晕染而显得眉目清秀(图 45)。这些飞天束发,神态恬静安详,身材苗条,但又不过分修长;细细的飘带随风舞

and *dhotis* floating in the breeze, producing an effect of wind blowing on the whole wall.

In Cave 248, a rather large number of *apsaras* are painted between the clay relief rafters and beams on the eastern and western slopes of the gabled ceiling. In these paintings, methods from the Central Plains were adopted. The thick and heavy *sfumato* technique, the pattern of color tinting from the Western Regions, is no longer there. Rather, lines are stressed, emphasizing the delicate features of the eyes and eyebrows (Fig.45). These *apsaras*, with their hair tied up,

Art Treasures: Murals and Painted Sculptures in Mogao Caves

图44 飞天 莫高窟第257窟北壁 北魏
Fig.44 *Apsaras*, North Wall of Mogao Cave 257, Northern Wei

动,飘带的末端形成的尖角,柔和自然。这种中原式的飞天到西魏以后便开始在洞窟中流行起来。

西魏第249窟正壁佛龛两侧各画出一组双飞天,左侧一身飞天,身体弯曲成直角,面朝后,正专注地吹奏笙篥。他身体的姿势仿佛从天上掉下。笙篥是一种

seem calm and peaceful; they look slim but not too tall, with narrow sashes floating in the wind and angling sharply at the end, creating a harmonious and natural effect. This type of *apsara* originated from the Central Plains and was commonly seen in caves beginning with the Western Wei.

Two *apsara* pairs, one on each side, are drawn on both sides of the main wall's niche in Cave 249, built during the Western Wei. The upper one on the left is bent into a

吹奏乐器，形似竖笛，比竖笛稍短，就是今天北方流行的管子。在敦煌隋唐以后的壁画中出现较多，应是当时北方一带流行的乐器。下面的一身飞天身体呈"U"字形，大幅度地弯曲，他伸起两手，好像正要拍击腰鼓，他的脸朝着中央的佛像，一腿尽量往前跨（图46）。右侧的飞天跟左侧的飞天相对，也是身体弯曲成90度，正吹奏横笛，下一身在拍击腰鼓。这4身飞天均裸上身，腿被夸张地画得很

right angle, facing backwards and playing the *bili* pipe attentively. Judging from his physical pose, it seems as if he is descending from heaven. The *bili* pipe is a type of double-reed woodwind instrument similar in appearance to a vertical flute but somewhat shorter. It is actually the modern day *guanzi*, which is quite popular in the northern part of China. More *bili* pipes are found in Dunhuang murals of the Sui and Tang periods, so it must have been a popular musical instrument in the north at the time. The lower one on the left is painted in a U-shape, bent sharply, facing the Buddha at the center, his two hands stretched out as if beating a waist drum. One of his legs seems to be trying its best to stride forward (Fig.46). The *apsara* pair on the right are drawn opposite the pair on the left. The figure of the upper one is also bent into a right angle. He is playing the transverse flute, while the

图45　飞天　莫高窟第248窟人字披西披　北魏
Fig.45　*Apsaras*, Western Slope of Gabled Ceiling, Mogao Cave 248, Northern Wei

Art Treasures: Murals and Painted Sculptures in Mogao Caves

图 46　飞天　莫高窟第 249 窟西壁龛内　西魏
Fig.46　*Apsaras*, Interior of Niche on West Wall, Mogao Cave 46, Western Wei

长，弯曲的幅度特别大，他们一上一下，有一种强烈的动感，又借助飘带和长裙飞舞而形成的曲线，构成优美的韵律。这几身飞天的服饰以及画法都是西域式的，但在动作上，特别是夸张地拉长了的身体和飘动的长裙，显然是受中原风格的影响。在第 249 窟南北壁两铺说法图中，也分别在佛的两侧相对画出 4 身飞天。

lower one is beating his waist drum. All four *apsaras* are unclothed from the waist up, with legs drawn exaggeratedly long and figures sharply curved. They are arranged one higher and one lower, bringing about a strong sense of motion. And thus, echoing the curved lines of the floating sashes and *dhotis*, a rhythm of beauty is composed. Both the clothing style and the painting method of these *apsaras* are from the Western Regions. However, when it comes to their dynamic state, especially the exaggeratedly lengthened body and the floating *dhotis*, influences from the Central Plains are quite obvious. In the two Dharma-preaching scenes painted separately on the north and south walls of Cave 249, four *apsaras* are drawn opposite each

下部飞天身体强壮，上身半裸，下着长裙，身体弯曲成圆弧形，形成一种强烈的张力。上面的飞天则穿着宽大的长袍，身体清瘦，飘带也画得细腻。上面的飞天更明显地表现出中原风格的所谓"秀骨清像"的特征，下部则是西域风格的飞天。这两种截然不同的飞天，一强一弱、一粗犷一纤细，又和谐地组合在一起（图47）。

最有特色的还是第249窟顶部的飞天。此窟的顶部是中国传统神话中的东王公、西王母及相关的朱雀、玄武、雷公、电母等形象，而传自佛教的飞天也与具有中国神仙思想的飞仙一起飞翔在这个奇妙的天国世界中。如画在南披的西王母，在凤辇的前后各有一身飞天、一身乘鸾仙人。画面上仙人、神兽、祥云、飞花，充满了飞动的气氛，以此烘托出仙境的场面（图48）。类似的表现在西魏第285窟的窟顶也可以看到。此窟的窟顶表现的主题是中国古代传说中的伏

other on each side of the Buddha. The lower ones are strong and partially clothed on the upper body, dressed in long *dhotis* and bent into the shape of an arc, bringing about a vigorous tension, while the upper ones wear long, wide *dhotis*, with slender bodies, and the narrow sashes are exquisitely rendered as well. The upper ones demonstrate more clearly the style of the Central Plains, that is, with features of "slim and smart figures", and the lower ones are painted in the style of the Western Regions. The two types of *apsaras*, the strong and the weak, the rugged and the delicate, are completely different, but are harmoniously composed together (Fig.47).

The most distinguished *apsaras* are those in Cave 249. On the ceiling of the cave are painted such figures as the King Father of the East, the Queen Mother of the West, and other related figures such as the Vermillion Bird (guardian spirit of the South), the Black Tortoise (guardian spirit of the North), the Thunder God, and the Lightning Goddess. All these figures profoundly reflect traditional Chinese concepts. *Apsaras*, which come from Buddhism, and flying immortals, which mirror the Chinese ideas of celestial beings, are all flying together here in a heavenly wonderland. An example is the image of the Queen Mother of the West on the southern slope of the ceiling, where an *apsara* and a celestial being riding a phoenix-like bird are paired respectively before and after the queen's cart. In the picture, the celestial beings, mythical beasts, auspicious clouds, and floating

Art Treasures: Murals and Painted Sculptures in Mogao Caves

图 47 飞天 莫高窟第 249 窟南壁 西魏
Fig.47 *Apsara*, South Wall of Mogao Cave 249, Western Wei

羲、女娲以及雷神、风神等，飞天也与这些神仙一起出现在云气飞扬、天花飘飘的空中。从第249、285窟的窟顶壁画中，可以看出佛教的飞天与中国传统神仙完美地结合在一起，共同表现出神仙思想。而这种神仙思想出现在佛教的洞窟中，实际上反映了

blossoms are painted together, creating an atmosphere of flying, thus setting off the scene of a fairyland (Fig.48). Similar paintings can also be found on the ceiling of Cave 285 from the Western Wei. Subjects expressed here are the legendary deities of ancient China: Fuxi, Nüwa, and others such as the Thunder God, the Wind God, and so on. *Apsaras* also join them in a universe of swirling clouds and floating heavenly blossoms. Murals on the ceilings of Caves 249 and 285 present a vision of Buddhist *apsaras* and

图48　西王母　莫高窟第249窟顶南披　西魏

Fig.48　Queen Mother of the West, Southern Slope of Ceiling, Mogao Cave 249, Western Wei

古代中国人最初是把佛教当成一种跟神仙思想一样的东西来认识的。这一点在很多历史文献中都有记载。

在第285窟南壁还画出了12身飞天，在云气缥缈、鲜花满天的背景中，他们一身接着一身，轻快地飞行。飞天均上身半裸，下着长裙，头梳双髻，面庞清秀，面带微笑，有的弹奏着箜篌，有的吹着横笛，有的一手支颐，一手前伸，显得矜持而娴雅（图49）。正如汉代文学家傅毅在《舞赋》中所写的："罗衣从风，长袖交横"，"绰约闲靡，机迅体轻"，体现着汉代以来的审美风范。

虽说在西魏时代中原风格已经大规模地传入了敦煌，但是敦煌地处丝绸之路要冲，不断地受到来自西方和中原的文化影响。到北周时一些洞窟的壁画又回到了西域风格，第428窟就是这样一个洞窟。这是一个大型的中心柱窟，窟内壁画基本上采用西域式的画法，在窟顶的平棋图案中，往往在

traditional Chinese immortals integrated perfectly, both expressing the concept of a supernatural world. Actually, when such concepts are illustrated inside Buddhist cave temples, it is evident that in the beginning the Chinese people understood Buddhism the way they did the supernatural world, which is in agreement with numerous historical accounts.

Another 12 *apsaras* are drawn on the south wall of Cave 285, against a background of misty clouds and abundant flowers. They are all partially clothed on the upper body and all dressed in long *dhotis*, flying briskly one after another, with pretty faces, gentle smiles, and hair tied up in double chignons. Some of them are playing the *konghou*; some are blowing transverse flutes; some are in a pose of one hand supporting the cheek and the other hand extending forward, looking elegant and reserved (Fig.49), just as the scholar Fu Yi of the Han Dynasty wrote in his *Ode to Dancing*: "Silk dresses wave in the gusting wind, with long sleeves rising and falling ", " Graceful and gentle poses, light and quick dance." All these embody the aesthetic style since the Han Dynasty.

During the Western Wei, the painting styles of the Central Plains had already been fully introduced into Dunhuang, but as the gateway to the Silk Road at that time, Dunhuang was constantly influenced by cultures from both the West and the Central Plains. During the Northern Zhou (557—581), Western Region styles recurred among murals

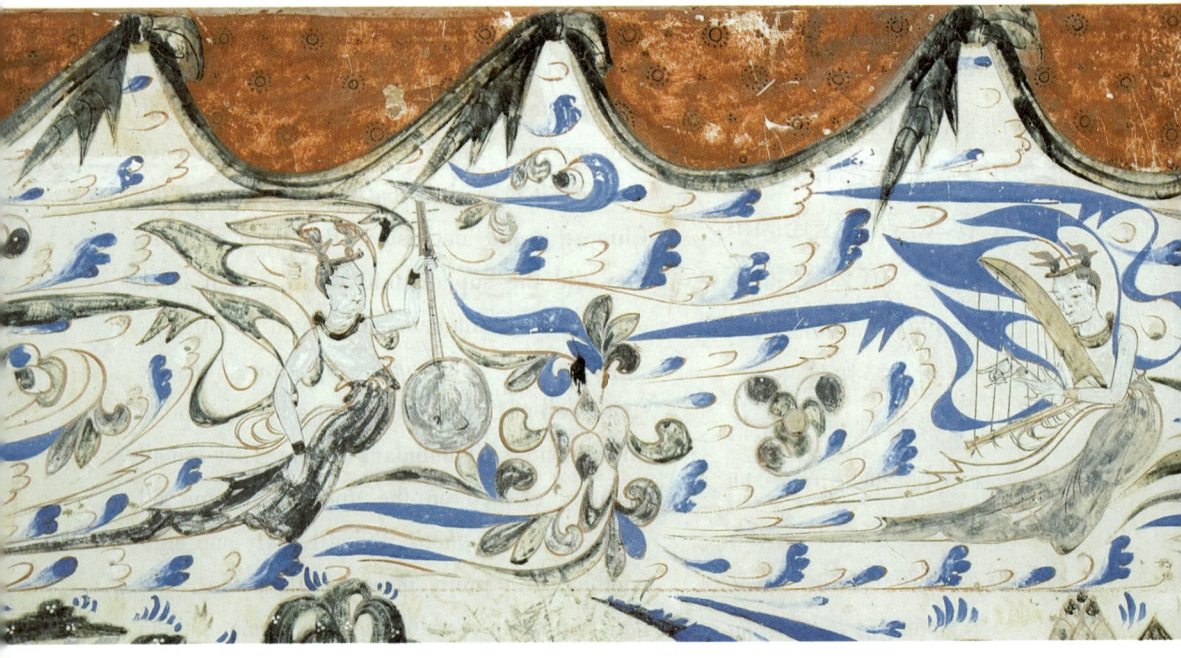

图 49　飞天　莫高窟第 285 窟南壁　西魏
Fig.49　*Apsaras*, South Wall of Mogao Cave 285, Western Wei

四角画出 4 个飞天的形象。这些飞天体格健硕，动感强烈，与北凉、北魏时期的飞天比较接近，从身体比例的准确性和动作的灵活性等方面，已显得非常成熟了。在顶后部的平棋中还出现了一些裸体飞天，均为男性，身体比例适度，动态自然（图 50）。裸体飞天在印度是十分常见的，但到了中国以后，出现较少。在新疆的克孜

in some of the caves. Cave 428 is an example. It is a large central pillar cave, where murals are painted adopting the techniques from the Western Regions. In flat ceiling designs, four *apsaras* are normally drawn at the four corners. These *apsaras* have sturdy physiques and are vigorously active, quite similar to those of the Northern Liang and the Northern Wei periods. The precise physical proportions and flexible movements indicate that the painting skills adopted here have become fairly mature. In the back part of the flat ceiling of this cave, some nude *apsaras* are painted as well. They are all males with realistic physical proportions and natural motions (Fig.50). Nude *apsaras* are quite common in India, but after their transmission into

尔石窟等处，还可以看到一些裸体飞天，但在中国内地的云冈、龙门等石窟则基本上没有出现。敦煌在北朝的一些洞窟中出现少数的裸体飞天，如北魏的第257窟、431窟和西魏的第285窟等。北周第428窟的裸体飞天形象清晰，色彩大体完整，从中可了解西域风格画法的特点。

第428窟南壁前部的说

China, they were rarely seen. In the Kizil Caves of Xinjiang, nude *apsaras* are still extant, but nearly none can be found in the Yungang or Longmen caves in interior China. There are nude *apsaras* in some of the caves of the Northern Dynasties in Dunhuang, but not many. Examples are Caves 257 and 431 of the Northern Wei, and Cave 285 of the Western Wei, among others. The images of nude *apsaras* in Cave 428 of the Northern Zhou are quite clear; the colors on them for the most part remain intact. Features of the Western Regions are identifiable from their painting styles.

图 50　裸体飞天　莫高窟第428窟窟顶　北周
Fig.50　Nude *Apsara*, Ceiling of Mogao Cave 428, Northern Zhou

法图中，有一组4身伎乐飞天。第一身回过头，怀抱琵琶；第二身抱着箜篌在专注地弹奏；第三身一条腿向前跨，正吹奏横笛；第四身双手拍着腰鼓（图51）。他们都裸着上身，着长裙，赤脚露在外面。由于变色，身体晕染部分都变成了较粗的黑色线条，仅在双眼和鼻子、下巴部位保存着白色，使人感到一种粗犷的效果，配合他们强健的身体和有力的动作，愈显得充满了力量感。

南壁靠后部说法图中的两身飞天也较有特色，左侧一身吹奏着竽篥，仿佛从天上直插下来，双脚上下拍打着，像个顽皮的孩子，憨态可掬。右侧一身与左侧的飞天相对，也是从上向下飞来，双手弹奏着琵琶。由于变色形成又粗又黑的线条，使飞天的形象更加简练完整，在土

A group of four *apsaras* who are musical performers can be seen in the Dharma-preaching scene on the south wall's front side in Cave 428. The first one carries a *pipa*[①] in her arms, looking back; the second one holds a *konghou*, playing it attentively; the third one is striding forth with one of her legs, playing the transverse flute; and the fourth one is beating the waist drum with both her hands (Fig.51). They are all unclothed on their upper torsos, but wear long *dhotis*, with feet exposed. Because of discoloration over the long expanse of time, the parts of the body that were originally drawn adopting *sfumato* techniques have turned into strong black lines with only the two eyes, the nose, and the jaw remaining white, creating a strong effect of starkness. Coordinating with their physical strength and their powerful motions, a sense of force is revealed more abundantly.

The two *apsaras* in the Dharma-preaching scene on the back side of the south wall in this same cave have their own distinguishing features as well. The one on the left is playing the *bili* pipe. He seems to be falling vertically from heaven, with his feet treading up and down, looking like a mischievous but charmingly naïve youth. The one opposite on the right is also falling downward, with both hands playing the *pipa*. The thick black lines that have resulted from discoloration over time make their images simpler,

---

① 4-stringed Chinese lute.

Art Treasures: Murals and Painted Sculptures in Mogao Caves

图 51 飞天 莫高窟第 428 窟南壁 北周
Fig.51 *Apsaras*, South Wall of Mogao Cave 428, Northern Zhou

红底色上,明快而富有韵律。飞天身上长裙的线条具有大写意的效果。

but still complete. Against the background color of red earth pigment, they look clear and lively, full of rhythm. The lines that define their long *dhotis* reveal signs of freehand brushwork used in traditional Chinese painting.

艺苑瑰宝
莫高窟壁画与彩塑

隋代的飞天
Apsaras of the Sui Dynasty

隋代的飞天多以群体飞天的形式出现，如第423窟、390窟、244窟等窟都在四壁上部接近窟顶的地方画出一道装饰带，其中飞天一身接着一身向中央佛的方向飞行。这些飞天小巧玲珑，灵活多姿，加上飘带简练流畅，造成一种快速飞行的气氛。第427窟也同样，在四壁上部画出天宫栏墙和飞天，在深蓝色的天空中，飞天的飘带配合流云构成轻快飞动的效果，造型简练优美、动作急速、色彩丰富变化是这个洞窟飞天的动人之处（图52）。由于变色的原因，底色形成了深褐色与蓝色交织的状况，犹如一道奇妙的色光，使这些飞天透出一种不可思议的神秘感。

第404窟的四壁上部，画家以蓝色作底，并有意表现出颜色由浅到深的变化，具有光的自然效果，非常真实地表现出飞天轻盈地飞行于天空的

Most *apsaras* of the Sui period were painted in groupings. For example, in each of Caves 423, 390, 244 and others, decorative borders are painted horizontally along the tops of all four walls, close to the ceiling. *Apsaras* within these borders fly one after another, towards the Buddha at the center. These *apsaras* are small and exquisite, limber and attractive. A feeling of rapid flight is created, compounded by the addition of their short, smooth sashes. Cave 427 is similar, where both *apsaras* and balustrades around the heavenly palace are painted in the upper part of the four walls, and the sashes of the *apsaras* go with the floating clouds against the dark blue sky, bringing about an effect of brisk flying. What is attractive about the *apsaras* here are the concise and graceful shapes, the rapid movements, and the rich colors (Fig.52). Because of discoloration, the background gives an impression of interwoven dark brown and blue, producing an effect of colored light and giving an incredible air of mystery to these *apsaras*.

In the upper part of the four walls of Cave 404, the artist based the painting on a blue background and deliberately showed the change of color from light to dark, bringing about the effect of natural light, and

图52 飞天 莫高窟第427窟南壁 隋
Fig.52 *Apsaras*, South Wall of Mogao Cave 427, Sui Dynasty

情景。如北壁上部的两身飞天，头梳双环髻，前一身飞天穿着大红的长裙，回头吹奏着笙，显得很悠闲；后一身飞天穿黑色长裙，一手托着一朵莲花，虔诚地向前飞去，在蓝天的背景中，给人一种脱壁欲出之感（图53）。

隋朝的艺术家对飞天的喜爱和描绘达到高峰，在佛龛上、藻井中、说法图中和四壁上部等很多地方都画满了成群结队的飞天。若单从飞天的数量来看，隋代的飞天不亚于唐代，在装饰画、藻井图案中，飞天往往与其他形象相配合，相得益彰，创造了很多杰出的作品。

隋代第305窟窟顶南北两壁分别画出了东王公、西

realistically displaying the scene of *apsaras* flying lithely across the sky. For example, the two on the north wall both have chignons arranged in double looped buns: the one in the front is dressed in a long red *dhoti*, turning her head to the side and playing the *sheng*, looking relaxed and carefree; while the one at the back wears a long black *dhoti*, lotus in each hand, flying ahead, looking devout. Against a background of blue sky, they seem to be flying off the wall (Fig.53).

The passion for *apsaras* reached its peak with the artists of the Sui Dynasty. Groupings and crowds of *apsaras* were rendered in all kinds of spaces such as niches, caisson ceilings (*zaojing*), walls, and Dharma-preaching scenes. If quantity is the only factor to take into account, the number of *apsaras* from the Sui period are no less than those of the Tang. In the decorative paintings and caisson ceiling motifs, *apsaras* were represented together with other images, contrasting and complementing one another. Many masterpieces were thus created.

艺苑瑰宝

莫高窟壁画与彩塑

图53 飞天 莫高窟第404窟北壁 隋
Fig.53 *Apsaras*, North Wall of Mogao Cave 404, Sui Dynasty

王母等形象。这一题材在西魏时期已经出现，但在这里，飞天的形象则大量出现了。如北披的西王母的凤辇前，上部有一身羽人引导，前面还有两身飞行的比丘，下部是三身飞天，各托鲜花飞去，凤车后面则是4身飞天飞舞着跟随。飞天拖着长长的飘带，与天空中的彩云和天花相伴，急速地向前飞去，呈现出浩浩荡荡行进的态势。南披的东王公龙车前后也表现了与北披一致的飞天及气氛（图54）。东西两披的

Images of the King Father of the East and the Queen Mother of the West appear on both of the ceiling's northern and southern slopes in Cave 305, from the Sui period. The subject itself appeared as early as the Western Wei, but presented here, large numbers of *apsaras* join in. For example, in the upper part of the northern slope, guiding the way ahead for Queen Mother's chariot is a flying deity, in front of whom are two flying *bhikṣus*; in the lower part are three *apsaras*, flying across with flowers in their palms. Behind the chariot follow four *apsaras*, flying and dancing, with their long *dhotis* trailing. They are flying swiftly ahead, accompanied by rosy clouds and heavenly blossoms in the sky, showing the vast

布局大体一致,都在中央画摩尼宝珠,两边各有 4 身飞天向着中心飞来。这样,窟顶画出了几十身飞天,在彩云飘扬、天花飞舞的空中,构成了一个飞天的世界,使整个窟顶的空间变得无限、辽阔、深远。

画在佛龛中的飞天也同样富有气势。第 420 窟正面龛的龛顶,共绘出 15 身飞天。与四壁上部天宫栏墙内的飞天不同,不是那种整齐排列朝着一个方向飞,而是自由自在,演奏着各自不同的乐器,纷纷从天

and mighty current of the group's forward progression. Similar *apsaras* and scenes are painted before and after the King Father of the East's chariot on the southern slope (Fig. 54). The overall arrangement on the eastern and the western slopes is roughly identical. A *mani* jewel is drawn in the center with four *apsaras* on each side, all flying toward the center. As a result, more than ten *apsaras* in total are painted in this cave. A world of *apsaras* is thus composed in a heaven of fluttering clouds and floating blossoms, and the whole ceiling is made boundless and expansive.

Apsaras painted in niches can also be rich in grandeur. In Cave 420, there are 15

图 54　飞天　莫高窟第 305 窟窟顶南披　隋
Fig.54　*Apsaras*, Southern Slope of Ceiling, Mogao Cave 305, Sui Dynasty

而降，使你目不暇接。几乎每个飞天都有不同的姿态，绝无雷同，有的柔和，有的强劲，有的迅疾，有的舒缓，各有个性。

第412窟本来是一个大型洞窟，现在大部已塌毁，但西壁的佛龛却完整地保留了下来。这个佛龛很大，里面塑出了佛和十大弟子彩塑，龛顶则画出26身飞天，可以说是飞天最多的一个佛龛。这些飞天有的手托莲花，有的持璎珞，有的弹奏乐器，有的在舞蹈散花。最特殊的是飞天中还有不少是身披袈裟的比丘，他们上下翻飞，自由翱翔，在土红底色的烘托下，更有一种热烈欢快的气氛（图55）。

apsaras on the ceiling of the main niche, which are quite different from those within the balustrades around the heavenly palace on the upper section of its four walls. They are not neatly arranged, flying in the same direction, but rather are carefree and at ease, playing different musical instruments and falling from heaven in succession, seemingly too many for the eye to capture them all. They each have different poses and none seems similar to another. Some are soft, and some are forceful; some are swift, and some are leisurely. Each one is unique.

Cave 412 was originally very large, but much of it has collapsed and been ruined. Fortunately the niche in the west wall is still extant and in good condition. This is quite a large niche, inside which are painted sculptures of the Buddha and his ten principal disciples. Twenty-six *apsaras* are depicted on the niche's ceiling. It is reasonable to say that this niche contains the greatest number of *apsara* images: some hold lotuses in their palms, some hold jeweled necklaces, some play musical instruments, and some dance and scatter blossoms. What is most special is that among them are quite a few *bhikṣus*, wearing *kasayas*. They effortlessly fly up and down with ease. Contrasting against the background color of red earth pigment, the *apsaras*' flight creates a warm and cheerful atmosphere (Fig.55).

图55 飞天 莫高窟第412窟龛顶 隋
Fig.55 Apsaras, Ceiling of Niche, Mogao Cave 412, Sui Dynasty

唐代前期的飞天
Apsaras of the Early Tang

初唐的飞天不像隋代那样飞得急速,而更多地表现出一种悠闲感。第329窟的飞天是较为突出的,窟顶中心是一个以莲花为主的藻井图案,在中心莲花的四周,深蓝色的底色中,有4身飞天随着流云自由自在地飞翔。在藻井外缘的帷幔外,又画出12身伎乐飞天,他们的背景是浅黄色的,与中央的蓝底色形成对比。在五彩祥云的衬托下,他们演奏琵琶、箜篌、腰鼓等乐器,朝着一个方向连续不断地飞去。华丽无比的图案以及他们活泼多姿的动态给观者以无限的遐想,你会感到天空是那样的宽广无垠,似乎充满着美妙的音乐之声(图56)。

在第329窟的龛顶两侧,分别画出佛传故事"乘象入胎"和"夜半逾城",表现的是释迦牟尼诞生前的预兆和为了修行而离家出走的情节。龛顶右侧画面中,画出一菩萨乘

Apsaras of the Early Tang do not appear to fly as swiftly as those of the Sui period. Instead, they exhibit more of a sense of leisure. Prominent examples are those in Cave 329, which has a caisson ceiling with a lotus design in the center. Around the central lotus, against the background color of dark blue, four *apsaras* fly freely amongst the floating clouds. Beyond the drapery around the outer edge of the caisson, there are 12 more musician *apsaras*, with a yellow background color, forming a contrast against the blue background in the center. The *apsaras* play musical instruments such as the *pipa*, *konghou*, waist drums, and the like, flying in one direction, one after another, amongst a setting of colorful auspicious clouds. The paintings are incomparably magnificent and the motions of the *apsaras* are dynamic and graceful, which can be quite thought-provoking to the viewers. One might feel that the sky is so vast and boundless, and yet it seems to be filled with sounds of sweet music (Fig.56).

Two painted narratives of the Buddha's life, "Queen Māyā's Dream" and "The Great Renunciation", appear on the sides of the niche's ceiling in Cave 329. They depict the foretelling of Sakyamuni's birth as well as his renunciation of royal family life to embark on

Art Treasures: Murals and Painted Sculptures in Mogao Caves

图 56　飞天藻井　莫高窟第 329 窟窟顶　初唐
Fig.56　*Apsaras*, Caisson Ceiling, Mogao Cave 329, Early Tang

象奔驰,前有乘龙仙人引导,前后有二菩萨侍立,又有雷神、风神跟随,前面有 4 身飞天迎着菩萨,或托花供养,或演奏音乐,载歌载舞,姿态优美,后面还有一身飞天演奏着乐器,天空弥漫着流云和鲜花,有一种热烈而欢

his spiritual journey. The painting on the proper right shows a bodhisattva riding a running elephant, with a celestial being on a dragon guiding the way. Two other bodhisattvas wait upon him, in front and behind, with the Thunder God and the Wind God following at the back. Four *apsaras* are ahead of the bodhisattva, facing him, either presenting flowers as offerings, or playing music, singing and dancing joyously in graceful poses. There is one more *apsara* following behind, playing his musical

107

快的气氛。龛顶南侧画面表现悉达多太子乘马而行，前面也有乘龙仙人引导，后有风神、雷神，前面也有4身飞天欢快地歌舞，后随2身飞天持花供养，伴随着彩云、鲜花。飞天们身体柔和，姿态优雅（参见图69、图70）。

第321窟在佛龛顶部画出天宫栏墙，沿着天宫栏墙有一群体态婀娜的天人，神情悠闲逍遥，有的在朝下散花，有的则好奇地看着下面的人间世界。正如唐诗中所写"飘飘九霄外，下视望仙宫"。佛龛上部以深蓝色画出天空，在靠近佛背光的地方，菩提树前相对画出两组飞天。右侧的飞天均一手托着花蕾，一手自然展开，长裙衬托着柔和的身姿，长长的飘带随风飞舞。左侧的飞天与右侧的飞天相对，也是身体朝下飞来，一手拈花蕾，一手轻柔地散花。这两组飞天体态自然而柔和，每一条飘带，每一个动作都显得那么完美（图57）。

盛唐时代是敦煌艺术的

instrument. Floating clouds and fresh flowers permeate the sky and the atmosphere is warm and jubilant. In the painting on the proper left, Prince Siddhartha is depicted advancing on horseback; ahead of him, there is also a celestial being riding a dragon guiding the way; the Thunder God and the Wind God follow behind too; four *apsaras*, as well, are moving towards him in front, singing and dancing joyously, and two other *apsaras* are holding devotional flower offerings at the back. Accompanied by rosy clouds and fresh flowers, the figures of the *apsaras* are soft and their movements are graceful (Figs. 69, 70).

In Cave 321, balustrades around the heavenly palace are depicted on the ceiling of the niche. Along the railings are graceful celestial beings. They look carefree and relaxed, some scattering flowers down, and some looking curiously at the human world below. This is exactly what was written in a poem from the Tang Dynasty: "Floating and fluttering in the sky beyond / Overlooking the heavenly palaces below". In the upper part of the niche, the sky is painted deep blue. Two groups of *apsaras*, symmetrically opposite, are painted near the aureole of the Buddha, in front of a Bodhi tree. All the *apsaras* on the right hold flower buds in one hand while extending the other hand naturally. Their long *dhotis* set off their soft figures and their long, narrow sashes wave in the wind. Those on the left, flying downward as well,

Art Treasures: Murals and Painted Sculptures in Mogao Caves

黄金时代,飞天的描绘也表现出成熟而完美的特点。第172窟西壁佛龛顶部,在华盖两侧各画出两身飞天。华盖右侧的飞天,一身头枕着双手,身体舒展,怡然而上,仿佛鱼在水中悠然游过;另一身头朝下,双手捧着花蕾,飘然而下(图58)。这两身飞天一个向上,一个向下,身旁的彩云也随着不同的方向翻卷,形成一个充满动势的结构。窟顶的藻井也比较独特。藻井中心画出莲花,外沿画出复杂

hold flower buds with one hand and gently scatter blossoms with the other. The two groups look soft and natural, and each ribbon-like sash and every motion appear as pure perfection (Fig.57).

The High Tang was the golden age of Dunhuang art, when paintings of *apsaras* were also characterized by maturity and perfection. On the ceiling of the west wall's niche in Cave 172, two *apsaras* are painted on either side of the canopy. On the right side, one of the *apsaras* clasps his hands behind his head, stretching and rising ebulliently, looking like a fish swimming

图57 凭栏下视的天人 莫高窟第321窟龛顶 初唐

Fig.57 *Apsaras* Looking Down from Balustrade, Ceiling of Niche, Mogao Cave 321, Early Tang

图 58 飞天 莫高窟第 172 窟西壁龛顶 盛唐
Fig.58 Apsaras, Ceiling of Niche on West Wall, Mogao Cave 172, High Tang

的图案,如卷草纹、团花纹、几何纹等层层递出,最外层则易方为圆,把四周垂角纹和流苏画成圆形,更具有华盖的真实感。在最外沿,圆形华盖与方井交汇形成的4个岔角中,分别画出4身飞天。飞天身材修长而柔和,长长的飘带体现出他们轻松的动态,简单的几朵彩云,衬托出他们无拘无束的身姿。有了这些飞天,壁画的空间似乎都变得辽阔了。北壁的经变画中几身飞天好像在不停地飞行。右上角的那身飞天仿佛刚从地面腾空而起,手托莲花正要献给佛陀。与她相对的右侧一身飞天也同样,双手张开,手托着莲花,一条腿轻提,正向上飞升(图59)。靠近中部也有两身飞天从不同的方向向着中央大殿飞去,右侧这一身飞天一手向前一手向后,好像是以很快的速度飞来。左侧这一身飞近楼阁,双手合拢,身体呈半蹲状,好像正要着地的一瞬间。这些身姿轻盈的飞天,在辽阔的空中自由翱翔,

leisurely in water; the other is heading downwards, floating while carrying flower buds in both hands (Fig.58). These two *apsaras*, one flying upwards and the other downwards, with nearby rosy clouds wafting in different directions, form a composition full of kinetic potential. The caisson ceiling at the top of this cave is also distinctive. Its center is a lotus motif, and the outer edges surrounding it are intricate designs expanding layer by layer, such as curling grass motifs, composite floral patterns, and geometric designs. The square frame at the center is set inside a large circle. Hanging triangle drapery motifs and tassels are drawn around the circle, giving the appearance of a tent canopy. The four corners where the round canopy meets the square outer edges of the caisson result in four semi-circular shapes, in each of which an *apsara* is painted. These *apsaras* are slender and supple. Their long sashes reflect their relaxed dynamic, and a few patches of simple pink clouds foil their unrestrained poses. Because of these *apsaras*, the space displayed in the murals seems expansive. There are also quite a few *apsaras* in the sutra illustrations on the north wall of this cave. They appear to be in a state of constant flight. The one in the upper right corner seems to shoot straight up into the air from the ground. She holds a lotus upon each palm and is ready to offer them to the Buddha. The one paired with her on the right is drawn in a similar manner, flying upwards with both hands extended, lotus upon palms, and one leg raised (Fig.59). There

图 59 飞天 莫高窟第 172 窟北壁 盛唐
Fig.59 *Apsara*, North Wall of Mogao Cave 172, High Tang

令人不禁想起李太白的诗："素手把芙蓉,虚步蹑太清。霓裳曳广带,飘拂升天行。"

第320窟南壁佛说法场面的上部画出4身姿态优美的飞天。以宝盖为中心,分两组相对画出。左侧这一组,前面的飞天头梳双丫髻,双手上举,正在散花,她的面庞微微向后,漫不经心地看着后面的飞天,长长的锦裙紧贴身体;后面的这身飞天双手高举,一条腿提起,一条腿伸直,动作强烈,好像正努力追赶着前面的飞天。一紧张,一舒缓,富有戏剧性。右侧的两身飞天形式上与左侧一致,两组飞天都裸着上身,穿着长长的锦裙,双脚藏在长裙中,结构单纯而完美。画家通过一张一弛的对比统一,表现了飞天的两个典型动态(图60)。

第39窟是一个中心柱窟,在西壁又开一个佛

are also two *apsaras* near the middle, flying towards the central hall from different directions. The one on the right extends one hand forward and the other hand backward as if flying close with great speed. The one on the left is flying towards the pavilion, hands folded together and body half-crouched, as if it is the moment when she is just about to land. These slim and graceful *apsaras* are flying freely through the vast sky, and inevitably remind people of the lines from a poem by Li Bai: "A lotus held in a soft, pale hand / Walking lightly in air on tiptoe / With rainbow raiment dragging wide sashes / Floating up to heaven."

In the Dharma-preaching scene on the south wall of Cave 320, there are four graceful *apsaras*, drawn in pairs at opposite sides, centered around the canopy. In the pair on the left, the one in the front wears her hair in double chignons. She raises both hands, scattering flowers. Her face turns back slightly as she looks at the one behind her, and her long brocade *dhoti* is worn skin-tight. The one at the back raises her hands high. One of her legs bends up, and the other extends straight. Her motions are full of strength, as if she is making great effort to catch up with the one in front of her. This pair, one tense and one relaxed, seems rather dramatic. The pair on the right is drawn in a similar pattern. Both pairs have nude upper torsos and wear brocade *dhotis* that are long enough to cover their feet. This arrangement of *apsaras* is simple but perfect. The artists displayed two typical dynamics of *apsaras* by contrasting and consolidating the elements of tension and relaxation (Fig.60).

Cave 39 is a central pillar cave. In its west

图60 双飞天 莫高窟第320窟南壁 盛唐
Fig.60 *Apsara* Pair, South Wall of Mogao Cave 320, High Tang

龛,内塑佛涅槃像。这是一个绘、塑结合的涅槃经变画。佛经中记载,当佛涅槃之时,诸天从天空散曼陀罗花等各种鲜花供养。于是在壁画中也画出了5身飞天从天而降,左侧一身飞天一手托着一盘鲜花,一手轻拈花蕾,一条腿正往前跨,身体向下倾,表现出飞速而下的瞬间。右侧的与之相对的

wall there is a niche, in which a nirvana Buddha is sculpted. This is a *Nirvana Sutra* illustration presented by combining painting with sculpture. According to Buddhist scriptures, when the Buddha was entering his nirvana, or final death, *devas* from all the Buddhist heavenly realms scattered all manner of flowers such as Datura blossoms from above, as offerings. Therefore, in the mural there are also five *apsaras* painted flying down from the sky. The one on the left holds a plate of fresh flowers in one of her palms as she gently picks up the flower buds with her other hand. One of her legs strides forward and her body leans down, displaying a moment of rapid descent. The one on the right is

一身飞天动作姿态都跟前者相对称。龛顶中央又有一身飞天,头朝下直落下来,两侧各有一身飞天相对向着中央飞来,都双手托着一盘花蕾,神情虔诚。这些飞天体态修长,配合着长长的飘带更显得潇洒自如。他们的飘带都飘出了龛外,突破了画面边界的限制,仿佛真的从龛外飞下来似的(图61)。

symmetrical to the other in both motion and pose. In the center of the niche's ceiling is another *apsara*, moving down. On either side of her *apsaras* fly towards each other, heading towards the center. They both look devout, each holding a plate of flower buds with both hands. These *apsaras* are slim and tall, and with their long sashes floating, they appear to be casual and elegant. Their sashes have even broken through the boundaries of the painting, floating out of the niche. It seems as if the *apsaras* are truly flying in from outside the niche (Fig.61).

图61 飞天 莫高窟第39窟西壁龛内 盛唐
Fig.61 *Apsara*, Interior of Niche on West Wall, Mogao Cave 39, High Tang

艺苑瑰宝
莫高窟壁画与彩塑

唐代后期的飞天
Apsaras of the Late Tang

中唐以后壁画中的飞天身体趋于肥胖，但仍表现出雍容的气质。经变画中的飞天与盛唐壁画中的飞天一样，小飞天穿梭飞行于佛国世界的宫殿楼阁之间，人物形象较小，画得更为小巧精致。如第 159 窟南壁西侧的法华经变上部两侧各有三身飞天，乘着彩云飞速地向中央飞来（图 62）；靠近中部宝塔的几身飞天则双手上举，半跪在云中。中央的阿弥陀经变上部有两身飞天，双手上扬正向上飞行。这些飞天形体虽小，却刻画细腻，真实地表现出飞天的不同动态。

在第 220 窟甬道南侧龛内也有两身小飞天，因这部分壁画是剥离了表层壁画而露出的，线条和颜色都很新鲜。飞天双手托花上举，上身半裸，穿红色长裙从天而降，比起盛唐的飞天来，衣饰不是那样华丽，也没有烦琐

In the period after the Middle Tang, *apsaras* in murals tended to become plump, but their elegant temperament remained. *Apsaras* in sutra illustrations are quite similar to those in the murals of the High Tang, with small figures shuttling back and forth among the palaces and pavilions of the Buddhist realms. The characters are smaller but rendered with more delicacy. For example, in Cave 159, three *apsaras* are drawn on each side of the upper part of the *Lotus Sutra* illustration in the right-hand section of the south wall. They ride rosy clouds and fly rapidly towards the center (Fig.62). Those close to the pagoda in the middle are painted with both hands raised, half-kneeling in the clouds. In the upper part of the central *Amitabha Sutra* illustration, two *apsaras* fly upwards with both hands raised. Small as these figures are, they are exquisitely portrayed and realistically display the different dynamics of *apsaras*.

Two small *apsaras* are drawn in the niche on the corridor's south side in Cave 220. Since this part of the mural was revealed after the original surface mural was peeled off, both the colors and the lines appear fairly fresh. The *apsaras* come down from heaven, dressed in long red *dhotis*, their upper torsos partially clothed. They hold up flowers in both hands. Compared with those of the High Tang, the clothing is no

图 62　飞天　莫高窟第 159 窟南壁　中唐
Fig.62　*Apsara*s, South Wall of Mogao Cave 159, Middle Tang

的花纹，但飞天的飘带翻卷而形成的圆圈却增加了，不仅具有装饰性，而且衬托出飞天的飞行速度较慢，亦显得雍容和穆。在绘画艺术上，画家更善于用寥寥数笔就勾勒出形体，色彩简淡，颇有写意的效果。

第 158 窟配合大型涅槃佛像，画出了涅槃经变

longer flowery, and the decorative motifs on them are no longer rich with intricate details. However, there are more curving and curling loops in the ribbon-like sashes, which not only presents a decorative effect, but also shows the slower velocity of the *apsaras*, making them more elegant and reverent. In terms of the art of painting, the artists were quite skilled in outlining the images with a few simple touches. The colors used here are light and soft, with the effects of freehand brushwork from traditional Chinese painting.

The *Nirvana Sutra* illustration paintings were created in Cave 158 to accompany the large

117

的内容。本窟的涅槃经变画突出地表现众弟子及世俗人物因释迦牟尼的离去而悲伤的场面。据佛经上说："尔时,帝释天及诸天众,即持七宝大盖、四柱宝台、四面庄严、七宝璎珞,垂虚空中,覆佛圣棺,无数香花、幢幡、璎珞、音乐、微妙杂彩空中供养。"(《大般涅槃经》)根据这些内容,壁画的上部还画出了不少飞天,有的双手托花,跪在云间;有的弹奏乐器;有的在空中散花。他们都神情庄重,飞行缓慢,与经变的气氛一致。特别是西壁的一身飞天,表情忧郁,双手持璎珞,缓缓地飞下来,表现出一种哀悼之情(图63)。这些都反映了中国人按中国式的思想来理解和表现涅槃这一主题。而飞天在其中,正是这种精神的表征。

晚唐以后,在窟顶藻井周围画出一周飞天的形式较为流行,并形成了一种模式。第161窟窟顶的藻井较为特别,井心画的是一身千

nirvana Buddha statue housed within. The *Nirvana Sutra* illustrations in this cave highlight the sorrowful scene among the disciples and lay followers caused by the Sakyamuni Buddha's imminent death. As detailed in Buddhist scriptures, "At that time, Indra and all the *devas* solemnly took the seven-treasure canopy, the four-pillared platform encrusted with jewels, and the seven-jeweled necklace of jade and pearls. They all descended from heaven and sheltered the coffin of the Buddha. Countless flowers, banners, jewels, music, and delicate colors appeared in the air as offerings" (*Nirvana Sutra*). Based on this account, quite a few *apsaras* are depicted in the upper part of the murals, some holding blossoms with both hands and kneeling among the clouds, some playing musical instruments, and some scattering flowers in the air. They all look solemn and move slowly. The atmosphere is completely consistent with the sutra illustrations in the cave. Special notice needs to be given to the *apsara* on the west wall, who looks despondent, while flying slowly down, holding the necklace of jade and pearls in both hands, showing an expression of mourning (Fig.63). All these denote that the Chinese people interpreted and expressed the concept of nirvana in a Chinese way of thinking. *Apsaras* are part of this conception, and they can well be regarded as manifestations of this spirit.

After the Late Tang, *apsaras* were painted around the caissons on cave ceilings. This type of painting became more and more popular, allowing

Art Treasures: Murals and Painted Sculptures in Mogao Caves

图 63　持璎珞的飞天　莫高窟第158窟西壁　中唐
Fig.63　*Apsara* Carrying Necklace of Jade and Pearls, West Wall of Mogao Cave 158, Middle Tang

手千眼观音菩萨,观音坐在莲花座上,他的千百只手形成一个圆圈,像一轮美丽的光环;观音两侧上部画有两身向上飞升的飞天。左侧的飞天两手伸开散花,右侧的飞天正吹奏着横笛,形象生

a new pattern to take shape. The caisson on the ceiling of Cave 161 is more distinctive. The painting in the center is a Thousand-Armed and Thousand-Eyed Avalokitesvara. Avalokitesvara sits on a lotus throne, hundreds upon hundreds of his hands forming a circle, resembling a beautiful halo. Two *apsaras* fly upwards on both sides above him. The one on the left extends both

119

动,色彩绚丽。在藻井四边各画出4身伎乐飞天,分别演奏着笙、排箫、笛、琵琶、腰鼓等乐器。他们一身接着一身飞行,不同的演奏姿态,不同的飞行动作,显得充满了活力。画家还往往在一列飞天之中画出一些特别的形象,造成一定的变化。如东披的飞天(图64),三身面向观众,而第二身吹笙的飞天则画成侧面形象,表现出专注的神情。南披4身飞天中,右起第一身飞天,双手握箫吹奏,身体向后倾,背向飞行方向,显得很悠闲。第二身飞天弹奏着琵琶,头朝下,倒着飞行。这些别致

hands, scattering flowers; the one on the right plays a transverse flute. Both of them are striking, with dazzling colors. An *apsara* musician is depicted on each of the four sides of the ceiling's caisson. They play musical instruments such as the *sheng*, panpipes, the flute, the *pipa*, and the waist drum, flying one after another. Their poses of playing and their manner of flying are each different, revealing a scene bursting with life and energy. It was also common during this period for artists to paint some unique images within a row of *apsaras*, giving a sense of variety. Examples are those on the eastern slope of the ceiling (Fig.64), where three of the four *apsaras* are rendered facing the viewer, while the second one, playing the *sheng*, is portrayed in profile, showing an expression of concentration. Among the four *apsaras* on the southern slope, the first one from the right plays the *xiao* with both hands. She leans back—and flies backwards as well—looking insouciant and casual. The second one plays the *pipa* as she flies upside down. These novel figures break with the conventional uniform patterns, so that the overall composition abounds in

图64　飞天　莫高窟第161窟东披　晚唐
Fig.64　*Apsaras*, Eastern Slope of Ceiling, Mogao Cave 161, Late Tang

的形象打破了整齐划一的格局,使画面富于变化。第80窟窟顶藻井的边沿也像第161窟那样画出一周共22身飞天。这些飞天或正面或侧面,或倒向飞行,自由变化,多姿多彩。飞天的旁边都画出色彩浓丽的五彩云朵,使她们看上去像在云雾中,别有风韵。

五代以后,莫高窟虽然仍在持续不断地开凿,甚至还开凿了不少大型洞窟,但由于与中原文化交流较少,在壁画艺术上没有更多的创新,飞天的描绘也呈现衰落的景象。西夏到元代,随着政权的更替,来自少数民族地区或者内地的艺术形式影响到了敦煌,出现了一些特别的画法,但数量不多。如第97窟正面佛龛中,在菩提宝盖两侧对称地画出两身童子飞天,都是秃发,在头两侧有小发辫,前额垂下两道红带子,身穿一种兽皮制的背带裈衫(类似背心的服装),脚穿红靴。这些都表现出回鹘民族的一些特征(图65)。两身飞天都面形丰满,略显出儿童的稚气,一手托着盘中的花朵,

changes. Just as in Cave 161, there are 22 *apsaras* drawn along the edge of the caisson ceiling in Cave 80. These *apsaras* are shown either in a frontal image, or in a side image, some flying in a backward direction with no restrictions, varied and graceful. Clouds in rich colors are drawn all around the *apsaras*, making them appear as if they are indeed among clouds and mists, lending them an elegant bearing.

After the Five Dynasties, more cave temples were constructed in succession at Mogao; quite a few were very large ones. However, due to a lack of cultural exchange with the Central Plains, there was not much innovation in mural art, and paintings of *apsaras* went into decline. From the Western Xia to the Yuan Dynasty, owing to changes in political regimes, Dunhuang art was influenced by the artistic forms of either ethnic minorities or those from China's interior. Some unusual painting methods were adopted, but such influences were rather limited and works of this type were not substantial in number. One example is the mural in the main wall's niche in Cave 97, where two child *apsaras* are drawn symmetrically on both sides of the Bodhi canopy. Both boys have shaved heads with small sidelocks of hair, and two red ribbons hang down over their foreheads. They each wear a kind of vest made of leather straps, and a pair of red boots. These show some of the features of the Uyghur people (Fig.65). Both

图 65 飞天 莫高窟第 97 窟西壁龛内 西夏
Fig. 65 *Apsara*, Interior of Niche on West Wall, Mogao Cave 97, Western Xia

一手扬起散花，彩云簇拥，飘带翻飞，映衬着孩童特有的丰腴的肌肤，使画面中的飞天颇有情趣。

元代第3窟的飞天也是以儿童的形象来表现的。在南北壁千手千眼观音像的上部两侧，各有一身飞天。南壁的飞天或跪或蹲于彩云上面，手托鲜花做供养状，神情虔诚。北壁的两身飞天较活泼，西侧这身飞天一手握着两枝长茎莲花，另一手托着一个花蕾，正从云中下视（图66）；东侧的飞天也是一手持长茎莲花，一手托花蕾，而身体倾斜，仿佛就要飞下来。这4身飞天身体较短，形象丰满，色彩浓丽，画家强调的是儿童的天真可爱。这也许与宋元以来民间对儿童画的喜爱有关。

总之，敦煌壁画中飞天可以说是无处不在，画家们以极大的热情来描绘飞天。飞天的存在使严肃的宗教绘画变得富有

boys have round faces, indicating childlike innocence. Surrounded by pink clouds, with sashes floating and fluttering, they hold a plate of flower blossoms in one hand while raising the other to scatter flowers. The unique figures of children are well-silhouetted against the background, making the general view of the *apsaras* pleasing to the eye and interesting.

The *apsaras* in Cave 3 from the Yuan Dynasty are also presented as figures of children. On both the north and south walls, two *apsaras* are painted over the images of the Thousand-Armed and Thousand-Eyed Avalokitesvara, one on each side. The two on the south wall either kneel or crouch over rosy clouds, holding fresh flowers for offerings, looking rather pious. The two on the north wall seem livelier. The one on the left side holds two long-stemmed lotuses in one hand and a flower bud in the palm of the other, looking down from the clouds (Fig.66). The one on the right side also has long-stemmed lotuses in one hand and holds a flower bud in the palm of the other. He is angled as if about to fly down. These four are relatively shorter *apsaras*, but their figures are filled with rich colors. The artists attached significance to the innocence and innate loveliness of children. This possibly could have something to do with the fact that people favored paintings of children, a trend beginning with the Song and Yuan periods.

In conclusion, it is safe to say that *apsaras* are a ubiquitous phenomenon in Dunhuang murals, and that artists painted them with great enthusiasm. As a result, serious religious paintings became interesting, dynamic, and vivid because of *apsaras*.

艺苑瑰宝
莫高窟壁画与彩塑

图 66　飞天　莫高窟第 3 窟北壁　元
Fig.66　*Apsara*, North Wall of Mogao Cave 3, Yuan Dynasty

情趣,生动活泼。敦煌飞天的造型与印度那种写实性较强的飞天不同,更强调一种理想的形式美,一种流动之美。长长的飘带,辅以流云,形成了一种飞动的韵律。这种形体的流动,又如书法一般,通过线条的流动感体现出一种畅快而生动的气韵。总之,敦煌飞天艺术是中国人物画艺术中的一朵奇葩,它介乎似与不似之间、真实与想象之间,创造了无限动人的形象。

Different from the more realistic ones depicted in India, the design of Dunhuang *apsaras* laid greater stress upon ideal aesthetic forms, namely a quintessential state of flowing beauty. The long, narrow sashes, accompanied by the floating clouds, resulted in a kind of flying rhythm. Just as the achievements in Chinese calligraphy gave rise to a type of structural flow, so the paintings of *apsaras* embodied a cheerful and lively style by creating a sense of linear flow. All in all, the art of Dunhuang *apsaras* is a wonderful flower in the artistic garden of Chinese figure painting. They lie somewhere between similarity and difference, reality and ideal—creating some immeasurably fascinating images.

艺苑瑰宝：莫高窟壁画与彩塑
Art Treasures: Murals and Painted Sculptures in Mogao Caves

佛教故事画

Buddhist Narrative Paintings

故事画是通过描绘一定的人物、动作以及人物之间的相互关系等来展示一个故事的发生、发展和结局，它综合了各种绘画手段为表达故事的思想内容服务。在古代印度的艺术中，故事性的雕刻和绘画也是十分流行的。早期的佛教艺术中，如建于公元前2世纪的山奇大塔、巴尔胡特大塔的塔门和周围的护栏中就有很多关于佛传故事、本生故事的浮雕。南印度的阿玛拉瓦提雕刻中也有不少故事性的内容。佛教传入中国之后，石窟、寺院的兴建很普遍，佛教故事画也同样在众多的寺院及石窟里流行起来。并且，由于中国已有故事画的传统，画家们结合中国的特点，绘出了有别于印度风格的故事画。

敦煌壁画中的故事画主要有四类：一是佛传故事，就是讲述释迦牟尼一生特殊经历的故事。二是本生故事，是讲述释迦

Buddhist narrative paintings portray the occurrence, development, and endings of Buddhist stories by depicting specific characters, their actions, and their relationships with each other. In such paintings, various methods are integrated for the purpose of expressing the ideological meaning and content of stories. In ancient Indian art, narrative-style sculptures and paintings were quite popular, and in the early period of Buddhist art, reliefs were carved on the doors and balustrades around stupas to illustrate *jataka* tales and narratives of the Buddha's life. The Great Stupa at Sanchi and the Great Stupa at Bhārhut, built in the 2nd century BC, are examples. Numerous stories can also be found in the carvings in Amarāvatī in South India. After Buddhism's dissemination into China, the construction of caves and temples became widespread throughout the land, and likewise, Buddhist narratives became popular in many temples and caves. Moreover, since China had already developed its own tradition in narrative painting, Chinese artists could integrate sinicized elements into narratives of Buddhist stories. Accordingly, paintings by Chinese artists bore rich Chinese features different from those in Indian patterns.

Buddhist narratives in the Dunhuang murals can be classified into four major types. The first type is the narratives of the Buddha's life, which tell about the unusual life experiences of the Sakyamuni Buddha. The second type is *jataka* tales, stories about Sakyamuni's previous births. According to Buddhism, a person is sure to undergo rebirth after death. If he commits virtuous

牟尼前世的故事。佛教认为人死后是要经过轮回的,如果做了善事,到下一辈子转生就会过好日子;反之,在转世后就会很惨。如果累世都做善事和修行,最终就会脱离轮回而成佛。释迦牟尼就是因为前世做了数也数不清的善事,终于成了佛。本生故事就是讲释迦牟尼前世的善行事迹。第三是因缘故事,主要讲与佛相关的一些因果报应故事。第四是佛教史迹故事,是讲佛教发展史上的一些高僧或某些地方的佛教圣迹的传说故事,也叫佛教感应故事。

deeds during his lifetime, he will enjoy better days after his rebirth. Otherwise, he will suffer after his transmigration. If a person practices good karma and spiritually cultivates himself during every rebirth of his life, he will ultimately escape from the cycle of Samsara, ultimately becoming a Buddha. As to Sakyamuni, it was because of the countless virtuous deeds he had committed during his previous rounds of existence that he finally became the Buddha. *Jataka* tales recount those deeds. The third type is *nidana* stories, mainly about karmic retribution related to the Buddha. The fourth type involves legends and stories of Buddhism's history, telling of eminent monks, legendary tales about sacred relics, or historical sites involved in the development of Buddhism. These narratives are also known as Buddhist tales of resonance (*ganying gushi*), indicating miracle stories.

艺苑瑰宝
莫高窟壁画与彩塑

佛传故事画
Narratives of the Buddha's Life

释迦牟尼本名乔达摩·悉达多,大约在公元前565年诞生于古印度的迦毗罗卫国,父亲是净饭王,母亲是王后摩耶夫人。关于悉达多太子的诞生,有着种种神异的传说。据说摩耶夫人梦见了一个菩萨乘六牙白象而来,于是身怀有孕。按古印度的习俗,妇女生育当回娘家。于是怀胎将满十月之时,摩耶夫人在很多宫女的陪伴下回娘家。途中经兰毗尼园,摩耶夫人觉得身体不适,便徐徐来到园中,当她手攀无忧树时,太子从她的右胁生了下来。原来,释迦牟尼不愿使母亲受到分娩之痛苦,就从腋下降生了。而太子刚生下来就能行走,他走了7步,每走一步后,脚下就生出一朵莲花。他用手指天指地说:

The historical name of the Sakyamuni Buddha was Gautama Siddhartha, who was born around 565 BC in Kapilavastu, a kingdom in ancient India. His father was King Śuddhodana and his mother was Queen Māyā. Diverse mystical legends abound on the subject of Prince Siddhartha's birth. It was said that in one of her dreams, Queen Māyā saw a bodhisattva come to her riding a white elephant with six tusks; after this dream she became pregnant. According to the customs of ancient India, a woman would return to her parents' home when she was about to give birth. Thus, when the time came that she had been pregnant for almost ten months, Māyā began the journey to her parents' home, accompanied by a retinue of palace women. When they were passing a garden at Lumbinī, she felt unwell, so she walked slowly into the garden. As she took hold of a sal tree for support, the prince was born from her right side, under her arm, since he was not willing to let his mother suffer the pain of childbirth. The prince was able to walk from the moment he was born. He strode seven paces, a lotus springing up from each footstep. He pointed to heaven and earth, declaring: "Foremost am I in the world." At that moment, nine dragons began to spray sweet dew to wash the prince. Queen Māyā and the baby Prince went back to the palace; King Śuddhodana was more

"天上天下,唯我独尊。"这时天上有9条龙喷洒甘露为太子沐浴。摩耶夫人和太子回到宫中,净饭王非常高兴,为太子取名叫悉达多。太子从小学文习武,受到很好的教育,并娶大臣摩诃那摩之女耶输陀罗为妻。他生活在宫中,享尽了人间的快乐。然而,太子常常感到忧郁。他在城外出游时看到人间有疾病、衰老和死亡等诸多痛苦,他陷入了苦苦的思索。这段经历称为"出游四门"。他想寻找一条解脱人间痛苦的途径,于是决定出家修行。在29岁那年,悉达多决定出家修行,为了避免国王阻拦,他在一个夜晚偷偷离城,到山中开始了苦修的生涯。这一经历称作"逾城出家"。他每天只吃一点豆羹以维持生命。经过了6年的苦行,他感到苦修并不能解决问题,于是到尼连禅河洗尽了6年的污垢,并接受了牧女施舍的牛乳,慢慢地恢复了体力。当他在菩提树下沉思默想时,战胜了心中的一切魔障,突然间得到了大悟,从此,明白了人间的真谛。

than pleased and named his son Siddhartha. From his childhood the Prince learned how to write and how to fight, receiving a very good education. He married Yaśodharā, daughter of Mahānāma, one of the ministers of the kingdom, and lived in the palace enjoying all the pleasures of the human world. However, the Prince often felt worried. When he visited the areas outside the city walls and witnessed various types of suffering in the human world, including disease, old age, and death, he was thrown into turmoil. This experience was called the "Four Sights". He wanted to find a way to escape human misery, so he made up his mind to renounce the world and undertake a spiritual path. At the age of 29, Prince Siddhartha decided to put his ideas into practice. In order to avoid being stopped by the king, he secretly left the city one night and went into the mountains to start his ascetic practice. This experience was known as "The Great Renunciation". Each day he only had a little dal porridge to survive and after about six years of practicing austerities, he felt that strict spiritual asceticism was not the way out. As a result, he went to the Nairañjanā River and washed off all the dirt from those six years. He accepted a bowl of rice milk offered by a shepherdess so that his physical strength gradually recovered. After he was absorbed in deep meditation under the Bodhi Tree and overcame the demon Māra, he suddenly experienced enlightenment and understood the true essence of existence. This event was

这件事称作"树下成道"。他开始收徒讲学,宣扬他的理论,这就是"初转法轮"。他所主张的教义就是佛教。他被尊称为释迦牟尼,意思是释迦族的圣人。后人又称他为佛陀,意为大彻大悟的人。佛教成立后,发展并不是十分顺利,释迦牟尼不断地到各地说法,扩大佛教的影响。公元前484年,释迦牟尼于拘尸那城的双树林中涅槃。

描绘释迦牟尼生平的佛传故事,大多是依据佛经中的有关记载来画的。佛经中往往把释迦牟尼神格化了,带有很多神异的色彩。这也是敦煌壁画故事画的一个特色。在莫高窟时代最早的洞窟——第275窟南壁就出现了佛传故事画,表现悉达多太子在出家前"出游四门",分别遇见老人、病人、死人及僧人的情景,由于壁面损毁,只剩下三个场景。人物形象具有西域人物的特征,而城门的建筑则是明显的中国传统建筑形式,门楼的屋檐及斗拱等历历可见。

called "The Great Awakening". He began to gather disciples, preaching to them and instructing them in the tenets of his teachings. The first sermon was known as the discourse on "Setting in Motion the Wheel of Dharma". The doctrines he advocated became known as Buddhism, and he was respectfully called Sakyamuni, meaning the Sage of the Śākya clan. Later people called him the Buddha, meaning the Awakened One. The development of Buddhism was not a very smooth process after its founding. Sakyamuni kept wandering from place to place, preaching the Dharma to expand its influence. In 484 BC, Sakyamuni entered his final nirvana, under the sal trees near the town of Kuśinagara.

Most narratives of the Buddha's life are based on related accounts from Buddhist canonical texts, in which Sakyamuni is usually deified with many divine mystical qualities. This is one of the features of Dunhuang paintings as well. In the earliest cave at Mogao, Cave 275, narratives of the Buddha's life were painted on the south wall. These depict the scenes of Prince Siddhartha as he encountered an old man, a diseased person, a corpse, and a religious mendicant, the "Four Sights" he came face to face with prior to renouncing the world. Because the surface of the wall is badly damaged, only three scenes remain. Though the human figures in these paintings carry the features of the Western Regions, traditional Chinese architectural patterns can be readily

石窟中的佛传故事画大多选取一两个有代表性的情节来表现。如释迦牟尼诞生前，摩耶夫人梦见白象的场景，称作"乘象入胎"。悉达多太子决定离家修行而骑马逾城的场景，称为"逾城出家"。这两个情节，一个象征着释迦牟尼的诞生，一个象征着释迦牟尼修行的开始，是壁画中最为常见的佛传场面。在隋及唐初的洞窟中往往在正面龛两侧分别画出这两个情节，具有装饰效果。如隋代第278窟西壁北侧上部"乘象入胎"（图67），画一菩萨乘六牙白象（颜色已变黑），正缓慢向前，身后有二伎乐正在演奏琵琶和箜篌，飞天在上空散花供养。南侧相对画出"骑马逾城"的场景，悉达多太子乘马跃起，有4个小天人分别托着马足，正急速飞行，前后有飞天手托莲花上下飞舞。这两幅画主题鲜明突出，用色质朴、单纯、稳健，造型凝重、典雅，而骑马逾城的场面有风疾电掣之

found in the city gates, where eaves and *dougong* brackets can be seen clearly upon the gate towers.

The plots in most narratives of the Buddha's life are presented by choosing one or two typical scenes. For example, the scene of Queen Māyā seeing a white elephant in her dream before Sakyamuni was born was called "Queen Māyā's Dream", while the scene of Prince Siddhartha deciding to renounce the world is called "The Great Renunciation". These two plots, one representing Sakyamuni's birth and the other the beginning of his spiritual journey, are the scenes that are commonly seen in Dunhuang narrative paintings of the Buddha's life. They are usually painted, as decorative scenes, on both sides of the main niche in caves from the Sui and the Early Tang. For example, "Queen Māyā's Dream" is painted in the upper part of the right side of the west wall in Cave 278 of the Sui Dynasty (Fig.67). In the painting, a bodhisattva rides a white elephant with six tusks (the colors have blackened from oxidation), advancing slowly, followed by two musicians playing the *pipa* and the *konghou*. Meanwhile, *apsaras* scatter blossoms in the air as devotional offerings. On the left side, the scene of "Departing the Palace on Horseback" is painted at the opposite position. Prince Siddhartha rides his charging horse, as four small *devas* support the four hooves of the horse, flying with great speed. In front of and behind the horse, *apsaras* hold lotuses in their hands,

艺苑瑰宝
莫高窟壁画与彩塑

图 67　乘象入胎　莫高窟第 278 窟西壁北侧　隋
Fig.67　Queen Māyā's Dream (the Conception), Right Side of West Wall, Mogao Cave 278, Sui Dynasty

图 68　夜半逾城　莫高窟第 278 窟西壁南侧　隋
Fig.68　The Great Renunciation, Left Side of West Wall, Mogao Cave 278, Sui Dynasty

感(图68)。

第209窟、329等窟的佛传故事画则更多地体现出初唐华丽热烈的精神气度。第329窟的佛传画构图较满,人物众多,刻画精致,具有华丽灿烂的装饰效果(图69、图70);而第209窟的画面中对骑马形象的轻盈和乘象的凝重等方面的刻画更生动而富于个性化。"乘象入胎"与"夜半

flying up and down. The themes of the two paintings are clear and distinct. The colors are simple, moderate, and unsophisticated; the designs are dignified and elegant. The scene of "Departing the Palace on Horseback" offers a sight as swift as the wind, and as quick as lightning (Fig.68).

Narratives of the Buddha's life in Caves 209, 329, and the like embody more of the intense, awe-inspiring spirituality of the Early Tang. Those in Cave 329 are densely packed with numerous figures, and are portrayed more delicately, with brilliant decorative embellishments (Figs.69, 70); while those in Cave 209 are livelier and more individualized depictions of gracefully riding on the

图69 乘象入胎 莫高窟第329窟西壁北侧 初唐

Fig.69 Queen Māyā's Dream (the Conception), Right Side of West Wall, Mogao Cave 329, Early Tang

艺苑瑰宝
莫高窟壁画与彩塑

图 70　夜半逾城　莫高窟第 329 窟西壁南侧　初唐
Fig.70　The Great Renunciation, Left Side of West Wall, Mogao Cave 329, Early Tang

逾城"两幅画由于内容和形式上的密切关系，构成了不可分割的组画形式，在洞窟中具有很强的装饰性。

"降魔成道"和"初转法轮"也是表现佛传的重要场面。前者表现释迦牟尼成道时，魔王波旬深恐释迦牟尼的成道威胁到自己，就率众魔军企图杀死释迦牟尼。面对众魔围攻，释迦牟尼镇定自如，以神通力击败了魔军，使众魔伏

horse and the majestic sense of riding an elephant. The two paintings, "Queen Māyā's Dream" and "The Great Renunciation", make up an inseparable combination, since they are closely related to each other in terms of both form and content. They also create strong ornamental effects in the caves.

Plot elements such as the "Defeat of Māra" and "The Enlightenment", as well as "Setting in Motion the Wheel of Dharma" also display important scenes from the Buddha's life. The former is a narrative of Sakyamuni's attainment of enlightenment: Māra deeply

首归降。表现这一主题的画面也称降魔变,在印度和犍陀罗的雕刻中就很常见。敦煌北魏壁画中的降魔变在构图上完全继承了外来的形式。如第254窟南壁(图71),表现佛安坐在中央,周围各式各样的妖魔手执各种武器,向佛袭来。画面下部则描绘魔军败北后跪在佛前的样子。画面下部左侧还描绘了三个美女正

feared that Sakyamuni's enlightenment would be a terrible threat, so he sent his minions to try to destroy Sakyamuni. However, when surrounded and attacked by these demons, Sakyamuni remained calm. He defeated all the demons with his supernatural strength, forcing them to surrender. Tableaux presenting this theme are often called the "Defeat of Māra", commonly seen among sculptures in India and Gandhara. Among the Dunhuang murals of the Northern Wei, the composition of subjugating Māra is a complete inheritance of exotic forms. The painting on the south wall of Cave 254 is an example, in which the Buddha sits quietly in the center while all manner of demons hold various

图71 降魔变 莫高窟第254窟南壁 北魏
Fig.71 Defeat of Māra, South Wall of Mogao Cave 254, Northern Wei

对着释迦牟尼搔首弄姿,右侧有三个面貌丑陋的老女人。这是表现魔王波旬见魔军不能战胜释迦牟尼,便施美人计,企图以美色来诱惑释迦牟尼,但释迦牟尼不为所动,并使神力,把美女变成了又丑又老的老婆子。

"初转法轮"表现的是释迦牟尼成佛后到鹿野苑第一次说法的情景,也称"鹿野苑说法"。通常描绘佛在说法,佛前有两只鹿象征着鹿野苑,并有三个圆形的法轮。佛两侧画有比丘5人,代表最早跟随释迦牟尼的5个比丘。在北魏第260窟、263窟都画有初转法轮图,特别是第263窟壁画保存如新。

涅槃也是佛传中的一项重要内容。释迦牟尼的涅槃意味着肉体的消失和灵魂的升华,从此进入不生不灭的状态。对于佛教来说,从此佛不再是一个实体的人物,而是一个永远存在的精神导师。因而涅槃就是佛教的最高境界。涅槃图在佛教艺术中具有十分崇高的地位,这一点与基督教

weapons, besieging and attacking him (Fig. 71). The lower register of the painting depicts a scene in which, defeated, demons kneel down and pay homage to the Buddha. Furthermore, on the left side of the lower register, three beautiful women are shown giggling and flirting, trying to seduce Sakyamuni, while three ugly old women appear on the right side of the same section. This indicates that when Māra realized his minions could not defeat Sakyamuni, he sent the women to ensnare him through sexual desire. But Sakyamuni remained unmoved, and with his superhuman powers, transformed the three beauties into three hags.

Narratives of "Setting in Motion the Wheel of Dharma" convey a scene in which, for the first time after his enlightenment, Sakyamuni went to Sārnāth to teach his doctrines. Thus it is also called "Preaching the Dharma in Sārnāth." It is often the case that when the Buddha is rendered preaching the Dharma, there are two deer symbolizing Sārnāth, and three round wheels of the Dharma. There are also five *bhikṣus* on both sides of the Buddha, representing the first five monks who followed Sakyamuni. In both Caves 260 and 263 of the Northern Wei, there are murals on "Setting in Motion the Wheel of the Dharma", and those in Cave 263 are especially preserved as if they were freshly painted.

Paintings on the Buddha's nirvana are also an important component of narratives of

艺术中描绘被钉在十字架上的耶稣表现的是同样一种宗教境界。北周第428窟西壁的涅槃图是莫高窟最早的涅槃图(图72),其表现方法与中亚的佛教艺术一致,描绘佛安详地卧在双树下,周围有众多的弟子环绕,弟子们表情悲哀,大弟子迦叶抚足恸哭。全图充满了伤感的基调。隋代以后,涅槃图形成了规模较大的独立的涅槃经变,增加了很多情节,这些内容将在下一章详述。

the Buddha's life. Sakyamuni's nirvana means the vanishing of flesh and sublimation of the soul, from which state neither birth nor death will ever be experienced again. For Buddhism, beginning with his nirvana, the Buddha is no longer a physical figure, but an ever-present spiritual guide. Nirvana is considered the ultimate state in Buddhism. Paintings about the nirvana enjoy a sublime status in Buddhist art. The religious realm depicted here is similar to that presented in Christian art by the Crucifixion of Jesus. The painting on the west wall of Cave 428 from the Northern Zhou is the earliest work of its kind in the Mogao Caves (Fig.72), where nirvana is rendered the same

图72 涅槃图 莫高窟第428窟西壁 北周
Fig.72 The Buddha's Nirvana, West Wall of Mogao Cave 428, Northern Zhou

最完整地表现佛传内容的壁画当数第290窟人字披顶的佛传图，表现了从佛的诞生、出家直到成道为止的故事，如连环画一样，以连续性的画面表现，形成长卷的形式。在人字披的两披各以三段长卷画幅相接续，共6段画卷，画出87个情节，可称为最长的连环画了。画面线描流畅而清晰，色彩简淡，以建筑、山水为背景，人物造型简练，体现出敦煌早期壁画中故事画艺术的成就（图73）。五代时期的第61窟也在南、西、北三壁的下部利用屏风画的形式，画出了完整的佛传故事，内容更为丰富，从佛诞生之前的种种传说到佛涅槃为止，共画出128个情节，是莫高窟内容最为丰富的佛传故事

way as Buddhist art from Central Asia. The Buddha is portrayed lying peacefully beneath the sal trees; many disciples surround him, looking despondent. The oldest disciple, Mahakasyapa, strokes the Buddha's feet and cries bitterly. The whole painting is filled with emotion. After the Sui period, paintings on nirvana were developed into *Nirvana Sutra* illustrations, which became extensive, independent works with more plot elements added. We will deal with them in detail in the next chapter.

The most comprehensive narrative murals of the Buddha's life are those on the gabled ceiling of Cave 290. They are painted in a series of pictures, covering tales from the Buddha's birth, through his renunciation of the world, to his attainment of enlightenment. The serial arrangements form a long panel of a continuous narrative painting. On each slope of the ceiling in this cave, the panel is divided into three successive bands or registers. The six registers in total on both slopes contain 87 scenes, which can be thought of as the longest continuous narrative painting. The lines in them are flowing, smooth, and clear, and the colors adopted are light and soft. Buildings, mountains, and rivers are painted as backgrounds, and the characters in them are portrayed simply and with brevity. The earliest artistic accomplishments in Buddhist narrative paintings in Dunhuang are embodied among the murals here (Fig. 73). Comprehensive narratives of the Buddha's life are also seen, in the form of screen paintings, at the lower parts of the north, south, and west walls of Cave 61 from the Five Dynasties. The content in these paintings is more extensive, with 128 scenes, covering a long range of events from various legends before the Buddha's birth up until his nirvana. These narrative

图 73　佛传故事（局部）　莫高窟第 290 窟人字披东披　北周

Fig.73　Narrative Paintings of the Buddha's Life, Eastern Slope of Gabled Ceiling, Mogao Cave 290, Northern Zhou

画,在现存的佛教艺术中也是十分罕见的。画面中还可以看到当时人们在社会生活中的种种面貌,如宫中生活、歌舞宴乐、骑射比武、市井生活、农耕景象等等,反映了当时社会的种种生活状况。

paintings contain the richest content of the Buddha's life in the Mogao Caves, unique among the Buddhist art that has been preserved until the present day. From these paintings, different aspects of everyday life can be traced as well, such as life in the palace, songs and dances and feasts, riding and shooting and fighting, daily affairs of the townsfolk, farming scenes, and so on. Consequently, living conditions of people from all walks of life are reflected within.

艺苑瑰宝
莫高窟壁画与彩塑

充满牺牲精神的本生故事
Jataka Tales Imbued With the Spirit of Sacrifice

本生故事是指释迦牟尼佛前生的故事。佛教认为人是会轮回转世的。佛就是经过了无数次轮回转世,并且每一次转世他都做了很多善事,或者是经过刻苦修行,最后才成为佛。佛经中记载了释迦牟尼佛在前世的无数善行故事,这些故事就称为本生故事。

九色鹿本生

九色鹿本生(图74)故事本来是古印度流传很广的传说,佛教产生后,这个故事也被编入了佛经中。故事讲的是在古代印度的恒河岸边,住着一只美丽的鹿,它的皮毛花纹斑斓,有9种颜色,所以称为九色鹿。一天,九色鹿正在河边散步,突然听到河里传来一阵急促的呼救声。九色鹿循声

Jataka tales refer to tales of Sakyamuni's previous lives and incarnations. According to Buddhism, people are bound to Samsara, the endless cycle of birth and death. A Buddha has experienced countless rounds of rebirth. During each of his rebirths, he has either gained merit by virtuous deeds, or undertaken strict spiritual cultivation, until finally becoming a Buddha. Accounts of Sakyamuni's countless virtuous deeds during his previous lives are recorded in Buddhist literature. These accounts are called *jataka* tales.

Jataka of the Nine-Colored Deer

The "*Jataka* of the Nine-Colored Deer" (Fig. 74) was originally a legend that was widespread in ancient India and was later adopted into Buddhist literature. According to the story, in ancient India, there lived by the Ganges River a beautiful deer, whose coat had bright markings with nine colors; thus he was known as the Nine-Colored Deer. One day the Nine-Colored Deer was walking by the river when he heard a burst of desperate shouts for help coming from the river. Following the sound, the deer ran over and saw that a man, who had fallen from the bank, was struggling in the rushing water. Upon catching sight of the man, the kind-hearted deer jumped into the torrent without hesitation, forgetting all about his own safety. He swam over to the man, put him on his back, and

跑去,只见一个落水的人正在急流中挣扎。善良的九色鹿见状,不顾自己的安危,毅然跳进激流中,游到落水人跟前,把那人背在背上,奋力游回了岸边。落水的人千恩万谢,跪在九色鹿面前说:"恩人啊,真不知道怎样报答你才好。"九色鹿平静地说:"不用感谢,但有一点请你答应我,就是你回去后千万不要把我所在的地方告诉任何人。人们贪图我的毛皮,可能会加害于我。"落水之人指天发誓说:"我决不把您的行踪告诉任何人。如果违背誓言,让我全身长满毒疮,痛苦而死。"当他回到城里时,看到城门口贴着一张告示,很多人正在围观。原来这个国家的王后做了一个梦,梦见一只十分美丽的九色鹿。醒来后,她要求国王把九色鹿捕来,取下毛皮为她做衣服。国王以为只不过是一个梦罢了,未必就真有九色鹿。但为了满足王后的要求,只好叫人贴出一张告示,上面写着:有知道九色鹿行踪者,愿意分一半的国土给他,并赏赐金、银无数。那个落

swam with all his might back to the bank. The man thanked the deer so profusely that he knelt down in front of him, saying: "You saved my life, I can never repay you enough!" The Nine-Colored Deer replied calmly: "You don't need to thank me, but you must promise me that after you return home you'll never tell anyone where I am. People are so greedy for my coat that they'll try to kill me either." Lifting his hand towards the heavens, the man swore an oath: "I promise to tell no one of your whereabouts. If I break my promise, may terrible sores grow all over me and may I die in bitter pain." When the man returned to town, he saw a notice on the town gate; many people were crowding around to read it. It announced that the Queen of the country had had a dream in which she saw a beautiful nine-colored deer. When she woke up, she asked the King to hunt down the deer so that his hide could be stripped off to make a coat for her. The King thought that it was merely the Queen's dream and that there was no such thing as a real nine-colored deer. However, in order to please the Queen, he had the notice posted on the gate. It read: Anyone who can reveal the whereabouts of a nine-colored deer will receive half the lands of my kingdom, and abundant rewards of gold and silver will be granted to him as well. The man who had fallen into the water saw the notice, and, tempted by the lucrative reward, was overwhelmed with greed. Forgetting all about

图 74 九色鹿本生(局部) 莫高窟第 257 窟西壁 北魏
Fig.74 Detail of *Jataka* of the Nine-Colored Deer, West Wall of Mogao Cave 257, Northern Wei

水人看到这一则告示，在重赏的诱惑下，顿生贪婪之念，便忘记了自己的誓言，向国王报告了九色鹿所在的地方。第二天，国王带着大批军队来到了恒河边的那一片树林。九色鹿根本不知道快要来临的大难，它正在林中午睡。它的好友乌鸦把它叫醒时，国王的军队已经把它团团包围了。九色鹿突然看见落水的那个人在国王前面带路，马上明白了一切。它昂首走向国王，对国王说："贤明的君主啊，我曾有恩于你的国家，为何却要杀我？"接着它把头一天在恒河边救人的事一五一十地告诉了国王。国王听了十分感动，他说："鹿为兽类，尚且知道善恶，而人却怎么做出忘恩负义的事？"于是下令从此以后，不许任何人伤害九色鹿。那个落水之人自从告密以后，浑身长满了毒疮，发出恶心的臭味，不久便痛苦而死。

这个故事画在莫高窟第257窟的西壁，画家采用了中国传统的长卷式连环画的形式，按两头到中央的顺序，详细描绘了故事发展的经过，把九

his promise, he told the King where the deer was. The following day, the King sent his troops into the woods by the Ganges River. The Nine-Colored Deer knew nothing about the imminent danger, for he was having his mid-day nap. When his close friend, the crow, woke him up, he was already surrounded by the king's troops. The deer suddenly caught sight of the man who had fallen into the river and who had shown them the way; he understood everything immediately. He went to the King with his head raised high, saying to him, "Your wise Majesty! I have done good for your country—why do you want to kill me?" Then he told the King in detail about what had happened by the Ganges River the previous day. The King was moved when he heard the tale, so he said, "Although this deer is a beast, he can still distinguish good from evil. How can it be that a man should be so ungrateful and treacherous?" He gave an order that from that moment on, no one was allowed to touch the Nine-Colored Deer. As to the man whom the deer had saved from the raging torrents, after he betrayed the deer, terrible sores developed all over his body which gave off a terrible smell. He did indeed die in bitter pain.

This *jataka* tale is painted on the west wall of Cave 257. The artists depicted in detail the plot development of the story,

色鹿向国王陈述事情经过的场面画在中央,突出了正直善良的九色鹿形象,特别是昂然挺立的九色鹿给人以深刻的印象。

萨埵本生

莫高窟第254窟南壁的"萨埵本生"故事画(图75),描绘了古代印度宝典国国王有三个儿子,最小的名为摩诃萨埵。一天,兄弟三人一起到山林中游玩,返回的路上,发现一只母虎躺在崖下,已饿得奄奄一息,旁边还有几只小虎,也饿得嗷嗷直叫。三人都很同情,但谁也想不出救助它们的办法。萨埵想找一些食物给老虎吃,但哥哥告诉他:"老虎只吃新鲜血肉,别的东西无济于事。"于是,萨埵太子暗自决定要救活这些老虎,他让两个哥哥走在前面,自己悄悄地返回了老虎所在的地方,躺在地上让老虎吃他。可是,几只老虎饿得连咬他的力气都没有了。萨埵很焦急,他找到一根木刺,爬到山崖上,用木刺刺破喉咙,然后跳下山崖,落在母

adopting the traditional Chinese style of serial pictures painted on long panels, and arranging the order from both ends to the center. The scene of the Nine-Colored Deer telling the King what had happened is painted in the center, reinforcing the image of the deer as virtuous and upright. The upright and bold Nine-Colored Deer makes a deep impression upon the viewer.

The Mahāsattva *Jataka*

The "Mahāsattva *Jataka*", painted on the south wall of Cave 254 (Fig.75), relates that in ancient India, there was a king named Mahāratha who had three sons, the youngest of whom was named Prince Sattva. One day the three brothers went out to the forest in the mountains. On their way back, they saw a tigress lying under a cliff, on the verge of starvation. Next to her were several cubs that were also crying because of hunger. The three brothers felt pity for them, but none could think of a way to help. Prince Sattva tried to find some food for them, but his elder brothers told him that tigers only eat fresh blood and meat, and that nothing else would work. Prince Sattva silently vowed to save the tigers. He told his two older brothers to go ahead, while he secretly returned to the spot where the tigers were. He lay down on the ground so that the tigers could eat him, but the tigers had become so weak that they did not even have

图 75　舍身饲虎　莫高窟第 254 窟南壁　北魏
Fig.75　Mahāsattva *Jataka*, South Wall of Mogao Cave 254, Northern Wei

虎身旁。母虎和幼虎舔食萨埵流出的鲜血，渐渐地有了气力，就把萨埵太子身上的肉吃光了。萨埵的两个哥哥发现三弟不见了，慌忙返回山中寻找，却见山崖下只有一堆白骨。他们顿时明白萨埵为救老虎已经舍身，不胜悲痛，便匆匆回到王宫，报

enough strength to bite him. Prince Sattva grew anxious. He saw a sharp thorn on a nearby cliff. He climbed up the cliff, stabbed his own throat with the thorn and leapt off, landing beside the tigress. The tigress and her cubs licked the fresh blood oozing from Prince Sattva. Gradually they regained enough strength to eat all his flesh. When the two elder brothers realized that the younger one was out of sight, they quickly returned to the mountains to look for him, but all they found was a pile of white bones. Immediately they knew that Prince Sattva had

告了国王。国王和王后闻讯哀伤不已，二兄弟忍痛收拾萨埵遗骨，造塔供养。

这个故事情节十分曲折离奇，画家把故事的全过程画在一个方形的画面中。画的中心是俩兄弟朝下观望，沿着他们的视线，我们看到右下侧一只面目狰狞的老虎，正在啃咬一个横躺着的人，这是全画面的中心。右侧描绘萨埵太子刺项、跳崖两个连续性的画面，正与"饲虎"这一场面衔接起来，使画面充满了悲壮的色彩。左下侧画萨埵父母抚尸恸哭，更烘托了画面的悲剧气氛。整个画面结构紧凑，色彩强烈，在视觉上给人以戏剧效果，是早期故事画的优秀作品。同样的内容也被画在北周第428窟东壁。在这里，画家通过上中下三段的长卷式画面，把萨埵太子与二兄离家、进山、见虎、饲虎直到造塔供养等共14个情节一一详尽地画出来（图76）。这种连环画的形式虽然不像第254窟画面那样集中、冲击感强烈，

sacrificed his own life for the tigers. Overwhelmed by sorrow, they hurried back to the palace and told the King what had happened. The King and the Queen were grief stricken. The two elder brothers had to overcome their emotions; they collected their younger brother's remains and built a stupa to make offerings to him.

The plot of this *jataka* tale is full of twists and turns. The artist painted the overall narrative in a square space, in the middle of which is the scene of the two brothers looking down. Following their line of sight, we can see that, on the lower right side, a ferocious tiger is gnawing a man lying on the ground, which is at the center of the whole composition. On the right are two successive scenes of Prince Sattva stabbing his own throat and jumping off the cliff, which are linked to the scene of feeding the tiger. An evocative and tragic essence is thus brought about within the picture. The scene of Prince Sattva's parents holding his body and crying bitterly is rendered on the lower left side, enhancing the heart-rending atmosphere. The whole painting, with a well-knit structure and forceful colors, produces a dramatic visual effect. It is a masterpiece among the earlier narratives of Buddhist stories. Similar content is painted on the east wall of Cave 428 of the Northern Zhou. The artist divided the long series of pictures into the upper, the middle and the lower registers, and

图 76 舍身饲虎（线描临摹） 莫高窟第 428 窟东壁 北周

Fig.76 Line Drawing Copy of Mahāsattva *Jataka*, East Wall of Mogao Cave 428, Northern Zhou

但却描绘具体，明白易懂。所以，北魏以后的壁画中，连环画形式更为流行。

尸毗王本生

北魏第 254 窟北壁，还有一幅"尸毗王本生"故事画（图 77），描绘古代一个叫尸毗王的国王乐善好施，立誓普救众生。一天，一只老鹰追逐一只鸽，鸽子生命危急，飞来飞去无处藏身，便来到了尸毗王的身边，请求尸毗王保护它。这

presented all 14 plots in detail, one by one, including Prince Sattva leaving home with his two elder brothers, going into the mountains, encountering the tigers, feeding the tigers, and finally the building of the stupa in his honor (Fig.76). Though the structure of the serial pictures is not as condensed, nor as striking, as the one painted in Cave 254, the scenes are concrete and easy to understand. Therefore, in murals after the Western Wei, serial pictures became even more popular.

The *Jataka* of King Śibi

On the north wall of Cave 254, constructed during the Northern Wei, there is another Buddhist narrative painting known as the "*Jataka* of King Śibi" (Fig.77). The story tells of a king during

Art Treasures: Murals and Painted Sculptures in Mogao Caves

图 77　尸毗王本生　莫高窟第254窟北壁　北魏
Fig.77　*Jataka* of King Śibi, North Wall of Mogao Cave 254, Northern Wei

时,老鹰已经追来,向尸毗王索要鸽子。尸毗王说:"我立誓要拯救一切生灵,希望你不要吃了这只鸽子。"老鹰说:"如果今天我不吃鸽子,便会受饿而死,你为何只救它却不救我呢?"尸毗王说:"我给你其他的食

ancient times named Śibi (sometimes spelled as Shivi), renowned for his charity and generosity, who vowed to save all sentient beings. One day, a hawk was pursuing a dove, and the dove's life was at stake. It flew hither and thither but could find nowhere to safely hide, so it came to King Śibi, seeking shelter from him. Just at that moment the hawk caught up with the dove and claimed it as his prey. King Śibi declared, "I have vowed to save all living things, so I pray you will not eat this dove."

149

品吧。"老鹰说:"我只吃新鲜血肉,其他一概不能吃。"尸毗王想到自己的誓言,既要救鸽子,又不能害了别的生灵,于是决定用自己的肉来换取鸽子的生命。他叫左右拿刀来,割自己腿上的肉给老鹰。老鹰对尸毗王说:"大王既然要用自己的肉代替鸽子,我也不敢贪多,就请用秤来称够与鸽子同样重量的肉吧。"尸毗王就让人找来一杆秤,一头放鸽子,一头放从自己身上割下的肉。说来也怪,国王把腿上的肉割尽,又把身上的肉也割完,还是达不到鸽子的重量。国王想到自己的誓言,为了彻底救助这只弱小的鸽子,毅然举身坐上了秤盘,决定把全身都施舍给老鹰。这时天地震动,诸天神为尸毗王散下鲜花,割下的肉一下子都复还到国王身上。只见帝释天与大臣满面笑容站在国王面前说:"恭喜你

But the hawk replied, "If I don't eat this dove today, I'll starve to death. Why do you only want to save the dove, but not me?" King Śibi asked, "Can I give you something else to eat?" The hawk replied, "But I can only eat fresh meat and blood, nothing else." King Śibi pondered his own vow. He should save the dove, yet at the same time he also didn't want to harm other living creatures. As a result, he decided to offer his own flesh in exchange for the dove's life. He told his attendants to bring a knife so that he could cut flesh from his leg to feed the hawk. Then the hawk said to King Śibi, "Your Majesty, now that you'd like to replace the dove's flesh with your own, I don't want to take more of your flesh than the weight of the dove. Please get a scale so that I can receive the amount of your flesh equal to the dove's weight." King Śibi had a scale brought to him. Then he placed the dove on one end of the scale, and put the flesh from his leg on the other end. It was rather strange—though the King cut off all the flesh from his legs and other parts of his body, it never equaled the weight of the dove. The King thought of his vow, and climbed onto the scale with determination. He decided to sacrifice himself to the hawk in order to save the small, weak dove. Just at that moment, both Heaven and Earth were moved, and all the heavenly deities and *devas* scattered blossoms down on King Śibi. The flesh that had been cut was returned and the King was made whole again. Indra and his retinue of ministers stood in front of King Śibi with smiling faces. Indra said, "Congratulations on the supreme

成就了无上正果。"原来,帝释天为了检验尸毗王对于施舍是否真诚,便与大臣分别变为老鹰和鸽子来试验,果然尸毗王对忍辱、施舍都意志坚定,符合佛教修行的要求。

壁画上,画家着力刻画了尸毗王这一形象,他头微向前倾,表现出慈祥大度而又无所畏惧的精神。他一手托着鸽子,一手扬起阻挡老鹰。在他的左侧,一个面目凶狠的人正在一手操刀,一手用力取肉。右边一人,一手提着秤,秤的一边放着鸽子,一边则是坐着的尸毗王。周围画出国王的眷属们悲伤痛哭,更衬托出国王的安详与平静。

spiritual state you have reached." It turned out that the gods Indra and Agni had taken the form of the hawk and the dove in order to test whether King Śibi's spirit of sacrifice was real. King Śibi had indeed shown resolve in not only tolerating humiliation, but also making sacrifices, completely fulfilling the requirements of the Buddhist path.

In this painting, the artist devoted his efforts in depicting King Śibi. The King's head leans slightly forward, demonstrating a spirit of kindness and magnanimity without fear. He holds the dove in one hand and raises the other hand to stop the hawk. On his left, a fierce looking man holds a knife in one hand, forcefully taking off the flesh with the other. The man on his right holds a scale, with the dove sitting on one plate and King Śibi on the other. All around, the king's family and dependents cry in despair, contrasting with the stoicism and calm demeanor of the king.

具有忠孝思想的佛教故事

Buddhist Narratives Marked by Loyalty and Filial Piety

佛教初传中国的时候,讲究修六度(也称六波罗蜜,指布施、持戒、忍辱、精进、禅定、智慧等6项修持内容)。因此,壁画中充满了关于施舍、忍辱和牺牲精神的本生故事,有的故事很难为中国人所接受。在南北朝时经历了较长时间的儒、释、道之间的斗争,北魏武帝和北周武帝的时候,就曾采取过大规模的灭佛行动,拆毁寺院,破坏佛像,迫使僧尼还俗等,给佛教以沉重的打击。这样,使佛教组织不得不采取更为灵活的措施来适应中国的道德观念、社会习俗和文化环境。为了与儒家思想妥协,宣扬忠孝思想的故事也就多了起来。于是壁画中就出现了像睒子本生、须阇提割肉奉亲、善事太子入海求珠、五百强盗成佛等与儒家思想接近的故事主题,表明佛教逐渐与中国传统文化相融合了。

When Buddhism first came into China, emphasis was placed on cultivating the six *pāramitās*—the "six perfections": generosity, morality, forbearance, effort, concentration, and wisdom. Therefore, among the murals, there are numbers of *jataka* tales on themes of generosity, forbearance, and self-sacrifice. Some of the tales were unacceptable to the Chinese way of thought. During the Northern and Southern Dynasties, struggles between Confucianism, Buddhism, and Daoism endured for quite a number of years. Buddhism suffered persecution during both the reigns of Emperor Wu of the Northern Wei and Emperor Wu of the Northern Zhou, when temples were demolished, statues of the Buddha were destroyed, and monks and nuns were forced to return to secular life. These events were a heavy blow to Buddhism. As a result, Buddhism was obliged to adapt more flexible measures to integrate itself into Chinese ideologies, social mores, and cultural milieu. An increasing number of tales advocating ideas of loyalty and filial piety were adopted by Buddhism in order to accommodate to Confucianism. Thus among the murals there appeared narrative paintings on such stories as the *jataka* of filial Śyāma, the tale of Prince Sujāta cutting his own flesh to feed his parents,

睒子本生

睒子本生，讲的是一个孝道的故事。古代迦夷国有长者夫妇双目失明，幸而晚年得子，取名睒子。睒子长大后对父母十分孝顺。长者夫妇早就向往着到远离城市的山中过清静的修行生活，儿子长大能够照顾父母时，他们一家便住到深山里去了。睒子与周围鸟兽和谐相处，每日到溪边汲水，专心侍奉父母。一天睒子身披鹿皮衣，去溪边汲水，这时正好迦夷国国王带兵到山中打猎，见溪边有不少野鹿，就弯弓射箭，却没想到射中了正在溪边取水的睒子。睒子惊叫道："你一箭射杀了三道士啊！"国王见射中了人，心中十分后悔，忙到跟前看望。听了睒子的话却十分不解，便问睒子是什么原因。睒子说明了盲父母将无人照顾，难以在山中生活，说完便死了。

Prince Kalyāṇakārin seeking treasure from the sea, and the conversion of 500 bandits to Buddhism. The themes of all these tales were closely aligned with Confucianism, which suggests that Buddhism was gradually integrating into traditional Chinese culture.

The Śyāma *Jataka*

The "Śyāma (sometimes spelled as Sama) *Jataka*" is a tale of filial piety—the devoted son. In the ancient Kingdom of Benares, there lived an old blind couple. Fortunately, a son was born to them when they were advanced in years, and they named him Śyāma. Śyāma treated his parents with great filial piety as he grew up. For a long time the old couple had been yearning for a quiet life in the mountains conducive to spiritual practice, far away from the city. As soon as the son was old enough to look after his aged parents, the family moved deep into the mountains. Śyāma got along very well with the birds and beasts there and every day he fetched water from a stream. He took care of his parents with whole-hearted devotion. One day, Śyāma dressed himself in his coat made from a deer hide and went to fetch water from the stream. Just at that moment, the King of Benares came hunting in the mountains with his men. Seeing a good many wild deer beside the stream, the King drew his bow and shot an arrow. Unexpectedly he shot Śyāma, who was collecting water. Śyāma, in shock, cried out, "You've killed three holy beings with one arrow!" The King felt intense remorse when he realized he

国王非常难过，表示要代睒子养活盲父母，便亲自到盲父母处，说明情况。睒子的父母随国王来到睒子死去的地方，失声痛哭。他们的哭声感动了天帝，于是天帝派人救活了睒子，并使盲父母双目复明。这个故事画在北周第461窟、438窟、299窟都有描绘，其中第299窟的最具代表性（图78）。画在洞窟顶部北侧沿藻井边缘的一条长画卷形式的壁面上，故事由两头向中间叙述，左侧由左至右描绘迦夷国王在宫中、乘马出行、射猎及睒子中箭等情节；右侧则由右至左描绘睒子在山中侍奉父母、国王引盲父母到溪边、抚尸痛哭等场面。把故事的结尾

had shot a man. Quickly he came close to see who the man was. He was totally confused by Śyāma's utterance, so he asked what he meant. Śyāma explained that after his death no one would take care of his blind parents, and it would be impossible for them to survive in the mountains alone. With these words he died. The King felt sorrow and promised to take care of the blind parents in Śyāma's place. He went to the old blind couple and explained to them what had happened. Śyāma's parents followed the King to the spot where Śyāma was killed. They lost control and burst into tears. Their tears touched Indra so much that he sent somebody down to bring Śyāma back to life and to restore the sight of the blind parents. The tale is painted in Caves 461, 438 and 299 of the Northern Zhou, among which the painting in Cave 299 is the most representative (Fig.78), where the tale is narrated from both ends to the middle, on the

图78　睒子本生（局部）　莫高窟第299窟窟顶北披　北周
Fig.78　Detail of Śyāma *Jataka*, Northern Slope of Ceiling, Mogao Cave 299, Northern Zhou

放在画面的中央，突出了睒子的形象。

善事太子本生

善事太子本生故事画在北周第296窟的窟顶（图79），讲的是古代宝铠国国王有二子，一名善事，一名恶事。善事太子心地善良，常常把国库打开，把宝物施舍给穷人。可是，时间长了，国库渐渐空虚，大臣们颇有非议。善事太子感到应该想一个更好的办法，让人们都能得到财富。这时，有人告诉他在海底龙王处有如意宝珠，要什么就有什么。善事太子决定到大

wall close to the top of the north side, arranged in a long continuous panel of narrative scenes along the edge of the caisson ceiling. From left to right, the left side shows scenes such as the king of Benares staying in the palace, riding out, hunting, and Śyāma being shot. And from right to left, the right side shows scenes including Śyāma looking after his parents in the mountains, the King leading the blind parents to the stream, and the old couple caressing Śyāma's body in their arms while crying. The end of the tale is painted at the center, highlighting the figure of Śyāma.

The *Jataka* of Prince Kalyāṇakārin

The "*Jataka* of Prince Kalyāṇakārin" is painted on the ceiling of Cave 296 of the Northern Zhou (Fig.79). In ancient times, there was a king who had two sons, one named Kalyāṇakārin ("Noble Doing") and the other named Papakārin

图79　善事太子本生（局部）　莫高窟第296窟窟顶东披　北周
Fig.79　Detail of *Jataka* of Prince Kalyāṇakārin, Eastern Slope of Ceiling, Mogao Cave 296, Northern Zhou

海里去找如意宝珠。这时，恶事太子也想跟着去。于是，善事与恶事辞别父母，分别率两条大船向大海深处进发。路上遇见金山、银山，贪婪的恶事搬了很多金、银上船，结果船载过重而倾覆。而善事太子坚持向前进发，在盲导师的带领下，经过很多艰难曲折，终于到达龙宫，向龙王求得如意宝珠。善事太子返回途中在一个岛上与恶事相遇，兄弟俩共述别离之情。恶事见善事取得宝珠，心生嫉妒，趁善事睡着的时候，用毒刺刺瞎了善事的双眼，抢走了宝珠，独自回国；又编造谎言，说善事太子已死，自己取得了宝珠。善事在梦中突然被刺瞎双眼，却不知是恶事所为。过了很久，有一牧牛人赶牛而过，牛用舌头舔出善事眼中的毒刺，善事太子随牧人来到了利师跋国。他请牧牛人帮他做一把琴，此后便每天在街

("Evil Doing"). Prince Kalyāṇakārin was a kind-hearted person, often opening the national treasury to distribute alms to the poor. As time went on, the national treasury started to dwindle, and the ministers started to talk about him behind his back. The Prince felt that a better solution must be found so that all people could obtain wealth. At that time, he was told that the dragon king living at the bottom of the sea had a *mani* jewel, from which people could get anything they wished. Thus he decided to go and search the sea for the *mani* jewel. Papakārin also wanted to go with his brother. Kalyā.ṇakārin and Papakārin bid farewell to their parents; each of them commanded a large ship, voyaging to the distant sea. On the way, they encountered gold and silver mountains. Greedy Papakārin loaded so much gold and silver onboard his ship that it overturned from the weight. Contrary to his brother, Kalyāṇakārin persisted in going ahead. Guided by a blind mentor, he reached the palace of the dragon king at last, after many trials and tribulations. He was successful in begging for the *mani* jewel from the dragon king. On the way back he encountered Papakārin on an island. The two brothers talked affectionately about the events that had taken place during their separation. Noticing that his brother had obtained the *mani* jewel, Papakārin became envious. He stabbed him in both eyes, blinded him with poisonous thorns, and robbed him of the *mani* jewel while he was sleeping. Papakārin returned to his country alone, started a rumor that Kalyāṇakārin was dead, and explained how he had gotten the *mani* jewel all by himself. Since he was asleep when it happened,

Art Treasures: Murals and Painted Sculptures in Mogao Caves

上以弹琴卖艺为生。不久，国王果园的人见他可怜，就让他帮助看管果园。善事太子用绳子系上铃铛，每听到鸟声，就拉铃赶鸟，闲时就在树下弹琴自娱。利师跋国王有一个美丽的公主，她到果园散步时，听到了善事太子的琴声十分动人，就常常来听善事弹琴，并与善事聊天。日子久了，她渐渐爱上了这个盲人。可是国王不同意他们结婚，公主却十分坚定，国王只得同意，让他们结婚了。后来才知道善事太子的来历，大家非常惊喜。其实，从前公主就已许配给了宝铠国的善事太子。于是，国王派很多人护送善事太子回国。这个故事画在第296窟窟顶，以两段横卷式画面由右至左的顺序表现，共描绘了42个情节。其中太子出游、施舍以及耕作、渔人捕鱼、乘船航海等场面都表现出细腻而富有浓厚的生活气息。

Kalyāṇakārin didn't know it was Papakārin who had blinded him. Time passed, and a herder came along, driving his cattle. One of the cattle licked the poisonous thorns out of Kalyāṇakārin's eyes. Kalyāṇakārin followed the cattle herder to his country, a neighboring kingdom. The cattle herder had a stringed musical instrument made for him and after that Kalyāṇakārin became a street performer, wandering along the roads, and making a living by playing music. Before long, the gardener in the King's orchard took pity on him and asked him to help take care of the orchard. Kalyāṇakārin tied a bell at the end of a rope, and as soon as he heard the sound of birds, he would pull the bell to scare the birds away. In his spare time he would make music to amuse himself. The King had a beautiful daughter. One day when she was walking in the orchard, she heard the music played by Kalyāṇakārin, which was very stirring. Thus, she often came to the orchard to listen to his music and chat with him. Days passed and she gradually fell in love with the blind man. The King would not permit them to marry, but the Princess was determined. As a result, the King finally agreed to their marriage. Only later on was the history of Kalyāṇakārin known to other people. To the delight of everyone, it was revealed that the Princess had been betrothed to Kalyāṇakārin long ago. Thus the King sent his men to escort the Prince back to his own kingdom. This *jataka* is painted on the ceiling of Cave 296. The horizontal painting is divided into two registers, going from right to left. Altogether 42 scenes are displayed.

五百强盗成佛

五百强盗成佛的故事,也叫"得眼林"故事。讲述古代印度某国有五百强盗经常抢劫作乱,后来国王派官兵与强盗激战,终于把五百强盗全部收捕,处以极刑,有的剜眼,有的割鼻,强盗们在树林中痛苦哀号。哭声惊动了天上之佛。于是,佛以慈悲心从天而降,为他们说法,使他们悔悟而争相皈依佛门,佛就洒下神药,使他们的伤口愈合、眼睛复明。五百强盗改邪归正,努力修行,终于个个得成正果。

这个故事表明即使是作恶多端的强盗,只要放下屠刀,也可以立地成佛。在莫高窟第 285 窟和第 296 窟都画有这一故事(图 80)。西魏时代的第 285 窟南壁,以长卷式连环画的形式描绘这个故事。画面从左至右绘出了官军与强盗作战,强盗被

Among them, a strong and exquisite essence of real life is revealed in such scenes as the prince going out travelling, distributing alms, as well as scenes of plowing, fishing, and nautical voyages.

Jataka of the Five Hundred Bandits

The tale of 500 bandits and their conversion to Buddhism is also called the Aptanetravana *Jataka*, "the Forest of the Recovered Eyes". According to this tale, there were once 500 bandits in a certain kingdom of ancient India, who kept forming insurrections and staging rebellions. Later the King ordered his troops to fight against them. The battles were fierce, and the bandits were captured in the end. They were sentenced to extreme penalties: some had their eyes gouged out, and some had their noses cut off. The bandits wailed bitterly in the woods. Their screams alarmed the Buddha in Heaven, who was merciful and came down to earth. He taught them the Dharma, and they were awakened from their evil deeds, eager to be converted to Buddhism. The Buddha sprayed some medicine on them, which healed their wounds and enabled them to regain their eyesight. The 500 bandits gave up their evil ways, becoming virtuous. They made great efforts in their spiritual progress, and finally they attained enlightenment.

The "*Jataka* of the Five Hundred Bandits", painted in Caves 285 and 296 at Mogao (Fig.80), shows that even if a person is a hardened criminal, he can become a Buddha as long as he lays down his weapons. On the south wall of Cave 285 from the

图 80　五百强盗成佛(局部)　莫高窟第 285 窟南壁　西魏
Fig.80　Detail of *Jataka* of the 500 Bandits, South Wall of Mogao Cave 285, Western Wei

捕、受刑、山中流放，佛为其说法，500 强盗皈依等情节。画家不仅画出了人物，而且对周围的环境也很注意，画出了高大的楼房，远处的山峦、树木和水池，以及在山中的禽兽等。特别是佛为强盗说法的场面，画出了山丘环绕的水池，池中绿水荡漾，还有鸭子、鹭鸶等水禽；山中可见鹿子、狐狸等兽类；在佛的身后是一片翠竹。如果抛开故事内容，那么，我们看到的完全是一幅情趣盎然的山水画。佛说法时的这种平和美丽的气氛与画面开始时表现的官兵与强盗作战时的残酷场面形成鲜明

Western Wei, the tale is painted in a long panel of continuous narrative pictures. The paintings are arranged from left to right, depicting such scenes as troops fighting with the bandits, the bandits captured, tortured, and exiled into the mountains, the Buddha expounding the Dharma to them, and the 500 bandits converted to Buddhism. Not only did the artist pay attention to portraying the characters, but he also laid plenty of emphasis on the setting. Tall buildings, distant hills, trees, and water pools as well as birds and beasts in the mountains can all be found in his painting. The scene in which the Buddha preaches the Dharma to the bandits requires special mention, where a water pool is seen surrounded by hills, ducks and egrets swim across the green, rippling pool of water, beasts such as deer and foxes roam in the mountains, and flourishing groves of green bamboo grow behind the Buddha. If we drift away from the contents of the tale, what we then see is a landscape full of fascination. When the Buddha is preaching the Dharma, the atmosphere is pleasant and tranquil,

的对比，具有很高的艺术性。第296窟南壁也描绘了同样的内容，也是采用长卷式的画面，自右至左详细表现了官兵出征、与500强盗激战、俘获强盗、对强盗处刑、强盗悲鸣、佛对强盗说法、强盗皈依等情节，画面强调对强盗的战斗和处刑，有意炫耀王权的力量。

but when the royal troops are fighting against the bandits, the sight is fierce and horrible. Thus, a sharp, highly artistic contrast is presented. Similar content is painted on the south wall of Cave 296, again in a long panel. Arranged from right to left, the pictures depict in detail scenes such as troops going into battle, fierce fights with the bandits, the bandits captured, tortured, crying piteously, the Buddha teaching them, and the bandits converted to Buddhism. In these pictures greater significance is attached to the fights and the torture of the bandits, which is purposefully meant to show off the king's power.

佛教史迹故事画
Narratives of Buddhist Legends and Transmission

壁画中有一类故事主题是讲述一些佛教历史上的故事，称为佛教史迹画。但这些故事往往加入了很多宗教性的神异传说成分，有人也把它称为佛教感应故事。建于初唐到盛唐之际的第323窟较为集中地绘出佛教史迹故事，此窟南北两壁的主要壁面上共绘制了八个佛教史迹故事画。这些故事并列绘于横长的画面上，既不是横卷式连环画，也不是单幅画的并列，而是以统一的全景式构图，各个故事穿插其间，形成自然的平衡。画家以绵延不断的青绿山水作背景，利用山峦的自然形态，隔出一个个空间来展开故事情节。由于青绿山水技法的成熟，这里不像早期

There is another type of tale among the murals, which deals with themes of certain historical events in Buddhism. Paintings with such themes are known as narratives of Buddhist legends and transmission. In these tales, it is often the case that many miraculous and mythical elements are added; in Chinese these narratives are also known as Buddhist "tales of resonance", another way of indicating miracle tales. Cave 323 was constructed in the High Tang, when narratives of Buddhist legends and transmission were created in dense compositions, such that altogether eight paintings are found on the main parts of both the north and south walls. These tales are created side by side on a horizontal space. However, they are not arranged in a horizontal sequence of serial pictures, nor are they a juxtaposition of single pictures, but rather they form an integrated panoramic composition. Different tales are placed within the frame of the painting, yet a natural balance is achieved. The artist applied continuous blue-green landscapes as the background, and by making use of natural formations of mountain ranges, different spaces were separated to develop plots. Because the skills adopted in painting blue-green landscapes are quite mature, the mountain ranges do not merely function as frames or dividers of scenes, or as symbolic background or ornamentation, as they did in the earlier paintings, but are made into vast settings by

艺苑瑰宝
莫高窟壁画与彩塑

那种装饰性山峦,仅仅起到分隔画面和象征背景的作用,而是利用山水透视构成一个巨大的空间环境。在整体布局上,山水决定着画面的均衡与变化,并且与人物巧妙结合起来,极大地增强了故事画的表现力。

佛图澄神异故事

佛图澄是晋、十六国时期西域的名僧,少年出家学道,精通佛法,曾帮助石勒建立了后赵。石勒死后,后赵皇帝石虎对佛图澄更加喜爱,封佛图澄为国师,很受世人的崇敬。据《高僧传》记载,佛图澄擅诵神咒、役使鬼神、观面相知人意、治疑难病、懂起死回生术等。所以,历代佛教徒撰写了很多佛图澄的神异故事。壁画(图81)的上部画佛图澄立于7层塔前,双手合十向人们解说塔檐的风铃声音有异,指出这是不祥的凶兆,他预言石虎和石韬将要火并。中部画佛图澄为石虎说法时,突然感到有异,告诉

way of landscape perspective. The mountains and rivers determine the balance and changes within the overall composition. When mountains and rivers ingeniously combine with human figures, the expressive force of the narratives are greatly enhanced.

The Miraculous Tales of Buddhcinga

Buddhcinga (also written in Chinese as *Fotucheng*) was a renowned Buddhist monk of the Western Regions during the era of the Jin Dynasty and the Sixteen Kingdoms. At a young age, he left home, started his study of Buddhism, and acquired a good command of Buddhist doctrine. He helped Shi Le to found the State of Zhao. After Shi Le's death, Shi Hu, the new leader of the state, favored him even more. The new ruler Shi Hu granted him the title of State Advisor, and everyone respected him. According to accounts in *Biographies of Eminent Monks*, Buddhcinga was credited with miraculous powers such as chanting magical incantations, making ghosts and spirits toil like beasts, reading people's minds by observing their faces, treating difficult diseases, and making the dead come back to life. Thus, through the ages, Buddhists wrote numerous miraculous tales attributed to Buddhcinga. In the upper register of the mural (Fig.81), Buddhcinga stands in front of a seven-storeyed pagoda, folding his palms together devoutly and explaining to the people that the sound of the wind chime that hangs upon the eaves of the pagoda is strange. He points out that it is an inauspicious omen, foretelling that

图 81 佛图澄的故事 莫高窟第 323 窟北壁 初唐
Fig.81.Miraculous Tales of Buddhcinga, North Wall of Mogao Cave 323, Early Tang

石虎，幽州四城门起火，并使出神力端酒向空中洒去。在场的众人将信将疑，石虎派人到幽州查验，回报说当日幽州发生火灾，后天降大雨而火灭，雨中有酒味。壁画的下部还画出佛图澄能洗涤自己的肠子。据说佛图澄左乳旁有一小洞，通彻腹内。平日，佛图澄常用丝棉堵塞小洞。如果他想读书时，就把丝棉拔掉，

Shi Hu and Shi Tao would fight against each other. In the middle register, Buddhcinga expounds Buddhist doctrines to Shi Hu, when he feels something unusual. He tells him that the four gates of the town of Youzhou have caught fire, as he immediately works his mystical powers and sprays wine into the air. People present are half believing and half doubting. Shi Hu sends his men to Youzhou to confirm the tale. Report comes that on that day a fire broke out in Youzhou, that the fire was put out because of a heavy rain, and that there was the smell of wine in the rain. In the lower register, Buddhcinga is depicted washing his own intestines. It was said that in his left breast, there was a small hole leading through to his entire belly.

艺苑瑰宝
莫高窟壁画与彩塑

则放出光芒使满屋子通亮，佛图澄就借此光诵读经书。每逢斋戒日，佛图澄来到河边，将肠子从中掏出，用河水清洗完毕后，还复内中。画面中是佛图澄赤裸上身，盘腿坐在水池边，正在河边洗肠的情景。

石佛浮江故事

画在莫高窟第323窟南壁西端（图82）的故事，讲的是西晋建兴元年（313年）在吴淞江口，渔民们远远看见两石像漂浮于海面上，以为是海神，遂敬香远迎。谁知海上风浪大作，渔民见此情景，心中害怕而返。有信道教者，以为是他们的天师降临，遂设醮坛，大兴法事。结果风浪不减，越来越盛。后来信奉佛教的居士朱应听说此事后，和东林寺僧人及佛教徒数人到江边，设斋向石像稽首唱赞歌，江面上立刻风平浪静，两个石佛踏水而至，佛像背后各有铭文，一名"维卫"，一名"迦叶"。朱

Usually he would plug the hole with cotton. If he wanted to read, he would pull out the cotton and the entire room would be illuminated by the light coming through the hole. Buddhcinga would then read the Buddhist scriptures aloud. During fasting days (*uposatha*), he would go to the riverside, pull out his intestines from his belly, and wash them in water. He would put them back after they were washed clean. Depicted in this section is the scene of Buddhcinga, unclothed from the waist up, sitting by the pool with his legs folded as he washes his intestines in water.

The Tale of the Stone Buddhas Floating in the River

The tale is painted on the right edge of the south wall of Cave 323 (Fig.82). In the 1st year of the Jianxing Era in the Western Jin Dynasty (313), some fishermen at the mouth of the Wusong River saw two stone statues floating in the distant sea. The fishermen thought the statues were gods of the sea, and burned incense to welcome them from afar. Unexpectedly, stormy waves began to rage violently. At such a sight, the fishermen were overcome with fear and headed back home. Some Daoists believed that the statues were Daoist Celestial Masters coming down to earth, so they set up an altar and conducted their grandest sacrificial ceremonies. Instead of subsiding, however, the storm became increasingly rough. Later, the news reached Zhu Ying, a lay Buddhist, who went to the riverside with several other Buddhists from the Donglin

图 82　石佛浮江的故事　莫高窟第 323 窟南壁　初唐

Fig.82　Tale of the Stone Buddhas Floating in the River, South Wall of Mogao Cave 323, Early Tang

应等人立即以船接迎,小舟运载两石佛像入通玄寺。

这幅画共有三个情节,从右上角开始:1. 远处江面有二石佛,岸边可见僧俗七八人注目礼拜;旁有榜题:"此西晋时有二石佛浮游吴淞江,波涛弥盛,飘飘逆水而降,舟人接得,其佛裙上有名号,第一维卫佛,第二迦叶佛,其像见在吴

Temple. They offered vegetarian foods, bowed in homage, and sang hymns of praise. The sea calmed down immediately. The two statues stepped across the water and arrived at the river bank. There were inscriptions on the back of each of them: one was named Vipaśyin and the other Kaśyapa. Zhuying and others welcomed the two statues onto their ship and took them into the Xuantong Temple with a small boat.

Starting from the upper right corner, three scenes are painted. Scene one: in the distance are two stone Buddha statues on the water;

郡供养。"2.绘巫祝三人在岸边扬幡设醮,后边有二人正在讲话,下有题记:"石佛浮江,天下希瑞,请□□□谓□道来降,章醮迎之,数旬不获而归。"3.绘一小船载二佛,船上比丘二人,扶持佛像者二人,船工二人。岸上有比丘跪拜,僧俗多人从远处赶向岸边。题记:"灵应所之不在人事,有信佛法者以为佛降,风波遂静,迎向通玄寺供养,迄至于今。"

这个故事利用山水分出三个情节,由远及近,推向高潮。曲折的河流把远景、中景、近景联系起来,画家着重刻画了故事的高潮——迎佛的场面。以佛为中心,周围的人们不约而同地向佛走去。这样,就把四周疏疏

seven or eight monks and lay followers look at them, worshipping; nearby a public notice reads: "These are the two stone Buddha statues found floating in the Wusong River during the Western Jin Dynasty. They came against the current, across the rough waves. Boatmen accepted them. They each had their names inscribed upon their *dhotis*, one the Vipaśyin Buddha, and the other the Kasyapa Buddha. Now the two statues are placed in the prefecture of Wu for people to venerate." Scene two: three men in charge of divination and sacrifice are performing a sacrificial ceremony while two others are talking behind them; the notice below reads: "It was rare but auspicious that stone Buddha statues were floating in the river. □□□ called Daoists □ were invited to summon them. The statues were welcomed with Daoist rituals and sacrificial ceremonies, but after several weeks [people] still could not bring the statues in, and the Daoists went back home." And scene three: a small boat is painted carrying the two stone Buddha statues; on board the boat are two *bhikṣus*, two men supporting the statues with their hands, and two boatmen; on the bank, the *bhikṣus* are kneeling and bowing, while more monks and lay followers are coming to the river bank from far away; the notice reads: "Whether or not the mystic message is true and effective is not determined by how people deal with it. The storm waves did not calm down until some Buddhists believed that it was the Buddha who had come to the world. The two stone Buddha statues were welcomed into the Xuantong Temple, and people have been making offerings to them to this day."

Space separated by mountains and rivers, three scenes are painted from far away to up close, pushing the tale step by step to its climax. The winding river joins the distant, the medium and the close views to one another. The artist made special efforts to paint the climax of the tale—the

落落的人群统一起来,构图形散而神不散。在统一中又有变化,不同的人物表现出不同的个性,如步履蹒跚、拄杖而行的老人和天真稚气的小孩等形象都描绘得细腻生动。

扬都出金像故事

画在第223窟南壁西起第二幅画,讲的是东晋咸和年间(326年),丹阳的地方官高悝在张侯桥发现水中有一尊金佛像放射着光芒。佛像没有背光和佛座。随后,高悝令人用牛车载像而归。当牛车走到长干巷口时,拉车的牛拒绝前行。众人决定让牛自行前走,众人紧随其后至长干寺。高悝等人将金像安置于此寺。扬都的百姓听说此事后,都感到很惊奇,争先恐后到长干寺供养礼拜金佛像。一年后,一渔民在海上发现了金像的莲花座,将此送到了扬都县衙中。扬都县衙又将佛座送到了长干寺安置在金像的足下,全然符合。又过了

scene of welcoming the Buddha statues. Taking the images of the Buddha as the center, people are walking towards them spontaneously from all around. In this way, scattered people are united so that the composition of the painting takes a loose shape but a compact spirit. Changes take place in unification. Different people show their diverse personalities. For example, there are the old people, who are moving unsteadily with the help of walking sticks, and the young children, who look innocent and naïve. All the figures are described exquisitely and vividly.

The Tale of the Golden Buddha of Yangdu

The second picture off the right edge of the south wall of Cave 323 relates the "Tale of the Golden Buddha of Yangdu". During the Xianhe Era of the Eastern Jin Dynasty (326), Gao Kui, the local county official of Danyang, saw a golden Buddha statue in the water below the Zhanghou Bridge. The statue was giving off light and shining brightly, but had no aureole or lotus throne attached to it. Gao Kui planned to have the statue hauled off with an oxcart to the government office. However, when the cart was passing by the entrance to Changgan Alley, the ox refused to move forward. People decided to let the ox go wherever he wanted, and, following the ox, they found themselves arriving at Changgan Temple. Gao Kui and his men placed the golden Buddha statue there. The people of Yangdu County were astounded by the news, going as quickly as

艺苑瑰宝
莫高窟壁画与彩塑

几年,到了东晋咸安元年(371年)间,一采集珍珠的人又在海底发现了金像的背光,均与长干寺金像吻合。历经多年,金像、佛座、背光三者才完全归于一体,并通过金像莲花台上的梵文文字,得知此金像是阿育王第四女所造。

此画与石佛浮江故事一样,在山水背景中表现人物的活动,特别是表现众人乘船从远处水中载佛像,由远而近,周围还有不同的人物前来观看。远近空间的处理以及不同人物的面貌与性格特征表现得十分生动自然。遗憾的是这一珍贵的壁画于1924年被美国人华尔纳用一种黏胶揭取而盗走,现藏于美国赛克勒博物馆。

possible to Changgan Temple to enshrine the statue, making devotional offerings to the golden Buddha. A year later, a fisherman found the lotus throne for the statue; he sent it to the county office of Yangdu. The government official had it sent to Changgan Temple and placed it under the golden statue. They matched perfectly. Many years later, in the 1st year of the Xian'an Era in the Eastern Jin Dynasty (371), a man collecting pearls found an aureole in the seabed, which also matched the statue in Changgan Temple. In the process of so many years, the three elements, namely, the golden statue, the seat, and the aureole, were finally joined together. After reading the Sanskrit inscription engraved on the lotus throne, it was discovered that the golden Buddha statue was made by the fourth daughter of King Aśoka.

Similar to the "Tale of the Stone Buddhas Floating in the River", everyday life in this painting is also portrayed within the setting of mountains and rivers, especially the scene of people carrying the Buddha statue across the water from far away, and that of many other people coming from all around to see the spectacle. Near and far spaces, as well as the features and mannerisms of various people are rendered vividly and naturally. Unfortunately, this invaluable painting was torn off with a kind of resinous glue and illegally removed by an American Langdon Warner in 1924, and is now kept in the Sackler Museum at Harvard University in the United States.

附属于经变画中的故事
Tales Affiliated with Sutra Illustrations

未生怨故事

The Tale of the Enemy While Still Unborn

王舍城的国王频婆娑罗（又称瓶沙王）有一太子名阿阇世，自小就受到国王和王后的百般宠爱。可是，太子长大成人后，一天忽然心生恶念，举兵政变，篡夺王位，将父亲幽闭在七重深牢，断绝食物，欲将父王活活饿死在狱中。王后韦提希夫人十分想念国王，而阿阇世不许她给国王送食物。王后就把蜜面涂在身上，以葡萄汁灌于璎珞之内，然后从身上取下蜜面给国王充饥。经过二十余日，国王并未饿死。阿阇世太子感到奇怪，就拷问狱卒，得知是王后所为，当即大怒，就用铁钉钉死父王，并持剑欲杀母后，因两位大臣苦苦相谏才作罢，遂将王后囚禁深宫。韦提希

According to this tale, Prince Ajātaśatru, the only son of Bimbisāra, King of Rājagṛiha, was doted upon in every imaginable way from childhood by the King and the Queen. However, after the Prince grew up, evil ideas suddenly occurred to him, seemingly overnight. He raised an army, staged a coup d'état, and seized the throne. He imprisoned his father in a jail which had a series of seven doors, and cut off his food, intending to starve the old King to death. Queen Vaidehī worried about the King very much, but Ajātaśatru did not permit her to send food to the King. As a result, she smuggled food to him, smearing her body with a paste of honey mixed with flour and hiding grape juice inside her jewelry. When she met with the King, she peeled off the paste for the King to eat. Over 20 days passed, yet the king was still alive. Prince Ajātaśatru felt it was rather strange. He tortured the prison guards to find out what had happened and learned that it was the Queen who was helping the King. He became so furious that he killed his own father by driving iron nails through his body. Then he drew his sword, intending to murder the Queen as well. Only after two of his vassals earnestly persuaded him from doing that did he put down his sword, but still he imprisoned the Queen deep

169

艺苑瑰宝
莫高窟壁画与彩塑

夫人被幽禁在深宫，每日向佛遥礼，她深为不解的是为何如此疼爱的儿子会产生杀心，将亲生父亲杀害？佛与目连、阿难二弟子来到王宫为她讲述了过去、现在的因缘：原来当初瓶沙王与王后年老无子，就盼望生一个儿子。于是请相师占相。相师告知当有一子，但此人在山中修行，要等他功德圆满后才来投生。国王心急，派人到山中断了修行者的水源，使之饥渴而死。但王后还是没有生子。国王又问相师，相师对国王说："你求子太急，已悖常理。如今他变为兔，在山中生活，只等兔子寿终，就来投胎。"国王仍不死心，派人到山中打猎，凡获兔子，都以铁钉钉死。于是，王后有孕，生下了太子阿阇世。

王后听了如此因缘，无限悔恨，专事念佛，别无它念。佛便教她十六种摆脱尘世烦恼而达到佛

inside the palace. While Queen Vaidehī was imprisoned she prayed to the Buddha daily. She simply could not understand why her son, whom they loved so dearly, could behave so cruelly! Why did he kill his own father? Eventually, the Buddha and two disciples, Mahāmaudgalyāyana and Ananda, appeared before her in the palace and explained to her the karma of the past and how it affected the present. In the past, both King Bimbisāra and his Queen were growing older, but the couple didn't have an heir. What they eagerly wished for was to have a son. They asked a soothsayer to predict the future by divination. The soothsayer told them that they would have a son, but the man was spiritually cultivating himself in the mountains. He could not be reborn until he reached the spiritual state of perfect virtue. The King was impatient and decided to speed the process along. He sent his men to the mountains and had the man's water source cut off. The man died of hunger and thirst, but no son was born to the King. Again the King asked the soothsayer, who replied, "You couldn't wait to have a son, but what you've done has gone against all decency. Now the man has been reborn as a rabbit, living in the mountains; the rabbit will be reincarnated into a new body after he dies." Still the King couldn't give up his obsession, and he sent his men to hunt in the mountains, ordering that all rabbits captured be killed by iron nails. As a result, the Queen became pregnant and Prince Ajātaśatru was born.

The Queen heard the *nidana* story and felt bitter remorse. There was nothing else for her to do

教极乐境界的方法，即"十六观"。

观无量寿经变画通常构图为：中间主要画面绘出极乐世界图，两侧以条幅的形式对称画出"未生怨（序品）"和"十六观"的内容。以竖条幅形式绘出的未生怨，第320、172等窟是较为典型的代表。如第320窟北壁，从下到上大致描绘6个情节（图83）：1.森严的宫门有一门卫，身后架上插着5支长矛；2.王子骑在马上，从人执缚国王；3. 王后探望国王；4.守卒禀告阿阇世；5.王子执王后举剑欲杀，旁二大臣进谏；6.王后礼佛，佛从空而降，为之说法。画家利用房屋建筑构成一个个独立的空间，把每个情节描绘在各自的空间环境。与早期横卷式故事画相比，这里每一个情节画面的独立性加强了，几乎可以分出明晰的界限来。对画面情节的选择与刻画，体现出更成熟的

but pray to the Buddha. The Buddha taught the Queen the 16 ways of casting off the worries and hindrances of this world and attaining supreme bliss, namely, the Sixteen Visualizations.

The usual arrangement of *Amitayurdhyana Sutra* illustration paintings is as follows: Sukhāvatī, the Western Pure Land of Buddhism, is painted in the center of the composition; the "Tale of the Enemy While Still Unborn" from the introductory chapter of the *Amitayurdhyana Sutra* and the Sixteen Visualizations are painted symmetrically on both sides in vertical panels. The "Tale of the Enemy While Still Unborn" in Caves 320 and 172 are typical of this. The one on the north wall of Cave 320, for example, presents six scenes from bottom to top (Fig.83): 1. At the palace gate stands a guard, and on the rack behind him are five long spears; 2. Prince Ajātaśatru rides on horseback, and his men tie up the king; 3. The Queen visits the King; 4. The guard reports to Ajātaśatru; 5. Prince Ajātaśatru captures the Queen, and raises his sword, intending to kill her, and two vassals dissuade him; 6. The Queen prays to the Buddha, and the Buddha comes from Heaven to teach her the Dharma. The artist has created separate spaces by making use of the structures of houses. Each scene is painted with its own space and setting. Compared with earlier Buddhist narratives in horizontal panels, the independent quality of each scene here has been intensified; the boundaries separating them can be clearly made out. The selection and depiction of scenes also show that the design of the pictures has become more mature. One example is the second picture. Prince Ajātaśatru rides a horse on the right

设想。如第二画面，右侧为阿阇世骑在马上，左侧是随从抓住国王，国王正竭力挣扎。这个矛盾冲突的瞬间，表现在画面上很富于戏剧性。又如王子执王后欲杀的场面，在第172窟南壁，选取了王子举剑欲斫，王后惊恐奔逃这个时刻；右侧一班大臣拱手而立，正战战兢兢地苦谏。左右两侧一动一静，各人的精神活动通过外在的动作表露无遗。这些富有表现力的画面，大大增强了故事画的感染力。

流水长者子故事

这个故事来自《金光明经》，讲的是古印度一个名叫持水的长者，有一个儿子叫流水。流水精通医术，治病救人，深得人民爱戴。一日，流水领着两个儿子水空与水藏到郊外散步，忽见很多鸟兽都朝一个方向跑去。他觉得奇怪，就跟踪而去，发现有个大水池，由于烈日

side, while on the left side, his men seize the King, who struggles desperately. Such a moment of rivalry and conflict is rendered full of drama. Another example is the scene in which Prince Ajātaśatru captures the Queen, intending to kill her. The moment is chosen when the Prince raises his sword and is about to hack her to death, and the Queen is terrified, trying to run away. The scene is painted on the left side of the south wall of Cave 172. On the right side of the same wall, vassals are standing aside submissively, trembling with fear and beseeching the Prince. The two sides, one dynamic and the other static, are painted differently. The inner intentions of the mind are thoroughly betrayed by the outer movements of the body. These expressive scenes greatly increase the effect of narratives of Buddhist legends.

The Tale of Jalavāhana the Virtuous Householder

This tale comes from the *Golden Light Sutra* (*Suvarṇaprabhāsottama Sutra*). In ancient India there lived a householder named Jaṭiṃdhara ("Water Bearer") who had a son, Jalavāhana ("Flowing Water"). Jalavāhana had an excellent command of medical skills. He could cure illnesses and save lives, enjoying immense love and respect from the people. One day Jalavāhana went for a walk to the outskirts of town with his two sons, when suddenly he noticed a great many birds and beasts moving quickly in the same direction. He had a strange feeling and followed them, arriving at a huge pond. Because of the blazing sun, the pond

Art Treasures: Murals and Painted Sculptures in Mogao Caves

图 83　未生怨的故事　莫高窟第 320 窟北壁　盛唐
Fig.83　Tale of the Enemy While Still Unborn,
North Wall of Mogao Cave 320, High Tang

图 84　流水长者子故事　莫高窟第 55 窟东壁南侧　宋
Fig.84　Tale of Jalavāhana the Virtuous Householder,
Right Side of East Wall, Mogao Cave 55, Song Dynasty

173

暴晒，池水即将干涸，池中一万条鱼面临着生命危险。这些鱼都注视着流水，求他救命。流水见此情景，急忙领着儿子四处寻找水源。他返回城中，向国王借了20头大象，又向人借了一些皮囊，疾驰河边，以皮囊盛水，大象驮运，很快来到水池边，将水注入池中，一万条鱼全部得救。流水颇为高兴，沿池边行走，发现池中之鱼仍然跟随着他，沿岸而游。他明白这些鱼为饥饿所迫，正向他求食。于是，他派遣两个儿子赶着一头大象回家向祖父取得鱼食，二子带回来了很多食物，流水即将食物撒于池中，鱼得饱食，嬉游水中。

一天，流水宴请宾客，酒后醉卧高楼。这时，池中的一万条鱼同日命终，升上忉利天，转世为一万天子。为了报答流水的救命之恩，一齐下到人间，来到了流水醉卧的高楼。流水正在熟睡，一万天子将无数的珍珠、璎珞放在流水周围，向天空翱翔而去。此时，天空出现了许多瑞相，光明如昼。第二天，国王询问大臣们

seemed to be rapidly drying up, and the 10,000 fish in the pond were in danger. All these fish fixed their eyes upon Jalavāhana and begged him to save their lives. Faced with such a sight, Jalavāhana and his sons hurried to find water. He went back to town, where he borrowed 20 elephants from the King and a number of leather bags from the people. Quickly they ran to the river, filled the leather bags with water and put the bags on top of the elephants; quickly they dashed towards the pond, poured the water into it, and filled the pond back to its normal level. The 10,000 fish were saved, and Jalavāhana felt very happy. As he walked along the edge of the pond, he noticed that the fish in the pond were still following him, swimming along the bank. He realized that the fish were now threatened by hunger and were begging for food, so he sent his two sons to ride an elephant home and fetch food for the fish from their grandfather. The two sons brought back plenty of food and Jalavāhana scattered it into the pond. The fish ate enough and swam happily in the water.

One day, Jalavāhana was entertaining some guests at home. He got drunk and lay sleeping that night in the multi-storeyed building. At that precise moment, the lives of the 10,000 fish in the pond ended. They rose to Trāyastriṃśa Heaven and were reincarnated as 10,000 princes known as "heavenly sons". In order to repay Jalavāhana for saving their lives, they came down to earth together, and to the building where Jalavāhana lay drunk.

为何昨夜光明如昼。有人告知可能是一万天子到流水家谢恩。于是,国王派人到池中检验,果然一万条鱼全部命终,池中充满了各种鲜花。

这个故事画在宋代第55窟东壁门南侧的金光明经变画右侧(图84)。在以净土图为中心的经变画两旁画出条幅的故事,这是盛唐以来观无量寿经变画形成的模式,后来在很多种经变画中都采用了这样的构成形式。这幅金光明经变画一侧画的是萨埵本生故事,一侧画流水长者子故事。画面自下而上,条理清楚地描绘了故事情节。

唐代后期,经变画中开始出现以屏风画配合经变画主题表现具体故事,上部绘极乐世界图,下部由几幅屏风表现其中的故事和相关内容。如第159窟南壁共绘制三铺经变画,下有9幅屏风画,《弥勒经变》下部为该经变的"嫁娶"等内容。《观无量寿经变》下部屏风

Since Jalavāhana was sound asleep, the 10,000 princes placed countless treasures and jeweled necklaces around him and then flew back to Heaven. Simultaneously, many auspicious sights appeared in the sky, shining bright as daytime. The next day the King asked his ministers why the night before was as bright as day. The King was told that probably it was the 10,000 princes that came to Jalavāhana's place to thank him for his favor. The King sent his men to check the pond. Sure enough, the lives of the 10,000 fish in the pond had ended, and the pond was filled with myriad kinds of blossoms.

The tale is painted on the right side of the *Golden Light Sutra* illustration, which is on the east wall, on the right side of the entrance in Cave 55, built during the Song Dynasty (Fig.84). The High Tang had introduced a new painting layout, with the Pure Land as the central element and Buddhist sutra narratives on both sides in vertical panels. This new style was first shaped while painting *Amitayurdhyana Sutra* illustrations, and adopted in many other sutra illustrations after that. On one side of this *Golden Light Sutra* illustration is the "Mahāsattva *Jataka*", while on the other side is the "Tale of Jalavāhana the Virtuous Householder". The pictures are arranged from bottom to top. The scenes of the tales are well organized and clearly depicted.

In the Late Tang, screen paintings began to appear depicting specific tales, aligning with the themes of sutra illustrations. Frequently, the upper register of the murals contains the Western Paradise, Sukhāvatī, while in the lower register

绘制"十六观""未生怨"等内容。"法华经变"下部绘制"随喜功德品""观音普门品"等内容。但也有很多屏风画与经变画无关,是独立的故事画。如晚唐第9窟中心柱东向龛内西壁屏风画分别绘"萨埵本生"和"闻偈施身"故事,北壁三幅屏风画为"须达拿本生"故事。其中"须达拿本生"较有代表性,第一幅屏风画自上而下绘出:1. 须达拿被驱出城;2.须达拿携妻子出走;3.遇人乞马,须达拿将马施人;4. 须达拿推车而行;5.遇人乞车,须达拿把车施人;6.须达拿一家步行前进。第二幅屏风画自下而上绘出:7.须达拿一家迤逦前行;8.山中结庐而居;9.婆罗门求施二小儿。第三幅屏风画自上而下绘出:10. 须达拿夫人痛哭;11. 婆罗门驱二小儿行走;12. 二小儿随婆罗门前行,路见

there are screen paintings depicting related tales and other related content. For example, there are three sutra illustrations on the south wall of Cave 159, the lower register of which are nine screen paintings. Under the *Maitreya Triple Sutra Illustration* are pictures on themes such as marriage, cited from the sutra. The screen paintings under the *Amitayurdhyana Sutra Illustration* illustrate the Sixteen Visualizations and the "Enemy While Still Unborn". Below the *Lotus Sutra* illustration are the "Chapter on the Merits of Joyful Acceptance" and "Chapter on the Universal Gate of Bodhisattva Avalokitesvara", from the *Lotus Sutra*. There are also many screen paintings that have little to do with sutra illustrations, which are simply separate, unrelated narratives of Buddhist legends and stories. Examples can be found in Cave 9 of the Late Tang. In the west side of the central niche, a screen painting illustrates the "Mahāsattva *Jataka*" as well as the *jataka* tale of a Brahmin who sacrificed himself to learn half a verse of the Dharma. The three screen paintings on the north wall of the cave depict the "Vessantara *Jataka*", also called the "Sudāna *Jataka*", which is a painting quite typical of the era. The scenes from top to bottom are as follows: 1. Sudāna is exiled from the town; 2. He leaves the town with his wife; 3. He meets a man who begs for his horse and he gives away his horse; 4. He continues ahead, pushing his cart; 5. He meets a man who begs for his cart and he gives him his cart; 6. He and his family continue the journey. From bottom to top in the second painting are the following scenes: 7. Sudāna and his family journey onward; 8. They make a thatched cottage to live in;

行人;13.婆罗门入城。从这个故事可以看出,屏风画仍然具有连环画性质,只不过没有明确的顺序,观众根据画中的榜题文字来辨别故事情节及发展顺序。几幅屏风相连接时,情节先自上而下,再自下而上,自然相衔接,便于观览。每一幅屏风画中又形成一个完整的画面,以山水为主体,穿插人物故事。

屏风故事画在唐代后期盛行以后,直到五代、北宋时期,仍然是故事画的主要表现形式,并产生了如第61窟的佛传故事、第98窟的贤愚经故事等规模较大的作品。

9. A Brahmin asks him for his two children; 10. Sudāna's wife cries bitterly; 11. The Brahmin takes the two children with him; 12. The two children follow the Brahmin onward and they meet passers-by; 13. The Brahmin enters the town. From the narratives above, it can be seen that screen paintings also share the characteristics of serial panels. The only exception is that the order of the pictures is not clearly marked. The plots of the tale and the order of its development have to be figured out according to text written within cartouches on the paintings. When several screen paintings are placed together, the plots are arranged first from top to bottom, and then from bottom to top, thus connecting with each other naturally, and making them easily readable. Each screen painting is presented as a complete picture, with mountains and rivers prominent in composition and characters and tales inserted in them.

Narratives of Buddhist tales and legends on screens were popular since the Late Tang. After that, they remained the major form of painting until the Five Dynasties and the Northern Song period. As a result, larger works were created, such as the paintings on narratives of the Buddha's life in Cave 61 and illustrations of the *Sutra of the Wise and the Foolish* in Cave 98.

艺苑瑰宝
莫高窟壁画与彩塑

故事画的艺术成就
Artistic Achievements in Buddhist Narrative Paintings

莫高窟故事画的发展,从北朝到隋代大体经历了单幅画到连环画的演变。从佛教故事的内容来看,早期的本生故事情节单纯,单幅画足可表达全故事的内容。但随着佛教的深入发展,故事内容越来越丰富,画家在单幅画里尝试做多情节处理,虽取得了很好的效果,但比起连环画来,它的短处是很明显的。因此,长卷式连环画应运而生,并逐渐发展完善。早期的单幅故事画较多地吸取了西域画法的长处,具有纯朴、豪放又富于装饰性的特点,但又有别于西域那种注重人体比例,精细而具有图案化效果的特征。西魏以后,画家们接受了来自中原横卷式构图和以山

During the period from the Northern Dynasties to the Sui Dynasty, Buddhist narrative paintings underwent an evolution from individual, single pictures to the pattern of long, continuous narratives. From the aspect of content, earlier *jataka* tales were simple enough to be contained entirely in a single painting. However, as the substance of the tales became richer with the further development of Buddhism, the artists attempted to depict stories with complicated plots within a single frame. The weaknesses were self-evident, however, compared with multi-framed continuous narrative paintings. As a result, long panels of serial pictures emerged out of necessity, and were improved and perfected as time went on. Early period narrative paintings of Buddhist stories took their strengths from the single-framed paintings of the Western Regions, and were characterized by simplicity, boldness, and ornamentation. But they were also different from those of the Western Regions, which stressed proportions of the human body and exquisite decorative effects. After the Western Wei, artists learned composition from the Central Plains, where paintings were created in long horizontal panels, and where landscapes and buildings were painted as background. At the same time, some of the advantages of single-picture paintings were also maintained. Therefore serial, continuous narrative pictures were created, with larger capacity, more

水、房屋衬托等优点,同时也吸取单幅画的一些长处,创造出了具有容量较大、情节设计灵活、首尾完整统一、线描造型手法规范等特点的连环故事画。北周到隋代,长卷式连环画成为表现佛教故事最流行的形式。唐代以后,长卷式故事画出现较少,隋及初唐时期多出现在佛龛两侧表现两个典型的佛传故事("乘象入胎"和"夜半逾城"),对称地表现,富有装饰性,在色彩处理上也独具匠心,通过对比色突出形象。盛唐以后,在一些经变画中,形成了较为成熟的连环画艺术。如很多洞窟中常见的观无量寿经变画中的未生怨故事,金光明经变画中的流水长者子故事等,代表了中国古代连环画艺术的重要成果。中晚唐以后屏风画流行,故事画又融入了壁画整体布局之中。

　　故事画对于佛教宣传来说具有十分重要的意义。在佛教传入中国的早期,由于佛陀释迦牟尼以及佛教

flexible scenarios, coherent beginnings and endings, and codified techniques in line drawing and design. During the Northern Zhou and the Sui Dynasty, long-panel serial pictures became the most popular format to present narratives of tales and legends. It was not until after the Tang Dynasty that the number of long-panel continuous narrative pictures decreased. During the Sui Dynasty and the Early Tang, they were mostly painted on both sides of a Buddha niche, presenting symmetrically the two quintessential narratives of the Buddha's life—"Queen Māyā's Dream" and "The Great Renunciation". Such paintings were decorative and inventive in dealing with colors, offsetting the images by contrasts in pigments. After the High Tang, the art of serial pictures was shaped more maturely in some of the sutra illustrations. For example, in many caves, such narratives as the "Tale of the Enemy While Still Unborn" in the *Amitayurdhyana Sutra* illustration and the "Tale of Jalavāhana the Virtuous Householder" in the *Lotus Sutra* illustration are frequently seen. These represent significant accomplishments in the art of continuous narrative paintings in ancient China. After the Middle to Late Tang period, screen paintings became popular, and narratives of Buddhist stories were integrated into the overall arrangement of murals.

　　Buddhist narratives were of great importance in disseminating the religion. In the early stages when Buddhism spread into China, the Sakyamuni Buddha, as well as considerable amounts of Buddhist doctrine, were not familiar

的很多教义还不为广大民众所熟知，佛教寺院和石窟壁画中十分重视表现与释迦牟尼佛有关的故事，往往画得十分详细。唐代以后，由于佛教的普及，那些佛教的基本教义和相关故事在广大信众中已经耳熟能详，壁画中就很少出现像北朝那种详尽地描绘佛传和本生故事的情况，而较多地出现以净土世界为主题的画面——经变画。但故事画并没有完全消失，只不过是处于从属的位置，画在经变画的侧边或下方。

to the common people. Thus Buddhist temples and murals in cave shrines often portrayed in full detail the legends and tales relating to Sakyamuni. After the Tang Dynasty, as Buddhism grew in popularity, the basic tenets and canon of tales became common knowledge among lay followers. Seldom were there such detailed mural renderings of the Buddha's life and *jataka* tales as there had been in the Northern Dynasties. Instead, more paintings appeared on themes of the worlds in the Western Pure Land—the sutra illustrations. This did not mean, however, that narrative paintings of tales and legends disappeared completely, but simply that they were now subordinate, painted beside or below the sutra illustrations.

艺苑瑰宝：莫高窟壁画与彩塑
Art Treasures: Murals and Painted Sculptures in Mogao Caves

佛国之境（经变画）

Realms of the Buddhist World: Sutra Illustrations

经变画就是概括地表现一部佛经的主要内容、情节较多、规模较大的画。它不像佛经故事画那样单纯地表现一个有头有尾的故事,而是综合地表现佛经所记的场面。佛经主要是讲佛教哲学思想和修行方法等理论的,有的佛经是利用很多故事来说明一些宗教的理论,这样的佛经表现在画面中就会描绘这些生动的故事。但有的佛经没有什么故事,画家通常就表现佛讲法的那个场面,往往是以佛为中心,周围还要表现众多的佛弟子、菩萨及天龙八部等众,以及世俗人物听法的场面。所以,经变画往往人物众多,场面宏大。在佛教传入中国的初期,讲述故事的佛经流传较多,佛教也需要通过浅显易懂的形式来宣传基本理论。到了隋唐以后,佛教在中国已经很流行了,佛教理论性的经典更受到重视。于是,经变画在佛教壁画中也就流行起来,很多经变画仅仅表现佛说法的场景,表现佛所在的净土世界。

根据经变画表现形式,大体又可分为两个类型:一是叙事性经变画,一是净土图式经变画。叙事性经变画往往有一定的故事情节,或者以一定的情节为线索来表现佛经教义,具有故事画的某些特征,画面可以按一定的顺序来看。如出

A sutra illustration (*jingbian*) is a large-scale, multi-faceted wall painting that outlines the central theme of a Buddhist scriptural text. It does not merely present a narrative with a beginning and an end—as with narrative paintings based on sutra stories—but presents a scene that comprehensively records a spectacle from Buddhist literature, presenting tenets of Buddhist philosophy and methodologies in spiritual practice. Some parts of the canon explain religious doctrines by making use of parables and stories. These texts, if presented in paintings, will contain dynamic portrayals. However, some sutras have no storyline whatsoever; thus, the artist simply creates a scene in which the Buddha is preaching the Dharma. Often in such a scene, the Buddha occupies the central space of the composition. He is surrounded by disciples, bodhisattvas, celestial beings from the Aṣṭasenā, and even mortals from the terrestrial world, all listening to him. As a result, a sutra illustration is typically characterized by a greater number of characters and grander scenes. During the earlier stages of Buddhism's dissemination into China, Buddhist narrative literature circulated among the people, and Buddhism also needed easy and simple forms to popularize its basic tenets. After the Sui and Tang dynasties, when Buddhism was already widely accepted in China, more attention was paid to the classic texts emphasizing Buddhist principles. Therefore, sutra illustrations became a prevalent form of Buddhist mural. Many of these paintings depict only a single scene of Dharma preaching, revealing the realm of the Western Pure Land where the Buddha dwells.

Two basic categories of sutra illustration wall paintings can be defined: narrative sutra illustrations and Pure Land sutra illustrations. The former normally have plots the way stories do, or use certain storylines to explain Buddhist doctrine. Thus, they share some features of narrative paintings, with scenes arranged according to a certain sequence. For example, paintings that appeared earlier than others, such as the

现较早的涅槃经变画、维摩诘经变画就属于此类。净土图式经变画则是以佛所在的净土世界为中心，表现佛教净土世界的种种场面。虽说有的经变画也有故事情节，但故事画面不占主要地位。代表性的经变画有阿弥陀经变、观无量寿经变、弥勒经变、法华经变等。唐代以后的石窟中通常都在左右两侧壁及门两侧各绘通壁巨制的经变画。中唐以后，经变画的种类越来越多，往往在一壁之中并列绘 2～3 铺经变画。五代的一些大型洞窟还有在一面壁上绘 5 铺经变画的情况。总之，经变画是唐代以后敦煌壁画的主要题材，在石窟中占着举足轻重的作用。经变画也是中国式佛教艺术的代表，体现着中国人对佛教的理解和中国人的审美观。古代画史中记载了隋唐和唐以后中原地区很多寺院壁画的经变画，其中有不少是展子虔、吴道子等著名画家所绘。可是，由于时代变迁，隋唐以至宋元的寺院大多不存，历史上那些有名画家的作品也无法领略了。所幸还有敦煌石窟这样的文化遗迹，保存了古代的大量绘制精美的壁画，我们从中可以推测历史上那些著名画家的绘画风格和特点。所以敦煌壁画的经变画具有十分重要的历史价值和艺术资料价值。

Nirvana Sutra illustrations and *Vimalakirti Nirdesa* illustrations, belong to this category. The latter are paintings which center around images of Sukhāvatī, the Pure Land of the West where the Buddha lives. Some of them may contain plot lines, but they do not occupy the main, central scene. *Amitabha Sutra* illustrations, *Amitayurdhyana Sutra* illustrations, Maitreya Triple Sutra illustrations, and *Lotus Sutra* illustrations, among others, belong to this category. After the Tang Dynasty, it was often the case in Mogao Grottoes that huge sutra illustrations covered entire walls of a cave temple, both the north and south walls, as well as those on both sides of the east entrance. After the middle of the Tang Dynasty, there were more varieties of sutra illustration paintings, and often two to three were presented side by side on the same wall. In some of the large caves from the Five Dynasties, there were even cases of five sutra illustrations on the same wall. Overall, sutra illustrations were the main subject of Dunhuang murals after the Tang Dynasty, and they were of great importance for the caves. They were also quintessential works of sinicized Buddhist art, embodying both the Chinese understanding of Buddhism and the aesthetic ethos of the Chinese people. Historical records on Chinese painting reveal that numerous temples in the Central Plains had sutra illustration murals during the Sui and Tang periods as well as after the Tang Dynasty. Many of those paintings were works by famous artists such as Zhan Ziqian and Wu Daozi. However, due to the ravages of time, most of the temples from that time, and even those of the Song and the Yuan dynasties, no longer exist. Works by these historically renowned painters are beyond our reach today. Fortunately, we still have cultural relics such as the Dunhuang Caves, where a great many exquisite ancient murals are preserved, allowing us to make some inferences from them about the style and features of famous artists. As such, sutra illustrations as seen in the Dunhuang murals are of great value, both as historical and artistic records.

涅槃经变

Nirvana Sutra Illustrations

涅槃经变画主要是根据《大般涅槃经》绘制的。在北周壁画中就已出现了作为佛传故事中一个场景的涅槃图，到隋唐时期则形成了规模宏大的涅槃经变画。

初唐第 332 窟的涅槃经变画是较典型的绘、塑结合的大型涅槃经变画，本窟建于武则天时代的圣历元年（698 年），是一个中心柱窟，在中心柱背后的洞窟西壁开一龛，内塑涅槃佛像，身长 5.6 米；龛内原有佛弟子塑像，现已不存。南壁在高 3.7 米、长达 6 米的壁面上配合涅槃像绘制了内容丰富的经变画。

画面从右下部开始，向左发展，然后由左向右，共描绘了 9 组情节：

1. 释迦牟尼临终说法。释迦牟尼结跏趺坐，手作转法轮印，为弟子们宣讲涅槃理论，周围众菩萨、弟子及天龙

Nirvana Sutra illustrations were mainly based on the *Mahāparinirvāṇa Sutra*. Although legendary scenes of the Buddha's nirvana had already appeared in murals from the Northern Zhou, it was not until the Sui and Tang periods that large-scale *Nirvana Sutra* illustrations developed.

The *Nirvana Sutra* illustrations in Cave 332 of the Early Tang, a combination of sculpting and painting, are immense works that are most typical of the kind. The grotto is a central pillar cave constructed in the 1st year of the Shengli Era in Wu Zetian's reign (698). In the west wall of the cave, behind the central pillar, there is a niche, in which a nirvana Buddha statue is sculpted 5.6 meters long. Originally, there were also images of disciples, but now they are no longer there. The south wall of the cave has a surface 3.7 meters tall and 6 meters long, on which sutra illustrations with profound details are painted, echoing the sculpted image of Buddha nirvana.

The illustration begins from bottom right part of the wall, first developing to the left, and then from left to right, revealing nine scenes:

1. Sakyamuni preaches the Dharma just before his death. He sits in a lotus pose, lecturing on the theory of nirvana for the disciples, hand giving the *mudra* of setting in

八部聆听佛的最后一次说法。在画面的上部还画了一座大山,山下有一比丘与一个婆罗门对话,表现佛弟子迦叶从耆阇崛山赶来,途中向婆罗门询问释迦牟尼的病情。

2. 画释迦牟尼躺在娑罗双树林中的七宝床上,众弟子焦急地围在释迦牟尼周围,询问佛是否涅槃。

3. 表现释迦牟尼于夜半时分入般涅槃,佛弟子们痛不欲生,哽咽流泪。拘尸那城的男女老少都来到佛所在的地方,悲痛流泪。佛弟子密迹金刚闷绝于地,须跋陀罗先佛入灭。

4. 拘尸那城的人们按转轮圣王的规格入殓释迦牟尼圣体,做成了用七宝镶嵌的金棺,众弟子菩萨等围绕金棺礼拜举哀。

motion the wheel of the Dharma. Around him are bodhisattvas, disciples and celestial beings from the Aṣṭasenā, all listening to him preaching the Dharma for the last time. There is a huge mountain in the upper part of the painting. At the foot of the mountain, a *bhikṣu* is talking to a Brahmin, representing the scene of Buddha's disciple Mahakasyapa hurrying along from Vulture Peak (Sanskrit: *Gṛdhrakūṭa*), asking the Brahmin about Sakyamuni's condition on his way back.

2. Sakyamuni lies on the seven-treasure bed under a sal tree at Bimbisāra. The disciples surround him, looking worried and asking the Buddha if he is beginning his final cessation.

3. Sakyamuni enters into *parinirvāṇa*. All the disciples are overwhelmed with sorrow, either choked with sobs or bursting into tears. All the people of the town of Kuśinagara, men and women, old and young, gather to where the Buddha is, weeping in grief. The Buddha's disciple, Guhyapāda Vajrapani, is so distraught he lies prostrate on the ground, while the newly-ordained Subhadra dies before the Buddha does.

4. The people of Kuśinagara enshroud his sacred body in the manner befitting a Cakravartin king, a monarch of the universe. They make a gold coffin, encrusted with the seven treasures[①]. The disciples and the bodhisattvas surround the gold coffin and commence with the funeral rites.

[①] The seven treasures refer to the seven jewels adorning Sukhāvatī, Amitabha's Pure Land in the West. Lists vary according to different texts, but a common assortment includes gold, silver, lapis lazuli, crystal, agate, ruby, and carnelian.

图 85　争舍利之战　莫高窟第 332 窟南壁　初唐

Fig.85　Eight Kings Battling for the Buddha's Śarīra (Bodily Relics), South Wall of Mogao Cave 332, Early Tang.

5. 佛母摩耶夫人听说释迦牟尼涅槃，匆匆自天而降，十分悲伤。释迦牟尼听到了母亲说话声，便自金棺中坐起，为母亲讲涅槃的意义。

6. 诸比丘抬着金棺出殡，前有 8 个菩萨持幡引路。众菩萨、弟子及天龙八部等送葬。

7. 佛棺焚化，众菩萨弟子及佛母在旁哀悼。在画面的右下方还画出 3 个比丘手舞足蹈，表现一些不守戒律的比丘幸灾乐祸，以为佛涅槃后再不会有人来管教他们了。

5. On hearing of Sakyamuni's nirvana, Queen Māyā, the Buddha's mother, returns to Earth in deep grief. Sakyamuni hears his mother's voice, sits up in the gold coffin and explains nirvana to her.

6. The *bhikṣus* carry the gold coffin to the cemetery, with eight bodhisattvas leading the way, holding long narrow banners. All bodhisattvas, disciples, and celestial beings from the Aṣṭasenā attend the burial.

7. The coffin of the Buddha is burned; bodhisattvas, disciples, and the Buddha's mother grieve over his death. In the lower right register of the mural, three *bhikṣus* are painted dancing with joy, indicating that there are some *bhikṣus* who do not observe the precepts and take pleasure in the Buddha's death, thinking they will no longer be subject to discipline after

8. 八国王为争舍利而战斗。佛经上说,佛于拘尸那国涅槃后,以摩竭国国王阿阇世为首的8个国王带兵前来,求分舍利,遭到拒绝,于是各自兴兵作战。画面右侧画出8人各骑战马,手执长矛奋勇冲杀,生动地表现出一幅古代战争图(图85)。

9. 经一位婆罗门调停,八王平息了战争,均分舍利,各自造塔供养。

按一定的顺序描绘故事的手法,继承了早期故事画的方法,但由于全画在一个完整的山水背景中展开,使经变画构图统一。人物、场景也不是画在固定的画幅中,而是根据具体场面安排大小,使全局统一,表现出宏大的空间关系。

盛唐第148窟是完全以涅槃经变画为主题的洞窟,洞窟主室形制为横长方形,这样的洞窟型制也称作涅槃窟。正面有一高1.4米的佛床,在佛床

his nirvana.

8. Kings from eight countries start a war for the Buddhist relics. It is written in Buddhist literature that after the Buddha's nirvana in Kuśinagara, kings of the other eight countries, led by King Ajātaśatru of Magadha, commanded their troops to Kuśinagara, demanding that the Buddha's relics be divided amongst them. But their request was denied, so armies were sent and fighting began. On the right side of the painting are seven men riding their horses, fighting bravely with long spears in hand—a life-like representation of ancient warfare (Fig.85).

9. A Brahmin intervenes in the dispute and the war of the eight kings comes to an end. The Buddha's relics are divided equally among them and they each build a stupa for worship and making offerings.

There is a codified narrative sequence to the painting, inherited from early-period Buddhist narrative painting methods. As a sutra illustration, however, the scenes are composed in an integrated scheme, since the whole picture is developed against a complete background of landscapes. The characters and the settings are no longer arranged in a fixed frame, but are dependent on the parameters of a specific scene to determine their size. The overall panorama is a unified whole, displaying spatial relationships within a grand setting.

Cave 148, constructed during the High Tang, is one that is solely devoted to the theme of nirvana. Its main hall is built according to a rectangular layout. A cave of this shape is also

图 86　分舍利　莫高窟第 148 窟西壁　盛唐
Fig.86　Dividing the Buddha's *Śarīra* (Bodily Relics), West Wall of Mogao Cave 148, High Tang

上面塑出长达 14.4 米的释迦牟尼涅槃像，塑像经后代重修，已失去盛唐风韵。佛像后面还有清代塑的 73 身佛弟子像。后壁和两侧壁画出了规模更为巨大的涅槃经变画。壁面高约 2.5 米，总长达 23 米。单从面积来说，这铺涅槃经变画可能是现存最大的涅槃经变画。主要描绘了 10 组画面，包括 66 个情节，出场人物达 500

known as a nirvana cave. On the main long wall of this cave is a Buddha platform 1.4 meters tall, on which a 14.4-meter nirvana statue of Sakyamuni rests. The statue was later reconstructed, so that the graceful bearings of the Tang Dynasty are lost. Behind the nirvana statue are sculpted 73 Buddhist disciples, created during the Qing Dynasty. The back wall and both the side walls are covered with large-scale *Nirvana Sutra* illustrations. The walls are two and a half meters high and their total length is 23 meters. These are possibly the largest *Nirvana Sutra* illustrations preserved today, in terms of area only. The murals are painted in ten groups, containing 66 scenes, with as many as 500 characters portrayed. Numerous story elements after Sakyamuni's nirvana are painted in sequential order

多。由南壁向西壁然后向北壁，按顺序画出释迦牟尼涅槃以后的诸多情节内容。主要的情节与第332窟一致，又增添了不少细节内容，以及更为细腻的刻画。如第二组画面表现"纯陀供养"，讲的是佛接受了纯陀等人的供养，食后因为背痛而入般涅槃。这一情节是第332窟没有的。在表现出殡图时，描绘出巍峨的中国式城郭建筑，表现得十分写实。八王争舍利的情节并没有表现八王战争，而是表现七王来求分舍利，被拒绝后悲愤而还的情景（图86）。画面中拘尸那城城门紧闭，戒备森严，七国王在城外想要舍利，城中停放着释迦牟尼金棺。帝释天从中取出佛牙舍利回天上供养等等。总之，第148窟的涅槃经变画内容丰富，表现细腻而生动，每个情节都描绘了众多的人物形象，并画出相关联的山水、城郭、道路等景观，更增强了写实感。特别是山水树木的描绘反映了唐代山水画的成果，成为中国美术史上重要的作品。

中唐的第158窟与第148

from the south wall to the west wall and then continuing on the north wall. In addition to the events that are illustrated in Cave 332, many more details and exquisite renderings are found here. For example, the second mural in the group displays what is known as "Cunda's offering". The Buddha accepted the food from Cunda, but after eating he felt pain in his back and soon died, achieving nirvana. This episode is not depicted in Cave 332. In the scene of carrying the coffin to the cemetery, lofty Chinese cities and buildings are displayed quite realistically. The scenario of eight kings contending for the Buddha's relics does not show the battle that breaks out among them, but instead shows seven kings returning in grief and indignation when their request to divide the Buddha's relics is refused (Fig.86). In the painting, the town gate of Kuśinagara is tightly closed and heavily guarded; the seven kings demand the Buddha's relics outside the town; the gold coffin of Sakyamuni is placed inside the town gate; and Indra takes the Buddha's teeth from the coffin and returns with them to Heaven to make offerings. In short, the *Nirvana Sutra* illustrations in Cave 148 are rich in content, meticulously detailed and dynamic in depiction, with many characters portrayed in each scene. Meanwhile, interrelated landscapes such as mountains, rivers, towns, and roads are added, enhancing the sense of realism. What is worth mentioning

艺苑瑰宝
莫高窟壁画与彩塑

窟一样，也是一个涅槃窟，佛床上塑出长达15.6米的涅槃佛像，洞窟南面塑出过去世迦叶佛、北壁塑出未来世弥勒佛，合起来组成过去、现在、未来"三世佛"。在佛像身后有众多的菩萨和弟子形象。这里的涅槃经变画没有详细描绘各种故事情节，而是重点在南壁画出众弟子举哀图，在北壁画出各国国王、王子们的举哀图。南壁画面中迦叶满眼泪痕，张口大哭，双手高举，身体前倾，身旁两弟子担心他倒地而将他拦住；阿难则一手遮耳，痛哭失声，其他几个弟子也都悲痛欲绝。北侧壁画中表现出各国国王和王子的悲伤表情，有的握剑剖腹，有的刺胸，有的割耳（图87）。这正反映了古代西域各民族表现悲痛时的不同。这些生动的场面给观者留下了深刻的印象。

here are the mountains, rivers, trees, and grass in the paintings. They represent achievements in blue-green landscape paintings of the Tang period, and have proved to be works of great significance in Chinese art history.

Similar to Cave 148, Cave 158 from the Middle Tang is also a nirvana cave. On the platform is a nirvana Buddha statue 15.6 meters in length. In the southern part of the cave is a statue of Kasyapa, the Buddha of the Past, while in the northern section is a sculpture of Maitreya, the Buddha of the Future. This combination forms the Trikāya Buddhas, the Buddhas of the Past, Present, and Future. Behind the Buddha statue, there are numerous bodhisattvas and disciples. Instead of depicting various plot elements in detail, the focus of the *Nirvana Sutra* illustrations in this cave is on both the north and south walls, where the sorrowful disciples and mourning kings and princes from different countries are painted. On the south wall, the disciple Mahakasyapa is portrayed weeping bitterly, eyes full of tears, and hands raised up high, leaning forward. Two disciples support him, for fear that he will collapse on the ground. Ananda loses control and cries out loud, covering his ear with one hand. The other disciples are all grief-stricken as well. On the north wall, kings and princes from every country appear inconsolable. Some stab swords into their bellies, some thrust weapons against their chests, and some cut their ears (Fig.87). These accurately embody the ways different people from the ancient Western Regions expressed their grief. Such graphic imagery leaves a strong impression upon the viewer.

图 87 涅槃经变中各国王子举哀图 莫高窟第 158 窟北壁 中唐
Fig.87 *Nirvana Sutra* Illustration Depicting Princes Grieving Over the Buddha,
North Wall of Mogao Cave 158, Middle Tang

《涅槃经》是大乘佛教十分流行的经典。佛教认为涅槃是一种崇高的境界。因此，从印度、中亚到中国的佛教艺术中，出现了很多表现《涅槃经》的雕刻和壁画。莫高窟共有14个洞窟画有涅槃经变画，很多都是绘、塑结合的，塑出涅槃像又在相应的位置画出经变。像第332窟、148窟中这样的大型涅槃经变画在世界佛教艺术中也是十分罕见的。

The *Nirvana Sutra* is a popular Mahayana Buddhist text. Buddhists view nirvana as the ultimate state. As a result, great numbers of sculptures and murals embodying the *Nirvana Sutra* have been created in Buddhist art, from India and Central Asia to China. Among the Mogao Caves, a total of 14 grottoes are dedicated to illustrations of *Nirvana Sutra*. Many of these sutra illustrations are composed by combining paintings with sculptures. That is to say, nirvana statues are sculpted in the caves, and *Nirvana Sutra* illustrations are painted at appropriate places. Large-scale *Nirvana Sutra* illustrations such as those in Caves 332 and 148 are rarely seen anywhere else in the world as far as Buddhist art is concerned.

维摩诘经变
Vimalakirti Nirdesa Illustrations

维摩诘经变画,是根据《维摩诘经》绘制的。佛经上说,维摩诘是个神通广大、能言善辩的居士,他不出家,却精通佛理。他经常在家称病,人们去探望他时,即向人们宣讲他的大乘佛理。经变画通常以佛派弟子去探望维摩诘这一事件为中心来展开。由于维摩诘善于辩论,佛的十大弟子都不敢前往,佛就让"智慧第一"的文殊菩萨率众到维摩诘的住所,于是产生了一系列戏剧性情节。先是佛弟子舍利弗暗自思忖:如此多的人众,哪儿有这么多的坐具?维摩诘心知舍利弗所想,即运用神通,须弥灯王便遣来了3.2万狮子宝座,进入方丈而不觉拥挤,这就是令人瞠目不解的"室包乾象"。维摩诘请众菩萨、弟子升座,道行较高的

Vimalakirti Nirdesa illustrations were painted based on the *Vimalakirti Nirdesa*, also called the *Vimalakirti Sutra*. According to Buddhist literature, Vimalakirti was a Buddhist layman who had far-reaching supernatural powers and a silver tongue. As a householder he did not renounce the world, but had a strong grasp of Buddhist doctrine. He often stayed at home malingering, claiming that he was ill, but when people went to visit him, he would explain to them the Dharma of the Mahayana sect. The *Vimalakirti Nirdesa* illustrations are often based on one particular episode in which the Buddha requested his disciples to visit Vimalakirti. Since Vimalakirti was quick-witted in debates, each of the ten leading disciples demurred, so the Buddha asked Manjusri, the Bodhisattva of Wisdom, to lead the others to Vimalakirti's place. This brought about a series of dramatic events. First, the Buddha's disciple Śāriputra thought to himself, "Where can this man find seats for so many people?" Vimalakirti knew what was going on in Śāriputra's mind; he made use of his supernatural powers and the Merudhvaja Buddha sent forth 32,000 lion thrones. The lion thrones were all placed in his 10-foot square dwelling, but the room did not seem crowded. This was known as "containing the universe in a 10-foot room", which astounded people. Vimalakirti then invited the bodhisattvas and the disciples to be seated. The

菩萨都能入座，舍利弗惭愧地说："此座太高，我不能升。"维摩诘道："你只要给须弥灯王行个礼，即可升座。"众弟子不得已，只好给须弥灯王合十行礼，才升上座。时至日中，佛弟子暗想："大家都饿了，到哪儿去吃饭？"维摩诘即知佛弟子的意念，便分身化为菩萨，飞往香积国，托来一钵香饭。又有佛弟子心中嘀咕："这小小一钵饭能够谁吃？"菩萨转过头，倾饭于地，顿时，香饭如山，饭香四溢，众人饱食，皆大欢喜。舍利弗问维摩诘："你从何处死后来到这里？"维摩诘反问道："你学的佛法有生死吗？"这时，佛告诉弟子："维摩诘来自妙喜国无动如来世界。"原来维摩诘舍弃清净国土，来到不净的世界，是为众生消除烦恼。于是大家都想见一见妙喜世界的样子。维摩诘一伸手，掌中现出妙喜国：其中有铁围山、须弥山等，山上有天宫，里

bodhisattvas, who had achieved a higher level of spiritual cultivation, could reach their thrones, but Śāriputra said timidly, "The throne is too high for me to sit on." Vimalakirti replied: "You can reach your throne as soon as you pay your respects to the Merudhvaja Buddha." The disciples devoutly placed their palms together in *añjali* as a greeting, after which they could reach their thrones. It was mid-day and the disciples thought to themselves, "Everyone is hungry, but where can we get our mid-day meal?" Vimalakirti could read their minds. He changed himself into a bodhisattva and flew to the Land of Fragrance, from where he fetched an alms bowl of delicious food. Some of the disciples again silently wondered, "Is it possible for this small amount of food to be enough for so many people?" The bodhisattva turned round and poured the food onto the ground. Immediately, the delicious food piled up like a mountain, filling the air with an appetizing aroma. Everyone ate their fill and was content. Śāriputra asked Vimalakirti, "Where did you live and die before you came here?" Vimalakirti responded by asking, "Are there birth and death in the Dharma you learned?" At that moment the Buddha told his disciples that Vimalakirti came from the Eastern Pure Land of Abhirati, the realm of the Akṣobhya Buddha. In fact, Vimalakirti gave up this Eastern Pure Land and came to the tainted mortal world in order to remove the worries of all sentient beings. Then everybody wanted to see what the Abhirati Pure Land was like. Vimalakirti extended his hand and

面有不动如来和菩萨，下面有溪谷、河流、大海、日月星辰、城邑村落和人们生活的情景等等。佛弟子惊叹不已。

由于维摩诘以智慧善辩著称，又可以不剃度出家而自由地在家修行，因此深受中国士大夫们的喜爱。魏晋以来，《维摩诘经》在中国十分流行，石窟中也大量出现雕刻或壁画形式的维摩诘经变画。中国现存最早的石窟炳灵寺石窟第169窟壁画中就画出了维摩诘与文殊菩萨的画面。北魏时期的云冈石窟、麦积山石窟等都有维摩诘经变的雕刻或壁画。莫高窟共有68个洞窟表现了维摩诘经变，最早出现于隋代洞窟，唐代以后已经十分流行。隋代洞窟通常是在佛龛两侧分别绘出维摩诘和文殊菩萨，如第276窟佛龛北侧画出手持麈尾，做辩论状的维

it appeared in his palm. There were the Cakravāḍa Mountains, Mount Sumeru, and other sights. Over the mountains there were heavenly palaces, where the Akṣobhya Buddha and bodhisattvas dwelled. Below the mountains there were valleys, rivers, and oceans, as well as the sun, moon, and stars. There were also towns, villages, and scenes of everyday life. All these won great admiration from the disciples.

Vimalakirti was known for his wisdom and eloquence, and he could remain a householder, free to cultivate his spiritual practice without tonsuring his head or leaving his family, so he was greatly favored by Chinese scholars and officials. The *Vimalakirti Nirdesa* was so popular since the Wei and the Jin dynasties that a good deal of its illustrations appeared in the form of carvings or murals in cave temples throughout China. For instance, images of Vimalakirti and Manjusri are found among the murals in Cave 169 of the Bingling Cave Temple, the earliest such extant caves in China. In the Yungang Caves and the Maijishan Caves of the Northern Wei, *Vimalakirti Nirdesa* illustrations are also seen in carvings and murals. Among the Mogao Caves, there are as many as 68 grottoes that contain *Vimalakirti Nirdesa* illustrations, the earliest of which were constructed in the Sui Dynasty. After the Tang Dynasty, *Vimalakirti Nirdesa* illustrations were a common theme of the Mogao Caves. In Sui period caves, it was normally the case that Vimalakirti and Manjusri were painted respectively on each side of a Buddha

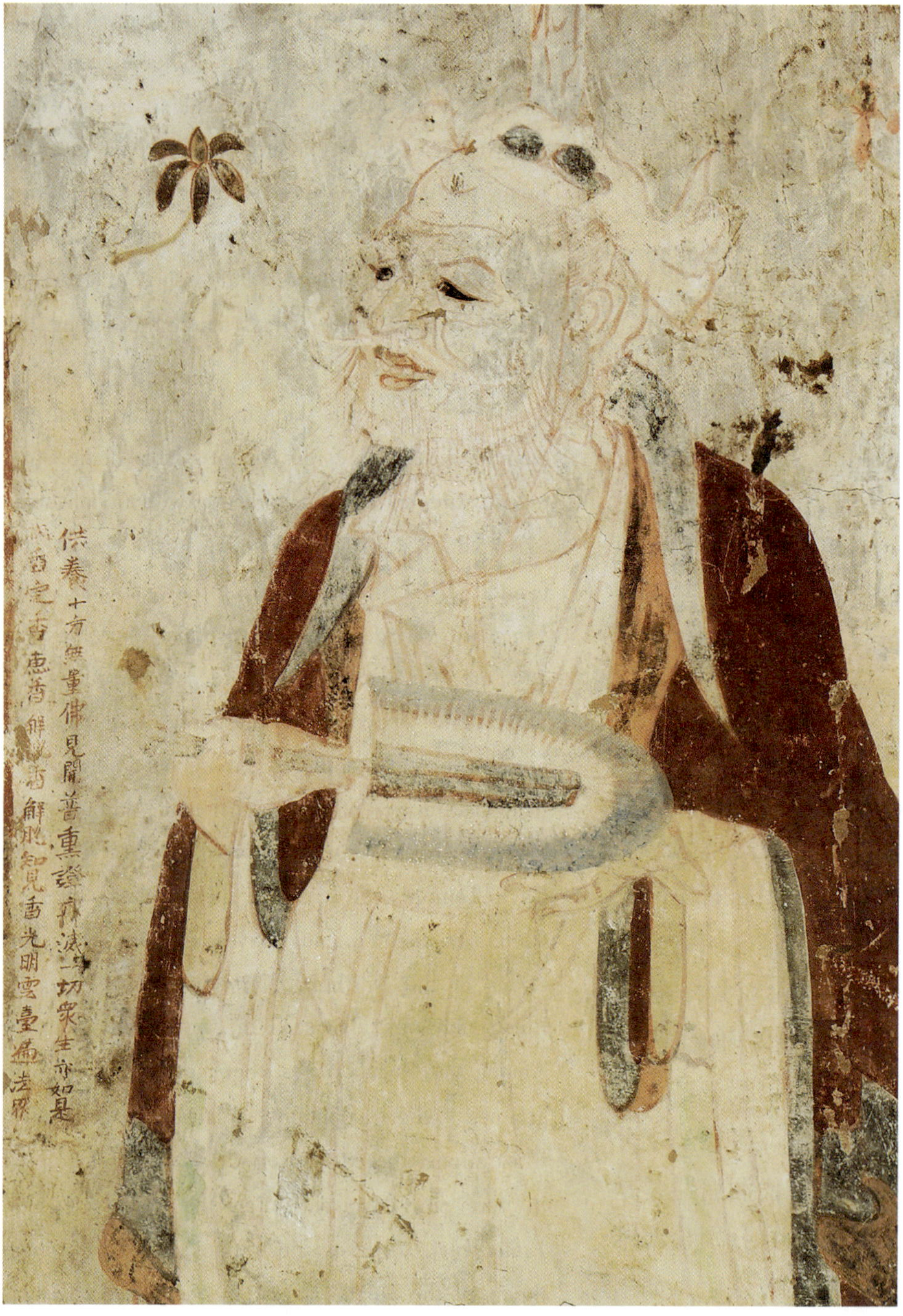

艺苑瑰宝
莫高窟壁画与彩塑

图88　维摩诘像　莫高窟第276窟　隋
Fig.88　Image of Vimalakirti, Mogao Cave 276, Sui Dynasty

摩诘形象(图 88),南侧画出文殊菩萨形象。唐代以后维摩诘经变画的规模更大,内容更为丰富,维摩诘与文殊菩萨周围往往描绘出众多的菩萨、弟子及世俗人物,还表现出各种相关的情节。往往利用整壁的壁面来描绘维摩诘经变,如初唐第 332 窟、335

niche. For example, on the north side of the niche in Cave 276 is a painting of Vimalakirti in the manner of a debate, yak tail whisk in hand (Fig.88), and on the south side is Manjusri. After the Tang Dynasty, *Vimalakirti Nirdesa* illustrations became broader in scale and richer in content. Numerous bodhisattvas, disciples, and lay people were painted around Vimalakirti and Manjusri, and a variety of related scenes were also represented. Often the surface of a whole wall was used for *Vimalakirti Nirdesa* illustrations. Examples can be found in Caves 332 and

图 89　维摩诘经变　莫高窟第 220　初唐
Fig.89　*Vimalakirti Sutra* Illustration, Mogao Cave 220, Early Tang

艺苑瑰宝
莫高窟壁画与彩塑

窟分别在北壁画出通壁巨制的维摩诘经变。还有不少洞窟中把维摩诘经变画在门两侧，如第220窟东壁门两侧分别画出维摩诘与文殊菩萨。南侧是维摩诘坐在帐中，手持麈尾，双目炯炯有神，神情激昂，沉浸在论辩的气氛中；香积菩萨托钵跪在前面（图89）。下部是各国王子听法的场面，上部则画出妙喜世界；门北侧是文殊菩萨和弟子、菩萨以及帝王、大臣听法。画中最有意义的是中国的帝王、大臣与少数民族国王的形象。皇帝戴冕旒，着衮服，两手伸开，仪态雍容，大臣们前呼后拥，显出至尊气派（图90）。这一形象与唐朝画家阎立本所画的《历代帝王图》很相似，但在整体气势上则远远超过了阎画。各国王子的形象包括南海、昆仑、西域各国的人物，相貌、服饰各不相同，大体上反映了唐朝与周围各族、各国的交往情况。

276 of the Early Tang, where huge *Vimalakirti Nirdea* illustrations are painted covering the entire north wall of each cave. There are also quite a few caves where *Vimalakirti Nirdesa* illustrations are painted on the walls on both sides of the entrance. For example, on both sides of the entrance, in the east wall of Cave 220, Vimalakirti and Manjusri are painted separately on each side. On the south side is Vimalakirti sitting in a tent holding a yak tail whisk with eyes shining brightly. He is passionate and deeply immersed in the atmosphere of a debate, and the bodhisattva in the Land of Fragrance is kneeling in front of him, holding an alms bowl (Fig.89). Painted below is a scene of princes from different countries listening to Dharma preaching, while painted in the upper section is the Pure Land of Abhirati. On the north side of the entrance is Manjusri, listening to Dharma preaching with disciples, bodhisattvas, emperors, and ministers. Most significant are the images of the Chinese emperor, ministers, and kings of the ethnic minorities. The emperor wears a tasseled ceremonial crown and imperial robe, with both hands extended, looking elegant and graceful. Escorted all around by ministers, he shows great dignity and supremacy (Fig.90). His manner here is quite similar to the *Emperors of the Past Dynasties* painted by Yan Liben, a well-known artist of the Tang Dynasty, but the overall style far exceeds the work of Yan Liben. The portraits of princes from different countries include figures from the South China Sea, Kunlun, and kingdoms of the Western Regions. Their dress and facial features are all different. The

Art Treasures: Murals and Painted Sculptures in Mogao Caves

在盛唐第 103 窟同样是把维摩诘经变画在东壁门两侧,南侧的维摩诘凭几而坐,身体略向前倾,手持麈尾,目光直视对手(图91)。画家以劲健的线描造型,微施淡彩,勾勒出一个气宇轩昂、雄辩滔滔的清谈家风采。维摩诘下部画出穿着不同服饰的各族王子形象。北侧的文殊菩萨端坐于高座上,表情恬静,

composition reflects the interaction and contact between the Tang imperial court, ethnic minorities, and neighboring countries.

Similarly, *Vimalakirti Nirdesa* illustrations are also painted on both sides of the entrance, on the east wall of Cave 103, constructed in the High Tang. On the right side of the wall, Vimalakirti is sitting by a small table, yak tail whisk in hand, leaning slightly forward, and looking his opponent directly in the eyes (Fig.91). With vigorous lines and light colors, the artist presented a dignified, eloquent man of elegant demeanor, who is skilled in intellectual discourse. Below Vimalakirti are images of princes

图 90　帝王图　莫高窟第 220 窟东壁北侧　初唐

Fig.90　Images of Chinese Emperors, Left Side of East Wall, Mogao Cave 220, Early Tang

199

图 91 维摩诘像 莫高窟第 103 窟东壁南侧 盛唐
Fig.91 Image of Vimalakirti, Right Side of East Wall, Mogao Cave 103, High Tang

一手执如意,一手向前打着手势,表现出从容论辩的样子。文殊菩萨身后的佛弟子们相互之间悄声说话。下部则画出中国式帝王及大臣们听法的情景。

中唐时期,由于吐蕃占领了敦煌,这时的维摩诘经变画中描绘各族王子的场面,一般都以吐蕃赞普的形象为首,形成了这一时期维摩诘经变画的一大特点。如第159窟东壁门的南北两侧分别绘制以维摩诘和文殊菩萨为中心的众多人物。在南壁维摩诘的下部,画出吐蕃赞普头戴红毡高帽,穿着虎皮翻领袍,腰系革带,佩长剑,右手持香炉立于一个方台上,身后还有侍从替他打着曲柄华盖。前面有一人持香炉,二人作前导,后面跟随着吐蕃大臣和其他民族的人物,这样的排场不亚于中原帝王,正好与北侧文殊菩萨下面的中原帝王形成分庭抗礼的形式(图92)。另外,第159

from different ethnic groups dressed in different costumes. On the left side of the wall, Manjusri is painted sitting straight on a high seat, looking tranquil. He holds a *ruyi* scepter in one hand and extends the other hand in a forward motion, revealing the unhurried manner of deliberate debate. Disciples behind him whisper to each other. In the lower register of the painting is a scene of Chinese emperors and ministers listening to a Buddhist lecture.

During the Middle Tang, Dunhuang was occupied by the Tubo Regime. As a characteristic of this period, the Tsenpo of Tubo was usually employed as the central figure of the *Vimalakirti Nirdesa* scene of the princes from different nations. For example, on both the right and left sides of the entrance on the east wall in Cave 159, a tableau of characters is painted, centering around Vimalakirti and Manjusri respectively. Below Vimalakirti on the right side, the Tsenpo is portrayed wearing a high hat made of red felt, a robe made of tiger skin with a lapel collar, and a leather belt around the waist. Equipped with a long sword, he stands on a square platform and holds an incense burner in his right hand. Behind him, his attendants hold a canopy on a curved pole over his head. In front of him, one attendant holds an incense burner, while another two guide the way. He is followed by Tubo ministers as well as figures from other ethnic groups. Such ostentatiousness and extravagance are no less than those shown by the emperors of China's Central Plains; indeed, a rivalry is formed with him standing as an equal to the emperors of the Central Plains, painted below Manjusri on the left side (Fig.92).

图 92　吐蕃赞普供养图　莫高窟第 159 窟东壁　中唐
Fig.92　Tsenpo of the Tubo Making Devotional Offerings, East Wall of Mogao Cave 159, Middle Tang

窟的维摩诘经变中，上部描绘维摩诘与文殊菩萨对谈的大场面，在下部则以屏风画的形式画出一些有趣的情节，如东壁南侧维摩诘的下部，画出阿难乞乳的场面。佛经上说释迦牟尼卧病在床时，佛弟子阿难持钵外出，为佛乞乳，遇上了维摩诘，维摩诘告诉阿难说："要是外道知道了，恐怕会耻笑释迦牟尼连自己的病都不能治，又怎能普度众生呢，你还是赶快回去

What is more, in the *Vimalakirti Nirdesa* illustration in Cave 159, the grand scene of dialogue between Vimalakirti and Manjusri is represented in the upper register, while in the lower register, some interesting scenes are shown in the form of screen paintings. For example, below Vimalakirti on the right-hand section of the east wall, there is the scene of Ananda begging for milk. According to Buddhist scriptures, when the Sakyamuni Buddha was sick in bed, his disciple Ananda went out with an alms bowl, begging milk for the Buddha. He met Vimalakirti, who said to him, "If the heretics hear about what you are doing now, they will possibly mock Sakyamuni saying, 'He can not even treat his own disease, so how can he deliver all living creatures from torment?' You'd better go back as quickly as you can." As painted in the mural, the scene presents Ananda waiting beside a cow, holding out the alms bowl to a milkmaid who is milking the cow. A calf is

吧。"这一场面在壁画上则表现为阿难托钵在一旁等待,一妇人正在母牛身下挤奶,旁边一头小牛正要向母牛而去,一个小男孩拼命拉住小牛,母牛回头看着小牛,生动地表现出舐犊之情。在东壁北侧的文殊菩萨的下部,还画出了维摩诘到人们赌博的地方劝化众人的故事。画中四个人围在一起赌博,维摩诘站在左侧观看,中间一人身穿蓝色衣服,双手叉腰,满脸凶相,右侧一人正举手掷骰,神情战战兢兢,唯恐输了的样子。生动地再现出古代市井赌徒的面貌和心态。

about to run towards the cow; a boy is trying hard to pull the calf back. The cow turns her head around, looking at her calf, presenting a lifelike display of maternal love. Below Manjusri on the northern part of the east wall is painted the tale of Vimalakirti urging people in a gambling den to commit virtuous deeds. In the picture, four men sit together gambling, with Vimalakirti standing on the left watching them. The man in the middle is dressed in blue, arms akimbo, looking rather fierce. The man on the right raises his hand to throw the dice. He trembles all over for fear he will lose. The scene graphically reproduces the expressions and inner psychology of gamblers in ancient times.

艺苑瑰宝
莫高窟壁画与彩塑

弥勒经变
Maitreya Triple Sutra Illustrations

弥勒信仰在佛教传入中国的初期就已流行,南北朝时期,不仅石窟和寺院,许多单独的造像碑也多刻弥勒菩萨的形象。但作为内容丰富的弥勒经变画则是在隋代以后才流行起来的。有关弥勒的佛经有很多种,主要流行的有《佛说观弥勒菩萨上生兜率天经》和《佛说弥勒下生成佛经》。隋代的弥勒经变画多描绘弥勒在兜率天宫说法的情景,这是表现《弥勒上生经》的内容。唐代以后,往往把《弥勒上生经》与《弥勒下生经》合起来,重点描绘弥勒下生经的内容。《弥勒上生经》主要讲弥勒降生于波罗奈国的婆罗门家,12年后入灭,上生到兜率天,成为一生补处菩萨,在净土院为诸天说法。《弥勒下生经》主要讲弥勒菩萨从兜率天宫下

Faith in Maitreya was already widespread in the early stages of Buddhism's transmission into China. During the Northern and Southern Dynasties, the image of Maitreya Bodhisattva was carved not only in caves and temples but also on individual votive tablets. However, Maitreya Triple Sutra illustrations, as forms of paintings with rich substance, were not prevalent until the end of the Sui Dynasty. There are many texts in Buddhist literature that relate to Maitreya, but the dominant ones are *The Sutra on the Contemplation of Maitreya Bodhisattva's Ascent to Rebirth in Tuṣita Heaven* (commonly known as the *Maitreya Contemplation Sutra*) and *The Sutra that Expounds the Descent of the Maitreya Buddha and His Enlightenment*. The Maitreya Triple Sutra illustrations from the Sui Dynasty mostly represented scenes of Maitreya preaching the Dharma in Tuṣita Heaven, essentially conveying the content of the *Maitreya Contemplation Sutra*. After the Tang Dynasty, the *Maitreya Contemplation Sutra* was often connected with *The Sutra that Expounds the Descent of the Maitreya Buddha and His Enlightenment*, with the latter being the focus. The *Maitreya Contemplation Sutra* mainly recounts that Maitreya was born into a Brahmin family in Vārānasi, and died when he was 12 years old. He was then reborn in Tuṣita Heaven and became a bodhisattva, limited to one

世,以修梵摩为父、梵摩耶为母,成道后教化众生,举行过三次规模宏大的讲法活动,化度数万人,称作"弥勒三会"。释迦牟尼涅槃之前,曾将自己的袈裟交给大弟子迦叶,并嘱咐道:"未来当有弥勒佛降世,他将接替我教化众生,你可把这袈裟转呈给弥勒佛。"弥勒成佛后,引众人到迦叶禅定之处,唤醒了深入禅定的大迦叶。于是,迦叶把释迦牟尼的袈裟送给弥勒佛。所以,弥勒成为继承释迦牟尼的未来佛。在弥勒世界,人们路不拾遗,夜不闭户,每天夜里有龙王洒水,罗刹扫地。还出现"一种七收""树上生衣"等奇迹,人们用力甚少,收获甚多。人寿八万四千岁,妇女500岁才出嫁。老人自知寿尽,便进入墓室平静地死去,没有痛苦。

more birth before becoming a Buddha. He preaches the Dharma to all Buddhist heavenly gods in the paradise of this Pure Land. *The Sutra that Expounds the Descent of the Maitreya Buddha and His Enlightenment* mainly foretells Maitreya's rebirth on earth from Tuṣita Heaven. According to the sutra, his father was Suvimala and his mother was Vimalapati. After attaining enlightenment, he began to preach Buddhist doctrine and instructed all sentient beings. Three times he hosted grand gatherings teaching Buddhism, and thousands upon thousands of people were enlightened. These were known as the Three Assemblies of Maitreya. Before entering nirvana, Sakyamuni handed his *kasaya* to his senior disciple Mahakasyapa, telling him, "In the future there will be a Maitreya Buddha descending to the world. He will preach the Dharma and instruct all sentient beings in my place, so please pass this *kasaya* on to the Maitreya Buddha." When Maitreya became a Buddha, he led people to the place where Mahakasyapa was meditating. He roused Mahakasyapa from that state, and then Mahakasyapa handed him Sakyamuni's *kasaya*. Thus Maitreya succeeded Sakyamuni and became the Buddha of the Future. In the world of Maitreya, passers-by do not touch others' lost articles on the road, and people can always leave their doors unlocked even at night. Every evening the Dragon King sprinkles water on the land and demons clean the ground. Miracles such as "one sowing brings seven harvests" and "clothes grow on trees" take place. People experience little suffering but receive many rewards. A human life span can reach 84,000 years, and women do not marry until they are 500 years old. Old people know when they will die and go to their

唐代以后的壁画中,画家们更热衷于描绘《弥勒下生经》中的种种景象,因为这些内容与现实生活更为贴近,使弥勒世界更具体可感。敦煌壁画中的弥勒经变画共98铺,仅唐代就有65铺,说明弥勒经变画深受人们喜爱。初唐第329窟南壁的弥勒经变画(图93),在上部约1/3的画面为上生经变。经文说:"兜率天宫

coffins when the time comes, dying peacefully without any suffering.

In murals after the Tang Dynasty, the artists preferred painting various scenes from *The Sutra that Expounds the Descent of the Maitreya Buddha and His Enlightenment*, for these scenes were closer to real life, making the world of Maitreya more concrete and easy to comprehend. There are 98 Maitreya Triple Sutra illustrations among the Dunhuang murals, and as many as 65 of them were painted in the Tang Dynasty, mirroring their popularity at the time. In the painting on the south wall of Cave 329 of the Early Tang (Fig.93), the upper one-third is devoted to the *Maitreya Contemplation Sutra*. According to accounts in

图93　弥勒经变　莫高窟第329窟南壁　初唐
Fig.93　Maitreya Triple Sutra Illustration, South Wall of Mogao Cave 329, Early Tang

有500亿天子，为供养弥勒菩萨，建造了华丽的宫殿，又脱自身摩尼宝冠化成供具，并从宝冠中变现出宝宫、宝树、龙王等异相。壁画中弥勒菩萨头戴宝冠，作善跏坐，两侧立有法音轮、大妙相两大菩萨，身后是500亿天子所造的宫殿。弥勒前面有众菩萨及天子、神王等。下半部约2/3的画面是下生经变，主要描绘弥勒降世成为未来佛，广度众生，以及弥勒世界的美妙景象。画中绿水荡漾，莲花盛开，亭台楼阁矗立其间。台上弥勒佛在中央说法，诸天圣众在周围听法。下部平台上，儴佉王正剃度出家。图中下部中央置一几案，上陈7宝，两侧画出男男女女正在剃度，后面有乐队奏乐。整幅经变画三座平台，中间有流水分隔，又有小桥通连，构图层次分明，色彩亮丽、单

Buddhist scriptures, there were 50 billion "heavenly sons" or princes in Tuṣita Heaven, who built magnificent palaces to make offerings to Maitreya Bodhisattva. They also took off their *mani* jewel coronets and changed them into sacrificial vessels. Extraordinary sights, such as jeweled palaces, jeweled trees, and the Dragon King, were created from these coronets as well. In the mural, Maitreya Bodhisattva is portrayed sitting in *pralambapādāsana*, legs pendant, wearing a jewel-encrusted crown. He is flanked by two attendant bodhisattvas, Bodhisattva of the Sound of the Dharma Wheel (*Fayinlun*) and Bodhisattva of Wonderful Appearance (*Damiaoxiang*), and behind him are the palaces built by the 50 billion heavenly sons. In front of him are bodhisattvas, heavenly sons, and *lokapalas*. The lower two-thirds of the painting is *The Sutra that Expounds the Descent of the Maitreya Buddha and His Enlightenment*, mainly depicting Maitreya's descent to earth. The painting portrays Maitreya as the Buddha of the Future, preaching the Dharma and enlightening countless living beings. The world of Maitreya is filled with scenes of splendor. In the picture, green water ripples and lotuses bloom with platforms, pavilions, and pagodas rising abruptly among them. On the platform, the Maitreya Buddha is preaching the Dharma in the center and *devas* from all Buddhist heavenly realms surround him, listening. On the platform below, a Cakravartin king (universal monarch) is having his head tonsured to become a monk. In the center of the lower middle section is a table, on which the seven treasures are arranged. On both sides of the table, men and women are having their heads tonsured. Behind the table an ensemble plays music. In the whole painting there are three

纯。

盛唐以后的弥勒经变画,内容更为丰富,并形成了与其他时期的经变画不同的格局。如第445窟北壁的弥勒经变画,中央上部画出弥勒所居的须弥山和兜率天宫,山前是弥勒佛说法及众天人围绕的情景。在画面的两侧及下部穿插表现弥勒世界的各种景象,中央下部以较大的画面描绘儴佉王及眷属们剃度出家的情景,真实地表现出男女老少剃度时的不同表情。在剃度场面左侧下部,还画出了婚礼图。这是为了表现经中所说"女人五百岁出嫁"的内容而画的:在一个大院的外面,有一个大大的帐篷,新郎新娘和众多的宾客们正在里面欢宴,有一人正在跳舞。这一场面反映了唐代婚俗中新婚之日,于户外搭"青庐"的习惯。在画面的右上部还画出了农夫辛勤耕作和收获的场面,这是表现经中所说"一种七收"的内容。

盛唐第33窟南壁的弥

platforms, separated by streams between them, while interconnected by small bridges over the water. It is composed with distinct arrangements and bright but simple colors.

The subject matter of Maitreya Triple Sutra illustrations after the High Tang was more profound, and new patterns had been developed, different from other such paintings. For example, Maitreya's abodes, Mount Sumeru and Tuṣita Heaven, are depicted on the north wall's upper middle section, in Cave 445. In front of Mount Sumeru is a scene of Maitreya Buddha preaching the Dharma as *devas* surround him. Interspersed on both sides and below the scene are various sights in the world of Maitreya. Occupying a large part of the lower middle section is a scene of the Cakravartin king and his family, having their heads tonsured to become monastics. Different looks of males and females, old and young, are realistically portrayed at their moment of renunciation. In the lower section, to the left of the tonsuring scene, there is even a painting depicting a wedding, illustrating that in Maitreya's abode women do not marry until they are 500 years old. In the scene, a large tent is set up outside a courtyard. The bride, bridegroom and crowds of guests enjoy the banquet in the tent while one person dances. The scene accurately reflects the Tang custom that on the wedding day, a hut would be specifically set up outdoors. In the upper right section of the painting is a scene of hardworking farmers planting and harvesting, which shows "one sowing brings seven harvests",

勒经变画，在构图上更集中，中央部分描绘弥勒说法的场面，上部表现上宽下窄的须弥山，山上各种宫殿楼阁，山下则是大海。周围描绘各种世俗生活的场面，于是把天上的世界与人间的世界明确地区别开来。中央下部描绘儴佉王及眷属们剃发出家的情景，在画面左上部描绘了在一个大帐子中举行婚礼的情景。新郎新娘向坐在右侧的双亲礼拜，新郎伏身跪地而拜，而旁边的新娘则欠身行礼（图94）。这也是唐代的风俗，即结婚典礼中，向双亲拜时，男跪女不跪。画面右上部画的是农民耕作的情形，下侧一农夫赶着两头牛犁地，上侧画两个农夫正在收割庄稼。在耕获图的下部画一座城池，城池上部一条龙翻卷着乌云，正在下雨，城外一罗刹鬼在扫地。表现的正是弥勒所在的翅头末城的情景。

由于弥勒经变画的很多场面与现实生活十分贴

as is written in Buddhist scriptures.

The Maitreya Triple Sutra illustration on the south wall of Cave 33 of the High Tang has a denser composition. The central part is a scene depicting Maitreya preaching the Dharma. The upper register reveals Mount Sumeru with a wide top and a narrow base. At the top of the mountain are various palaces, temples, pavilions, and pagodas while at the foot of it lies the sea. All around are scenes of secular life. Thus the heavenly world and the human world are clearly delineated. A scene of the Cakravartin King and his family having their heads shaved to become Buddhist monks and nuns is also painted in the lower middle section. The upper left section reveals a wedding scene, taking place in a large tent. The bride and groom pay their formal respects to their parents sitting on the right. The groom prostrates and kneels on the ground to kowtow, while the bride beside him merely bends down as she performs her part of the ritual (Fig.94). This, too, was a custom of the Tang Dynasty. In a wedding ceremony, when the newly-wedded couple paid formal respects to the parents, the groom was required to kneel down while the bride was not. In the upper right section is an agricultural scene of farmers at work, two farmers plowing the fields with two oxen in the lower part, and two farmers harvesting their crops in the upper part. Below the farming scene is a city with a dragon swirling overhead creating dark clouds and rain showers. Outside the city, a demon sweeps the ground. The painting is an epic scene of Maitreya's

图 94　婚礼图　莫高窟第 33 窟南壁　盛唐
Fig.94　Wedding Scene, South Wall of Mogao Cave 33, High Tang

近,深受人们喜爱。盛唐以后的弥勒经变画中,如剃度图、婚嫁图、耕作图等场面成了弥勒经变画中必不可少的内容,而且随着时代的变化,往往有着相应的变化。如中唐时期,吐蕃族统治了敦煌一带,于是在榆林窟第 25 窟的弥勒经变画中,婚嫁图中描绘了藏族妇女与汉族男子结婚的场面,反映了古代敦煌地区多民族共同生活的历史。这些都成为记录古代社会生活的典型画面。

abode.

Since a great many of the scenes in Maitreya Triple Sutra illustrations were fairly close to real life, they were widely appreciated among the common people. After the High Tang, images such as tonsure ceremonies, weddings, and agricultural work were indispensable parts of Maitreya Triple Sutra illustrations. Furthermore, they were always changing with time. For example, during the Middle Tang, Dunhuang was ruled by the Tubo Regime, so in the Maitreya Triple Sutra illustration in Cave 25 at Yulin, a wedding is depicted with a Tubo woman marrying a Han man, mirroring the different ethnic groups coexisting in Dunhuang during that historical era. Thus, these paintings are typical scenes recording the social life back then.

阿弥陀经变、无量寿经变、观无量寿经变
Amitabha Sutra, *Sukhavativyuha Sutra*, and *Amitayurdhyana Sutra* Illustrations

　　阿弥陀佛的信仰是大乘佛教中最流行的信仰之一。小乘佛教认为，一个人即使累世修行，有了善根，最快也要经过三次轮回转世才能成佛。而大乘佛教则认为，人人皆可成佛，而且还有一个最简便的修行办法，就是念佛，只要念阿弥陀佛，就可以进入西方净土世界。于是，大乘佛教信仰迅速地在中国南北大地流行起来。阿弥陀佛也译作无量寿佛，崇奉阿弥陀佛的经典主要包括《阿弥陀经》《无量寿佛经》《观无量寿经》，也称"净土三经"。净土宗就是以这三经为宗旨的宗派。

　　根据《阿弥陀经》《无量寿经》和《观无量寿经》绘制的经变画，主要是描绘阿弥陀佛所在的西方净土世界，所以都可以称作西方净土变。但在壁画中，这三种经变画也有很多细微的区别。

　　Faith in Amitabha is one of the most prevalent beliefs in Mahayana Buddhism. The Theravada sect believes that even if a man has undertaken spiritual cultivation in repeated rounds of life and has firmly planted the seeds of virtue, the minimum amount of time it can take for him to achieve enlightenment will be three lives. However, Mahayana believes that everybody can become a Buddha, and furthermore, there is an easier way to achieve enlightenment, which is to chant the Buddha's name. As long as a person keeps chanting Amitabha, he can enter Sukhāvatī, the Western Pure Land. As a result, the Mahayana sect spread rapidly all over China. In translation, Amitabha is also rendered as Amitayus. The Amitabha Buddha canon of sutras primarily includes the *Amitabha Sutra*, the *Sukhavativyuha Sutra*, and the *Amitayurdhyana Sutra*, known as the Three Sutras of the Pure Land. The Pure Land School refers to the sect that takes these three sutras as the foundational texts for its faith.

　　Sutra illustrations that are painted according to the *Amitabha Sutra*, the *Sukhavativyuha Sutra* and the *Amitayurdhyana Sutra* mainly portray the Pure Land of the West, where Amitabha dwells; thus, they can all be designated as Western Pure Land sutra illustrations. In murals, however, there are several distinctions among the three. According to Buddhist texts, the Western Pure Land is also the

211

根据佛经，西方净土世界也就是极乐世界。在这个世界中，没有痛苦，只有快乐，人们丰衣足食，所需物品，皆得满足，也没有劳作之苦。阿弥陀佛与观世音菩萨、大势至菩萨生活在这里，有天人做音乐舞蹈，一片歌舞升平气象。通常的人是由胎生的，而进入西方净土世界则要从莲花中生出来，称作化生。化生表明进入净土世界，到了生生不灭的境地。

唐代以后，净土信仰流行全国。贞观十五年（641年），净土宗大师善导就在长安绘制了300幅阿弥陀经变画，后来，武则天以此为蓝本，制作了400幅阿弥陀净土的大绣帐。在这种风气的影响下，莫高窟也绘出了大量的西方净土变。经专家研究，敦煌壁画中能确认的阿弥陀经变画有38铺、无量寿经变画38铺、观无量寿经变画84铺。其他又有60多铺简略的净土变，但还不能

Western Paradise. In such a realm, there is no suffering, but only pleasure. People enjoy ample food and clothing, and every need can be satisfied with none of the hardships of labor. The Amitabha Buddha presides over the land with the bodhisattvas Avalokitesvara and Mahasthamapraptapta. *Devas* play music and dance for them. The atmosphere is made up of singing and dancing, in celebration of peace. Ordinarily, people are born from parents, but when they enter Sukhāvatī, the Pure Land of the West, they are born from lotus flowers, a form of "spontaneous birth" *(upapādukayoni)*. This also indicates that entering the world of the Pure Land means being reborn into a deathless realm.

During the Tang Dynasty, faith in the Pure Land prevailed throughout China. In the 15th year of the Zhenguan Era (641), Shandao, the master of the Pure Land School of Buddhism, created 300 *Amitabha Sutra* illustrations in Chang'an. Later, Empress Wu Zetian had 400 huge embroidered silk pieces made on the theme of Amitabha's Pure Land. Influenced by this trend, large numbers of Pure Land sutra illustrations were also painted in the Mogao Caves. According to experts, 38 *Amitabha Sutra* illustrations, 38 *Sukhavativyuha Sutra* illustrations, and 84 *Amitayurdhyana Sutra* illustrations have been identified among the Dunhuang murals. In addition, there are over 60 other paintings that are brief or simplified versions of Pure Land sutra illustrations, but it is yet to be clarified which of the three types they belong to.

Among the murals of the Northern Dynasties in Dunhuang, there were already paintings of the Amitayus Buddha preaching the Dharma. However,

确认是哪种净土变。

敦煌北朝壁画中就已绘制了无量寿佛说法图,但作为经变画的形式则是唐代以后才流行起来的。几种净土变都主要通过巍峨的宫殿建筑来表现净土世界。无量寿经变与阿弥陀经变的区别在于无量寿经变强调"三辈往生",即根据生前修行所积累的功德高低程度,在进入西方净土世界时,就分为上辈、中辈和下辈的不同等级。这样的情况,在壁画中是通过莲花化生的形象来表现的。

初唐第 220 窟南壁的无量寿经变画(图 95),中间画碧绿的水池,这是表现佛经所说的七宝池、八功德水。在水池中有朵朵莲花,莲花上面坐着的儿童就是化生。还有一些透明的莲蕾,可以看到也有儿童在其中,说明这些化生要进入净土世界还需一段时间。水池中央无量寿佛坐在水中的莲花

it was not until after the establishment of the Tang Dynasty that *Sukhavativyuha Sutra* illustrations became popular as a form of that genre. All Pure Land sutra illustrations present the world of the Pure Land by painting images of splendid and lofty palaces. *Sukhavativyuha Sutra* illustrations are different from *Amitabha Sutra* illustrations in that the former emphasize the "three grades of rebirth". That is to say, when one enters the Western Pure Land, he will be assigned into one of the three levels, the top grade, the intermediate grade, or the bottom grade, according to the amount of spiritual practice in his previous life, the amount of meritorious actions he performed, and the intensity of his aspiration for enlightenment. These differences are signified in the murals by different lotus images indicating spontaneous rebirth from lotus flowers.

In the *Sukhavativyuha Sutra* illustration on the south wall in Cave 220, constructed during the Early Tang, a green water pool is painted in the center (Fig.95), representing the seven-treasure pool and the eight-merit water mentioned in Buddhist scriptures. Blooming lotuses appear here and there; the children sitting on them have been spontaneously reborn. There are also some transparent lotus buds, with children visible inside, meaning that it takes some time for a lotus child to be reborn into the world of the Pure Land. The Amitayus Buddha sits on a lotus seat in the center of the pool, preaching the Dharma. Standing one on each side are Avalokitesvara and Mahasthamapraptapta, and numerous bodhisattvas surround him as they listen. Above wafts heavenly

图95 西方净土变 莫高窟第220窟南壁 初唐
Fig.95 Western Pure Land Sutra Illustration, South Wall of Mogao Cave 220, Early Tang

座上说法,两侧是观世音、大势至菩萨,周围有众多的听法菩萨。上面有不鼓自鸣的天乐,下面的平台上有两身舞伎在小圆毯上翩然起舞,其两侧还各有一个乐队。画面以佛为中心,人物众多,但神形各异,有主有从,繁而不乱。用色以青绿为基调,配色不多却华丽灿烂。画家对人物的动态和衣服的质感表现得非常细腻真切。

阿弥陀经变画一般没有化生,但很注重表现华丽的

music, playing spontaneously on its own. Below him, two dancers move gracefully on a small round carpet on a platform, with an ensemble playing on each side. The painting, with the Buddha as its center focus, gives all the characters their own spirit and personality despite the great number. Some are primary figures in the composition, while others are secondary or subordinate. Although numerous, they are arranged neatly. The colors are mainly blue and green, without many other coordinating pigments, but the overall look is bright and sumptuous. The motion of the characters and the texture of their clothing are exquisitely and realistically rendered.

Generally speaking, *Amitabha Sutra* illustrations do not depict spontaneous rebirth of

宫殿楼阁。如第 329 窟南壁的阿弥陀经变画,描绘出绿色的宝池上建有 7 座华丽的平台,台上楼阁高耸,平台的地面铺满了有花纹的地砖,并有金银装饰。这是表现阿弥陀世界里七宝铺地的景象。阿弥陀佛居中央,结跏趺坐,双手作说法印,神态庄严慈祥。观世音菩萨、大势至二菩萨分立两侧,其他听法菩萨或坐或立,有的合掌捧花,有的低头思考。她们头梳云环髻,戴宝冠,斜披天衣,腰束锦裙,璎珞环饰,姿态婀娜。画面的上端,流云飘动,飞天穿行,天乐不鼓自鸣。图下端中部画一组舞乐,舞蹈者面向佛陀,身体呈"S"形弯曲,左手平伸,右手上举,舞姿奔放有力。左右各有三身伎乐,分别演奏着琵琶、筝、箜篌、竖笛。她们的手随着音乐的旋律边舞边奏,动感强烈。宝池中还有人头鸟身的迦陵频伽,仿佛也

children from lotus flowers—the emphasis is instead laid upon displaying magnificent palaces, temples, and pagodas. An example can be found in the painting on the south wall of Cave 329, in which there is a green-jeweled pool. Constructed in the pool are seven grand platforms, covered by patterned floor bricks as well as gold and silver ornaments. Pavilions and towers stand high on the platforms. This is to show that the ground in Amitabha's world is paved with seven treasures. The Amitabha Buddha is at the center, sitting in lotus pose, his two hands in the *vitarka mudra* of Dharma preaching, looking serene and kind. Avalokitesvara and Mahasthamapraptapta stand on both sides. Other bodhisattvas listening to the Buddha reveal different postures and positions: some sit, some stand, some hold flowers with both palms folded together in *añjali*, and some lower their heads in thought. They wear jeweled coronets, flowing celestial clothing, brocaded *dhotis*, jeweled rings and necklaces, coiled hair like clouds, looking attractive and elegant. In the upper part of the painting, clouds float and swirl, *apsaras* fly back and forth, and divine music comes spontaneously from the air. In the middle of the lower section is an ensemble of musicians and a dancer. The dancer is facing the Buddha, her body bent in the S-shaped *tribhanga* posture, her right hand extended horizontally, and her left hand raised. Her dancing is bold and forceful. On either side of her are three musicians, playing the *pipa*, the *konghou*, and the vertical flute. Their hands move to the rhythm of the melody while playing, showing strong dynamics. In the jeweled pool, there is a *kalavinka*, a celestial being that has a human head

正随着优美的乐曲载歌载舞。图下部的两侧各绘有一组供养菩萨,其中西侧的四身菩萨动态极为优美:左起第一身菩萨正侧身款款而行,手捧香炉,神态虔诚;第二身菩萨一手持花于胸前,正举步欲行;第三身上半身微侧,似在招呼身后的一位,体态优美,颇有动感;最后一位面向观众,头微侧向身后的佛,好像仍沉浸在佛的教诲中。这组菩萨颜色已变,形象也有些模糊,若仔细观察,仍能感受到唐代人物画的神韵和风采。

净土经变画中最有特色的还有净水池,在池中描绘莲花化生。根据佛经记述,要进入西方净土世界,须从莲花中化生而出。所以化生就是进入净土世界的象征。唐代的净土变中,对净水池的描绘成为一个重要的内容。文献记载长安的赵景公寺有"范长寿画西方净土变

and a bird's body, who seems to be singing and dancing to the sweet tune. On either side of the lower section of the painting groups of bodhisattvas make offerings. The motions of the four on the right-hand section are enchanting. The first one on the left holds an incense burner with both hands while walking sideways in slow steps, looking devout. The second one holds flowers close to her breast with one hand, raising her foot with the intention of stepping forward. The third one leans slightly to one side, apparently greeting the one following her, with a lovely bearing and a sense of movement. The last one faces the viewer, with head slightly inclining toward the Buddha behind her, as if still immersed in the Buddha's teachings. The pigments have changed over time, and their images are not perfectly clear. But if observed carefully, the elegance and charm of the painted Tang period characters can be felt.

Another feature that is unique to Pure Land sutra illustrations is the clear water pool, where spontaneous birth from lotus flowers is depicted. According to Buddhist literature, if a person wants to enter the Western Pure Land, he needs to be spontaneously born from a lotus flower. Therefore, spontaneous birth symbolizes entering the realm of the Pure Land. In the Pure Land sutra illustrations of the Tang Dynasty, clear pools of water were one of the most important subjects. According to records, in Chang'an there was a temple called Zhao Jinggong, where "Fan Changshou painted Western Pure Land sutra illustrations with 16 other pictures matching it. In the paintings, the water pools are exceptionally well done. If you look at them carefully, you will feel

Art Treasures: Murals and Painted Sculptures in Mogao Caves

及十六对事。宝池尤妙绝,谛视之,觉水入浮壁"。范长寿画的宝池使人感到好像水在流动一样,可见画家技艺之精。

净土变中通常在净水池上绘出台榭和宫殿楼阁。水上的台榭又画出舞乐的场面,表现歌舞升平的气象(图96、图97)。于是,为了表现天国的美好景象,歌舞的场面也就越来越大,有时甚至占据了画面三分之一的地方。

唐代以后,观无量寿经变画急剧地流行起来。它与无量寿经变和阿弥

that water is flowing into the wall and the wall is floating above water." The water painted by Fan Changshou gives viewers the impression that it is flowing, revealing the perfection of the artist's skills.

In Pure Land sutra illustrations, it is normally the case that platforms, pavilions, palaces, pagodas, and temples are painted over a pool of water, with scenes of dancing and playing music painted on the platforms, enhancing the atmosphere of prosperity and peace. (Fig.96, 97). As a result, to represent these beautiful sights of heavenly realms, scenes of singing and dancing increasingly expand in size, so that sometimes they cover one third of the whole painting.

After the Tang Dynasty, *Amitayurdhyana Sutra* illustrations spread rapidly. Different from either *Amitabha Sutra* illustrations or *Sukhavativyuha Sutra* illustrations, *Amitayurdhyana Sutra* illustrations were usually painted according to the

图96 乐舞图 莫高窟第220窟南壁 初唐

Fig.96 Scene of Playing Music and Dancing, South Wall of Mogao Cave 220, Early Tang

217

艺苑瑰宝
莫高窟壁画与彩塑

图 97　乐舞图　莫高窟第 220 窟北壁　盛唐
Fig.97　Scene of Playing Music and Dancing, North Wall of Mogao Cave 320, High Tang

陀经变的区别在于：除了在中央部分画出与前二者类似的净土世界以外，往往在画面的两侧以条幅的形式画出《观无量寿经》的《序品》和《十六观想》的内容。序品即前一章所讲的"未生怨故事"。"十六观"就是佛所讲述的达到佛教境界的 16 种修行办法。这"十六观"包括：日想观、水想观、地想观、树想观、八功德水想

following pattern. In addition to the world of the Pure Land in the center, such content as the introductory chapter and the Sixteen Visualizations from the *Amitayurdhyana Sutra* were presented on both sides, in the form of vertical panels. The introductory chapter refers to the *nidana* story of the "Enemy While Still Unborn", mentioned in the previous chapter. The Sixteen Visualizations, which refer to 16 instructions given by the Buddha for meditation so as to attain rebirth in the Pure Land, include visualizations on the setting sun, pure water, a beryl ground, jeweled trees, eight-merit water, the universe, the lotus throne of Amitabha, Amitabha himself, the characteristics of all physical bodies, the true physical body of Avalokitesvara, the

观、普想观、华座观、真身观、遍观一切色身相、观世音菩萨真实色身相观、大势至菩萨色身相观、观想无量寿佛化身无数、杂想观、上辈生想观、中辈生想观、下辈生想观。对这"十六观"的解释也是《观无量寿经》的主要内容,其中发展了三辈往生的思想,从而形成了"九品往生"的思想。即进入西方净土世界有9种不同的级别,分别为上品上生、上品中生、上品下生、中品上生、中品中生、中品下生、下品上生、下品中生、下品下生。《观无量寿经》讲解了比阿弥陀经和无量寿经更为细致而具体的修行途径,唐代以后更为流行。

第172窟是莫高窟盛唐时期的代表窟之一,南北两壁的观无量寿经变画是此窟的主要内容。由于画家的高超技艺,相同的内容在同一洞窟不仅不显得重复,而且令人感到丰富多彩、目不暇接。这两铺观无量寿经变画都采用三联式构图,即中间大部空间表现西方极乐世界,两边以条幅的形式分别画出"十六观"和"未

physical body of Mahasthamapraptapta, the countless incarnations of the Amitayus Buddha, random thoughts, the highest level of rebirth, the intermediate level of rebirth, and the bottom level of rebirth. Interpretation of the Sixteen Visualizations is also the primary content of the *Amitayurdhyana Sutra*, in which the concept of three grades of rebirth is developed to such a degree that beings who succeed in being reborn into the Western Pure Land are further subdivided into nine grades, i.e., the uppermost in the top grade, the intermediate in the top grade, the lowest in the top grade, and so on down the classes of rebirth. The *Amitayurdhyana Sutra* gives more concrete and detailed instructions for spiritual practice than either the *Amitabha Sutra* or the *Sukhavativyuha Sutra*, so it became more popular after the Tang Dynasty.

Cave 172 is representative of the High Tang. The *Amitayurdhyana Sutra* illustrations on both the north and south walls are its main subjects. Owing to the superb skills of the artists, similar content painted in the same cave do not appear repetitive, but rich and varied. They are a feast for the eyes. Each of the two paintings is composed of three sections. Most of the space in the middle displays the world of the Western Paradise, and on both sides are the Sixteen Visualizations and the *nidana* of the "Enemy While Still Unborn" in vertical panels (Fig.98). The mural on the north wall has the Buddha as its center, with bodhisattvas listening to him like myriad stars circling the

生怨"的故事(图98)。北壁的经变画以佛为中心,听法菩萨似众星捧月,围绕成弧形。这些菩萨个个体态优美,面含笑意,有的身体前倾,双手捧香炉供养;有的合掌低头,静思默想;有的抚掌微笑,若有所悟;有的仰首注视,全神贯注;有的正襟危坐,充满敬意;有的抱膝冥想,若探求佛理。这些不同的动作构成了变化而和谐的整体旋律,使这幅经变画宏大而不单调,丰富而不繁乱。在画的下部还描绘了乐舞场面。乐舞是为了娱佛的,所以也被称作供养乐伎。北壁经变画中有两组乐伎共16人演奏乐器,中间舞伎两人正挥袖起舞,那急速、有力的舞姿使我们感觉到一种强烈而欢快的音乐节奏。南壁与此有所不同,虽然左右两侧也分别有8人的乐队在演奏,但中间两个舞人,却是一人挎腰鼓,一个反弹琵琶。从乐队的乐器来看,打击乐器和吹奏乐器居多,连舞伎也拍打腰鼓而舞,其节奏感应该是很强的,旋律也一定是雄壮铿锵的。反弹琵琶舞在唐朝壁画中经常出现,大约是当时流行的精彩舞蹈绝技,而今它也已

moon. The bodhisattvas each have graceful posture, with smiling faces. Some lean forward, holding an incense burner with both hands to make an offering; some fold their hands, lowering their heads, and meditate. Some clap their hands and smile gently as if having realized something; some raise their eyes, looking at the Buddha attentively. Some sit upright, full of respect; and some clasp their knees, thinking deeply as if contemplating the Dharma. The different dynamics make up the overall "melody" of the mural: varied but harmonious, making it grand but not monotonous, expansive but not disorganized. In the lower part of the painting is a scene of music and dance. The purpose of music and dance is to entertain the Buddha. Such devotees are called "musical performers making offerings". In the center of the painting, two ensembles of 16 performers play musical instruments while two others dance, waving their long sleeves. From their quick and forceful movements, we can sense a sort of strong and pleasing musical rhythm. There is something different in the mural on the south wall. Again two ensembles of eight performers play musical instruments, but of the two dancers in the middle, one holds a waist drum and the other plays the *pipa* behind the back. Most of the instruments appear to be percussion and woodwinds. Even the dancer is beating her waist drum while she dances, so it is certain that the

图98 观无量寿经变 莫高窟第172窟北壁 盛唐
Fig.98 *Amitayurdhyana Sutra* Illustration, North Wall of Mogao Cave 172, High Tang

成为人们追寻唐代舞蹈风采的最耀眼的标志了。这两组乐舞图，向我们展示了1000多年前唐代音乐舞蹈的辉煌壮观的场景。

第172窟这种以中央净土图为主，两侧又辅以条幅的形式，在盛唐以后便成为观无量寿经变画的主要形式。如第320窟、103窟、148窟等洞窟都有着同样的表现。第171窟也是以观无量寿经变画为主题的洞窟，在南、北、东三壁都

rhythm must be strong and the melody majestic and sonorous. The image of playing the *pipa* behind the upper back is frequently seen in the murals of the Tang Dynasty, and likely it was the most marvelous dance skill, popular at that time. Today it has become an iconic symbol of Tang choreography. These two groups of music and dance paintings reveal to us the splendid spectacles of the Tang Dynasty, over 1,000 years ago.

After the High Tang, the prevalent pattern of *Amitayurdhyana Sutra* illustrations was a composition dominated by the Pure Land in the center, complemented by vertical panels on both sides. Cave 172 is typical, and

画出了通壁的观无量寿经变画，同样是三联式的构成。但未生怨故事的表现较为特别，采用格子形式，每个格子画一个情节，连续起来表现一个完整的故事。如北壁东侧表现未生怨故事共画出了横4格、纵8格的格子，由上而下详尽地表现故事的具体情节。此画是唐代连环故事画代表之一，在中国绘画史上有着独特的地位。

similar representations are found in Caves 320, 103, 148, and others as well. Cave 171 is also one that has the *Amitayurdhyana Sutra* illustration as its main theme, completely covering the surfaces of the north, south, and east walls. Similarly the paintings are composed of three sections, and the *nidana* story of the "Enemy While Still Unborn" is presented in a more novel way. It is painted in a grid layout. Each section of the grid contains a part of the storyline, and a succession of grids makes up the complete tale. The tale is presented in the painting on the right side of the north wall. Horizontally there are four grids and vertically there are eight grids, and the tale is arranged within them, showing the detailed plot from top to bottom. The work is a quintessential continuous narrative painting from the Tang Dynasty, enjoying a unique position in the history of Chinese painting.

药师经变

Bhaisajyaguru Sutra Illustrations

药师经变画也称东方药师净土变，同属于净土经变，是根据《药师如来本愿经》等经典绘成，也是敦煌壁画中十分常见的经变画。佛教认为药师佛能治病救人，凡"无救、无归、无医、无药、无亲、无家"之人，只要供养药师佛，就可以得救。药师佛便成了深受苦难的人民心目中的救星。于是，药师崇拜也就盛行起来。《药师经》还渲染了人世间的很多种意想不到的灾难，称作"九横死"。横死指死于非命，如生病求医，而得到并不对症的药而误死；受冤枉被王法处死；酒色无度而死；火灾而死；水灾而死；被猛兽咬死；堕落山崖而死；因毒药等致死；饥饿而死；等等。在壁画中还绘出了药师佛曾发下的"十

Bhaisajyaguru Sutra illustrations belong to the genre of Pure Land sutra illustrations, and are also known as Pure Land sutra illustrations of Bhaisajyaguru, the Medicine Buddha of the Eastern Pure Land. They are based on details from the *Bhaisajyaguru Sutra* (*Medicine Buddha Sutra*) and are commonly seen among the Dunhuang murals as well. Buddhists believe that Bhaisajyaguru can heal illnesses and save lives. Those who are "hopeless, helpless, homeless, cureless, and kinless" will be saved, as long as they make offerings to the Bhaisajyaguru Buddha. Thus he became a savior in the eyes of afflicted people, and worship of him flourished. The *Bhaisajyaguru Sutra* also details unexpected disasters of the human realm known as the "Nine Violent Deaths". Violent death means an unnatural death, referring to the following examples: when one is ill and goes to a doctor, but receives the wrong medicine and suffers a wrongful death; when one is unjustly accused, and is sentenced to death by mistake; when one dies because he is immoderate in wine and women; when one dies from a fire; when one dies from a flood; when one is killed by a fierce beast; when one dies falling off a mountain cliff; when one dies of poison; and when one dies of hunger. In the murals, Bhaisajyaguru's "Twelve Great Vows" are also presented, mainly illustrating the promises he made on how he would deliver people from suffering after he became a Buddha.

二大愿",主要内容就是药师佛未成佛之前发愿,如果成佛将拯救人民于水火之中等事。

在敦煌石窟中现存有97铺药师经变画。唐代洞窟中往往把西方净土变与药师经变相对画出。如初唐第220窟南壁画无量寿经变,北壁就画药师经变。这样,西方阿弥陀佛(即无量寿佛)、东方药师佛就与正龛塑释迦牟尼佛组成了"横三世佛"。

大多数药师经变画的构图与观无量寿经变画一致,中央画净土世界,两侧以条幅的形式画出"九横死""十二大愿"等内容。如盛唐第148窟东壁门北侧巨幅药师经变画,中央表现东方药师净土世界,与西方净土变同样通过华丽无比的楼阁来象征庄严的净土世界(图99)。与这些高楼相接的是建于净水池中的平台,在

There are 97 extant *Bhaisajyaguru Sutra* illustrations in the Dunhuang caves. In Tang Dynasty caves, *Bhaisajyaguru Sutra* illustrations are usually painted directly opposite Western Pure Land sutra illustrations. For example, in Cave 220 of the Early Tang, the *Sukhavativyuha Sutra* illustration is painted on the south wall, while the Bhaisajyaguru illustration is painted on the north wall. Thus the Amitabha Buddha (that is, the Amitayus Buddha) of the West, the Bhaisajyaguru Buddha of the East, and the image of the Sakyamuni Buddha sculpted in the main niche combine into a parallel representation of the Trikāya Buddhas.

The composition of most *Bhaisajyaguru Sutra* illustrations is similar to that of the *Amitayurdhyana Sutra* illustrations. The world of the Pure Land is painted in the center and themes such as the "Nine Violent Deaths" and the "Twelve Great Vows" are painted in vertical panels on both sides. An example can be seen in Cave 148 from the High Tang, where a huge *Bhaisajyaguru Sutra* illustration is painted on the left side of the east wall, next to the entrance. In its center is the Eastern Pure Land of Bhaisajyaguru. Similar to Western Pure Land sutra illustrations, this serene world is also symbolized by unparalleled splendid pavilions and pagodas (Fig.99). Joined to these tall buildings are platforms constructed in the clear pools of water. On the platforms are celestial musicians and dancers who play different musical instruments, singing and dancing. Though the instruments they play are heavenly ones, what is really presented is the grand musical culture of the Tang Dynasty. There are as many as 33 people dancing and playing music in this painting. The two

这些平台上,都有歌舞作乐的伎乐天。她们弹奏着各种乐器,虽然表现的是天乐,却展示了宏大的唐代音乐文化。这铺经变画的乐舞人数达33人,中央二人对舞,两侧各有两组乐队,演奏着箜篌、琵琶、横笛、拍板等乐器。这样庞大的乐队,可以称得上是最早的交响乐队了。从这些乐队的规模及乐器配置等方面,可以看出唐代中国音乐的发达状况。而净土世界中复杂的殿宇、楼阁则展示了唐代建筑的完美结构。中央大殿前面是大平台,这一平台前面延伸出来,通过一座小桥又与画面最前部的一组平台相连。这一组平台为三联式,中央为"凹"字形平台,两侧各有一方形平台,平台之间各有虹桥相连。中央大殿的后面有长廊,通向两旁的侧殿。而长廊后面可见两层殿宇,其两侧也各有两层楼阁,在左右两个角建有圆形亭。这些复杂的建筑令人想起唐代宫殿建筑的雄伟气象,反映

in the middle dance in a pair, on either side of whom are two orchestra ensembles, playing musical instruments including the *konghou*, *pipa*, bamboo flute, and clappers. An ensemble of this size deserves to be called the earliest symphonic orchestra. From the size of the ensembles and the configuration of the musical instruments, we can see how advanced Chinese music was during the Tang Dynasty. Additionally, the complex pavilions and temples demonstrate the perfection of Tang style architecture. In front of the main hall is a large platform, which extends forward and is joined by a small bridge to a group of platforms in the front part of the picture. The group of platforms is made up of three sections. The one in the middle is in a U-shape, and on either side of it is a square platform. Rainbow-shaped bridges connect the platforms. At the back of the main hall is a corridor leading to the halls on both sides. Behind the corridor is a two-storeyed hall, on each side of which is a two-storeyed tower. In each of the left and right corners is a round pavilion. These elaborate structures remind us of the majestic palaces and temples of the Tang Dynasty, and they represent the brilliant architectural achievements in ancient China.

Bhaisajyaguru Sutra illustrations increased in Dunhuang during the Middle and Late Tang, becoming more popular. In an era of social unrest, people hoped that the Bhaisajyaguru Buddha could protect them from unexpected disasters. After the Late Tang and the Five

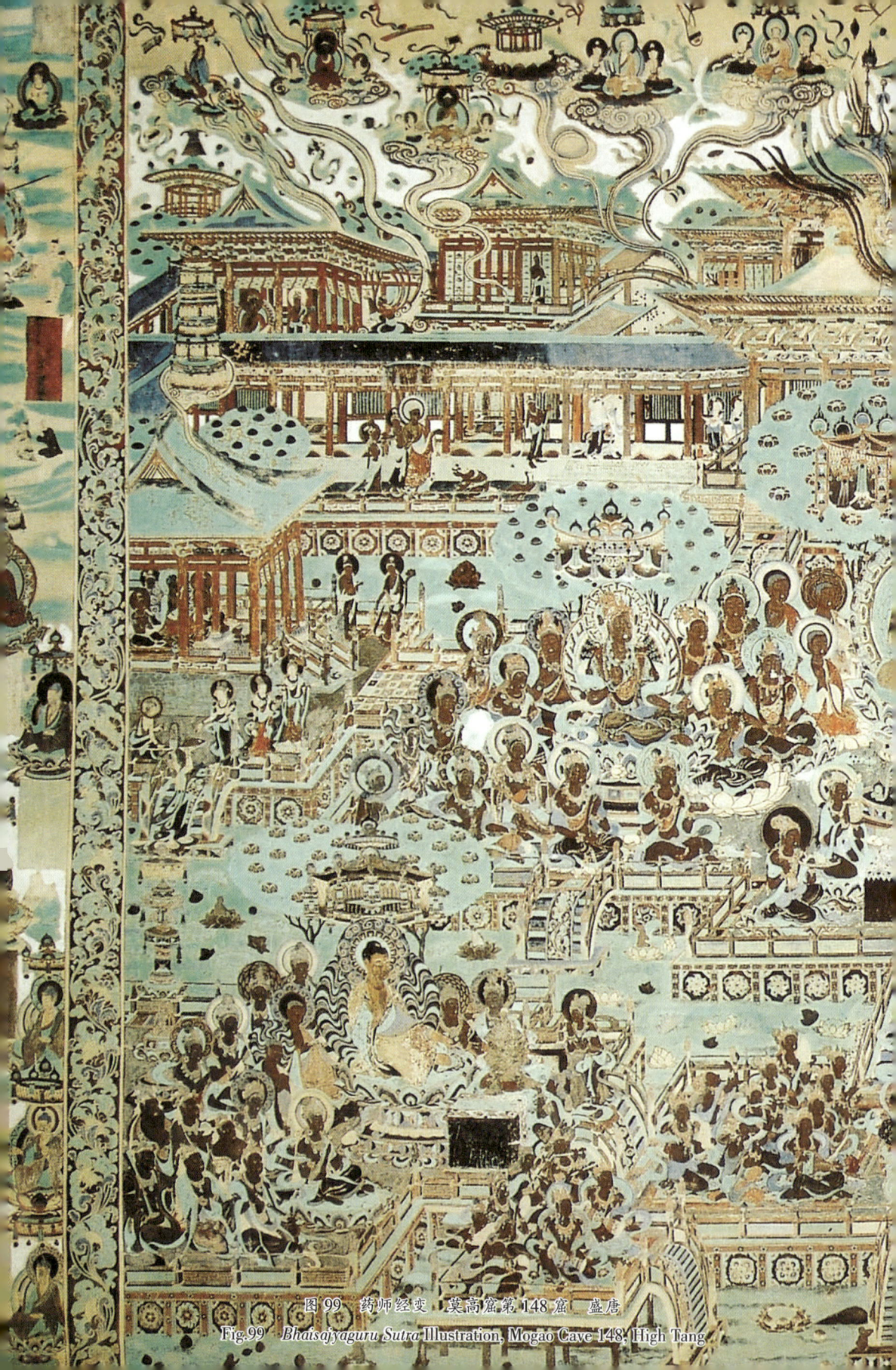

图 99 药师经变 莫高窟第 148 窟 盛唐
Fig.99 *Bhaiṣajyaguru Sutra* Illustration, Mogao Cave 148, High Tang

了中国古代建筑艺术的辉煌成就。

中晚唐以后，药师经变画在敦煌更为流行。在社会动荡不安的时代，人们希望得到药师的保佑，避免那些意想不到的灾难。晚唐、五代以后，药师经变画的构图形式有一点改变，就是往往把画于两侧的"九横死""十二大愿"的内容画在下部的屏风式画面中，而中心的东方净土世界图则没有大的变化。

Dynasties, the composition of *Bhaisajyaguru Sutra* illustrations changed a bit. Instead of painting the "Nine Violent Deaths" and the "Twelve Great Vows" in vertical panels on both sides, they were normally arranged in the lower register, in the form of screen paintings. No obvious changes occurred in the central section, however, with its scene of the Eastern Pure Land.

法华经变
Lotus Sutra Illustrations

《法华经》是《妙法莲华经》的简称，是佛教传入中国后最流行的经典之一，南北朝时期有多种译本，其中鸠摩罗什翻译的《妙法莲华经》最受欢迎，敦煌壁画中也大多依据《妙法莲华经》绘制经变画。《法华经》强调大乘是佛教的唯一法门，强调众生通过自己的觉悟而获得佛性，并指出了许多方便法门，任何人只要护持、诵读、书写《法华经》就可能成佛。《法华经》中还塑造了一个大慈大悲、救苦救难的观世音菩萨的形象，人们在危难之时，只要口念观世音菩萨名号，即可得救。于是，长期以来，观世音菩萨在中国深入人心，可以说是家喻户晓，《法华经》也因此得到最广泛的传播。

敦煌北魏石窟中就已出现了《法华经》的内容。如第259窟中龛内就塑出释迦、多宝二佛并坐的形象。同样的

The title *Saddharmapuṇḍarīka Sutra*, meaning *The Sutra of the White Lotus of the True Dharma*, is simplified in English as the *Lotus Sutra*. It became one of the most widespread sutras after Buddhism spread into China. During the Northern and Southern Dynasties, there were several versions in Chinese, the most popular of which had been translated by Kumārajīva. The majority of the sutra illustrations in Dunhuang are based on the text of the *Lotus Sutra*, which stresses that Mahayana is the only way leading to Buddhahood, and that all beings acquire Buddhahood through their own enlightenment. The sutra also introduces many practical approaches or "Dharma doors", maintaining that anyone can become a Buddha as long as he reveres, recites, and copies the *Lotus Sutra*. It also portrays the image of Avalokitesvara, who shows great mercy on people and who delivers people from suffering and distress; as long as they chant his name, they will be delivered from danger. Consequently, Avalokitesvara became a household name and has long been venerated by the Chinese people. The *Lotus Sutra* thus became the most widely disseminated sutra in China.

Themes from the *Lotus Sutra* appeared in Dunhuang caves as early as the Northern Wei.

形象，在西魏第285窟北壁、北周428窟西壁也以壁画的形式表现出来。经典中记载，佛在为弟子们宣讲《法华经》之时，突然从地下冒出一座宝塔，弟子们十分不解；佛告诉大家在若干年前，有一位叫多宝的佛曾预言："我灭度以后，于十方国土中有说《法华经》处，我将涌现其前作证明。"此塔当是多宝塔。佛正说着，宝塔便开了，里面的多宝佛让出一坐，请释迦入内，于是二佛并坐为大众说法。

隋代以后，壁画中描绘了很多《法华经》中的内容。如第420窟的顶部描绘出了《法华经》的《序品》《方便品》《见宝塔品》《化城喻品》和《观世音菩萨普门品》等内容，是法华经变的早期形式。隋代第303窟顶部还单独描绘了《观世音菩萨普门品》的内容。到了唐代，法华经变画的艺术形式才臻于完善，其代表性的作品是绘于盛唐

For example, statues of Sakyamuni and Prabhutaratna sit side by side in the niche of Cave 259. Similar images were also presented in murals on the north wall of Cave 285 of the Western Wei and the west wall of Cave 428 of the Northern Zhou respectively. According to Buddhist scriptures, the Buddha was lecturing to his disciples on the *Lotus Sutra*, when suddenly a stupa emerged from underground. The disciples were completely bewildered. The Buddha explained to them that many years ago, a Buddha named Prabhutaratna predicted, "After my nirvana there will be an occasion when a lecture on the *Lotus Sutra* will be given in a certain land in the universe, and I will spring up in front of him to witness the scene". The Sakyamuni Buddha went on to explain, "This must be the stupa of Prabhutaratna." While he was talking, the door of the pagoda opened and Prabhutaratna inside moved over, making space for Sakyamuni, and invited him in. Thus they sat side by side, preaching the Dharma to all.

After the Sui Dynasty, a great deal of thematic material from the *Lotus Sutra* appeared in murals. For example, on the ceiling of Cave 420 are paintings illustrating sections from the sutra including the "Introductory Chapter", "Chapter on Expedient Means", "Chapter on the Vision of the Jeweled Stupa", "Chapter on the Parable of the Conjured City", "Chapter on the Universal Gate of Bodhisattva Avalokitesvara", and so on. These are the earlier forms of *Lotus Sutra* illustrations. On the ceiling of Cave 303 from the Sui Dynasty,

第217窟南壁的法华经变画。

第217窟是一个方形覆斗顶窟,正面开一大龛,北壁绘观无量寿经变画,南壁绘法华经变画。两铺经变画都是唐代经变画的代表作品。法华经变画中央绘佛于灵鹫山说法的景象,这里表现《序品》中灵鹫会的盛大场面:释迦牟尼于中央说法,周围众菩萨围绕。在佛的上部有一座上部宽下部窄的山峰,这就是灵鹫山。山上有诸多宫殿楼阁,表现的是释迦牟尼的白毫照耀东方万八千世界中的色究竟天,即佛教所说的十八重天上的最上一层天。

画面的左右及下部,分别绘制《法华经》诸品的内容,呈"凹"字形环抱着中央的画面。这一区域并没有按一定的顺序来表现各品,而是根据画面的构图安排,利用山水、树木把全画联系起来,使经变画整体成为一幅规模宏大的山水人物画。特别引人注目的是画面右侧

"Chapter on the Universal Gate of Bodhisattva Avalokitesvara" appears as an independent work. However, it was not until the Tang Dynasty that the artistic forms of *Lotus Sutra* illustrations reached their perfection. The south wall in Cave 217, from the High Tang, contains just such a quintessential painting.

Cave 217 is a square cave with a truncated pyramid ceiling. A huge niche is constructed in the main wall. On the north wall is an *Amitayurdhyana Sutra* illustration, while on the south wall is a *Lotus Sutra* illustration. Both of them are representative works of the Tang Dynasty. A scene of the Buddha preaching the Dharma at Vulture Peak occupies the center of the *Lotus Sutra* illustration. This is a rendering of the grand gathering at Vulture Peak where Sakyamuni preaches the Dharma at the center, surrounded by all the bodhisattvas, as recorded in the "Introductory Chapter" of the *Lotus Sutra*. Above the Buddha is a mountain peak with a wide top and a narrow bottom, representing Vulture Peak. Palaces, temples, and pavilions are constructed on top of it, indicating that this is Akaniṣṭha, the highest level of the 18 pure abodes among the 18,000 worlds to the East, which is illuminated by the light-beaming white whorl of hair (*ūrṇā*) between the Sakyamuni Buddha's eyebrows.

On both sides and in the lower register of the painting, arranged in a U-shaped layout, are different chapters of the *Lotus Sutra*, embracing

表现《法华经·化城喻品》的内容,画出了一幅完整的青绿山水图(此图将在下一章详细介绍)。

在左侧的画面中,表现了《方便品》《如来神力品》《妙庄严王本事品》等内容。其中表现《方便品》中拜塔斋僧的内容:画面中央空地上有一座宝塔,一些人正在塔前礼拜;塔后面是一座寺院的走廊,廊下并列坐着四位僧人,廊前空地上还有三位俗人正陪着僧人们吃斋;右侧的院子里走出僮仆、婢女分别提壶、托盘正忙着给僧人们送饮食。这些生动的画面,正是唐代寺院生活的真实写照。

在经变画下部中央表现《药王菩萨本事品》中"如子得母、如病得医"的内容:在一座柳树荫的庭院里,一位妇人正坐在正房内华丽的床上,另一位妇女怀抱婴儿相对而坐;在屋外的院子里,一位瘦骨嶙峋的医生拄杖而来,身后一侍女捧着药箱,小心翼翼地跟随而来;

the scene in the center. Rather than arranging the chapters in order, the layout is determined instead by the compositions of the pictures. The artist made use of mountains, rivers, and trees to connect the whole work so that the sutra illustration appears to be a grand painting of landscapes and figures. Worthy of special attention is its right section, which presents the "Chapter on the Parable of the Conjured City" from the *Lotus Sutra*. It is an example of a complete blue-green landscape painting, which is to be examined in detail in the next chapter.

The left side of the painting presents sections such as "Chapter on Expedient Means", "Chapter on the Spiritual Powers of the Tathāgata", "Chapter on the Past Deeds of King Wonderful-Adornment", and others. Subjects such as stupa worship and monastic meals from the "Chapter on Expedient Means" are rendered here. The scene reveals a stupa in an empty space in the center. In front of the stupa some people engage in worship; a covered corridor to a temple is behind the stupa. Four monks are seated side by side in the corridor, while three lay followers sit in the open space in front of the corridor, accompanying the monks over their meal. Servants and maids come out into the yard on the right side, carrying kettles and trays, busily offering food and drink to the monks. These lifelike depictions are an accurate portrayal of life in Buddhist temples during the Tang Dynasty.

前有一少女引路,少女面带忧愁,一副弱不禁风的样子。《法华经》中说信奉《法华经》可以得到12种快乐,"如子得母、如病得医"就是其中两种快乐。这本是一种比喻,但画家却描绘出了当时社会生活的一个真实的场景,使我们能够从中看到1000多年前普通人的生活景象。其价值远远超过了本来的宗教意义。

在法华经变画流行的盛唐时代,还出现了全窟绘制法华经变画的第23窟,有人把这个洞窟称作法华窟。本窟西壁开龛,除了顶部北披和西披以外,南、北、东三壁及顶南披和东披画的都是法华经变的内容,详尽地描绘了《法华经》的《药草喻品》《方便品》《信解品》《见宝塔品》(图100)等13项内容。特别是北壁中央主要绘"灵鹫会",南壁中央绘"虚空会",以这样的空间形式来图解《法华

The center of the lower register presents the analogies, "like a child finding his mother" and "like a sick person finding a doctor", as recorded in the "Chapter on the Past Deeds of the Medicine King Bodhisattva". In the scene, a woman sits on a magnificent bed in the main chamber next to a willow-shaded courtyard; another woman sits opposite her, carrying a baby at her breast. In the courtyard outside the chamber, a doctor arrives, bony and emaciated, with the aid of a walking stick; following the doctor a maid comes carrying a medicine chest with the utmost care. A young girl guides their way, looking frail and heavy-hearted. According to the *Lotus Sutra*, those who have faith in the sutra may receive 12 kinds of happiness, two of which are likened to "a child finding his mother" and "a sick person finding a doctor". Originally this was meant to be just an analogy, but the artist painted an accurate reflection of the social life of the time, enabling us to see the authentic condition of common people over 1,000 years ago. The value of the painting goes far beyond its original religious significance.

In the High Tang, the *Lotus Sutra* became so popular that there were even cave temples devoted exclusively to illustrating it, such as Cave 23. Thus, some have called it the *Lotus Sutra* Cave. This cave has a niche cut in the west wall. Except for the northern and western slopes of the ceiling, all other surfaces are covered with *Lotus Sutra* illustrations. Thirteen individual subjects such as the "Chapter on Medicinal Herbs", "Chapter on

图 100　法华经见宝塔品　莫高窟第 23 窟顶南披　盛唐
Fig.100　Vision of the Jeweled Stupa from the *Lotus Sutra*, Southern Slope of Ceiling, Mogao Cave 23, High Tang

经》的义理,表明了洞窟壁画有着完整的设计思想。另外,不少细节描绘也十分生动有趣,如北壁的《药草喻品》,描绘了一幅雨中耕作的图景。画面上部乌云密布,暴雨倾盆,一位农夫正在冒雨辛勤地耕作,另一位农夫挑着东西冒雨疾行。画面下部,表现在地头休息的农家三人,右侧是父子俩正吃饭,给他们送来午饭的农妇坐在左侧和父子俩聊天。多么恬静的一幅田园生活场景(图101)!

《法华经·观世音菩萨普门品》往往被信徒们单独诵读,简称作《观音经》。隋代的壁画中已出现了观音经变画,唐代第23窟和217窟在表现法华经变时,又以单独的壁面来描绘《观世音普门品》的内容。第45窟南壁则整壁绘制了观音经变画,中央画观世音菩萨立像,两侧上部画观世音菩萨现身说法,下部画观世音救苦救难的情节。观世音信仰主要是由于观世音能在人们受难之时前来救助。经中说若在大

Expedient Means", "Chapter on Belief and Understanding", and "Chapter on the Vision of the Jeweled Stupa" are painted in detail (Fig.100). Special attention should be paid to scenes including the gathering at Vulture Peak in the central section of the north wall, as well as the scene of the audience rising into the sky to see the two Buddhas, Sakyamuni and Prabhutaratna, in the floating jeweled stupa, located in the central section of the south wall. It is evident that murals in this cave were painted based on an overarching concept of design, for spatial form is used to illustrate the principles of the *Lotus Sutra*. In addition to this, many detailed, slice-of-life depictions are also quite interesting. For example, the "Chapter on Medical Herbs" on the north wall presents a scene of farming in the rain. Thick clouds have gathered in the upper part, and it is raining hard. One farmer works arduously, while another carries something on a shoulder pole as he hurries through the downpour. In the lower register, a family of three relaxes in the field. On the right, the father and son enjoy their meal, and on the left, a country woman sits and chats with them, having just delivered their meal. Without doubt, it presents a peaceful and idyllic scene of daily life (Fig.101).

The "Chapter on the Universal Gate of Bodhisattva Avalokitesvara" of the *Lotus Sutra* is usually read as an independent scripture by adherents, so the chapter is known as the

海中航行之时，遇到大风浪，且有各种魔怪缠绕时，只要口念观世音名号，就可得到解脱。依据这一内容，在壁画的右侧画出大海中有一条大帆船，船周围的水中有很多凶猛的怪物向船

Avalokitesvara Sutra for short. *Avalokitesvara Sutra* illustrations appeared in wall paintings as early as the Sui Dynasty. When *Lotus Sutra* illustrations were painted in Caves 23 and 217 from the Tang Dynasty, separate walls were allocated for content from the "Chapter on the Universal Gate of Bodhisattva Avalokitesvara". The entire south wall of Cave 45 is devoted to an *Avalokitesvara Sutra* illustration. At the center is a standing image of Avalokitesvara, and

图 101　雨中耕作　莫高窟第 23 窟北壁　盛唐
Fig.101　Scene of Plowing in the Rain, North Wall of Mogao Cave 23, High Tang

攻击,船上的人们心惊胆战,有两人跪在船上,大家都双手合十。这一画面虽是图解经文,但也反映了当时海上航行的某些历史场面(图102)。在壁画的右侧还描绘了一群商人牵着毛驴,带着很多行李在山中行进,突然从山后窜出来几个手执武器的强盗,商人们诚惶诚恐,战战兢兢,前面的商人已把行李放在地上。这是表现《观音经》所说:"若有商人遇到强盗,性命财产不保之时,只要口念观世音菩萨名号,自然得到解脱"。画中强盗的骄横凶狠、商人们害怕求饶的表情描绘得栩栩如生。在胡商遇盗图的上部,还画出一个窈窕美丽的少女,旁边有一男士正拱手向着她说话。这是表现经中所说的"离淫欲"的内容。本来,佛经中说若

on both sides, the upper registers contain scenes with manifestations of Avalokitesvara preaching the Dharma, while the lower registers contain scenes of Avalokitesvara saving people from suffering and distress. Faith in Avalokitesvara is mainly based on the belief that Avalokitesvara can come to the rescue of people who are suffering and in danger. It is stated in the sutra that when people are voyaging at sea, and if they get caught in storms or are threatened by monsters, these disasters can be dispelled by chanting the name of Avalokitesvara. Based on these texts, a huge ship is depicted on the right side of the mural, sailing in the sea. Many fierce monsters attack the ship from surrounding waters as all the men on board tremble in fear. They fold their hands devoutly in prayer; two men kneel on the deck. Though the image is painted to illustrate Buddhist scriptures, it does reflect some of the historical details of sea navigation at that time (Fig.102). On the right side of the mural, a group of merchants are painted advancing through the mountains. They drive their donkeys, carrying heavy loads of cargo. Suddenly, armed robbers rush out from behind the hills. The merchants are panic-stricken, trembling with fear, and those in the lead of the group have already laid their baggage down on the ground. This is to illustrate what is recorded in the *Avalokitesvara Sutra*. When merchants meet robbers and their life and property are in danger, they will surely be saved as long as they call on Avalokitesvara. In the picture, the robbers are arrogant and fierce; the merchants are terrified and beg for mercy. Their emotional expressions are precisely captured and depicted with realism. Over the scene of merchants waylaid by robbers, a young man talks respectfully to a

Art Treasures: Murals and Painted Sculptures in Mogao Caves

图 102　观音救难　莫高窟第 45 窟南壁　盛唐
Fig.102　Avalokitesvara Saving Those in Peril, South Wall of Mogao Cave 45, High Tang

有人被淫欲困扰，不能解脱，只要口念观世音菩萨名号，即得解脱。而壁画上却画出了一位男士向少女求爱的场面。画面的上部表现观音现身说法，有时现天王身，有时现大将军身，有时

gentle and beautiful maiden. This theme of "fleeing from lust" is mentioned in the scriptures. According to Buddhist scriptures, if one is stranded by lust and cannot free himself, he can chant the name of Avalokitesvara to be extricated. However, a young man courting a maiden also appears in the murals. The upper register of the painting displays scenes of Avalokitesvara in his various manifestations, preaching the Dharma in different situations.

239

现女人身等等，根据情况以不同的身相为人们说法。画家以写实的手法，表现了观音的种种现身，再现了唐代不同身份的人物的形象，反映了当时社会的生活风貌。

Sometimes he is in the guise of a Heavenly King, sometimes he is a great general, and sometimes he appears as a woman. The artist portrayed various forms of Avalokitesvara by adopting a style of realism, representing people from different walks of life in the Tang Dynasty, and reflecting the styles and scenes of the age.

报恩经变及其他经变画
Sutra of Requiting Kindness Received Illustrations and Others

敦煌壁画中的经变画总计有30多种,包括了依据大乘佛经及密教经典所绘的经变画。现存的遗迹中,像敦煌壁画这样数量庞大、艺术精湛的经变画是任何地方都无法比拟的,可以说是经变画的宝库。以上几种是其中最流行的经变画,也是在艺术上较有特色的经变画,还有很多其他经变画,都大大丰富了佛教艺术的内容。由于经变画表现的领域很广,从不同的侧面反映了当时的社会生活,为我们提供了生动的历史画面,其意义远远超出了佛教思想的范畴。

报恩经变画是依据《大方便佛报恩经》而绘的。这部佛经不是从印度传来的,而是中国的僧人为适应中国的国情编造的佛经,在佛教界把这样的经典称作"伪经"。它融合了儒、佛两家的

There are altogether over 30 varieties of sutra illustrations in Dunhuang wall paintings, including those created according to the scriptures of Mahayana Buddhism as well as Esoteric Buddhism. Among such historical relics preserved today, Dunhuang murals, with their large numbers and exquisite art, are unparalleled in any other place in the world. It is safe to say that Dunhuang is a treasure house for sutra illustrations. The types of sutra illustrations that have been introduced above are not only the most prevalent but also the most distinguished in terms of artistic features. There are, however, many other types, and all of them contribute greatly to the enrichment of Buddhist art. Due to the wide range of subject matter presented, sutra illustrations reflect different aspects of the social conditions at that time. Providing us with lifelike historical images, their significance goes far beyond the scope of Buddhist religious ideology.

The full title of the *Sutra of Requiting Kindness Received* is the *Sutra of the Great Good Means by Which the Buddha Requites Blessings Received*. The sutra itself did not originate in India but was compiled by Chinese monks, who adapted it to conditions in China. In Buddhism this group of texts is known as the Apocrypha. Apocryphal texts synthesizes the thinking of Confucianism and Buddhism and advocates the

思想,宣扬报恩精神,即所谓"上报佛恩、中报君亲恩、下报众生恩"。其中又以中报君亲恩为重点。这样的思想与儒家的忠孝思想完全一致。《报恩经》中的故事大多从别的佛经中选取符合报恩思想的内容改编而成。由于《报恩经》主要通过很多故事来说理,易为大众所接受,因此在唐代以后,《报恩经》十分流行。据经典所绘的报恩经变画也自然流行了起来。盛唐以后,莫高窟壁画中出现了报恩经变画,到晚唐五代更为盛行。

报恩经变画中的很多故事,其实在北朝时期就已出现了,但同样的故事却是依据别的经典所绘,如"恶友品"就是北朝的善事太子入海故事,"孝养品"即须阇提割肉奉亲的故事。此外还有一些新出现的故事,如"论议品",讲罗波奈国山上住着一仙人,仙人常于泉边便溺,一雌鹿常于泉边饮水,不久

spirit of repaying kindness, referring to "requiting the greatest kindness of the Buddha, the middle kindness of the Emperor and parents, and the lower kindness of all sentient beings". The concept of requiting the kindness of the emperor and parents was especially emphasized among the three. Ideologies like this were consistent with the Confucian conception of loyalty and filial piety. Tales in the *Sutra of Requiting Kindness Received* were mostly selected and rewritten from other Buddhist sutras that focused on themes of repaying kind deeds. Since the ideas in it were mainly explained by tales and easily accepted by ordinary people, the sutra was very popular during the Tang Dynasty. Naturally, paintings based on it became popular as well. *Sutra of Requiting Kindness Received* illustrations appeared among the murals in the Mogao Caves beginning with the High Tang, and during the Late Tang and the Five Dynasties they became even more prevalent.

In fact, many of these tales appeared as early as the Northern Dynasties. However, similar tales were painted on the basis of other Buddhist canonical texts. For example, the "Chapter on the Evil Friend" was the tale of Prince Kalyāṇakārin seeking treasure from the sea; the "Chapter on Filial Piety" was actually the tale of Prince Sujata cutting his own flesh to feed his parents. There were also new tales such as "Chapter on Discourses" and "Chapter on Close Relationships". "Chapter on Discourses" is a narrative. In the mountains of Vārānasi, there lived an immortal who used to urinate by a spring. A doe often came to the spring to drink water. Before long the doe

鹿产一女，与人无异，不能养育，便送至仙人处，仙人将女养大，美丽无比。一日国王入山游猎，见鹿女美貌，便娶为夫人。不久鹿女怀孕,生下一朵大大的莲花。国王十分失望,贬夫人为普通宫女,将莲花抛入池中。一日国王与群臣在池边游戏,忽见池中莲花发出灿烂的光芒，便派人察看，原来莲花中有500儿。国王知为鹿母所生,便向鹿母悔过,重新封为第一夫人。500个儿子长大后,力敌千人。邻国有侵略者，自往讨伐，每战必胜。从此四境安宁，国家昌盛（图103）。

"亲近品"讲的是金毛狮子坚誓的故事。波罗奈国仙圣山中有一狮子名叫坚誓，毛呈金色，美丽无比,英姿威武。它经常接近沙门,听僧人们诵讲佛经。有一猎师对金毛狮子早已垂涎三尺,他想射死狮子，把皮毛献给国

gave birth to a daughter who appeared completely human. The doe was unable to raise the girl, so she handed the baby over to the immortal. The immortal brought up the doe's daughter, who was incomparably beautiful. One day the King went hunting in the mountains. He was struck by the beauty of the girl, married her, and made her Queen. Before long the doe's daughter became pregnant and gave birth to a huge lotus. The King was so disappointed that he demoted the Queen to the rank of ordinary palace maid and threw the lotus she birthed into a pool of water. One day the King and his ministers were cavorting by the pool when he saw the lotus shining brightly in the water. He sent his men to investigate: it turned out there were 500 sons within the lotus. The King realized that they were born from the Mother Deer, so he repented to her and reinstated her as Queen again. When the 500 sons grew up, each of them was strong enough to resist 1,000 men. Whenever there were invaders from neighboring countries, they would fight and defeat the enemy. Thus the kingdom enjoyed lasting peace and prosperity (Fig.103).

The "Chapter on Close Relationships" relates a tale about a golden-furred lion. In the enchanted mountains of Vārānasi, there was a lion called Resolute Vow. He had beautiful golden fur and looked incomparably fascinating and majestic. He always went close to the śramaṅas, listening to the monks chanting and reciting sutras. A hunter had long been casting his greedy eyes upon the lion. He wanted to shoot the lion and offer his fur to the king so that he could get a large reward. However, he feared that the lion was brave and fierce, and it was

图 103 鹿母夫人的故事 莫高窟第 85 窟 晚唐
Fig.103 Tale of the Mother Deer, Mogao Cave 85, Late Tang

王;以获重赏。可是又害怕狮子勇猛,难以下手。于是,他伪装成一个虔诚的信徒,吸引狮子亲近,最后用毒箭射死了狮子。狮子深受佛教熏陶,中箭未死之时,并不对猎师进行报复。猎师剥了狮子的皮献给国王。当国王得知狮子皮的来历后,十分痛心,即处死猎师,用香火焚化了狮子的遗骸,收取舍利,建塔供养(图104)。

在中唐第231窟中详细描绘了鹿母夫人的故事,这个

hard to kill him. As a result, the man pretended to be a devout Buddhist, ensnared the lion into a close relationship with him, and finally shot him with a poisonous arrow. But the lion was a pious Buddhist; even though he had been shot, he did not take any revenge upon the hunter as he was dying. The hunter skinned the lion and offered the fur to the King. When the King learned how the lion's skin was obtained, he was extremely distressed. He put the hunter to death without hesitation, burned the lion's body over a funeral pyre of sandalwood, collected the relics, and built a stupa for worship (Fig.104).

Cave 231, built during the Middle Tang,

图104　金毛狮子坚誓的故事　莫高窟第85窟　晚唐
Fig.104　Tale of Resolute Vow, the Golden-Furred Lion, Mogao Cave 85, Late Tang

故事成为各时代报恩经变中较多选绘的题材。在中唐第112窟的报恩经变画中,上部两侧画出鹿母夫人的故事,左侧画一鹿在池边喝水,后面是幽静的山谷,山洞里有一仙人正在坐禅修行。右侧的画面表现国王领着随从骑马入山的情景(图105)。画的背景是奇崛的山崖,体现出中唐以后水墨山水画的风格。壁画的下部描绘"亲近品",即金毛狮子坚誓的故事。画一比丘正在讲经,很多人围在一起听经。左侧画一猎人向金毛狮子射箭的场面,右侧画猎人向国王献狮皮的情节。

晚唐第85窟的报恩经变画是内容较丰富,描绘较成功的代表作品。中央表现佛说法会,上部右侧画鹿母夫人的故事,左侧画金毛狮子坚誓的故事。下部左侧画"恶友品"(善事太子入海的故事),右侧画"孝养品"。以山水

contains a detailed painting of the "Tale of the Mother Deer", as it is one of the most frequent themes among the *Sutra of Requiting Kindness Received* illustrations throughout different historical periods. The painting in Cave 112 of the Middle Tang presents the tale on both sides of its upper register. On the left, a doe drinks water by the pool, with a secluded, peaceful valley in the background. In a mountain cave an immortal sits in meditation, cultivating himself spiritually. On the right, the scene shows the King on horseback advancing into the mountains with his men (Fig.105). The back ground is composed of strangely-shaped mountain cliffs, revealing the ink-and-wash style of land scape painting after the Middle Tang. The lower register presents the "Chapter on Close Relationships", the tale of the lion named Resolute Vow. In the picture a *bhikṣu* gives a lecture on a Buddhist sutra and many people gather around him listening. On the left side the hunter shoots at the golden-furred lion, and on the right side the hunter offers the lion's skin to the king.

The *Sutra of Requiting Kindness Received* illustration in Cave 85 of the Late Tang is a quintessential work, more substantial and successful in execution than others. In the center is a gathering with the Buddha preaching the Dharma. The right side of the upper register is the tale of the Mother Deer, while the left side depicts the tale of the golden-furred lion, Resolute Vow. The left side of the lower register contains the "Chapter on Evil Friends" (the *jataka* tale of Prince Kalyāṇakārin), and the right side presents the tale from "Chapter on Filial Piety". Events from the tales are developed

图105　报恩经变　莫高窟第112窟北壁　中唐
Fig.105　*Sutra of Requiting Kindness Received* Illustration, North Wall of Mogao Cave 112, Middle Tang

Art Treasures: Murals and Painted Sculptures in Mogao Caves

图 106 屠夫 莫高窟第 85 窟窟顶东披 晚唐
Fig.106 Scene of a Butcher, Eastern Slope of Ceiling, Mogao Cave 85, Late Tang

自然景物为背景来展开故事情节，具有画面统一而又真实可感的特点。如表现善事太子入海求珠的过程，包括善事太子眼睛被刺、成为盲人，在树下弹琴自娱、与公主邂逅等场面，描绘得细腻而生动，展示了画家的艺术水平。

除了报恩经变画外，壁画中还有金光明经变、华严

against a background of natural scenery such as mountains and rivers. The composition is thus unified and appears realistic and coherent. A good example is the tale of Prince Kalyāṇakārin seeking treasure from the sea. The events are clearly delineated, including scenes such as the Prince's eyes being stabbed, the Prince playing a musical instrument under the tree, and the Prince's unexpected encounter with the princess. The descriptions are exquisite and true to life, reflecting the artistic level of the painter.

In addition to the *Sutra of Requiting Kindness Received* illustrations, there are yet

249

经变、金刚经变、楞伽经变等经变画。由于佛经内容较为抽象,壁画中大多以表现佛说法的场面为主。其中穿插一些图解佛经的情节,也颇有生活气息。如楞伽经变画中画出了屠夫卖肉的场面(图106),工人制作陶器的场面等,使我们对古代社会增加了许多感性认识。

more sutra illustrations, including the *Golden Light Sutra* illustrations, *Flower Garland Sutra* illustrations, *Diamond Sutra* illustrations, *Laṅkāvatāra Sutra* illustrations, and more. The contents of these Buddhist sutras are abstract to some extent, so the murals are mostly dominated by scenes of the Buddha preaching the Dharma. There are also some situations inserted to illustrate the sutras, lending a touch of verisimilitude to the paintings. Examples can be found in the *Laṅkāvatāra Sutra* illustration, in which are portrayed scenes of a butcher selling meat and a craftsman making pottery (Fig.106). They give us considerable awareness of social life during ancient times.

经变画的艺术成就
Artistic Achievements in Sutra Illustrations

唐代以后,中国绘画在空间处理方面取得了令人瞩目的成果,这就是在平面的画面中,描绘出接近于三度空间的场景。这一点体现在唐代流行的经变画中。当然这样的空间表现方法还不能算是科学的透视法,但在公元7世纪至8世纪的时代,能表现出较为真实的空间关系来,在当时也是令人吃惊的事情。因而,经变画深受人们喜爱而在各地流行起来。据《历代名画记》等文献的记载,当时首都长安以及东都洛阳的寺院里,绘制了大量的经变画。经变画是隋唐以来中国石窟及寺院壁画的主要绘画形式,是最富有中国特色的佛教艺术形式。

建筑画是经变画中的重要组成部分,尤其是在净土图式的经变画中,如果没有建筑恐怕也就没法表现净土世界了。隋代画家展子虔和杨契丹都以建筑画而著名,而当时宫

During the Tang period, Chinese painting made remarkable achievements in the treatment of space and depth, creating scenery that appeared three-dimensional on a flat surface. This can be seen in sutra illustrations popular throughout the Tang era. Of course, such a spatial representation method was far from the use of perspective today, but it was amazing that fairly realistic use of space could be shown in paintings as early as the 7th and 8th centuries. As a result, people enjoyed them so much that sutra illustrations became popular everywhere. According to works such as *Famous Paintings through the Ages*, huge numbers of sutra illustrations were created at the time not only in temples in the capital city Chang'an, but also in temples of the eastern capital Luoyang. During the Sui and the Tang dynasties, sutra illustrations, the dominant genre of wall paintings in caves and temples throughout China, were Buddhist art forms conveying the most profound Chinese characteristics.

Architectural paintings are an important part of sutra illustrations, especially in those representing the Pure Land. Without architectural structures, it would be impossible to portray such realms. Artists Zhan Ziqian and Yang Qidan of the Sui Dynasty were both

殿建筑实物也给画家们提供了写生的对象。《历代名画记》曾记载当时的画家杨契丹长于画建筑,郑法士想要借他的画本(底稿),"杨引郑至朝堂,指宫阙、衣冠、车马曰:此是吾画本也。由是郑深叹服"。说明那时的画家是以现实的宫殿建筑为依据来画的。由于这些画家们的努力,使隋唐时代的建筑画达到了极高的水平。特别是唐代以后的建筑画在表现远近的空间关系方面取得了很大的成果。

这些建筑都是中轴对称的形式,中央描绘一座大殿,两侧又有数幢殿堂,建筑物之间以回廊相通,通常在画面下部还要绘出平台。当然,画里表现的建筑群也并不是唐代建筑的完整再现,可能仅仅是那时佛寺的大殿及相关的建筑。画家们主要是通过这些建筑来作为佛说法的背景,并象

renowned for their architectural paintings, and it was true that real structures in palaces provided them with objects for sketching. According to *Famous Paintings through the Ages*, Yang Qidan excelled at painting buildings, and Zheng Fashi wanted to borrow his sketchbook. "Yang showed Zheng around the imperial palace, pointing at the buildings, clothing, carts, and horses, and said that those were his sketchbook. And Zheng gasped in deep admiration." The record reveals that artists of the time worked on their paintings on the basis of real palaces and buildings. Thanks to the efforts of these artists, the architectural paintings of the Sui and Tang dynasties reached a very high level. In particular, those painted during the Tang period made great accomplishments in expressing the spatial relationships concerning distance.

In Dunhuang mural art, all architectural paintings are axially symmetrical, with a large palace in the center and several halls on both sides. Corridors connect the different buildings, with platforms usually painted below. Of course, architectural complexes depicted in these paintings are not necessarily an exact representation of Tang Dynasty architecture. Most likely they are just halls and their related buildings in Buddhist temples of that time. The artists mainly painted these structures as backgrounds for the Dharma-preaching scenes and as symbols for the Buddhist world of the Pure Land. Thus they may not be entirely realistic, and probably there are elements of imagination at play. In contrast to representations of real buildings, when working on these paintings the artists often expressed the forms and positions of architectural

征佛教净土世界。因此,也许并不全是写实的,也会有想象的部分。相对于描绘真实的建筑,画家常常会从绘画构成的角度来表现建筑的形体及其位置。但从隋入唐,建筑画逐渐向三度空间发展则是一个大致的倾向。

画家们还采用山水与建筑相配合来表现空间关系。如有的阿弥陀经变画和观无量寿经变画中,在建筑物周围描绘一定的山水树木,把建筑物没有完成的一些空间补充了出来。如第172窟北壁的观无量寿经变画,在建筑物后面画出一些远景山水,给人以无限远之感。这样的方法改变了初唐那种舞台式背景的不足,而使画面的空间表现达到完满。中唐以后综合处理山水与建筑的经变画较多,通常建筑物作为近景,山水作为远景,把远近空间有机地联系起来。如中唐第231窟北壁的弥勒经变画,第112窟南壁的金刚经变画,晚唐第85窟南壁的报恩经变画等等。

印度、中亚的佛教美术虽

structures from the perspective of scene composition. However, from the Sui Dynasty through to the Tang Dynasty, it had been the general trend that architectural paintings were gradually developing toward three-dimensional space.

The artists also combine landscapes and architecture to express spatial relationships. Examples can be found in some of the *Amitabha Sutra* illustrations and *Amitayurdhyana Sutra* illustrations, in which mountains, rivers, trees, and grass are painted around the buildings, complementing the unfinished space. For example, in the *Amitayurdhyana Sutra* illustration on the north wall of Cave 172, some distant landscapes are painted behind the buildings, leaving an impression of infinite space. Such a method remedied the defects of the musical stage backgrounds from the Early Tang, enabling space to be more fully and completely expressed. After the Middle Tang, an increasing number of sutra illustrations treated scenery and architecture in an integrated manner, with buildings normally painted in the foreground while landscapes were painted in the background, organically connecting the spaces far and near. Examples are the Maitreya Triple Sutra illustration on the north wall of Cave 231, and the *Diamond Sutra* illustration on the south wall of Cave 112 from the Middle Tang, as well as the *Sutra of Requiting Kindness Received* on the south wall of Cave 85 from the Late Tang.

然也表现背景，但主要以人物为主，尤其是雕刻作品中几乎看不出对空间的表现。敦煌的经变画从隋朝开始出现，唐代兴盛起来，而且在空间表现方面形成了人物群像、建筑、山水等综合表现的方法。净土图式经变画中建筑艺术在这个时期达到极盛。盛唐以后，山水画的成分在经变画中不断增加，以山水画为主要背景的经变画也越来越多。建筑画和山水画的成熟而使唐代的经变画构成臻于完善。而经变画的意义不止于此，它表现出一个完美、丰富的净土世界，使佛教的理想境界变得十分具体可感。经变画表现的是佛国之境，然而，这些建筑、山水则是人间的风景，它反映了中国人对风景审美的需要。而这种审美风气又促使画家进行空间探索，从而形成了中国画空间处理的一些规律和特色，也形成了有别于印度和西域的中国式佛教绘画艺术。

The Buddhist art of India and Central Asia also shows background, but works are normally dominated by characters, and especially in sculptures, little is seen regarding spatial representation. Sutra illustrations began in Dunhuang during the Sui Dynasty, and flourished in the Tang Dynasty. Furthermore, an integrated method of representing groups of figures, architecture, and scenery was used to express space. The art of Pure Land sutra illustrations reached its zenith in this period. After the High Tang, landscape elements were increasingly added to painting composition, with ever more sutra illustrations including landscapes as background. The maturity of architectural and landscape paintings contributed to the perfection of sutra illustrations of the Tang period. However, the significance of sutra illustrations was more than that. They portrayed a perfect and profound world of the Pure Land, making this ideal realm of Buddhism concrete and comprehensible. They portrayed the Buddhist world, but the architecture and landscapes were scenery from the human world, reflecting the Chinese people's aesthetic desires. This type of aesthetic setting in turn promoted the artists' exploration of spatial relationships. Thus, not only were the rules and characteristics of spatial representation shaped in Chinese painting, but the unique art style of Chinese Buddhist paintings also emerged, different from that of India and the Western Regions.

艺苑瑰宝：莫高窟壁画与彩塑
Art Treasures: Murals and Painted Sculptures in Mogao Caves

青山绿水看唐风

Blue–Green Landscape: Styles of the Tang Dynasty

在敦煌石窟壁画中，除了有丰富的佛像画、经变画、故事画及装饰图案以外，还保存有绚丽多姿的山水画场景。这些数量可观的山水画，展示出了一部公元4世纪至14世纪系统的中国山水画史。从中不仅可以观赏到古代的山水画实例，还可以探寻北朝至元代1000年间石窟壁画中山水画发展演变的过程。

敦煌石窟是作为佛教信徒修持和礼拜场所开凿的，因此，壁画都是与佛教相关的内容，山水图像主要是作为装饰和人物活动的背景出现的。尽管如此，敦煌壁画中的山水画数量之多、描绘之精、时代延续之久在古代艺术中也是绝无仅有的。而在印度和西域壁画中，虽也画出一些植物和简单的象征性风景，但绝没有像敦煌壁画这样大量的山水画。表明了中国传统山水审美意识对佛教壁画的强烈影响。

Dunhuang wall paintings, in addition to being abundant in Buddhist iconography, sutra illustrations, Buddhist narratives, and decorative motifs, also include considerable numbers of gorgeous, varied landscapes, revealing the history of Chinese landscape painting from the 4th to the 14th centuries. Not only do the paintings provide classical examples for our appreciation today, but they also enable us to trace the development and evolution of landscapes among cave-temple murals during the 1000-year period which span from the Northern Dynasties to the Yuan Dynasty.

The Dunhuang caves were constructed for Buddhist adherents to carry out their religious rituals and to worship the Buddha; thus, the mural subjects all relate to Buddhism. Landscapes are painted primarily as ornamentation or background for the characters and their actions. However, because of the large collection of works, their exquisite presentation, and their long history of continuity, they are classical art unmatched by anything else. Although there are plants and basic stylized scenery seen in murals from India and the Western Regions, nowhere else provides so large a number of landscapes as Dunhuang. This indicates the strong influence of traditional Chinese aesthetics of landscape painting on Buddhist murals.

隋唐时代的山水画色彩丰富，称为青绿山水。到唐末、五代以后，水墨山水画逐渐成了山水画的主流。北宋以后，画论中出现了"着色山水"这个词，说明那时大多数山水画是不用色的。如果用了色，就得专门强调是着色的，而宋人仿唐的所谓"青绿山水"也与唐人的绘画有一定的距离。特别是水墨山水画兴起以后，唐代流行的那种青绿山水就渐渐受到冷淡。在唐代画家们的作品基本上失传了的今天，人们对唐代山水画的认识就显得十分不足。而敦煌壁画中现存大量的山水画正是解开中国宋代以前山水画史之谜的一把钥匙。

Paintings of the Sui and Tang dynasties were rich in color, and as such they were called blue-green *shanshui* (landscapes). During the Late Tang and the Five Dynasties, ink wash gradually became the main trend. After the Northern Song Dynasty, the phrase "colored landscapes" was used in the theory of painting. Inferences can be made that colored pigments were not used in most of the landscapes of that time, and if colors were used, it would be specifically designated as a colored painting. Furthermore, in terms of "blue-green landscapes", the Song artists' imitations of their Tang counterparts were actually quite different from the original paintings of the Tang. After ink wash paintings grew in popularity, blue-green landscapes gradually lost their momentum in spite of their previous widespread presence. Today, in an age when most of the works by Tang artists have been lost, huge gaps exist in our knowledge of landscapes of that time. Thus the considerable number of landscapes preserved within the Dunhuang murals is an important key in unlocking the mysteries of Chinese landscapes in the pre-Song period.

艺苑瑰宝

莫高窟壁画与彩塑

北朝至隋代的山水画

Landscapes from the Northern Dynasties to the Sui Dynasty

北魏洞窟基本上都是中心塔柱窟，多在四壁下部画金刚力士，金刚力士的脚下就画出一列起伏的山峦，通常用土红、石绿等色以粗线条画出轮廓，或全部平涂。这样的山形一直延续到隋朝。此外，在说法图中，还画出象征着佛所居的灵鹫山，如第254窟西壁的白衣佛等画面。在第254窟南壁的降魔变、第263窟降魔变还可见到表现魔军中有手托山峦的形象。这一类山峦的样式和画法，与汉代画像石、画像砖中的山峦非常接近。

在佛经中有许多关于须弥山的记载。佛经上说，一个大千世界包括1000个中千世界，一个中千世界包括1000个小千世界，而每个世界上都存在着"九山八海"，其中心就是须弥山。须弥山上有忉利天宫，金刚力

Almost all grottoes built during the Northern Wei are central pillar caves. More often than not, *lokapalas*, with rolling hills under their feet, are painted in the lower sections of each of the four walls. Normally these hills are outlined with strong lines in red earth or malachite green pigments, or simply painted flatly. This method of painting hills lasted until the Sui Dynasty. Besides this, Vulture Peak also appears in the Dharma-preaching scenes painted in this period, symbolizing the Buddha's dwelling. The white-robed Buddha on the west wall of Cave 254 provides an example. In the demon-subjugating sutra illustrations on the south wall of Cave 254 and in Cave 263, we can see images of demon troops holding hills in their hands. The painting techniques and shapes of the hills are very close to those employed in images engraved in Han Dynasty bricks.

There are abundant descriptions of Mount Sumeru in Buddhist sutras. According to texts, in each major chiliocosm (i.e., universe) there are 1,000 medium chiliocosms, and in each of the medium chiliocosms there are 1,000 small chiliocosms. In each individual chiliocosm there are "nine mountains and eight oceans", with Mount Sumeru at the center of all. Mount Sumeru contains the heaven Trāyastriṃśa, with its palaces guarded by *lokapalas*. There are images of

士就镇守在须弥山四周。壁画中画出了金刚力士，在他们的脚下就是象征着须弥山的山峦了。

北魏时期壁画中山岳出现较多的在第254窟、251窟、248窟等窟中。山峦的画法几乎都是近似三角形的形式，一面平滑，一面还有两三道波形线，山头与山头相连或叠压，并分别以红、黑、白、绿、蓝等色染出，色彩在这里仅仅起装饰作用。由于它的形状像连续的驼峰，有的学者把这样的山峦称作"驼峰式"山峦。

第257窟，是北魏时期的代表洞窟。西壁画有著名的《九色鹿本生》故事画，表现九色鹿从河里把溺人救出等情节，描绘出山峦和河流。在长卷式画面的下部是长长的一列山峦。画面的左侧因烟熏而模糊，但仍能看出一条河自左上部向右下侧流下，河水用线描出波纹，并以青绿色晕染。河中的九色鹿背负溺人向岸边走去，沿河两岸各画出一列斜向排列的山峦，画面的中部也画出几列这样斜向的山峦。这样，与河流的作用相同，这些山峦也表现出纵深的空间感。另外，这些山峦还有一个作用就是在横

lokapalas in the murals, with hills under their feet symbolizing Mount Sumeru.

Among the murals of the Northern Wei, Caves 254, 251, and 248 contain the largest number of mountain images. Almost all of them are presented in a roughly triangular shape, with one side smooth and the other side created with two or three wavy lines. The peaks are either linked or overlapped, dyed with colors such as red, black, white, green, or blue. They serve solely as an ornament or decoration. They resemble a series of camel humps, and as such were designated "camel hump" hills by certain scholars.

Cave 257 is representative of the Northern Wei, with the iconic "*Jataka* of the Nine-Colored Deer" on its west wall. Mountains and rivers help illuminate such scenes as the Nine-Colored Deer saving the drowning man from the river, and at the bottom of the panel is a long range of mountains. The right side of the painting is obscured by smoke damage, but a river can be seen running from top left to bottom right. Waves in the river are sketched with lines and the water is dyed blue and green, adopting a *sfumato* technique. The Nine-Colored Deer carries the drowning man, moving toward the river bank. Along each bank are slanting hills, and several ranges of similar slanting hills are painted in the center as well. In this way, the hills, like the river, give a sense of depth and space.

长的画面中分隔出一个个场面，用于表现故事发展的一个个情节。这是北朝故事画构图的基本形式。

北魏末至西魏，中原的山水画新风也传入了敦煌。第249窟、285窟的壁画就体现出了中原传来的新风格。西魏第249窟窟顶四披除了画出阿修罗外，还画出了中国传统的神——东王公、西王母的形象。阿修罗王的身后是高大的须弥山。须弥山的形状很独特，上部较大，下部较小。在须弥山上有一些宫殿，那就是帝释天所居的忉利天宫。须弥山下有大海，阿修罗王双脚站在大海中，但大海还没有淹过他的膝盖。这些充满神话色彩的内容，使山水画也增添了几分神奇。在本窟覆斗顶四披下部描绘出连绵不断的山峦，比起北魏时期的故事画来，这里的空间更大，山水树木得到更为自由的表现。对山头的晕染则往往通过同类颜色的深浅变化来表现山峦的层次。这种深浅相递变化

Additionally, in a long horizontal painting, another function of the hills is to separate the scenes for different subplots of the tale. This is the basic pattern in the composition of narrative paintings of the Northern Dynasties.

From the end of the Northern Wei to the Western Wei, fresh trends swept into Dunhuang; the murals in Caves 249 and 285 embody this new style introduced from the Central Plains. On the four slopes of the ceiling of Cave 249, in addition to the image of *asuras*, traditional Chinese deities are drawn—the King Father of the East and the Queen Mother of the West. Behind an *asura* king stands lofty Mount Sumeru, the shape of which is quite unique, with a larger top and a smaller bottom. The palace complex at the top of the mountain, called Trāyastriṃśa, is the heavenly abode where Indra lives. At the foot of Mount Sumeru lies the sea. An *asura* king stands in the sea with both feet in the water, but the water is not deep enough to reach his knees. Such images, full of the flavor of mythology, add mysticism to the landscapes. Rolling hills are painted in the lower sections of the four slopes of the truncated pyramid ceiling. Compared with the narrative paintings of the Northern Wei, the space here is larger, and mountains, rivers, trees, and grass are displayed with greater freedom. By applying *sfumato* techniques in painting the mountaintops, different gradations of mountains are presented by varying shades of the same color. This progressive change in the depth of color is more decorative. On the northern slope of the ceiling

更富有装饰性。窟顶北披画出一群活动于山中的野猪,野猪的上部又画出三座山峰,与下部的山峰相对,表现出一定的远近关系。在西侧的狩猎场面中,也有类似的表现(图107)。

第285窟窟顶画出伏羲、女娲等中国传统的神话题材,其中山水的布局与第249窟十分接近,也是在窟顶四披的下沿画出山水树木。在这里主要为表现在山中修行的禅僧,画出僧人们在草庵里坐禅的形象。草庵外是起伏的山峦和树林,山中还有走兽出没。树木茂密,树叶连成一片,像一顶顶帽子,罩在山峦上部的丛林上,具有浓厚的装饰意味。

第285窟南壁的《五百强盗成佛图》,描绘出500强盗在山林中的活动及听佛说法的情节。随着故事情节的发展,用斜向排列的山峦分隔出一个个空间,表现各个场次,具有连环画的效果。同时斜向的山峦表现出了一定的深度。这里值得注意的是树木大量出现了,摇曳多姿的杨柳、亭

are a herd of wild boars wandering in the mountains. Above the boars are three peaks, opposite those painted below, showing the use of perspective. Similar application of perspective is also shown in the hunting scene on the west part of the ceiling (Fig.107).

Traditional Chinese myths—such as legends of Fuxi and Nüwa—appear on the ceiling of Cave 285. The arrangement in this cave is similar to that of Cave 149, where mountains, rivers, trees, and grass are also painted along the lower edges of the four slopes of the ceiling. The main subject presented here are monks undertaking their spiritual practice in the mountains: images of monks in thatched huts, sitting in *chan* meditation, can be seen. Outside the huts are rolling hills and woods, among which beasts wander about. The woods are dense and their leaves are thick. They are linked up into a row of cap-like peaks, covering the trees on top of the hills. The decorative effect here is impressive.

The "*Jataka* of the Five Hundred Bandits" on the south wall of Cave 285 depicts the actions of the 500 bandits in the mountains as well as scenes of their listening to the Buddha preaching the Dharma. As the tale progresses, obliquely arranged hills are used to separate spaces and represent events, bringing about the effect of serial pictures. Meanwhile, slanting hills lend some depth to the scenes. Remarkable here is the abundance of trees: poplars and willows sway gently, bamboo groves stand slender and graceful, and even

图 107 狩猎图与山水 莫高窟第 249 窟窟顶北坡 西魏
Fig.107 Hunting Scene with Landscape, Northern Slope of Ceiling, Mogao Cave 249, Western Wei

Art Treasures: Murals and Painted Sculptures in Mogao Caves

亭玉立的竹林,以及很多不知名的树木,使山水景物变得丰富多彩了。此外,画家还在山峦和树林的旁边画出水池,池中碧波荡漾,水鸟嬉戏其间,别有情趣(图108)。

北周以后,横卷式故事画高度发达,作为故事画背景的山水也得以大量表现。如第428窟的《萨埵本生》和《须达那本生》便是代表作。这两铺故事画都是以三道横长

unknown varieties of trees appear, all rendering the landscape and the scenery rich and colorful. Furthermore, beside the hills and woods are water pools, with green waves rippling and water birds playing between the ripples. The impression is enduring (Fig.108).

After the Northern Zhou, horizontal panels of Buddhist narratives reached a high degree of development. Landscapes, as background of stories, were also painted in large numbers. Two quintessential works are the "Mahāsattva *Jataka*" and the "Vessantara *Jataka*" in Cave 428. These two paintings are both arranged in a continuous narrative format, in three horizontal panels, displaying the scenes in detail. Continuous lines of hills, rivers, trees, and grass are painted as background. The hills

图108　山水　莫高窟第285窟南壁　西魏
Fig.108　Landscape, South Wall of Mogao Cave 285, Western Wei

的画面相连续,详细地表现故事情节内容。作为背景画出了连绵不断的山水和树木。山峦的画法是一个个山头斜向连续,在横长的画面中形成波浪式的起伏,同时把画面分隔成一个个小小的单元,按时间顺序条理清晰地把故事描绘出来。山头用石青、土红等色平涂,看起来是为了表现一种装饰性。另外,这些错落起伏的山峦从画面整体来看,还表现出一种韵律和节奏的美,使横长的画面显得活跃而充满生气。树木穿插于山峦之中,表现各种不同的样式。如婆娑摇摆的柳树、挺拔的杨树、枝繁叶茂的槐树等。特别是东壁南侧的《萨埵本生》故事画中,描绘萨埵太子的两个哥哥得知太子已舍身饲虎的消息后,快马加鞭地赶回宫中报告父王这一情节,背景中的树木也随着两人骑马奔跑而向前倒,表现在风中摇曳的树木,十分生动逼真(图109)。

第299窟的窟顶北披的《睒子本生》,描绘了睒子在山中侍奉父母,却不幸被进山打猎的国王误射而死,由于睒子的善行感动了帝释天,终于被天人救活。

are arranged in a succession of slanting ranges, creating undulating waves. Meanwhile the picture is divided into smaller units, and the tale is arranged in clear chronological order. Hilltops are tinted with malachite green and red earth in smooth washes, seemingly as a decorative touch. In addition, these undulating hills, taken as a whole, demonstrate the beauty of metrical rhythm. The whole picture in the horizontal scroll looks active and full of life. Trees intersperse with hills in a variety of ways; willows wave gracefully; poplars stand straight up, and locust trees are lush with thick leaves. There is also something special in the painting of the "Mahāsattva *Jataka*", located on the right side of the east wall. When the two elder brothers learn that their younger brother has given up his own life to feed the tigers, they return quickly back to the palace to report the tragedy to their father, spurring on the flying horse. So realistic is the scene that while the two men race forward on horseback, the trees in the background also lean forward, showing that the trees are waving in the wind (Fig.109).

The "Śyāma *Jataka*" on the northern slope of the ceiling in Cave 299 tells the story of Śyāma who took care of his parents in the mountains. Unfortunately, Śyāma was accidentally shot by the king on his hunt. The virtuous deeds of Śyāma moved Indra, and finally he was brought back to life by

艺苑瑰宝
莫高窟壁画与彩塑

图 109　太子回宫　莫高窟第 428 窟东壁　北周
Fig.109　Prince Sattva's Brothers Racing Back to the Palace,
East Wall of Mogao Cave 428, Northern Zhou

这幅画主要表现睒子在泉边取水，被国王误射的场景：茂密的树林中，一条小溪流过，睒子在溪边取水，画面左侧国王及侍从骑马奔驰而来。一边是幽静而安详的山林，一边是奔驰而来的人马，这一动一静的对比，烘托出一个富有戏剧性的气氛，完美地表现出这个动人的故事。色彩浓丽的山水画则作为故事画的舞台背景，显示出了十分重要的作用。

celestial beings. The painting mainly depicts the scene of Śyāma collecting water from the spring when he is mistakenly shot by the king: a stream flows through the thick woods, and Śyāma fetches water from the stream; on the left, the king and his attendants ride horses and rush closer. Thus one side of the painting contains peaceful quiet mountains and woods, while the other side of it shows men and horses dashing along. The contrast between the static and the dynamic sets off a dramatic tension, a perfect presentation of the moving story. Landscapes with rich, strong colors play an important role, setting a stage background for the narratives.

隋朝壁画中，故事画大量出现,内容空前丰富,表现手法也细腻而精致。在长卷式故事画中，山水景物也大量地描绘出来。虽然这是北魏以来就流行的形式，但隋代壁画中山水树木刻画之精细与繁富却是前代所无法比拟的。如第419窟、420窟、423窟、303窟等窟中的山水树木都是较有代表性的。隋代画家展子虔等都擅长画宫殿楼阁，在敦煌壁画中也可看出隋代的建筑画很发达,故事画、经变画中的建筑物画得很多,反映了中原新画风的影响。隋末第276窟的壁画还出现了对表现岩石的新技法，对唐代绘画的发展产生了深远的影响。

隋代故事画继承北周的传统，依然用山水树木作背景。但山水树木在画面中所占有的比重越来越大，人物相对来说画得较小。开凿于开皇四年(584年)的第302窟,在人字披

Among the murals of the Sui Dynasty, narrative paintings abound, with unprecedented rich content and exquisite representations. Large quantities of landscapes and scenery are also depicted in them. Although paintings in long panels had been popular since the Northern Wei, the renderings of mountains, rivers, trees, and grass in the murals of the Sui Dynasty were so exquisite and intricate that they were unparalleled by those of any previous age. Typical examples can be found in Caves 419, 420, 423, and 303. Artists such as Zhan Ziqian of the Sui Dynasty were skillful in painting palaces, temples, and pavilions. It can be seen from Dunhuang murals that architectural paintings of the Sui period were also quite advanced. Many of them were included in narrative paintings and sutra illustrations, and influences of the new style from the Central Plains are obvious. Additionally, among the murals in Cave 276 of the late Sui, new techniques were adopted to depict rocks, creating a profound impact on the paintings of the Tang Dynasty.

Narrative paintings of the Sui Dynasty continued the traditions of the Northern Zhou, with mountains, rivers, trees, and grass still painted as background. However, they occupied increasingly larger proportions of the composition, while characters became relatively smaller. On the gabled ceiling in Cave 302, constructed in the 4th year of the Kaihuang Era (584), the "Mahāsattva *Jataka*" and a *Merit Field Sutra* illustration are painted in horizontal panels. Brown hills and green trees are

顶上画出了横卷式故事画《萨埵本生》和《福田经变》，作为故事的背景，以赭色的山峦、绿色的树木分布在素面的墙上，显得质朴而简淡。这一时期不像北朝故事画那样把人物形象挤满画面，而是留出了一定的空白，画面上部还有天空中飞翔的小鸟。这些富于想象力的表现，使画面产生了一定的空间感。

隋代第303窟在四壁及中心柱的下沿横卷式画面中，稀稀落落地分布着山峦和树木，树林中还画出鹿、羊等动物，或在觅食，或在奔跑，表现出山林自然的气息。树林的表现也很有趣味，有的整齐排列，有的则枝干弯曲，呈现出如舞蹈般的动态。树叶大都具有装饰性。驼峰式的山头也体现出不同的形态。山峦的用色简淡而和谐，除了赭红色以外，就是

distributed as background on the uncolored surface of the wall, appearing plain and simple. During this period, characters were not crowded into the paintings the way they were in those of the Northern Dynasties. Instead, a certain amount of space was set aside. In the upper part of the picture there are even birds flying in the sky. These presentations, full of imagination, create a sense of space.

In the horizontal panels along the lower edge of the four walls and the central pillar in Cave 303 of the Sui Dynasty, hills and trees are thinly interspersed. Deer and goats are painted in the woods; some forage for grass and some run about, lending the natural atmosphere of mountains and forests. The trees present an interesting display: some are arranged in neat rows, while some are painted with curved branches and bent trunks, showing the motions of dancing. The leaves of the trees are mainly decorative. The "camel hump" hills are also rendered in a different way. The hills are tinted in light, subtle, but harmonious colors. Black and white are commonly used in addition to brown. The deep-to-shallow range of shades on the hills are evocative of the later "wrinkle technique" (*cunfa*)[①] texturing in Chinese painting. Since the Northern Wei, such areas in a cave were usually painted with *lokapalas*, with landscapes serving merely as their background. But in this cave, landscapes are depicted, independent of any

---

① a technique in Chinese painting, employing the paintbrush sidewise with comparatively less ink to show the texture, lines, and cracks on the surface of rocks, bark, and similar objects.

黑色、白色。山峦上由深到浅的着色方法,似乎类似于后来的"皴法"的特点。北魏以来,在洞窟中的这一位置通常是画金刚力士的,山水是金刚力士的背景。而在这个洞窟,第一次描绘出没有佛教内容的山水(图110)。看起来最初是由于佛教的需要而画出山水作为背景,在这里则已经把本来固有的佛教内容抛开,成为纯粹的山水画了。尽管山峦形象及色彩的表现依然是汉画的古老传统,但这个洞窟的山水画却标志着山水画的审美意识已超越了佛教主题。

第419窟在窟顶人字披两侧绘出须达那太子本生和萨埵太子本生故事画,第420窟在窟顶绘出

Buddhist thematic material, for the first time (Fig.110). Apparently, landscapes were originally painted as background for Buddhist content, but the content is abandoned here, and paintings have become pure landscapes. Although the shape of the mountain ranges and the palette clearly have their roots in the ancient traditions of the Han Dynasty, the paintings in this cave reveal that aesthetic concepts of landscapes have gone beyond serving the needs of Buddhist themes.

The "Mahāsattva *Jataka*" and the "Vessantara *Jataka*" are represented on the two slopes of the gabled ceiling of Cave 419, while *Lotus Sutra* illustrations are painted on the ceiling of Cave 420. The techniques used in these two caves

图110　山水　莫高窟第303窟南壁　隋
Fig.110　Landscape, South Wall of Mogao Cave 303, Sui Dynasty

法华经变画。这两窟的画法非常相似。在山岳的表现上，比起北周以前那种光秃秃的山头来，隋代壁画中的山峦层次丰富。如第419窟的萨埵本生故事画中，在山峦的上部往往画出一层绿色的植物，就像一顶帽子一样，在其中画出细密的线条，如草，如苔。山峦重叠时，层次就变得非常丰富（图111）。这一手法，一直影响到唐代壁画中的山水表现，如盛唐第217窟的山头上就有类似的表现。这两窟的山峦都用石绿、石青、赭石等以及多种颜色混合染出。由于时代久远，壁画大多已经变黑，但当初一定是十分绚丽灿烂的。

第420窟窟顶西披，表现法华经变中群鸟听法的场面。佛坐在高台上说法，前面有很多鸟伸长脖子在聆听佛法，山丘后画有水池，水池中也有很多水鸟面佛静听。佛的身后是长长垂下的柳树，环境优美，衬托出佛法的庄严。

在同窟窟顶东披还画出观音救难的场面：右侧一条

are very similar. In terms of presentation of mountains, more color gradation was revealed in Sui period murals, compared with the stark, bald peaks from before the Northern Zhou. For example, in the "Mahāsattva *Jataka*" in Cave 419, the mountain ranges are topped by a layer of green plants, resembling a cap, with fine and closely woven lines, resembling grass or moss. Where there are overlapping mountain ranges, there is plenty of gradation (Fig.111). Such techniques have influenced the landscapes in the murals of the Tang Dynasty, and similar presentations on the mountain peaks in Cave 217 of the High Tang can be seen as an example. The mountain ranges in these two caves are all tinted with malachite, azurite, red ochre, and many other blended mineral pigments. Most of the murals have darkened over the years due to oxidation, but originally they must have been bright and colorful.

On the western slope of the ceiling in Cave 420 is a scene from the *Lotus Sutra*, in which birds listen to the Buddha's teachings. The Buddha sits high on a platform preaching the Dharma, and in front of him, birds listen, stretching their necks. Behind the hills is a pond, where more water fowl also listen attentively, facing the Buddha. Behind the Buddha are long willows hanging down. The beautiful environment reflects the grandeur of the Buddhist Dharma.

Scenes with Avalokitesvara helping

Art Treasures: Murals and Painted Sculptures in Mogao Caves

图 111 山水 莫高窟第 419 窟窟顶 隋
Fig.111 Landscape, Ceiling of Mogao Cave 419, Sui Dynasty

河流由远而近流下，河中有人遇难，河边画出慈祥的观音菩萨向河里伸手，正在搭救溺水者。曲折的河流上部细下部宽，体现出远近的空间距离。左侧是大海中有人遇难的情景，左边画出数人乘小船航行于大海，遇大风浪的

people out of harm's way are on the eastern slope of the cave's ceiling. A river flows from far to near on the right section of the scene, with a man dangerously trapped in the current. Kind-hearted Avalokitesvara, on the river bank, extends his hands into the waters to rescue the drowning man. The winding river is narrow in the upper part and wide in the lower part, reflecting the spatial distance far and near. On the left side of the ceiling is a scene of people in danger at sea. A

图 112 观音救海难 莫高窟第 420 窟 隋
Fig.112 Avalokitesvara Aiding Those in Distress, Mogao Cave 420, Sui Dynasty

危急状况。右边也画出数人乘船航行于大海，一只张着大口的怪兽正朝小船虎视眈眈，表现在大海中遇到各种怪兽的情景（图112）。佛经上说若遇到这样的灾难时，只要口念观音便可以消灾免难。画家由此画出大海及波浪。但当时的画家还未掌握描绘大海的技法，画出的大海仍像水池一样，在水池中还画出莲花。左边描绘海浪，令人想起彩陶纹饰中的波浪纹，那样图案化的处理方法仍是一脉相承的。

隋代壁画的另一大特色是房屋建筑大量进入了故事画的背景中。从佛经故事的内容画看，除了在野外山林中的故事外，还有很多情节是发生在宫殿、房屋内的。在早期壁画中也有少量的建筑出现。到了隋代，房屋建筑已成为背景的重要内容，表明壁画表现出写实化的倾向。同时，建筑

scene is painted on the left, in which several people in a boat at sea encounter a violent storm. The right side presents a sight of several people at sea with a monster glaring fiercely at their boat, with its mouth wide open. Different situations of encountering various monsters at sea are presented here (Fig.112). Mahayana Buddhist sutras maintain that in the event of such calamities, disaster can be avoided as long as people chant the name of Avalokitesvara. The artists of the time painted the sea and the waves on the basis of these scriptures. However, they had not yet mastered the techniques of depicting the ocean, so what they painted still resembled a pool, complete with lotuses. The ocean waves on the left are reminiscent of the decorative wavy lines on painted pottery. Undoubtedly the patterned treatment can be traced in the same vein.

Large numbers of houses and buildings in the background are another distinctive feature of Sui period murals. Based on content of parables and tales in sutras, with the exception of those stories set in forests and mountains, many events took place inside palaces, temples, or houses. Indeed, there were some buildings depicted in early murals, but during the Sui Dynasty, houses and buildings became an important feature in the background, showing that murals were manifesting a tendency toward realism. Meanwhile, buildings played an important role in the composition of a painting. In the *Lotus Sutra* illustration in Cave 420, houses break the conventions of continuous narrative horizontal panel paintings. Twists and turns along

物在构图中起着重要的作用。在第420窟《法华经变》中，由于房屋的作用，突破了横卷式构图的约束，由建筑物的转折而形成了蛇行线，把画面分成一个个单元，构成一种独特的空间。山水风景中，山峦通常都是圆弧的形状，而建筑则往往是直线和角形，山峦与建筑相接，直线与弧线，使画面刚柔相补，丰富多彩。建筑物的增多也使画家更注重人物与景物的比例关系。隋代绘画在比例方面比起北朝的故事画有了重大的进步。

在第423窟人字披顶的《须达那本生》故事中，通过连续起伏的山峦，形成波浪状的曲线，组合成一个个单元，在这些圆形的画面中，展开一个个故事情节。从画面构成来说，打破了北朝以来那种横长画面整齐但却单一的格局。这样极其自然地表现山峦，也使中国画山水的表现走向一个新的阶段。

the building structures form a winding line, dividing the picture into a succession of individual units, one after another. The separated spaces are unique. In landscapes, mountains are crescent-shaped, while architecture is normally created with straight lines and angles. By combining buildings and mountains, straight lines and arcs, the rigidness and softness complement each other, making the picture rich and graceful. The increasing use of architecture also made artists pay more attention to balancing the proportions between figures and scenery. In terms of proportion, the composition of narrative paintings from the Sui period manifest significant improvement, compared with those of the Northern Dynasties.

In the "Vessantara *Jataka*" on the gabled ceiling of Cave 423, units are shaped one after another along the wavy curves formed by continuous, undulating mountains. Pictorial scenes unfold one by one in these round spaces. Seen from the composition of the painting, the neat but monotonous pattern of horizontal panels in use since the Northern Dynasties has been broken. This type of natural representation of mountains also leads to a new stage in Chinese landscapes.

In Cave 276 from the late Sui, strangely shaped peaks are drawn separately, close to the intersections where the north and south walls meet the west wall. For example, a hillside is painted at the bottom next to the bodhisattva on the left side of the north wall (Fig.113), while at

图113 菩萨与山水 莫高窟第276窟北壁西侧 隋
Fig.113 Bodhisattva with Landscape, Left Side of North Wall, Mogao Cave 276, Sui Dynasty

Art Treasures: Murals and Painted Sculptures in Mogao Caves

隋末第276窟在南北两壁与西壁交接处附近,分别画出奇崛的山峰。如北壁西侧菩萨的旁边,最下部是一个山坡(图113)。上部画出坚硬的岩石,顶部岩石向右翘出,显得很险峻。岩石用赭红线条勾勒,在有的部分染出石青和赭红色,表现出岩石的阴阳向背。在岩石上还画出一些树木。岩石与树木、人的比例还不太协调,但这与传统的山岩画法已完全不同,不再停留在对山峦的概括而笼统的描绘,而是把山岩作为近景来刻画,强调岩石细部的质感。此后,敦煌壁画中的山峦表现开始注重近景与远景的区别,空间关系的表现进入了一个新阶段。在第276窟南北两壁的说法图中,还可以看出树木的具体刻画。北壁的菩萨身后的松树体现出挺拔直立的特点,西壁的树木表现出梧桐枝繁叶茂的特征,每一张树叶都用线描具体地勾出轮廓;南壁的树类似槐树,树叶采用"介"字点法。在每一棵树粗壮的树干上,都仔细地画出了树的纹理。

the top are hard rocks, with the highest one sloping up to the right, looking rather precipitous. The rocks are sketched with reddish brown lines and some parts are colored with malachite and red ochre, showing the sunny and the shaded sides. There are even some trees painted above the rocks. The proportional ratio between rocks, trees, and human figures is not quite in harmony, but the methods adopted here are completely different from traditional paintings of rocks. No longer did artists just give a brief and general outline of mountains, but they presented them in the foreground, stressing the detailed texture of the rocks. From this point in Dunhuang mural art, emphasis began to be laid upon the differences between close and distant scenery when mountain ranges were painted. The representation of spatial relationships thus progressed to a new stage. In the Dharma-preaching scenes on both the north and south walls, specific renderings of trees can also be seen. The pines behind the bodhisattva on the north wall are straight and upright; the Chinese parasol trees on the west wall are lush with foliage, each leaf outlined in detail. Trees on the south wall look like Chinese scholar trees with leaves dotted by a light brush. The lines of each trunk's wood grain are carefully executed.

雍容华美之风——唐代前期壁画中的山水
Pursuit of Grace and Beauty: Landscapes in Early Tang Murals

唐前期，唐王朝积极开拓西域，敦煌成为控制西域政治军事的要地。随着中国与西域诸国的频繁交往，处于丝路要冲的敦煌已成为一个佛教文化的中心，长安、洛阳的艺术风格很快就能传到敦煌，敦煌壁画的发展差不多与中原完全同步。文献中记载的长安、洛阳一带佛教寺院壁画的经变画等内容，绝大多数都能在敦煌壁画中找到，说明当时敦煌壁画艺术与中原寺院壁画艺术密切相关。在当时如吴道子、朱审、韦偃等画家曾经在寺院壁画中画出了独立的山水画。敦煌虽然没有出现完全独立的山水画，但如第 217 窟、103 窟、148 窟等窟的壁画中的山水画已具有相对独立的意义了。

初唐第 209 窟南壁西侧、西壁和北壁西侧的故事画，都采用纵向布局的形

The central government was actively exploring the Western Regions during the Early Tang. Dunhuang thus played the role of a military and political strategic stronghold for controlling those regions. With frequent exchange between China and countries in the Western Regions, Dunhuang, a vital communication hub along the Silk Road, was turned into a center for Buddhist culture, and the artistic features of Chang'an and Luoyang rapidly spread into Dunhuang. Indeed, the development of Dunhuang murals was almost completely synchronous with those of the Central Plains. According to historical records, virtually the same sutra illustration content seen in Buddhist temples of Chang'an and Luoyang could also be found in Dunhuang murals. This reveals that the art of Dunhuang murals was closely related to that of the Buddhist temples in the Central Plains. Artists of the time, such as Wu Daozi, Zhu Shen, and Wei Yan, painted individual landscapes in the wall paintings of Buddhist temples. Although no completely stand-alone landscapes have been found in Dunhuang, those painted among the murals in Caves 217, 103, and 148, can in fact be regarded as comparatively independent works.

Narrative paintings are all arranged vertically on the entire west wall, as well as the west side of both the north and south walls in Cave 209 of the

式，作为故事画背景的山水景物画得很大。南壁西侧，右边一重山占了将近四分之一的画面；左边主要画了三重山，其间以曲折排列的树木相连，近处是大河前横。两组说法图，分置于山与山之间，远处画了三座小山表示远景，云霞飘动，意境深远。树的形式，主要作为装饰，沿山的轮廓线画出，远处高大，近处矮小，甚至有的如小草一般。大约画家为了突出人物，又要考虑山、树的装饰作用，画树不按比例。这种山和树的装饰性，仍然承袭了早期山水画的特点，但已注意到了山水景物的空间层次感。色彩上改变了早期那种青绿相递叠染的方法，而用大面积的绿色染出，又以赭色相间，以表现层次。第209窟西壁佛光两侧，还保存赭红色线条勾出的山石轮廓。对照隋代第276窟的山水画，可以看出它们的一致性。大面积的青绿染色，烘染出草木朦胧的效果，使山水画的意境更加完整。

Early Tang. Landscapes and scenery provide expansive background for the stories. On the right side of the south wall, one of the mountains on the right takes up nearly a quarter of the painting, while the main object on the left is three mountains, connected by winding rows of trees. A nearby river flows in front of the mountains, between which two Dharma-preaching scenes are arranged. The three small hills painted in the background indicate distance, and, together with the drifting pink clouds, provoke an ambience of remoteness. The trees, painted along the outline of the mountains, are mainly ornamental. The distant ones are tall and large; the closer ones are short and small—some even as short and small as the grass. They are not painted according to scale, probably because the artist wanted not only to highlight the characters, but also to treat the trees and mountains as embellishments. The decorative nature of the mountains and trees still embodies the characteristics of earlier landscapes, but spatial gradations among them are noted. As to the color scheme, the earlier methods of alternately overlapping blue and green are changed here, and gradations are shown by large areas of green interspersed with reddish brown. On both sides of the Buddha's aureole on the west wall of the same cave, the reddish brown lines that outline the mountains are still preserved, and compared with the Sui period landscapes in Cave 276, identical features can be found between them. Large areas of green create a hazy effect of vegetation, completing the artistic conception.

Both the north and south walls in Cave 323

第323窟南北壁中部均画佛教史迹画，但画家没有像以前的故事画那样按故事发展的顺序来构图，而是以山水统摄全图。在山水画分隔出的空间里，描绘一个个故事场面，山水画成了壁画构图中首先考虑的问题了。南壁共有三组故事画，画家用两组山脉把壁面分成三段。左侧的山脉呈"之"字形，左下部又有一组小山相呼应。右边一组山脉大体呈"C"形，环抱故事画，壁画最右侧上部又有一组山崖与之相照应。在两组山脉之间，还有一组山峰耸立，把两组山脉联系起来，这样，两组山脉在横长的画面中形成了稳定的结构，主宰着全壁，使山水联成一气，绵延壮阔。远景的山水则通过曲折的流水相联系，由近景到远景，层次丰富而境界辽阔。

本窟山水画中最引人注目的是远景的画法。如北壁《张骞出使西域图》，近处描绘张骞辞别汉武帝的场面，人物画得很大。在左侧的山峦中，画出张骞与随从人员渐渐远

contain paintings of Buddhist historical sites and events. The artists did not compose the scenes according to a plot sequence as in previous paintings, but instead, the whole picture is governed by landscapes. Scenes are depicted one after another in spaces separated by mountains and rivers, and therefore landscapes become the first element to be taken into consideration in the composition of these murals. On the center of the south wall there are three groups of narrative paintings. The artist divided the wall into three sections by two ranges of mountains. The range on the left is presented in the shape of a Z with another group of small hills echoing it on the bottom left. The range on the right is presented in a C-shape, embracing the scenes, with a coordinating group of cliffs on the top right. A group of high peaks stands between the two ranges, joining the mountain ranges to each other. Thus they form a stable structure in a horizontal extension of paintings, dominating the whole wall, so that the landscapes are unified into one continuous and grand panorama. Distant scenery, from close up to far away, are connected by a winding river, creating varied gradations and vistas.

The most striking aspect of the landscapes in this cave is the method employed for displaying distant scenery. One example is the painting on *Zhang Qian's Diplomatic Mission to the Western Regions*. The foreground, in which the characters are quite large, shows Zhang Qian bidding farewell to Emperor Wu of the Han Dynasty. In the mountains on the left,

Zhang Qian and his men gradually move further away. The further away they are, the smaller the figures are painted. The proportions of people and mountains are in harmony, showing a sense of natural perspective. The "Tale of the Stone Buddhas Floating in the River" on the south wall depicts the legend of two stone statues of the Buddha, seen floating in the Wusong River during the Western Jin. On that occasion, stormy waves began to rage violently. People pulled the statues to land with a small boat, placed them in the local Buddhist temple, and made offerings, and the storm subsided immediately. Three groups of people are portrayed in the picture. The distant scene in the upper part shows a group of people looking at the dazzling light from the Buddhas' halos, gesticulating while talking. The people in this group are the smallest, with generally visible figures but unclear features. The group in the middle venerate the stone statues of the Buddha by the river. People in this group are larger than those in the distant scene. The scene in the lower foreground depicts people greeting the stone statues. Figures are painted larger and in more details. Thus, from far away to close up, scenes are connected by the river, presenting perspective. The proportions among mountains, river, and people are pleasing and harmonious. Since the ratios between distant and close scenes tend to be correct, the realism of the paintings is considerably enhanced, and at the same time, the landscape on the whole wall is more integrated.

The artist seemed to take great pride in rendering distant mountains, and the boats sailing in the distance in particular, which reflects a strong

是画家的得意之笔,特别是远景中画出帆船,颇有意境。本窟北壁"康僧会的故事"上部表现康僧会从海上来的情节,画出大海中一叶扁舟,隐约可见舟中数人(图114)。南壁的故事画中,上部远景中几处画出了小舟,与山水相映成趣,表现了烟雨迷蒙的江湖景色。尽管线色脱落,但是仍可看出近处

creative concept. The legend of Kang Senghui appears in this cave's upper section of the north wall. In one of the scenes, Kang Senghui comes from the sea. On the sea is a small rowboat, with several faintly visible figures (Fig.114). In the narrative painting on the south wall, a small boat is painted in the distant scene in the upper part, which forms a delightful contrast with mountains and rivers, presenting a scenery of rivers and lakes in the hazy mist and rain. Although the color of the lines has deteriorated, the waves nearby and the rivers in the distance are still visible. The sails in the distance particularly remind us of the artistic conception: "a solitary sail merges into the blue sky, like a shadow

图114 远山与小船 莫高窟第323窟北壁 初唐
Fig.114 Small Boat with Distant Mountains in Background, North Wall of Mogao Cave 323, Early Tang

的波浪和远处的河流,特别是远景的点点帆影,颇有"孤帆远影碧空尽"的意境。由于变色比较严重,山水及人物的轮廓线都看不清了,远山的颜色都变成了黑色,因此有人误认为本窟的壁画是"没骨画",或者甚至认为是水墨画。这是不了解敦煌壁画变色的情况而产生的误解。当时的壁画中都染出了绚丽的色彩,而且,按照唐人绘画的习惯,都是采用线描施彩的办法,并不存在没骨画。

值得注意的是第323窟还有几处表现云的场面。本来在早期的壁画中就已出现很多云,但大多是描绘佛、菩萨及天人等乘云来去的场面;那样的云是佛、菩萨、天人等的乘骑,带有很强的想象性,并不是自然风景中的云。在第323窟北壁中描绘了佛图澄举杯洒酒化为雨,扑灭幽州城大火的神异故事。画面中高僧佛图澄举杯向上,一朵乌云向上升去,上部画出山峦的后面有一座城,城楼中火焰升天,上面的乌云化为大雨,倾盆而

remote". Due to serious discoloration, the lines that sketch the landscapes and people are blurred, and the distant mountains have blackened. As a result, such works have been mistakenly regarded as "boneless paintings (*moguhua*)" by some people, or they are even regarded as ink wash paintings. This is a misunderstanding, resulting from a lack of knowledge about mural discoloration. At the time of their creation, all Dunhuang murals would have been tinted with brilliant hues, and furthermore, according to the customs in the Tang period, the method adopted then would have been line contouring filled with color painting. Therefore, these are not boneless paintings at all.

Several scenes involving clouds in Cave 323 are worthy of special notice. It is true that there were already clouds in early-period murals, but most of them depicted scenes of the Buddha, bodhisattvas, and *devas* riding on them, and as a result, clouds of this type were only painted for this purpose. They were not from landscapes, but from the imagination. The miraculous tale of Buddhcinga, who turned a cup of wine into water to put out a fire in the city of Youzhou, is depicted on the north wall of this cave. In the painting, the eminent monk raises his wine cup while a black cloud rises to Heaven. The upper register shows a city behind the hills. Flames rise to the sky from the city tower. Dark clouds over the city are changed into heavy downpours of rain. On the right side of the south wall in the same cave, a patch of

下。同窟南壁西侧，在远景中描绘出一朵云霞，由于变色，我们无法得知当时是什么色彩，但在远山中的一片云霞，的确是很美的。南壁东侧，表现隋代昙延法师祈雨的故事。城内昙延法师坐于高台之上，正作法求雨，上部的天空中乌云滚滚，向中央聚集。中央部分的云中已降下了大雨。这些故事虽然充满了神话色彩，但画面中却是按现实中的自然现象描绘出来的。大火燃烧，烈焰熊熊；乌云翻滚，大雨如注，都可以形成独特的风景。唐代画家们最早注意到并描绘出了这些自然奇观，这些都是中国绘画史上的珍贵资料。

建于大历十一年（766年）的第148窟，是盛唐后期的规模较大的洞窟，在本窟的巨型经变画中，山水画也体现出空前绝后的水平。特别是在其西壁、北壁画出的涅槃经变和天请问经变中，成功地画出了气势壮阔的山水，空间表现又与人物故事情节完美地结合起来，实在是佛教壁画中不可多得的山水佳作。

clouds appears in the distance. Because of the faded colors, it is impossible for us to know how it was tinted, but the pink clouds in the distant mountains present a beautiful scene. On the left side of the south wall is the tale of Buddhist master Tan Yan of the Sui Dynasty, praying for rain. Inside the city, Master Tan Yan is seated on a high platform, praying. Up in the air, black clouds roll towards the center. In the center section, heavy rain pours down from the clouds. These tales are redolent of mythology, but the paintings themselves are based on natural weather phenomena: raging fires with whirling flames, dark clouds swelling with torrential rain—all can create striking scenes. Tang artists were the first to capture and depict these natural wonders, leaving invaluable resources in the history of Chinese painting.

Cave 148, constructed in the 11th year of the Dali Era (766), is a comparatively large cave from the later High Tang period. In the large-scale sutra illustrations here, landscapes also reflect an unprecedented achievement in art history. The *Nirvana Sutra* illustration and the *Heavenly Inquiry Sutra* illustration on the north and west walls are particularly special, in which magnificent landscapes are successively painted, and spatial presentations are perfectly combined with characters and events in the tales. Indeed, they are masterpieces rarely found among the Buddhist murals.

In the *Nirvana Sutra* illustration, there

Art Treasures: Murals and Painted Sculptures in Mogao Caves

本窟的涅槃经变共画出10组画面，66个情节，人物数百，山水也极其壮观。其顺序先是从南壁西侧开始，由西壁全壁到北壁西侧，主要画面在宽达16米左右的西壁上。西壁的南侧，表现释迦牟尼在双树林入般涅槃的时候，画面在空旷的原野中展开，远处有山崖耸立，中部引人注目的是画出雄伟的城楼，表现拘尸那城（图115）。这样高大的城楼与西安附近出土的懿德太子李重润墓壁画中的建筑很相似。虽然莫高窟第148窟比李重润墓壁画要晚70年左右，但那种雄强的盛唐风格是一脉相承的。由这一组建筑，形成了画面的一个高潮，城门外是一片开阔的原野，远景的山峦绵延相接，一直连到城楼后面，近景的缓坡也在这里交接，景物的远近空间关系表现得十分真切。在北壁的"分舍利"场面，可以说是这铺经变画的高

are 10 groups of scenes including 66 events and hundreds of characters. The landscapes in this cave are also magnificent. The paintings start from the right side of the south wall, extending all the way across the west wall to the left side of the north wall. The main section, about 16 meters wide, is on the west wall. On the left side of the west wall is a scene of Sakyamuni entering nirvana under a group of sal trees. The scene unfolds across the vast open land. Cliffs rise high in the distance; stately, eye-catching city towers stand in the middle, representing the town of Kuśinagara (Fig.115). Such high city towers are quite similar to the buildings painted in the tomb murals of Li Chongrun, Prince Yide, unearthed near Xi'an. Though the murals in Cave 148 at Mogao were painted about 70 years later than those in Li Chongrun's tomb, the strong, prosperous style of the High Tang is in the same vein. The climax of the painting is thus shaped by this complex of buildings. Outside the city gate is a vast stretch of land. Distant hills run on and on until they reach the city tower, joining the gentle slopes in the foreground at the back of the tower. The space in the scenery is expressed realistically, whether nearby or far away. The scene of dividing the Buddha's relics, on the north wall, can be regarded as the climax of this sutra illustration. A multitude of characters surround the platform where the relics are stacked. Imposing mountains are presented in the upper section of the background. Steep crags rise high behind the open land, and a white cloud covers the hillside. In the

图 115　城楼　莫高窟第148窟西壁　盛唐
Fig.115　High Buildings in Town, West Wall of Mogao Cave 148, High Tang

潮，众多的人物围绕在堆放舍利的台前。背景的上部，山势表现得十分雄奇。在辽远的原野后面，危崖耸立，其中还画出一片白云把半山腰遮住。画面上部，与青绿重彩的山峦相对的是橙黄色的彩云，仿佛是夕照中的晚霞，具有一种动人心魄的力量（图116）。从这铺涅槃经变，我们可以看出唐代壁画表现故事，不仅仅停留在把故事内容图解出来，而且更注意到壁画作为美术的一种视觉感受，充分调动山水画的技法，体

upper register of the wall painting, orange clouds are depicted as if reflecting the glow of the sunset, in sharp contrast with hills in deep blue and green, revealing an inspirational power (Fig.116). From this *Nirvana Sutra* illustration we can understand how Tang period murals expressed narratives. Stories were not merely presented as graphic illustrations, but instead more emphasis was placed on the visual experience of murals as works of fine art. Thus the techniques for painting landscapes are fully deployed, majestic and powerful artistic conceptions are conveyed, and the pinnacle of beauty is achieved.

图 116　山水　莫高窟第 148 窟西壁　盛唐
Fig.116　Landscape, West Wall of Mogao Cave 148, High Tang

现出雄奇壮阔的意境,达到了画面美的顶点。

第217窟南壁西侧,是根据《法华经·化城喻品》来绘制的山水图景。画面的顺序大体是上部从右至左,再从左至右。右上角是危崖耸立,有二人骑马一远一近行进。透过山崖,可见远方曲折流淌的河流,境界辽远。中部两座高峰之间,一道飞瀑涌泻而下,山下的旅人被这大自然的奇景所吸引而驻马观赏。马匹半掩在山后。左部也是一条曲折的河流,在近处被山崖遮断。下面的山峰,悬崖突出,青藤蔓草悬垂。有三人仿佛是长途跋涉而疲惫不堪,一人牵马,一人躺倒在地,一人在水边,欲饮山泉。中间靠右是旅人向一座西域城堡走去,路旁桃李花开,春光明媚(图117)。

《法华经·化城喻品》本是叙述一群人往一宝地取宝,路途遥远险恶,"迥绝多毒兽,又复无水草"。众人走了很久,苦于道路险阻,不愿再前行。这时,聪明睿智的导师以神通力化出一座城池,让众人进城休

In Cave 217, on the right side of the south wall, there is a landscape based on the "Chapter on the Parable of the Conjured City" from the *Lotus Sutra*. The painting begins in the upper section of the wall, arranged in an order first from right to left, and then from left to right. In the upper right corner, steep crags rise high and two men advance, riding their horses, one close and the other distant. A winding river flows through the crags, moving to a vast, remote area. Between the two high peaks in the middle, a waterfall gushes down in torrents. Travelers below are attracted by the wonders of nature and stop to watch, with horses half-hidden behind the peaks. To the left is also a winding river, cut off by the cliffs nearby. The peaks below are painted with protruding crags and overhanging vines and creeping tendrils. Three men appear to be completely exhausted from the long arduous journey: one leads his horse, one lies on the ground, and the third one remains by the water, about to drink from the mountain spring. To the right, a traveler walks towards a castle in the Western Regions. It is a bright spring day with peach and plum trees in full bloom (Fig.117).

The "Chapter on the Parable of the Conjured City" tells the tale of a group of people seeking treasures from a land of wealth. It was a long and dangerous journey, and "the road was remote and far away, always menaced by vicious animals; there was neither water nor grass". The group traveled for a long

息。众人休息好了，化城消失，又继续赶路。法华经用这个故事来象征佛引导众生走向彼岸。但是，画家并没有机械地按照经文画出那种穷山恶水的荒凉景象，而是渲染了一路曲径通幽、草木葱茏的秀丽景致，使之成为"可居""可游"的游春图景。说明画家是从美的角度来进行创作，有意识地创造山水意境。这幅山水画，主要表现了4组山峦：左侧一组山峰刻画颇细，以石绿和浅赭相间染出，峰峦上的树形除了沿用过去那种装饰性的树形外，又相应地描绘了树的枝叶细部，还画了许多悬垂的藤蔓。右侧是潺潺的流水。中部是一组平缓的山丘，与左侧的山崖相映成趣，用很单纯的笔法勾描，平涂石绿色并刻画了不同的树木，花开烂漫，一片春色。右上一组山峦最引人注目，飞流而下的瀑布，虽已变色，但仍使人感到充满生意，仿佛点睛之笔，是画面中最传神之处。左上部的远景，尽管不如前面几组富有特色，但在画面的构图上是必不可少的，它把左侧近景山崖与右侧

time, until, exhausted, they felt they could go no further. At that moment, a wise master conjured up a city with his magical powers, so that the people could enter the city and refresh themselves. After the group rested, the city disappeared and they resumed their journey. The *Lotus Sutra* uses this parable to show that the Buddha guides all sentient beings to the "other shore", i.e., nirvana. However, the artists did not mechanically follow the scriptures in painting desolate scenes of barren mountains and unruly rivers, but rendered beautiful scenes of winding paths and verdant vegetation. As a result, the painting portrays a land of springtime that is "comfortable to live in, and comfortable to wander around". This indicates that the artists painted with an eye for beauty and purposefully created an artistic ambience for landscapes. The painting mainly presents four groups of mountain ranges. The group of peaks on the left, tinted with malachite and light ochre alternatively, is painted in fine detail. Trees on the peaks display detailed branches and leaves as well, apart from those following the decorative forms used in the past. There are also creeping vines, and, on the right, a babbling brook. In the center is a group of gentle hills, contrasting nicely with those on the left. They are sketched with simple lines and colored by a smooth wash of malachite pigment. Various trees are also presented with bright flowers in full bloom, creating an overall vision of springtime. The

图117 化城喻品 莫高窟第217窟南壁 盛唐
Fig.117 The Parable of the Conjured City from the *Lotus Sutra*, South Wall of Mogao Cave 217, High Tang

一组山峦有机地联系在一起，在两组山崖之间还画出一行大雁飞向远方，使山水显得较有纵深感。

第103窟的《化城喻品》，更像一幅独立的山水画（图118）。上部远景中，绘有一群人从右向左前行，前面一人牵着大象，大象驮着很多行李；后面一人戴风帽，骑着毛驴，像一个贵族妇人，身后又有二人步行跟随。下部描绘近景山水，左侧是一座险峻的悬崖，上面垂下青藤翠蔓，岩石间一道山涧凌空流下。崖下是曲折的河流。与左侧的悬崖相对，右侧也是一座高耸的山峰，山脚下旅行的人们在这里休息。这一景色成了画面的主要内容。经变画本来的图解佛经内容的意义被淡化了，而倒像是一幅完整的山水画。此画是唐代青绿山水画的代表作品。

在第103窟、217窟的山水画中，画家们充分调动了山水的各个要素，山峰、河流、瀑布、树木、藤蔓等都各得其宜，表现得十分协调。山峰有耸立的危崖，有平缓的小丘，有近景的岩石，有远景的峰峦。河流也各有曲

group of hills in the upper right section is the most attractive. The cascading waterfall, though discolored, still gives off an impression of life and vitality. It contains highlights, similar to the way pupils of the eyes are depicted when painting a dragon. The distant scene in the upper left section is not as rich as the previous groups, but it is indispensable in terms of the painting's overall composition. It organically joins the cliffs in the close scene on the left to the group of hills on the right. Even a row of wild geese is added between the two groups of cliffs, creating a sense of depth and breadth upon the landscapes.

The "Chapter on the Parable of the Conjured City" wall painting in Cave 103 appears more like an individual landscape (Fig.118). In the distant scene in the upper section, groups of people advance from right to left. The one in the front leads an elephant laden with baggage. Behind them, a traveler riding a donkey wears a winter hat—she appears to be a noblewoman. Two others follow them on foot. The lower part contains scenery in the foreground. On the left is a precipitous cliff with green vines and vegetation hanging from it. A stream flows down between the rocks, and below the cliff is a winding river. On the right is another high cliff, opposite the one on the left, at the foot of which travelers stop and rest. This scene seems to be the main subject of the painting. A sutra illustration

图 118 化城喻品 莫高窟第 103 窟南壁 盛唐

Fig.118 The Parable of the Conjured City from the *Lotus Sutra*, South Wall of Mogao Cave 103, High Tang

折,远景河流细细如线,近景中波浪翻滚,还有山崖上喷出的瀑布、泉水,体现出透明之感。树木更是种类繁多,开花者如桃如李,近景中柳树婆娑,松树挺立;悬崖上青藤垂下,草丛茂盛。从野外到城里,人物来来往往。这一切构成了一幅完美的山水人物图。

以莫高窟第217窟、103窟为代表的山水画,线描细腻,以青绿色为主,画面绚丽灿烂。这样的山水画也就是画史记载的"青绿山水"。唐代李思训(653—718年)、李昭道父子以画青绿山水著称。《唐朝名画录》盛赞李思训"山水绝妙""国朝山水第一"。《历代名画记》说李思训"其画山水树石,笔格遒劲,湍濑潺湲,云霞缥缈,时睹神仙之事,窅然岩岭之幽。时人谓之大李将军其人也"。从这些记载中,我们看到李思训一派山水画的特点在于:注重以线描勾勒;注重明亮色彩。这

is meant to be a painting that interprets Buddhist scriptures. The concept of that interpretation is weakened here, and instead it looks like a complete landscape on its own, making it a representative work of Tang period blue-green landscapes.

In the paintings in Caves 103 and 217, the artists made full use of various landscape elements such as hills, rivers, waterfalls, trees, vines, and so forth. They allowed each one to play its part in the composition, and all of these are in complete harmony. In terms of peaks, some are towering cliffs, some are gentle hills, some are nearby rocks, and some are distant ranges. The rivers wind in their own way, following their own course. The distant ones are painted as thin as mere lines; the nearer ones swell with magnificent currents; there are even springs and waterfalls gushing out of cliffs, appearing transparent. There are a variety of trees, as well: peach and plum trees bloom; willows dance, and pines stand straight and high in the foreground. Green vines hang on steep cliffs, and lush grass flourishes. People come and go between rural areas and towns. All these make up a perfect image of landscape and people.

Landscapes are painted in exquisite line sketches, with blue and green as the dominant colors, bright and brilliant. Typical works of blue-green landscape paintings, as they are known, can be seen in Caves 217 and 103. Father and son artists, Li Sixun (653–718) and Li Zhaodao, of the Tang period were famous for this type. *Anthology of Prominent Paintings of the Tang Dynasty* praised Li Sixun highly, stating that he was "excellent in

两点也就是青绿山水画的一般特点。这样的山水画在唐代是很受欢迎的,所以李思训赢得了那样高的声誉。敦煌壁画唐代前期的山水画在画法上与青绿山水画是一致的。莫高窟第 217 窟约开凿于景云年间(710—711 年),大致与李思训同时或稍晚,受到李思训一派山水风格的影响是很自然的。从敦煌壁画中我们也可以探索唐代青绿山水画的发展状况。

第 172 窟观无量寿经变中的山水画与别的山水画不同,在重重楼阁的两侧画出山水景物,不是画成高山的样式,而是画出一望无际的原野,其中有河流曲折地流下,画面上部留出部分空白。在象征着净土世界的建筑物后面,表现出了真实的空间透视,体现出画家驾驭山水的熟练程度。在净土世界的两侧还以条幅的形式画出了"未生怨"和"十六观"的内容;在两个条幅的上部往往画出山水场景,具有相对的独立性。"日想观"是《观无量寿佛经》中所说 16 种

painting landscapes" and "second to none in our dynasty". *Famous Paintings through the Ages* also made mention of Li Sixun: "Mountains, rivers, trees, and rocks in his paintings are vigorous. He can portray rushing torrents, gentle streams, and illusory clouds. He seems to present a heavenly world in front of the eyes, but actually what he does is depict the natural scenes of cliffs and ranges, obscure and remote. People call him Grand General Li." Judging from these accounts, we can see that the key features of Li Sixun's style are sketching with clean lines and tinting with the bright colors commonly used in blue-green landscapes. Such paintings were widely appreciated in the Tang Dynasty, explaining why Li Sixun was so highly honored. The landscape techniques of Early Tang Dunhuang murals were consistent with those used in blue-green landscape paintings. Mogao Cave 217 was constructed in the Jingyun Era (710–711), approximately the same time as, or slightly later than, Li Sixun's works. It was natural that landscapes were influenced by Li Sixun's style, and the development of blue-green landscape paintings in the Tang Dynasty can be explored through the Dunhuang murals.

The landscapes in the *Amitayurdhyana Sutra* illustration in Cave 172 are unique. Scenes painted on both sides of the numerous pavilions and towers are not high mountains, but a boundless stretch of open land where rivers meander, and even blank space is

修行方法即"十六观"之一，是通过对落日的"观想"，并进而使意念进入到佛国净土世界。壁画中则通过描绘自然的山水景物来表现这样的"观想"场面。在第172窟北壁的日想观中，右侧画出高耸的山崖，韦提希夫人坐在山下，左侧一条河流环绕，上部画出淡蓝色的远山及彩云。青绿色画出远景中的原野，与近景中赭红色的山崖形成强烈的对比，华丽而不流俗（图119），充分显示出唐代山水画的成就。同一内容，在本窟南壁也有成功的表现，而且盛唐第320窟、172窟的这一内容，也都是表现出完整的山水场景（图120）。

第172窟东壁北侧的文殊变上部山水也表现出了相似的空旷的风景。图中共画出三条河流，由远而近流下，在近处汇成滔滔洪流，左侧是一组壁立的断崖，中部是一处稍低矮的山丘，右侧是一组山峦。沿山峦一条河流自远方流下，近处则表现出

adopted in the upper part. Thus true spatial perspective is displayed behind the buildings that symbolize the world of the Pure Land. This shows how skillful the artists were in controlling the elements such as mountains and rivers. On each side of the Pure Land scene, the *nidana* of the "Enemy While Still Unborn" as well as a scene of the Sixteen Visualizations are painted in vertical panels. Normally the tops of these two panels would be mountains and rivers, which are relatively independent. The visualization on the setting sun, one of the Sixteen Visualizations, is one of the 16 methods from the *Amitayurdhyana Sutra* for meditation practice. The method intends to help the practitioner's mind go into the Buddhist world of the Pure Land by observations and contemplations on sunsets. In the murals, such visualizations are represented by depicting natural scenery, including mountains and rivers. In the "Visualization on the Setting Sun" on the north wall of Cave 172, high cliffs are painted on the right, and at the foot of the cliffs sits Queen Vaidehī. A river circles around on the left, with rosy clouds over the river and distant mountains in light blue. The blue and green open land in the distance and the reddish brown cliffs nearby form a sharp contrast, making the view magnificent and not coarse or common (Fig.119). The remarkable achievements in landscapes of the Tang Dynasty are on full display here. The south wall of this cave also presents similar material just as successfully. Furthermore, in both Caves 320 and 172 of the High Tang, this same subject is displayed in the form of complete landscapes (Fig.120).

图 119　日想观　莫高窟第 172 窟北壁　盛唐
Fig.119　Visualization on the Setting Sun, North Wall of Mogao Cave 172, High Tang

艺苑瑰宝
莫高窟壁画与彩塑

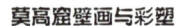

图 120　日想观　莫高窟第 320 窟北壁　盛唐
Fig.120　Visualization on the Setting Sun, North Wall of Mogao Cave 320, High Tang

汹涌的波浪,远处河两岸的树木越远越小,与远处的原野连成一片,表现出无限辽远的境界。河流的表现引人瞩目,特别是表现出汹涌澎湃的波浪,具有大江大河的气势（图121）。

盛唐石窟的青绿山水画大多是从中原传来的粉本,或丘峦秀丽,绿树环合;或烟霭

Cave 172 displays similar scenes of open landscapes. In the upper register of the Manjusri illustration painting, located on the left side of the east wall, three rivers flow from far away and converge with a torrential current nearby. On the left is a group of sheer cliffs, in the center is a cluster of lower hills, and on the right is a range of mountains. One of the rivers flows down along the range from far away. As it comes near, the water turns into tempestuous waves. In the distance, there are trees on either side of the river. The farther away the

图 121　山水　莫高窟第172窟东壁　盛唐
Fig.121　Landscape, East Wall of Mogao Cave 172, High Tang

雾锁，山水迷蒙；或大海扬波，舟楫帆影……这些都不是西北地区的自然风光，但是敦煌的画家们受到内地山水画审美意识的深刻影响，自觉或不自觉地把西北的风光融入了青绿山水画中，尽管经过了美化加工，但仍能寻其端倪。如第172窟的山水画对于辽阔原野的表现，显然不是南方的自然风光。仔细观察沟壑的特点，就会发现，这种仿佛断裂的沟壑，在西北很多地方都可以看到。敦煌附近就能找到类似的景观，只是由于干旱，现在没有那样汹涌的流水了。而在唐代，莫高窟附近曾有过"左豁平陆，目极远山，前流长河，波映重阁"（莫高窟第148窟碑文）的景色，这就为当时的画家们提供了素材，并激发他们的灵感，进而创作出这种富于地方特色的山水画来。

trees are, the smaller they look, merging into the far open land, and showing a sense of infinite remoteness. The river is remarkable, particularly the surging waves which convey the majesty of huge rivers (Fig. 121).

The majority of Dunhuang's blue-green landscapes created during the High Tang period were based on drafts from the Central Plains. Green trees embrace the tall and lovely hills; mists and clouds shade the mountains and rivers all around; sea waves swirl and rock the distant ships and sails. None of the scenes are native to the terrain of Northwest China. However, deeply influenced by interior China's aesthetic concepts on landscape, artists in Dunhuang integrated—whether intentionally or not—the scenes of Northwest China into blue-green landscape paintings. Although they were beautified and processed artistically, clues to their origin can still be traced. For example, it is obvious that the wide-open spaces displayed in the landscapes in Cave 172 are not from South China. A close inspection of the features of gullies reveals topographical fissures that can be seen in many places in Northwest China. Similar scenery can even be found near Dunhuang. Nowadays, there are no longer swelling rivers due to the arid climate. However, near the Mogao Caves, during the time of the Tang Dynasty there used to be such scenery as "open land extending to the left, hills as far as the eyes can see, long rivers flowing in front, and numerous pavilions reflected in the waves"—as quoted from the stele inscription in Cave 148. This provided material for the artists of the time and triggered their inspiration, enabling them to work out landscapes rich in regional flavor.

恬静淡泊之景——唐代后期壁画中的山水
Peaceful and Simple Scenery: Landscapes in Late Tang Murals

经过盛唐的发展和完善，山水画在中唐以后更加丰富了，这个时代的每个洞窟几乎都画有山水景物，能够表现山水的地方，画家都尽量画出相应的山水。尽管山水仍然是人物活动的背景，在佛教石窟里始终没有取得独立的地位，但这一时期山水画大量普及，已经成为壁画中不可缺少的部分。一些经变如观无量寿经变、法华经变、金刚经变、楞伽经变等已经形成了与佛经内容相适应的固定的山水模式。盛唐时期取得很高成就的全景式青绿山水画，在这一时期得到进一步发展。这一时期，水墨画技法传入了敦煌，给壁画中的山水画艺术带来了新的气息。这些具有水墨画特征的山水画为我们探索唐代水墨山水画技法的兴起和发展，提供了重要的参考资料。唐代后期山水画描绘较多，且有特色的洞窟有第 112 窟、154

Due to their development and refinement in the High Tang period, landscape paintings became more abundant during the Middle Tang, appearing in almost every cave of that era. The artists tried their best to create suitable landscapes wherever there was an opportunity. Although landscapes still functioned as the background for people and events, and could never be the independent subject of wall paintings in Buddhist caves, they grew in popularity during this period, becoming indispensable parts of the murals. *Amitayurdhyana Sutra* illustrations, *Lotus Sutra* illustrations, *Diamond Sutra* illustrations, *Lankavatara Sutra* illustrations, and others acquired codified landscape schemes based on Buddhist texts. Panoramic blue–green landscapes, having achieved great success in the High Tang, were further developed in this period. Meanwhile the technique of ink wash was introduced into Dunhuang, breathing fresh air into the art of mural landscapes. Wall paintings characterized by ink wash provide important reference material for us to explore the history of landscapes, i.e., the rise and development of this painting technique during the Tang Dynasty. Numerous landscapes were painted during the Late Tang as well, and Caves 112, 154, 468, 361, 369, 85, and 9 are

窟、468窟、361窟、369窟、85窟、9窟等。

第369窟南壁西侧的金刚经变,主要表现佛在金刚山中说法,周围环绕众多的菩萨和弟子。画面上部主峰耸立于画面正中,两侧层峦叠嶂,与主峰共同构成如金字塔一般的形式,充满了宗教的庄严感。同窟的南壁东侧经变画中,却把中央空出来,表现平缓的原野和丘陵,两侧分别画出山崖,形成平远的景色(图122)。这两铺经变画的构图形式,虽然在唐前期已经出现了,但本窟对山峰的表现十分突出。画家通过山峰表现出了佛教的气氛,把山水的境界与佛教的境界统一起来。比起唐前期的山水画来,那种鲜艳的青绿颜色用得较少,大多仅用赭色染出;线描也用极淡的色彩勾出,以致在很多地方如果不仔细看,往往看不出轮廓线。这是唐代后期山水画的一个倾向。

第231窟北壁的山水画也是这样。在北壁弥勒经变的上部两侧,分别画出山水景

among those that possess distinctive features.

The *Diamond Sutra* illustration on the north wall's left side in Cave 369 mainly presents a Dharma-preaching scene in the Diamond Mountains, with the Buddha surrounded by many bodhisattvas and disciples. The main peak stands tall in the center of the painting's upper register, with multiple hills on both sides. These hills, together with the main peak, constitute a pyramid-like formation, full of an awe-inspiring feeling of the sacred. By contrast, in the same cave's sutra illustration on the left side of the south wall, the central section is left open with uncultivated plains and gentle hills; on both sides, mountain cliffs are painted as a foil to the flatland scenery (Fig.122). Although this pattern of the two sutra illustrations appeared in the Early Tang, mountain peaks in this cave's wall paintings figure quite prominently. The artists evoked a Buddhist atmosphere through mountain peaks which unified the Buddhist realms with the landscapes. Unlike those of the Early Tang, the landscapes in this cave were mostly painted in reddish brown, with fewer bright colors such as blue and green. The colors within the sketched lines are so light that in many parts they are almost invisible if not examined closely. This is a tendency in landscapes of the Late Tang.

So it is with the scenery on the north wall of Cave 231. There are mountains and rivers on both sides of the upper section of the Maitreya Triple Sutra illustration. On the right is a group of towering cliffs, with a winding river running

Art Treasures: Murals and Painted Sculptures in Mogao Caves

图 122　山水　莫高窟第 369 窟南壁　中唐
Fig.122　Landscape, South Wall of Mogao Cave 369, Middle Tang

物；右侧是一组高耸的岩崖，在两道峭壁之间，有一条河水曲折地流出，近处的河道越来越宽，山脚下绘出修行的草庐。靠近中部的山，阳面是一个缓坡，有几只鹿悠闲地吃草，上部的远山也烘托出辽远的效果，左侧的山峦较平缓，通过河流的曲折线条表现出苍茫的原野，远景中也有几只鹿。对于远景的处理，加强了写实性，表现出深远的意境。比起盛唐第148窟的气势壮阔而强烈的气氛来，第231窟更多地表现出安详而宁静的风格。同窟南壁的法华经变及西壁的文殊变、普贤变中都画出了山水画。如文殊变中的山水在文殊菩萨的身后，远方耸立着几座峻峭的山峰，山的峰顶都比较尖，在山峰的顶部以石青色晕染，山峰之间还有白云缭绕。近处的原野上画出树丛，色彩明快。把平远与深远的景色结合起来，富有真实感。

晚唐第85窟东壁门上部画出萨埵本生故事。这个

between two of them; the closer it flows, the wider it becomes. At the foot of the cliffs is a thatched cottage used for spiritual practice. Near the mountains in the middle section, several deer graze leisurely on a sunny, gentle slope. The distant mountains above also create an effect of vastness and boundlessness. Hills on the left slope gently, and a wide expanse of land is shown by the winding course of the river. There are a few more deer in the distance as well. In terms of dealing with distant scenery, the realism is enhanced, revealing a profound artistic ambience. Compared with the imposing and intense atmosphere of Cave 148 of the High Tang, Cave 231 demonstrates a more serene and tranquil mood. In this same cave, landscapes also appear in the *Lotus Sutra* illustration on the south wall, and the Manjusri illustration and Samantabhadra illustration on the west wall. For example, there are landscapes behind Manjusri Bodhisattva in the Manjusri illustration. In the distance rise a series of steep peaks with pointed summits, colored by *sfumato* technique in malachite, white clouds coiling around them. Groves of trees are painted in bright colors in the fields nearby. A profound sense of realism results from combining the close and the distant scenes.

The "Mahāsattva *Jataka*" was painted above the entrance on the east wall of Cave 85, constructed during the Late Tang. This *jataka* tale was one of the most popular themes of the Northern Dynasties, but by the Tang period it was seldom painted on its own. In this cave, the *jataka* is on both sides of the *Golden Light Sutra*

故事是北朝最流行的题材之一,唐代以来单独画出的极少。此窟是作为金光明经变的一个部分画出的,却画在经变的旁边,采用了连环画的形式描绘故事内容,但没有像早期的那样分段画成长卷形式,而是以山水为骨干,均衡地分布情节,山脉相连,很难分隔开来。山峦的画法与唐前期的山水画相比,有了一些微妙的变化:首先是山的形状由圆润变为坚硬,山头多为角形,注重对岩石的刻画。在色彩上,唐前期是以石绿为主,而这里则以石青为主。中唐以后,壁画的色彩趋向于简淡,但进入晚唐以后,青绿重色再一次受到重视。尽管如此,色彩简淡的倾向似乎是难以阻挡的潮流。同样是青绿山水画,唐前期那种色彩丰富而绚丽的气氛、山势雄浑的境界不复出现。如第9窟的壁画中,在窟顶经变中也画出了连绵的山峦,但山峰与山峰之间的联系显得不太自然,由远景山峰到近景平地间也缺乏一个有机的过度。但峰峦显得坚硬,近景岩石的表现加强了,这是新的倾向。

illustration, as a part of it. It is not painted in the form of long narrative panels divided into sections as was done in the earlier period. Rather, the events are evenly distributed with the landscape forming the backbone, continuous and difficult to separate. Subtle changes also occurred in terms of painting technique, compared with landscapes of the Early Tang. The shapes of mountains changed from round, smooth peaks to stiff ones, most of which were painted with angled tops; emphasis was placed on the depiction of rocks. As to coloring, paintings of the Early Tang were dominated by malachite, but here the principal color is azurite. After the Middle Tang, the color of murals tended to be light and simple, but in the Late Tang, importance was attached to heavy blues and greens again. However, the tendency toward light, simple colors seemed to be an irresistible trend. Blue and green landscapes were the same, but they lacked the atmosphere of the rich, gorgeous colors and majestic mountains of the Early Tang. For example, in the murals in Cave 9, a range of hills is included in the sutra illustration on the ceiling, but the connection between the peaks seems unnatural. There is also a lack of organic transition from distant peaks to nearby plains. The hills appear to be hard and stiff, and the rocks in the foreground are depicted in an enhanced way. This is a new trend.

Cave 112 of the Middle Tang is a small

艺苑瑰宝
莫高窟壁画与彩塑

中唐第112窟是一个小型洞窟，在南北两壁各画出了两铺经变，北壁的报恩经变和南壁的金刚经变都画出了山水画。报恩经变上部画的是"论议品"，即鹿母夫人的故事。左侧画出一座山中有一大石窟，窟中一人在修行，窟外一鹿正在饮水。右侧也画出石窟内一人修行，窟外一女子行走，身后有很多莲花，前面有一王者正骑马经过。画家着意刻画了山崖和岩石，体现出一种幽静的气氛（图123）。

这里的山水则是全新的样式，山头几乎都是尖锐的角形，轮廓线转折强烈，似乎表现岩石的特征；颜色也极为清淡，仅用少量的石绿。值得注意的是，在墨线勾勒之后，又用淡墨渲染，这样的方法是水墨画的特征。第154窟也有同样的表现。该窟东壁门北侧的金刚经变及北壁观无量寿经变中，山水都以水墨画出，虽然也用石

one, with a sutra illustration painted on each of its north and south walls. Landscapes appear in both the *Sutra of Requiting Kindness Received* illustration on the north wall and the *Diamond Sutra* illustration on the south wall. In the upper register of the *Sutra of Requiting Kindness Received* illustration is the "Chapter on Discourses", namely the tale of the Mother Deer. On the left is a mountain with a huge rocky cave, in which a man is meditating, and outside, a doe is drinking water. On the right, again, a man meditates in a rocky cave, and outside the cave a woman walks by. Lotus blossoms trail behind the woman as a king on horseback rides by in front of her. The cliffs and rocks are depicted with care and effort, illustrating a quiet and secluded atmosphere (Fig.123).

Landscapes here are painted in a completely new style. Almost all hilltops are drawn with pointed angles, sketches contoured with sharp turns, seeming to display the features of rocks. The colors are extremely light and soft, tinted with only a little malachite pigment. What is noteworthy is that after the sketches are made with lines of ink, the landscapes are then filled in with light ink, characteristic of ink wash style. Similar features can be found in Cave 154 as well. The landscapes in both the *Diamond Sutra* illustration on the east wall, to the left of the entrance, and the *Amitayurdhyana Sutra* illustration on the north wall are created in ink wash. Despite being painted with malachite, the color does not obscure the ink lines. These features are also evident in the wall paintings in Cave 25 at Yulin—a

图 123 鹿母夫人的故事 莫高窟第 112 窟北壁 中唐
Fig.123 Tale of the Mother Deer, North Wall of Mogao Cave 112, Middle Tang

绿染出,但颜色并没有遮盖墨线。这种特征在中唐的代表窟——榆林窟第 25 窟壁画中,也可以明显地看出。

敦煌壁画中的水墨山水画显然是受到长安一带画家影响的产物。从藏经洞出土的唐代绢画中,水墨山水画之例也很多。如大英博物馆所藏的一幅有公元 836 年题记的药师经变,右上角的峰峦较尖,全有水墨晕染,薄施青绿色,

quintessential grotto of the Middle Tang.

Ink wash landscapes in Dunhuang murals were clearly influenced by artists from places such as Chang'an. Examples abound among Tang silk paintings discovered in the Library Cave, one of them being the *Bhaisajyaguru Sutra* illustration with inscriptions from the year 836, held in the British Museum. In this painting, the hills in the upper right corner are rendered with pointed tops and dyed overall with ink wash, applying the *sfumato* technique, but with blue and green tones, making the whole picture vigorous and dignified. Another example is a *Sutra of Requiting Kindness*

显得浑厚凝重。另一幅时代大体相近的报恩经变，画面构图与敦煌壁画一致，即中央画出净土图，两侧以条幅的形式画出佛教故事画。图中描绘须阇提父母从山间走出，左侧是峻峭的山崖，二人行走在山下的平地上。山崖以浅赭色染出受光面，阴面以水墨晕染，与莫高窟第112窟的画法一致。由于壁画与绢的质地的差别，绢画更能体现出水墨画的优点。而且，从绢画中，我们更能清楚地看出笔墨的方法。所以，从绘画的效果上看，绢画的水平往往高于壁画。

大英博物馆藏品中的另一幅佛传故事画中，山水的表现具有盛唐时期的很多特征，如山峰较圆、青绿色较重等。在构图上，画面左半部画出耸立的山崖，右侧画出远景，山势的布局与盛唐第320窟北壁的山水完全一致，但用墨线画出的强烈的轮廓线，以及山峰上面树丛的样式，则透露出了新的时代特征。同时还可以清晰地

Received illustration from the same period. Its composition is the same as that of the Dunhuang murals, namely, the Pure Land occupies the center and narrative paintings flank both sides with vertical panels. Painted within are Sujātā's parents as they come out of the mountains. On the left are high steep cliffs, and the couple walk below along the plains. The sunny side of the cliffs is tinted light reddish brown while the shady side is dyed in ink wash, using *sfumato*. The techniques adopted here are the same as those in Cave 112 at Mogao. Due to the differences between wall plaster and silk, silk paintings can better reflect the advantages of ink wash. Moreover, on silk paintings, we can see more clearly the method of brush and ink. As a result paintings on silk are often of higher quality than murals.

The landscape in another narrative painting in the British Museum reveals many of the characteristic features of the High Tang, including smooth round peaks, strong blue and green colors, and so forth. The picture is composed of high cliffs in the left half and distant scenery in the right half. The overall arrangement of mountains is identical to the landscapes on the north wall of Cave 320, from the High Tang period. However, the new features of that period are presented by the strong ink outlines and patterns of the forest groves on the peaks. Meanwhile, the wrinkle method can be clearly discerned. Due to the weak permeation of paint into the plaster, wall paintings in Dunhuang were normally tinted with deep colors,

看出皴法的运用。与敦煌石窟壁画相比,壁画的渗透效果较差,颜色往往涂得很厚,而绢画的颜色相对较淡,往往露出起稿的线条,或者当时就是一次起稿后,不再描线。反过来受其影响,中原以后的壁画也往往用较浓的墨线起稿后,施淡彩,不再画定形线。

while silk paintings were created using thinner, lighter hues, leaving the draft lines visible. Or, after the draft was made, there was no need to go over the sketch lines again. Murals of the Central Plains were in turn influenced by this technique of creating a draft in thick ink lines, then painting them over with light colors, so that final contour lines for shapes were no longer essential.

艺苑瑰宝
莫高窟壁画与彩塑

屏风画中的山水
Landscapes in Screen Paintings

中唐以后的经变画通常在上部表现净土世界，下部以屏风的形式表现经变中的具体故事或相关细节。这种形式称为屏风画。屏风画为山水画的表现提供了新的场所，虽然壁画都是以连屏的形式来描绘佛经故事，但每一扇屏风都具有一定的独立意义。画家可以利用屏风自由地进行山水布局，于是，屏风画的山水呈现出无限丰富的状况。第 159 窟五台山图的屏风画是比较独特之例（图 124），把金字塔形的五台山图画在屏风的中央，这是否就是当年吐蕃到内地求得的《五台山图》呢？由于屏风画形式呈纵向的画轴形式，通常都把画面分隔成几段以表现故事情节。但也不是截然分开，而是用山水把画面有

After the Middle Tang, it was often the case that the Pure Land was presented in the upper register of a sutra illustration, while in the lower register, specific narratives or related details of the sutra were represented in a form that somewhat mimicked a standing painted folding screen. These murals were known as screen paintings, and they provided new spaces for landscapes. Although a succession of screens in murals were used to depict stories from Buddhist sutras, each screen was relatively independent of the others. The artists could take advantage of the screen format to freely arrange mountains and rivers, resulting in infinitely abundant landscapes. One distinctive example is the *Map of Mount Wutai* in Cave 159, in which the pyramid-shaped mountain is painted in the center of the screen (Fig.124). Is this the fabled *Map of Mount Wutai* that the Tubo Kingdom was seeking in interior China? As screen paintings are arranged in vertical panels, the picture would normally be compartmented into several sections to display the plot of a story. However, here the sections are not completely separate, instead, the whole painting is coherently connected by landscapes. As for the landscapes, the composition of the painting tends to be more complete. An example is provided by the screen painting in Cave 231, inside the niche, where the "Mahāsattva *Jataka*" is presented. Actually three scenes are painted in the screen: at the bottom

图 124　屏风画五台山图　莫高窟第 159 窟西壁　中唐
Fig.124　Screen Painting of *Map of Mount Wutai*, West Wall of Mogao Cave 159, Middle Tang

机地联系起来。从山水画的角度来说，则是在构图上更趋向于完整了。如第231窟龛内表现萨埵太子舍身饲虎的屏风画，实际上有三个场面：下面画出萨埵太子山中见到饿虎的情节；中央画出萨埵太子舍身饲虎的场面；上部画出亲属为萨埵太子起塔供养的情节。由于人物较小，山水成了壁画的主体，屏风画的中心是萨埵太子饲虎的场面，山水也是以此为基准。下部的场面为近景，上部的画面处理为远景，中央则详细描绘山水景物，右侧是突兀的悬崖，悬崖下面是一片平地，地上画出众虎围绕萨埵太子啖食的场面。画面左侧画出一组低矮的山峦，中央这部分的山水布局，显然是延续了盛唐以来的样式。在山水构图上十分完整，山与树木、人物十分和谐。在色彩的运用上，山崖的顶部有较淡的石青色，下部的山坡和原野都用石绿画出，其中又以赭色相间，表现阴阳向背。大量的石绿色把画面统一起来，造成均衡的效果，虽然不像盛唐山水画那种鲜明、强烈而

register, the prince sees the hungry tigers in the mountains; in the middle, he sacrifices his own life to feed the tigers; and at the top, his relatives build a stupa to commemorate him. As the figures are rendered very small in the screen, the landscapes become the focal point. The landscapes are based on the central scene of Prince Sattva sacrificing his life for the tigers. The bottom displays a close-up view, while the top deals with a distant view, and in the middle, landscapes are depicted in detail. On the right are towering cliffs; below is a stretch of land where tigers surround the prince, eating his flesh. A group of low hills is on the left. The arrangement of landscapes in the middle is obviously a continuation of the High Tang style, in that the composition is quite complete and mountains, trees, and people are harmoniously integrated. In terms of color, the cliff tops are painted in light azurite; slopes and open land at the bottom are all in malachite; and red ochre alternates to show the sunny and shady sides. Abundant green pigments are applied to unify the whole painting, bringing about a balanced effect. The painting is not as bright, vigorous, or appealing as those of the High Tang, but the techniques in detailed treatment of landscapes are improved. The depiction of rocks turns out more natural, whether with the application of the wrinkle method or *sfumato* with thin ink, thus shaping a new formation of landscapes.

富有感染力，但对山水细部的处理则有所进步，不论是对岩石的皴笔还是淡墨的晕染都比较自然，形成了一种新的山水结构。

从构图上来看，通常每一扇屏风中要画出 2~4 个情节，因此往往利用山水或建筑分隔出一个个小环境，从中描绘故事情节。第 231 窟龛内南北西侧的屏风画表现报恩经变中"善事太子入海求宝"的故事，共有 4 个情节，通过自上而下的呈"S"形的一条河流，把画面联系起来；在河的两岸画出山峦，从全画面看来体现出山水画的构思。第 238 窟龛内南壁的屏风画中，也是表现"善事太子入海求宝"的故事，构图较疏朗，通常一扇屏风里描绘三个场景。如南壁西侧的屏风画中，下部是表现一群牛走过，中部是山丘和树木，上部在山崖旁有二人做对谈状，最上部是远山及远景的树丛（图 125）。分开来看，可以看作是两个场景；合起来看，山水风景由近及远，又是

In terms of composition, usually two to four narrative scenes are arranged in one screen. Therefore, landscapes or buildings are often used to separate spaces for individual scenes. The "*Jataka* of Prince Kalyāṇakārin" from the *Sutra of Requiting Kindness Received* is presented in the screen paintings on both the north and south sides of the niche in Cave 231. The painting is made up of four scenes, connected by a river sinuously running in an S-shape from top to bottom. Mountain ranges flank both banks of the river. The whole work expresses the artist's construct of landscape painting. In Cave 238, the same tale is presented in the south side of the niche. The composition here is rather loose, with three scenes arranged in one screen. For example, in the screen on the right side of the south wall, a herd of cattle walks along at the bottom. Hills and trees are painted in the middle. In the upper register, two men seem to be engaged in conversation beside a cliff. And at the top, mountains and groves of trees appear in the distance (Fig.125). Viewed separately, it can be regarded as two independent scenes, and taken as a whole, it is a complete landscape with mountains, rivers, and scenery from faraway to nearby. Many screen paintings are like this. Comparatively speaking, the fewer events or scenes a screen painting depicts, the more complete the landscapes are. The screen painting on the west side of the niche in Cave 54 is an example, in which there are only two scenes of Dharma preaching. Mountain peaks

图 125 屏风画 善事太子入海故事 莫高窟第 238 窟龛内南壁 中唐
Fig.125 Screen Painting of *Jataka* of Prince Kalyāṇakārin,
South Wall inside Niche, Mogao Cave 238, Middle Tang

一幅完整的山水画。这样的屏风画，数量不少。相比之下，情节较少的屏风，山水布局相对较完整，如第54窟龛内西壁的屏风画，只有两组说法场面，画面左侧画出山峰及树木，右侧则是平缓的山坡，上部画出远山，色彩极其简淡。第468窟龛内的屏风画是较为成功的例子。这里每一扇屏风都画出两组说法图，全画面呈平远景色，没有雄伟高大的山崖。在说法场面中只画出一两棵老树，两个场景之间以曲折流下的河流分隔开来，画面最上部画出远山，由远及近画出疏疏落落的树丛。这样自然和谐的山水意境，代表了这一时代的风格。

中唐第154窟龛内两侧的屏风画大多没有画出人物情节，似乎是没有佛经内容的山水画。当时，龛内本来曾有一些菩萨和弟子的塑像。这些屏风式的山水画是作为菩萨或弟子的背景画出的。现在塑像已失去，壁画完全露了出来，但往往左侧或右侧有一半的空白，使山水画看起来不完整。由此我们知道，在唐代后期的确出现过没有佛教内容的纯粹的山水画。在第156窟的维摩诘经

and trees are painted on the left, while on the right are gentle slopes. In the upper part are distant hills, tinted in extraordinarily simple, light colors. More examples of somewhat successfully executed screen paintings can be found in the niche in Cave 468, in which two scenes of Dharma preaching are painted on each screen. Overall the scenery is distant and flat, and there are no imposing cliffs. One or two old trees appear in the Dharma-preaching scene; the two scenes are merely separated by a winding river flowing downward. The top register shows distant mountains; scattered groves of trees appear from faraway to close by. The atmosphere revealed in such natural and harmonious landscapes represents the style of the period.

Cave 154 was constructed during the Middle Tang. There are no narrative scenes or characters in the majority of the screen paintings on either side of the niche, so they seem to be landscapes that have little connection with Buddhist scriptures. Originally there were statues of bodhisattvas and disciples in the niche; the screen painting landscapes were there to serve as background. Now that the statues are gone, the murals are completely exposed. But still many of the landscapes appear to be incomplete, as some of the left or right sides appear

变中，我们还可以看到在维摩诘像的身后画出一组屏风，屏风上都绘有山水画。这大约是当时现实生活的真实写照。屏风在唐代贵族的家庭流行，而屏风中画山水则是十分普遍的。

half-empty. However, from these paintings we can see that in the later years of the Tang there were indeed pure landscapes, having no connection with Buddhism. In the *Vimalakirti Nirdesa* illustrations in Cave 156, we also see a group of screen paintings behind Vimalakirti. Landscapes are painted in them all. Probably such paintings were a portrayal of real life at the time, for screens were popular with the Tang nobility and landscapes painted on screens were a common phenomenon.

五台山图

The *Map of Mount Wutai*

五代到北宋，正是中国山水画由着色山水向水墨山水转变的重要时期。这一时期由于西北地区的政治形势非常严峻，敦煌与中原的往来十分困难，文化艺术的发展处于相对停滞状态。曹氏统治者仿照中原王朝在敦煌设立了画院，壁画都由画院的画工们制作，从而形成了一种敦煌地区的"院体"画风，也使这一时期的绘画具有一定的保守性。

这一时期值得一提的是第 61 窟的《五台山图》。五台山位于山西省境内，山有 5 个顶，称为五台。由于海拔较高，山中气温很低，即使在盛夏也很凉爽。这些特点与佛经所记载的文殊菩萨所居的清凉山十分一致。早在南北朝时期，佛教信徒们就把五台山与文殊菩萨联系在一起，产生了种种传说，这样就使五台山的佛教

The *Map of Mount Wutai* in Cave 61 from this period is worthy of discussion. Mount Wutai lies in Shanxi Province (west of the Taihang Mountains), and gains the name from its five peaks. The temperature there is quite low owing to its elevation, and it is fairly cool even in the middle of summer. These features are nearly identical with the mythic Mount Qingliang ("Clear and Cool Mountain"), which according to Buddhist scriptures is the abode of Manjusri, the Bodhisattva of Wisdom. As early as the Northern and Southern Dynasties, Buddhist adherents had already associated Mount Wutai with Manjusri, giving rise to various legends. As

317

艺苑瑰宝
莫高窟壁画与彩塑

寺院越来越兴盛。到了唐代，高宗还专门派使臣会颐去五台山检验佛迹，会颐命随行人员画出了《五台山图小帐》带回。于是，《五台山图》连同五台山信仰就在全国传播开了。远在西南的吐蕃赞普也曾派人到唐朝求取《五台山图》。日本遣唐高僧圆仁曾专门访问过五台山，在他回日本时，还把《五台山图》带回了日本。可见《五台山图》流传之广。

敦煌壁画中最早出现《五台山图》是中唐时期的第159窟、361窟等。可能与文献记载的吐蕃遣使求取《五台山图》有关，这几幅《五台山图》都画成屏风画的形式，也许就是模仿唐代会颐所创的《五台山图小帐》。五代时期，《五台山图》更为流行，并与文殊变结合起来，内容更丰富了。榆林窟第19窟、32窟中的《五台山图》都是作为文殊变的背景画出的，由于山水的面积很大，使全图具有山水画的意味。榆林窟第32窟的文

a result, there was a proliferation of Buddhist temples in Mount Wutai. During the Tang Dynasty, Emperor Gaozong sent his imperial envoy Huiyi to Mount Wutai to inspect Buddhist sites of historical interest. Huiyi had *An Album of Mount Wutai* drawn up and dedicated it to the emperor. Thus the *Map of Mount Wutai* and faith in Mount Wutai as a spiritual site spread throughout the country. Even the Tsenpo of the Tubo Kingdom sent envoys to the Tang Dynasty for a copy of the map. The eminent monk Ennin, sent to the Tang imperial court from Japan, paid a special visit to Mount Wutai. When he returned to Japan, he also brought back a copy of the *Map of Mount Wutai*. This was a testimony to how widely the picture spread.

The *Map of Mount Wutai* first appeared in Mogao Caves 159 and 361 during the Middle Tang. Possibly this had something to do with the historical accounts of the Tubo Kingdom sending an envoy for the map. The murals in these caves were all in the genre of screen paintings, and most likely they were modeled on *An Album of Mount Wutai* created by Huiyi of the Tang Dynasty. During the Five Dynasties, the *Map of Mount Wutai* became more popular, and combined with Manjusri illustrations, the content became richer. Those in Yulin Caves 19 and 32 are painted as backgrounds of Manjusri illustrations. Because mountains and rivers occupy large parts of the painting, the overall sense is that is a landscape. The Manjusri illustration in Cave 32 at Yulin centers around a scene of Manjusri mystically appearing in Mount

殊变是以文殊菩萨在五台山化现为中心画出的。中央画文殊菩萨骑狮子从云中化现，四周则画出五台山和山中的寺院。与之相对应的普贤变，也画出普贤菩萨化现于云端，周围画出山水及毗沙门天王决海的情节。两铺壁画都褪色严重，皴法及晕染效果已看不出来了。

第 61 窟的《五台山图》可以说是《五台山图》在敦煌发展的最高表现。第 61 窟开凿于 947—951 年，本窟主要供奉文殊菩萨，所以也叫"文殊堂"。西壁配合文殊像画出巨幅《五台山图》，全长 13.45 米，高 3.42 米。画中详细描绘了东起河北正定、西至山西太原方圆 500 里的山川地形及社会风情。画面左侧为南台（图 126）、西台；下部为太原城至五台山的道路；上部画毗沙门天王、阿罗汉等赴会的情景；右侧为北台、东台，下部分别画出由河北道镇州（今河北省正定县）到五台山的道路。全图以中台及其下的文殊真身殿、万菩萨楼为中轴线，两边各以 5 座大寺分布在东、南、西、北四台之间。南下角是太原城；靠近中部有河东道

Wutai. He emerges from the clouds at the center, riding a lion. Surrounding him are Mount Wutai and its temples. At the opposite position, in the Samantabhadra illustration, Samantabhadra is also painted emerging from the clouds, surrounded by landscapes and the scene of Heavenly King Vaiśravaṇa leaping out of the sea. Both murals are so badly discolored that the effects of the wrinkle method and *sfumato* technique are hardly discernible.

The *Map of Mount Wutai* in Cave 61 at Mogao can be regarded as the zenith of its evolution in Dunhuang. The cave, constructed between 947 and 951, was primarily consecrated to Manjusri, so that it is also known as the Hall of Manjusri. A huge *Map of Mount Wutai*, measuring 13.45 meters long and 3.42 meters high, is painted on the west wall along with an image of Manjusri. The painting lays out in detail all the mountains, rivers, terrain, and even social life in the 500 *li*-area stretching from Zhengding in Hebei Province in the east, to Taiyuan in Shanxi Province in the west. On the left section are the south (Fig.126) and the west terraces. Below the terraces the road from the city of Taiyuan winds to Mount Wutai; above that is the scene of Heavenly King Vaiśravaṇa and an arhat on pilgrimage. On the right section are the north and the east terraces. Below them is the road leading to Zhenzhou (present day Zhengding County of Hebei

图 126　五台山图(局部)　莫高窟第 61 窟西壁南侧　五代
Fig.126　Detail of *Map of Mount Wutai*, Left Side of West Wall, Mogao Cave 61, Five Dynasties

山门；与之相对的北下角是镇州城，靠近中部有河北道山门。这样通过大山和大型建筑构成骨架，使画面形成了一个基本对称的格局。这样的布局无疑是受到了经变画构图的影响。山水画表现基本是沿袭唐代以来的传统表现手法。5座主峰基本上呈金字塔形，山头较柔和，令人想起董源山水画中常见的稳重而庄严的山峰。在近景表现中有所变化，画出尖锐的山峰，皴法则类似斧劈皴，笔力雄健。

在藏经洞出土的绢画中也有一幅《五台山图》(EO.3588，法国吉美博物馆藏)，其创作时间大约在曹氏

Province) of Hebeidao①, and Mount Wutai respectively. The middle terrace, the Temple of the True Manjusri, and the Pavilion of Ten Thousand Bodhisattvas below form the central axis for the whole map. On both sides of the axis, five grand temples are distributed among the east, the south, the west, and the north terraces. In the lower south corner is the city of Taiyuan and close to the central part is the gate leading to Hedongdao②. Opposite it, in the lower north corner, is the city of Zhenzhou and close to the central part is the gate leading to Hebeidao. In this way, the picture is framed by huge mountains and large buildings, so that overall it is composed in a symmetrical scheme, doubtlessly influenced by sutra illustrations. Techniques adopted in this painting follow, in general, traditions since the Tang Dynasty. The five main peaks are arranged basically in the shape of a pyramid, with gentle hilltops, reminiscent of the sedate and stately mountain peaks commonly seen in landscapes by Dong Yuan. There are some changes in the presentation of scenes in the foreground, where pointed mountain peaks are seen. The wrinkle method results in deep axe-cut texturing in the mountains, revealing the strong and energetic work of the paintbrush.

Among the silk paintings discovered in the Library Cave, there is also the *Map of Mount Wutai* (EO.3588), kept in the Guimet Museum in France. It is a work from the later *Guiyijun* period, when Dunhuang was ruled by the Cao clan. Manjushri is painted in the center, and

---

① Hebeidao, an administrative region in the Tang Dynasty, so named because it was located to the north of the Yellow River (Hebei, "to the north of the Yellow River" in Chinese).

② Hedongdao, an administrative region to the east of the Yellow River.

归义军晚期。画面中央是文殊菩萨,背景画满了山水,即五台山。这幅山水画是以着色为主的,山的轮廓线较柔和,山峦的形状较单调,以绿色晕染,值得注意的是山上树木的画法,在山上分布着同一形状的树木。

敦煌壁画中的山水画,对于佛教石窟来说,并不是主要的内容。由于唐五代以前中国山水画迹所存极少,而敦煌石窟中有大量作品保存下来,从它的发展历程,我们可以探索出中国山水画发展变迁的重要信息。

surrounding background consists of landscapes, namely, Mount Wutai. It is primarily a colored painting. The mountain contours are gentle and soft, and the shape of hills are uniform, tinted green with the *sfumato* technique. The painting method adopted in presenting trees on the mountains is noteworthy due to the similar tree shapes scattered all over.

The landscapes within Dunhuang murals are by no means the primary content of Buddhist caves. However, very few Chinese landscapes before the Tang and the Five Dynasties have been preserved, and a large number of works can still be seen in Dunhuang caves. From the course of their development, Dunhuang murals can provide important clues and information about the historical changes in Chinese landscape painting.

艺苑瑰宝：莫高窟壁画与彩塑
Art Treasures: Murals and Painted Sculptures in Mogao Caves

装饰的艺术

The Art of Ornamentation

广义地说，石窟艺术本身就是一种装饰艺术，因为所有的彩塑和绘画都体现着艺术家的装饰意图和匠心。莫高窟的彩塑、壁画基本上都包含着佛教的意义，有很多是直接根据佛经内容画出来的。这些题材如何进行组合、排列，如其中的构图、色彩等方面的考虑，就是石窟装饰的思想。自古以来，为了让幽暗的佛教石窟散发出迷人的光彩，画家们在装饰上花费了很多心血，营造出十分诱人的佛国世界。这些艺术上的构思，我们在前面各章对石窟建筑、彩塑以及壁画的各项内容中大多已经涉及了。本章主要谈一谈洞窟壁画中的图案画。

石窟中最引人注目的就是装饰于洞窟顶部的图案。北朝时期中心柱窟流行，洞窟前部顶为人字披，后部为平顶，于是为了体现出木构建筑的特点，前顶往往在人字披两披各浮塑出一些椽子装饰，在人字披主梁的两头还做出斗拱的形式。在椽子之间通常绘出的是莲花与忍冬纹组成的图案，有时也

Broadly speaking, cave temple art is itself a type of ornamentation, for all the painted sculptures and murals embody the artists' decorative intentions and ingenuity. Essentially all the works reflect Buddhist ideas, and a good many of them are directly based on Buddhist scriptures. However, ideas on how content is grouped, how it is arranged, and specifically how pictures are composed and what colors are used are the basis of cave ornamentation. Since ancient times, artists have put painstaking efforts into the decoration of dim cave shrines, so that they shine with beauty and the Buddhist world within them is captivating. Artistic elements and concepts have mostly been covered in the previous chapters, including cave structures, painted sculptures, murals, and so on. In this chapter, our focus will mainly be on decorative motifs for the wall paintings.

The most striking motifs are those painted as ornamentation on cave ceilings. During the Northern Dynasties, central pillar caves were in vogue. In this type of cave, the front part contains a gabled ceiling, while the back ceiling section is flat. Therefore, in order to indicate the features of a wooden structure, the front part of the ceiling is often decorated with clay relief rafters along both slopes, and *dougong* brackets are made at either end of the main beam. Lotus and honeysuckle motifs are often painted between the rafters, and sometimes images of bodhisattvas or the Buddha are also painted

画出菩萨或佛像与莲花忍冬纹组合成的图案。如第251窟人字披图案,下部表现一个从莲花中诞生出来的化生,从旁边有一根弯曲成"S"形的莲茎向上伸展,连接起上部的三朵莲花,弯曲而长的莲茎与盛开的莲花有一种动感,使画面充满活力。第254窟、263窟的人字披图案大体与前者一致,但下部画出的是站着的菩萨,更

in combination with lotuses and honeysuckles. Those on the gabled ceiling of Cave 251 are an example. In the lower part is a lotus child spontaneously reborn from that flower. Beside the baby is a lotus stem stretching upward in a curving S-shape, connecting with three lotuses in the upper part. The winding, growing stem and the blooming lotuses bring about a sense of movement, filling the picture with vitality. On the gabled ceilings in Caves 254 and 263, similar motifs are painted, but the pictures are made more vivid by the bodhisattva standing in the lower section (Fig. 127). There are numerous lotuses with flourishing petals on the gabled ceiling in Cave 288, constructed in the Western Wei. Peacocks and

图 127 人字披图案 莫高窟第 263 窟窟顶 北魏
Fig.127 Designs on Gabled Ceiling, Mogao Cave 263, Northern Wei

显得生动（图127）。西魏第288窟的人字披则画出有很多花瓣繁盛的莲花，还把孔雀、鹦鹉等禽鸟也组合到图案中来，使图案更为华丽而丰富（图128）。

中心柱后部的平顶通常是以方形连续纹组成，称为平棋。平棋图案一般有数重交错叠涩，层次较为丰富。平棋的中心是一朵大莲花，在4个岔角处画莲花或火焰纹。西魏以后，在平棋四角画飞天的情况较多。

parrots are even included in the motif, making it richer and more splendid (Fig.128).

The flat section of the ceiling at the back of a central pillar—known simply as a "flat ceiling"— is often made up of a sequence of square designs. Flat ceiling motifs are usually composed of overlapping squares within squares, set at angles to each other, resembling a laternendecke ceiling from Central Asia. In the center of each individual square is a large stylized lotus, and in each of the four corners are lotus or flame motifs. After the Western Wei, *apsaras* were usually added in the four corners of the flat ceilings.

图128　人字披图案　莫高窟第288窟窟顶　西魏
Fig.128　Designs on Gabled Ceiling, Mogao Cave 288, Western Wei

以忍冬纹、莲花纹为主的图案,形成了北朝装饰画的主旋律。但在西魏北周时期,图案中逐渐加入禽鸟、动物的图案。如北周第428窟顶部图案中不仅画出鹦鹉、孔雀,还画出了虎、鹿、猿等动物形象,并与周围的忍冬纹、莲花纹、几何纹等有机地组合起来,体现出自由奔放的气质(图129)。

隋代第427窟人字披顶部,画家不厌其烦地绘出一道精致的图案:在深绿的底色上,以缠枝莲茎和忍冬纹,按

Motifs dominated by honeysuckle and lotus designs formed the main trend of decorative painting during the Northern Dynasties. However, during the Western Wei and the Northern Zhou, birds and beasts were added to them. For example, in the motifs on the ceiling of Cave 428 of the Northern Zhou, not only are there parrots and peacocks, but also tigers, deer, and apes. These images are combined with lotuses, honeysuckles, and geometric patterns, displaying a free and unrestrained ambience (Fig.129).

At the top of the gabled ceiling in Cave 427 from the Sui period, the artist spared no effort in creating a border with exquisite motifs. Against a background of dark green, a pattern

图129 平棋图案 莫高窟第428窟窟顶 北周
Fig.129 Flat Ceiling Pattern, Mogao Cave 428, Northern Wei

波浪形延续，构成一个个环形空间，其中画出盛开的莲花以及坐在莲花上的化生童子。这些化生童子显然象征着往生极乐净土的途径。图中的童子坐在莲花上，有的怀抱琵琶，有的吹奏竖笛，一副无忧无虑、愉快欢歌的神态。这条长长的装饰带随着起伏的莲茎，充满了动感的旋律（图130）。

在殿堂窟中，顶部中心是藻井，这里成为全窟装饰的重点。北朝的洞窟如西魏第249窟、第285窟的藻井大体与平棋图案一致，以莲花纹为主。第285窟在藻井四周增加了两层垂幔纹，并在四角画出长长的流苏，使藻井具有华盖的意义。隋代以后，洞窟越来越重视藻井装饰，创造出很多美丽的藻井图案。如第407窟藻井，中心是一朵八瓣莲花，花瓣重叠，显得厚重。花心是一个绿色的圆圈，圆中画出三只奔跑的兔子。这三只兔子共有三只耳朵，可是不论你看哪一只兔子都有两只耳朵。这

of twining lotus stems and honeysuckles repeats, resulting in a row of circle-shaped spaces. Within each circle is a lotus in full bloom, upon which sits a lotus child. It is clear that these boys symbolize the route to the paradise of the Pure Land. The boys sit on lotuses, some holding a *pipa* in their arms, some playing the vertical flute; they appear light-hearted, and full of joy. This long decorative border is bursting with rhythm with its undulating lotus stems (Fig.130).

In a hall cave, at the center of the ceiling is a sunken caisson, providing the focal point of the entire cave's embellishment. The caisson ceiling motifs in caves of the Northern Dynasties are generally similar to flat ceiling designs, dominated by lotuses. Examples can be found in Caves 249 and 285 of the Western Wei period. Around the caisson ceiling in Cave 285, two layers of hanging drapery are added, with long tassels painted in the four corners, giving the impression of a tent canopy. After the Sui Dynasty, emphasis was increasingly placed on the decoration of caisson ceilings, resulting in the creation of many stunning designs. One example is the ceiling in Cave 407. In its center is an eight-petaled lotus. The petals pile up, looking thick and luxuriant. At the heart of the lotus is a green circle, with three rabbits running counter-clockwise inside. These three rabbits appear to have, in total, three ears, but no matter which rabbit you look at, it actually has just two ears. This is the iconic three-rabbit pattern (Fig.131). The artist made skillful use of the

图 130　卷草图案　莫高窟第 427 窟窟顶　隋
Fig.130　Scrolling Grass Motif, Caisson Ceiling of Mogao Cave 427, Sui Dynasty

就是有名的三兔造型（图 131）。画家巧妙地利用图案共用原理，形成了有意味的三兔图案。在大莲花四周的蓝色底色上又有 8 身飞天环绕莲花飞行。这些飞天手托鲜花，兴高采烈地行进，长长的飘带伴随着流云，空中充满了鲜花，具有热烈的气氛。飞天旋转飞行与中央奔跑的兔子相呼应，充满了生机勃勃的情调。三兔藻井图案在隋代还有不少，但并不雷同。如第 420 窟的藻井，中心也绘三兔，藻井向外有三重叠涩，四边形成的岔角里画飞天。

唐代以后，洞窟形制以殿堂

sharing principle in the design, which imbues the three-rabbit pattern with its fascination. Against a blue background, eight *apsaras* appear around the central lotus, blossoms in hand, long sashes flowing with the floating clouds, and fresh flowers filling the air. They fly exuberantly, creating a warm atmosphere. The rotating *apsaras* in flight echo the rabbits running in the center, full of vitality. During the Sui Dynasty, more three-rabbit motifs were painted on caisson ceilings, but none were identical. For example, three rabbits were painted in the center of the laternendecke ceiling design in Cave 420 as well, with an *apsara* in each of the four corners of the square design.

窟为主,藻井的装饰也越来越华美。初唐第329窟的藻井(图132),井心用14个卷曲莲瓣和14朵卷云纹环绕莲心绘成一朵大莲花,花心以白色的弧线画成波状旋转形,似莲花正在旋转的色轮上放光,正如《华严经》中说:"莲花妙宝为璎珞,处处庄严净无垢,香水澄淳具众色,宝华旋布放光明……"在方井的四角与中心相对应又各画出莲花的一角,莲花的外缘具有石榴纹样。这些巧妙的组合使造型简单的莲花变得无比华丽丰富。中心莲花的周围,在

During the Tang period, hall caves became the predominant type of architectural layout; the designs on caisson ceilings became ever more magnificent as a result of this trend. The ceiling of Cave 329 of the Early Tang is an example (Fig.132). At the center of the caisson is a large lotus made up of 14 curling petals and 14 cirrus cloud motifs. The lotus is surrounded by white wave-like arcs; the floral design resembles a spinning colored wheel giving off light, exactly as stated in the *Flower Garland Sutra*: "As fine a treasure as jade and pearls is the lotus; Stately and pure all over, a unique universe; Clear yet colorful, its fragrance is permeating; Elegant and splendid it shines while whirling ..." Corresponding to the center, in each of the four corners of the

艺苑瑰宝
莫高窟壁画与彩塑

图 131 三兔藻井 莫高窟
第 407 窟窟顶 隋
Fig.131 Iconic Three-Rabbit Design on Caisson Ceiling, Mogao Cave 407, Sui Dynasty

图 132 莲花飞天藻井
莫高窟第 329 窟窟顶
初唐
Fig.132 *Apsaras* with Lotus Design on Caisson Ceiling, Mogao Cave 329, Early Tang

深蓝色的底色中，画出4身衣袂飘飘、手持鲜花的飞天，她们在蓝天中轻飞曼舞，身边浮云流动。井心以外是卷草纹、联珠纹、垂角纹帷幔等。在藻井外缘的帷幔外侧，又画出12身飞天，在五彩云的衬托下，他们演奏着琵琶、箜篌、腰鼓等乐器，朝着一个方向连续不断地飞去。华丽无比的图案以及他们活泼多姿的动态给人以无限遐想。这个藻井生动绚丽，变化丰富，不愧为唐代装饰画的杰作。

唐代装饰图案把莲花、牡丹、石榴等各种花纹的图案组合在一起，在色彩、花纹构成等方面争奇斗艳，美轮美奂。初唐第322窟的藻井，井心由葡萄蔓网纹构成，四边又以团花、棱格、矩形纹等组成边饰，外层画成帐幔的形式。四周又画出十几身飞天各自弹奏着乐器，在蓝天白云中轻快地飞翔，色调明净而绚丽。第209窟的藻井在中央以4个石榴对称排列，8串葡萄交错组织，通过

ceiling is painted one quarter of a lotus, the outer edge composed of pomegranate motifs. These ingenious combinations enable simple lotuses to be incomparably beautiful and rich. Around the lotus in the center, against a background of dark blue, are four *apsaras*. *Dhotis* floating, and fresh flowers in hand, they fly gently and freely, dancing in the blue sky, with clouds flowing beside them. Around the center are curling grass motifs, linked pearl motifs, and triangular hanging canopy motifs. Another 12 *apsaras* are painted beyond the outer edge of the canopy, along the sides of the ceiling. Set off by rosy clouds, playing musical instruments including the *pipa*, the *konghou*, and the waist drum, they fly one after another in the same direction. The matchlessly gorgeous motifs and their varied dynamics captures the viewer's imagination. The ceiling design in this cave, vivid and brilliant, full of constant change, is truly a masterpiece among the decorative paintings of the Tang Dynasty.

In Tang period decorative painting, different flowers such as the lotus, peony, pomegranate, and others were combined together as motifs. In terms of color and composition, they were beautiful and fantastic, almost seeming to compete with each other. Take the caisson ceiling in Cave 322 from the Early Tang, for example: the center is composed of a network of grapevines; its four sides are decorated with floral, lozenge, and geometric motifs; the surrounding border is painted with a canopy design of hanging triangular pendants. Over a

藤蔓联系起来。四周分别为连珠纹、鱼鳞纹、矩形纹等,最外层为垂幔,色彩简淡而典雅(图133)。盛唐第320窟的藻井中央为团花纹。这种结构复杂的团花纹,可以看出莲花、牡丹等花瓣的特征,但它又不像某一种花。在中央方井以外,有着层次丰富的边饰,菱形纹、团花纹、鱼鳞纹、垂角纹及流苏的纹饰无不描绘细腻,色彩丰富。全图以大红为主色调,用不同色度的青、绿、黄、白等色描画纹样,显得强烈、厚重而又华贵,体现出唐人的审美气质。

五代以后,除了唐代以来的团花图案外,中国传统的龙凤图案开始流行起来。画面色调倾向于清淡,以绿色为主,常常辅以描金,表现出华丽的效果,并开始采用沥粉堆金的新手法,表现出类似浅浮雕的效果。西夏以后,更进一步在图案中推广这种手法,特别是藻井中,表现龙凤图案时,大量采用堆金的方法,体现出高贵的气质。

dozen *apsaras* are painted in the outermost border along the edges of the caisson, each playing a different musical instrument, flying with carefree ease among the white clouds in the blue sky. The colors are dazzling and beautiful. In the center of the caisson ceiling of Cave 209, four pomegranates are arranged symmetrically, with eight bunches of interlaced grapes, joined together by the vines. Around them are linked pearl, fish-scale, and rectangular motifs, with an outermost band of hanging triangular pendants, all tinted in soft, simple, elegant colors (Fig.133). In Cave 320 of the High Tang, the center of the caisson ceiling is a complex composite floral motif, in which features of lotus and peony petals are detected, but which does not resemble any particular flower. Beyond the central square, there are rich decorative borders with lozenge, composite floral, fish-scale, and triangular pendant motifs, as well as hanging tassels. All are superbly executed with abundant colors. The overall color scheme is red, but motifs are depicted in different accent colors of blue, green, yellow, and white, looking bold, elegant, and luxurious, embodying the aesthetic ethos of the people during the Tang Dynasty.

After the Five Dynasties, in addition to composite floral motifs in vogue since the Tang, traditional Chinese motifs such as the dragon and phoenix were also popular. The color tones tended to be light and simple, predominantly green, normally complemented by outlining in gold, creating a gorgeous effect. Meanwhile, the new technique of applying gypsum powder

Art Treasures: Murals and Painted Sculptures in Mogao Caves

图 133　莫高窟第 209 窟藻井　初唐
Fig.133　Caisson Ceiling, Mogao Cave 209, Early Tang

五代第 146 窟的藻井，方井以土红为底色，中央以青绿色画出团花，花心在绿底色上画一条龙。在团花的四面各画一对鹦鹉，四角又饰以半团花。方井周围分别画方胜纹、卷草纹等。色彩别致，风格清新。西夏时期以龙凤形象为主的装饰图案更为盛行，绿色调成为此时的基调。第 16 窟藻井中心也是

mixed with glue and then gilding (*lifen–duijin*) was adopted, which could produce an embossed or relief effect. After the Western Xia, the technique became even more widespread in motif designs, especially in caisson ceilings. It was widely applied in dragon and phoenix motifs, lending an air of nobility.

The background color of the caisson ceiling in Cave 146 of the Five Dynasties is earthly red, against which a flower cluster in blue and green is painted in its center. At the center of the flower is a dragon drawn against a background of green. Pairs of parrots are painted on each of the four sides, and all four corners are decorated with flower clusters. Around the caisson are geometric square motifs as well as curling grass motifs with unconventional colors and fresh

以红色为底色,在团花的花心,画出一只凤凰,在花的四周则画出4条龙。龙凤图案都以沥粉堆金的方法画出,有一种浮雕的效果。四周的边饰也以同样的方法画出卷草纹,显得层次丰富,形象华美。第130窟的顶部藻井也是西夏时期所绘,中心是一条团龙,四周画出4条小龙。龙的形象也是以沥粉堆金的方法画出,周围配合团花纹及彩云图案,造成华丽庄严的效果(图134)。

styles. During the Western Xia, ornamental motifs dominated by dragon and phoenix images grew in popularity, with green as the main color scheme of the time. The background of the caisson ceiling in Cave 16, however, is red. The center of the flower cluster contains a phoenix; the outside of the flower is surrounded by four dragons. The dragons and the phoenix are created using the *lifen-duijin* technique of applying gypsum powder mixed with glue and then adding gold leaf. Similarly, decorative curling grass motifs are painted along the four sides with rich gradations, looking gorgeous. The caisson ceiling in Cave 130 is again the work of the Western Xia, the center of which is a coiling dragon with a smaller dragon on each of the four sides. These dragons are also painted with the *lifen-duijin* technique of embossing and gilding. Complemented by composite floral motifs and rosy clouds, the dragons create a majestic, extraordinary effect (Fig.134).

图 134　莫高窟第 130 窟藻井　西夏
Fig.134　Caisson Ceiling, Mogao Cave 130, Western Xia

艺苑瑰宝：莫高窟壁画与彩塑
Art Treasures: Murals and Painted Sculptures in Mogao Caves

敦煌壁画的风格与成就

Style and Artistic Achievements of the Dunhuang Murals

六朝至唐代的著名画家,如顾恺之、曹仲达、吴道子等都曾画过大量的佛像画,像吴道子这样的画家主要作品几乎都在寺院壁画中。说明佛教绘画在当时成为中国绘画的新潮流,在这一股潮流的冲击下,中国的绘画便飞速地发展起来。

敦煌壁画是保存至今数量最多、时代延续最长、绘制最精美的艺术宝库。从敦煌壁画中,我们可以看出公元4世纪至14世纪中国佛教壁画发展的大致轨迹,特别是对于考察中国早期人物画、建筑画、山水画的发展具有重要的意义。

敦煌壁画北凉至北魏时期的绘画主要受西域壁画的影响,佛、菩萨较多地体现着印度式或犍陀罗式的形象特征。佛和菩萨多为正面形象,只有药叉、伎乐飞天等次要的神格和世俗人

From the Six Dynasties[①] (222–589) to the Tang period, famous artists—including Gu Kaizhi, Cao Zhongda, and Wu Daozi—all painted large numbers of Buddhist images. Almost all the important works by artists such as Wu Daozi were murals painted in Buddhist temples, reflecting that Buddhist art was a new trend in China at that time. Chinese painting developed rapidly under the impact of this trend.

Dunhuang is a treasure trove of fine art. The number of caves still preserved today is the largest, the history of construction is the longest, and the painting skills revealed there are the most exquisite. From the wall paintings, we can see the general evolutionary track of Buddhist murals in China from the 4th to the 14th centuries, which is of great significance to investigating the development of earlier Chinese paintings of figures, landscapes, and architecture.

From the Northern Liang to the Northern Wei, paintings in Dunhuang were primarily influenced by mural art of the Western Regions. The Buddha and bodhisattva were mostly characterized by styles from India and Gandhara, in which they were portrayed in an obverse position facing the viewer, while secondary *devas* such as *yakṣas*, musical performers, and *apsaras*, as well as mortals, were painted only in profile. In the Northern Liang murals in Caves 272 and

---

① The Six Dynasties in the southern part of China in history, including Wu of the Three Kingdoms, Eastern Jin, and the Southern Dynasties, which is one geographical part of the Northern and Southern Dynasties, made up of four successive shorter dynasties, Song, Qi, Liang and Chen.

物出现侧面像。北凉第272窟、275窟,北魏第251窟、254等窟的壁画中,人物的比例合度、形体健壮,菩萨的身体多呈"S"形弯曲,上身半裸,下着长裙。飞天和药叉动作幅度较大,充满力量感。特别是重色晕染的技法,是传自古代龟兹艺术的典型技法,现存的克孜尔石窟就保存着大量的西域风格壁画。西域风格的画法由于用色厚重,晕染层次丰富,在1500年后的今天,大多变色严重,形成了线条粗犷、"小字脸"等奇特的形状。

东晋、南朝时期,南方贵族阶层崇尚清谈和神仙思想,对那种身体清瘦、飘飘欲仙的人体形象有特别的爱好,这就是所谓"秀骨清像""褒衣博带"的审美风格。在南方和中原一带出土的画像砖中就发现了这样的仙人和世俗人物形象。在北方,由于北魏孝文帝改革,大力倡导学习汉民族文化,南方的文化艺术便大举影响到北方,以龙门石窟为中心的北方佛教艺术中就体现出了南方所欣赏的秀美的风

275, as well as the Northern Wei murals in Caves 251 and 254, human figures are sturdy and well-proportioned, while bodhisattvas are painted in the *tribhanga* S-shaped pose with the upper body partially clothed, and the lower body dressed in a long *dhoti*. *Apsaras* and *yakṣas* appear in vigorous motion, full of the sense of power. In particular, the *sfumato* technique of heavy color saturation is a characteristic technique borrowed from ancient Qiuci art. Large numbers of murals in the Western Region styles are still found in the Kizil Caves today. Due to heavy color dyeing and rich gradations in *sfumato* technique, most of the paintings we see today, 1,500 years later, have undergone such dramatic discoloration that strange shapes like rough lines and "small shape faces" have resulted.

During the Eastern Jin and the Southern Dynasties, the aristocratic class in the South were interested in lofty, intellectual discourse and Daoist immortalism, so they naturally gravitated toward slender, ethereal human images. This was the so-called aesthetic style of "slim and smart figures" and "broad robes with broad sashes". Such images of immortals and mortal humans were found on engraved bricks unearthed in the South and in the Central Plains. Meanwhile in the North, because of reforms led by Emperor Xiaowen of the Northern Wei, it was strongly advocated that the culture of the Han people be widely studied and imitated. As a result, the art and culture of the South greatly influenced the

格。敦煌则是在西魏以后，接受了传自中原的造型风格，以第249窟、285窟为代表的壁画中，出现了人体比例修长、身体苗条、眉目清秀、动作飘举、如神仙般的形象。在技法上则注重线描，色彩简淡，不重立体感，而追求一种平面的装饰性。这是当时追求的一种形式美，在人物造型上体现了汉代以来中国传统艺术的新发展。

但这种风格没有维持很长时间。到了北周时期，西域特色的造型再次出现在敦煌壁画之中，如第428窟的佛、菩萨像脸形浑圆，比例适中，色彩晕染厚重。与此同时，西魏出现的中原式造型风格并未消失，而是在很长一段时间与西域式造型并存于洞窟中。这是由于在当时的中原绘画中也存在着多种风格。

在南北朝时期，传自西域的画法在中国内地也同样被一些画家所吸收和

North. Therefore Northern Buddhist art centering on the Longmen Caves reflected the beautiful and graceful style appreciated in the South. However, it was not until the Western Wei that Dunhuang adopted the style of lines and shapes coming from the Central Plains. Among the representative murals in Caves 249 and 285, there are tall, slender figures with delicate eyes and eyebrows, and immortal-like floating movements. In terms of technique, emphasis was placed on lines, with simple, lightly saturated hues. Attention was not paid to achieving a sense of three-dimensional representation, but rather to decorating a flat two-dimensional surface. This was the type of formal beauty pursued during this period. In terms of figure portrayal, it was the newest development in traditional Chinese art since the Han Dynasty.

However, the trend did not last long. In the Northern Zhou, characteristic figure shaping of the Western Regions appeared once more in Dunhuang wall paintings. For example, the Buddha and bodhisattva in Cave 428 are shaped with round faces and moderate physical proportions, bearing the thick, heavy colors of the *sfumato* technique. Meanwhile, the Central Plains styles that began with the Western Wei did not disappear, but coexisted in caves with Western Region styles for many years. This was because there were several painting styles in the Central Plains at the time.

During the Northern and Southern Dynasties, painting techniques from the Western Regions were also absorbed or adopted by artists of interior China. For example, Cao Zhongda, an artist of the Northern Qi, painted clothes with thick and

采用。如北齐画家曹仲达的绘画具有衣纹稠迭如出水之状，因而被称为"曹衣出水"。这样的手法其实是来自印度笈多时代佛像造型的风格，在南北朝佛教美术大兴的时代，印度式的佛像画法传入中国并不罕见。南朝的张僧繇曾采用西域传来的"凹凸法"在南京一乘寺绘制壁画，"远望如凹凸，就视乃平"在当时传为佳话。人们把一乘寺称作"凹凸寺"。张僧繇的画法正是敦煌壁画北凉至北魏壁画中较为流行的西域式画法。六朝时代，张僧繇是与顾恺之、陆探微并称的著名画家，张彦远评价说，"象人之貌，顾得其神，陆得其骨，张得其肉"。中国绘画讲究神韵，能够传神的艺术应是最高的，因此顾恺之的人物画在当时评价最高。陆探微的绘画很讲究用笔，所谓"骨法用笔"，就是指在线

overlapping lines, as if they had just been pulled out of water; consequently the style was called "garment lines in Cao Zhongda style". However, this was actually the style of Buddhist statues from the Gupta period in India. In the Northern and Southern Dynasties, when Buddhist art flourished, it was not uncommon for Indian Buddhist painting techniques to be introduced into China. In the Southern Dynasties, Zhang Sengyao adopted the "concave-convex method" borrowed from the Western Regions, and painted murals in Nanjing's Yicheng Temple. The comment "Seen from far away, it seems to contain both the concave and the convex, but examined closely, the painting is flat" became such a favorite saying of the time that Yicheng Temple was called the "Ao Tu Temple"[①] by some people. Zhang's method was borrowed from the very style of the Western Regions, popular in the Dunhuang murals from the Northern Liang to the Northern Zhou. During the Six Dynasties, Zhang Sengyao was a famous artist who enjoyed a similar reputation to Gu Kaizhi and Lu Tanwei. Artist Zhang Yanyuan made the following remarks: "To paint what a person looks like, Gu portrays the spirit, Lu the bones, and Zhang the flesh." Chinese painting was particular about revealing inner qualities, so art which conveyed the spirit was considered the best. As a result, figure paintings by Gu Kaizhi were the most highly praised at the time. Lu Tanwei devoted special attention to the use of his brush, and thus the

---

① A transliteration: *Ao* means concave and *Tu* means convex in Chinese.

描方面的成就，他代表了以线描造型的传统绘画方法。而"张得其肉"，就是把人物身体表现出一种立体感而具有真实性。张僧繇就是吸取和融合了西域绘画技法而取得了较高成就。

顾恺之、陆探微的绘画风格注重用笔，形体清瘦的中原式绘画虽然在西魏时期已经传入了敦煌，但并没有很快在敦煌石窟中普及。敦煌仍然在不断地接受着来自西域的影响，所以北周和隋代的洞窟都出现了西域式和中原式两种风格并存的局面。这一局面也反映了当时中原内地的绘画多种风格并存的状况。

隋代以后，中原式的造型与西域式的造型逐渐融合，形成了新的造型风格。它既不同于西域式那种只强调晕染，不注重神采的造型，也不同于中原式那种只注重线描，不注重形体的概念化的造型，而是注重神韵而兼顾写实，以线描为主兼顾色彩晕染的写实主义的造型艺

so-called "bone painting" referred to his achievements in line drawing. He was the quintessential representative of traditional painting using lines. "Zhang portrays the flesh" meant the presentation of figures in three dimensions, and demonstration of representational style. Zhang was the artist who absorbed and assimilated painting methods from the Western Regions and made the most remarkable accomplishments.

The style of Gu Kaizhi and Lu Tanwei emphasized the use of paint brush. Painting style of slim and smart figures from the Central Plains was introduced to Dunhuang as early as the Western Wei, but it was not popularized in the Dunhuang caves rapidly, because Dunhuang was still under constant influences from the Western Regions. Therefore, in the caves from the Northern Zhou to the Sui Dynasty, there was a coexistence of styles from both the Central Plains and the Western Regions, which in turn reflected the situation of the multi-styled paintings of the Central Plains.

After the Sui Dynasty, the design forms of the Central Plains and that of the Western Regions gradually merged and a new style was formed. Not only was the new style different from that of the Western Regions, which mainly stressed *sfumato* technique and paid little attention to revealing inner qualities, but it was also different from the style of the Central Plains, which focused only on line drawing without attaching enough importance to conceptualized styling or design. But rather, it stressed spiritual

术。隋代壁画中出现了两种造型风格：一种是描绘细腻，注意色彩晕染和装饰性的"细密派"，以第419窟、420窟、427窟等窟为代表；一种是注重用笔，色彩较少，甚至不加晕染的"简淡派"，代表洞窟有第276窟、303窟等。

唐代以后，由于统一的国家经济文化高度发达，敦煌美术与中原美术发展几乎同步，以当时的首都长安为中心的中原地区流行的风格很快影响到敦煌。敦煌壁画进入了极盛时期，画家们熟练地运用不同的手段，塑造不同性格的形象，留下了许多杰出而生动的作品。唐代以后的绘画很难看出明显的外来风格与中原风格的区分，但当时中原画家的风格流派也或多或少地影响到了敦煌，使敦煌壁画呈现出百花齐放的局面。

初唐画家阎立本以写实精神创作了《凌烟阁二十四功臣图》《秦府十八学士图》等，都是直接对当时的人物进行写生而创作的，在当时

revelation while giving consideration to realistic representation. The new style was an art of realistic modeling that not only gave priority to line drawing but also paid attention to color dyeing adopting *sfumato* technique. In the murals of the Sui Dynasty, two design styles were reflected: One was the "school of the miniature", which emphasized delicate presentation, *sfumato* techniques in color application, as well as ornamentation; representative grottoes include Caves 419, 420, and 427. The other was the "school of brevity and simplicity", which stressed the use of paint brush with less color and essentially no use of *sfumato*. Typical caves for this school are Caves 276 and 303.

During the Tang Dynasty, due to the highly unified empire, developments in Dunhuang art were almost synchronous with that of the Central Plains. Popular styles in the Central Plains, with the capital city Chang'an as their center, would soon influence Dunhuang, and Dunhuang murals entered their golden age. The artists made skillful use of different methods, depicting figures with different personalities, and created many lively and outstanding works. From the Tang period on, it was rather difficult to distinguish foreign from interior Chinese styles in painting. However, different schools and styles from the Central Plains might have more or less influenced Dunhuang, so that Dunhuang murals underwent a phase of free development of different artistic forms and styles.

Yan Liben, an artist of the Early Tang, painted *Twenty-Four Meritorious Statesmen at*

赢得了很高的声誉。他还创作了表现外国人物的《职贡图》，表现帝王的《步辇图》和《历代帝王图》。如果对比现存于波士顿美术馆的《历代帝王图》以及宋人模刻的《凌烟阁功臣像》（现存陕西省麟游县），可以发现敦煌壁画中就有不少类似的绘画作品。如初唐第220窟东壁、第335窟北壁的维摩诘经变中有帝王图，第323窟佛教史迹画中的国王与大臣形象，第45窟观音经变中的部分人物像等。这些人物形象写实，服装规范与阎立本画中一致，无疑是在阎立本一派画风影响下创作的。由于阎立德、阎立本兄弟在初唐宫廷中先后长期担任负责建筑与装饰的长官（将作大匠），阎立本后来更被提升为右相，参与国家大事。所以，阎氏的绘画风格在全国范围内产生较大的

Lingyan Pavilion and *Eighteen Scholars from the Qin Family* in the spirit of realism, both of which were created by basing the human figures on real people, earning him a great reputation at the time. He also created other paintings, such as *Foreign Dignitaries Presenting Tributes* portraying foreigners, *Devotions in Imperial Carriages* presenting Tubo diplomatic envoys, and *Emperors of the Past Ages* showing the Chinese emperors. Compared with *Emperors of the Past Ages*, currently housed in the Museum of Fine Arts in Boston, and *The Portraits of Meritorious Statesmen at Lingyan Pavilion*, presently kept in Linyou County in Shaanxi Province, a number of similar works can be found among the Dunhuang murals. Noteworthy examples include portraits of emperors in the *Vimalakirti Nirdesa* illustration on the east wall of Cave 220 and the north wall of Cave 335 from the Early Tang, paintings of emperors and the ministers in narrative paintings of Buddhist legends and transmission in Cave 323, and some of the people in the *Avalokitesvara Sutra* illustration in Cave 45. These figures were painted realistically, with a clothing style and standards similar to works by Yan Liben. Influences from Yan's school were evident. The brothers Yan Lide and Yan Liben were officials in charge of architecture and decoration for many years in the Early Tang imperial court, and later, Yan Liben was promoted to Grand Chancellor of the Right, administering national affairs in the legislative bureau, so it is understandable that Yan's style exerted wide influence on paintings all over the nation.

During the High Tang, Wu Daozi, known as the

影响也是很好理解的。

盛唐时期,被称为"画圣"的吴道子活跃于画坛,把中国人物画艺术推向了高峰。苏轼评论唐代的艺术,说"故诗至于杜子美,文至于韩退之,书至于颜鲁公,画至于吴道子,而古今之变,天下之能事毕矣"。说明吴道子在中国绘画史的地位。吴道子在当时长安和洛阳一带的寺院中创作了大量的壁画,其中如地狱变等绘画使观者"腋汗毛耸,不寒而栗"。据说许多屠夫见了长期都不敢再从事屠宰的行当,说明其感染力是很强的。而吴道子创造了兰叶描的技法,"其势圆转而衣服飘举",即所谓"吴带当风"。这种线描的特点在于"用笔磊落"而富于变化,能表现完整的气韵。所以,吴道子奉诏画嘉陵江山水,一日而就。而当时的山水画家李思训画同一题材则用了三个月。由于吴道子的线描水平极高,他常常画

"Saint of Painting", was active in fine art circles, pushing the art of Chinese figure painting to its peak. Su Shi once made a comment on art in the Tang Dynasty, saying: "Therefore, all innovations and transformations of the past and present reach the pinnacle when poetry arrives at Du Zimei, prose at Han Tuizhi, calligraphy at Yan Lugong, and painting at Wu Daozi." Such remarks illustrate the venerated status Wu Daozi holds in Chinese painting. Wu painted a large number of murals in the temples around Chang'an and Luoyang. His *Illustration of Hell* made viewers "sweat from their armpits and tremble with fear, hair standing on end". It was said that many butchers and fishermen feared taking up their trade after they saw his paintings. His works had a powerful appeal. Wu Daozi created the orchid leaf painting technique, by which "the shape is round and smooth and the clothes are floating". His technique was known as "Wu's sashes undulating in the wind". His line drawing was characterized by a "liberality of the paint brush" and rich variety, which was capable of presenting an integrated artistic conception. Thus, when he received an imperial order to paint the landscapes along the Jialing River, he completed the task within a day; it took Li Sixun, the renowned landscape artist of the time, three months to finish the same subject. Because of his supremely high skill in line drawing, it was often the case that he finished the lines first and then asked his students to color them in. But his students did not dare paint over his lines and often

完线描，让弟子们上色；弟子们不敢覆盖了他的线描，常常用淡色，以突出他的线描，于是就形成了重线描而减淡色彩的风格。盛唐以后的敦煌壁画中也出现了很多线描技法优秀的壁画作品，可以看作是吴道子一派的绘画风格。如第103窟维摩诘经变、第217窟龛内南北壁经变画中的人物形象以及第158窟涅槃经变中的人物形象等。

盛唐时期李思训、李昭道父子开创了青绿山水画，以青绿重色表现出富丽堂皇的气象，深受时人喜欢。李思训官至右武卫大将军，人称"大李将军"，而把他的儿子李昭道称为"小李将军"。唐代的评论家说李思训为"国朝山水第一"，可惜他的山水画真迹已经不存。台北故宫有传为李思训的《江帆楼阁图》和传为李昭道的《明皇幸蜀图》，都是后人临摹品。敦煌壁画中有不少青绿山水画，为我们了解李思训一派山水画的原貌

used light colors to highlight them. Thus, the style of stressing lines and reducing colors was formed. After the High Tang, outstanding works were created in Dunhuang murals with the technique of line drawing. They could well be regarded as paintings in Wu's style. Examples are the figures in the *Vimalakirti Nirdesa* illustration in Cave 103, those in the sutra illustrations on the north and south walls of the niche in Cave 217, and in the *Nirvana Sutra* illustration in Cave 158.

In the High Tang, Li Sixun and Li Zhaodao, father and son, initiated the style of blue-green landscapes, producing paintings with an atmosphere of majestic splendor by using heavily saturated colors of blue and green. Their works were widely loved by people of the time. Li Sixun's official court position was Grand General of the Right Guard, so he was known as "Senior General Li", while his son Li Zhaodao was called "Junior General Li". Critics during the Tang claimed that Li Sixun was "second to none in landscapes in our dynasty". Unfortunately none of his authentic works remain today. Some people say that *River Sails and Storeyed Pavilions* was painted by Li Sixun and that *Emperor Minghuang's Journey to Sichuan* was the work of Li Zhaodao. Both paintings are kept in the National Palace Museum in Taipei, but both are actually copies made by later artists. There are, however, many blue-green landscape works among the Dunhuang murals, providing an

提供了依据。莫高窟盛唐第217窟、103窟、148窟、172窟等窟都有不少青绿山水画,特别是第217窟和103窟的《法华经·化城喻品》,具有相对的独立性,山水构图完整,线描劲健,色彩绚丽而不俗,体现出李思训画风的特色。

五代以后的敦煌曹氏政权偏安一隅,与中原的联系时断时续,中原绘画的变化不太容易影响到敦煌。曹氏政权仿照中原王朝的体制,建立了画院。这一时期的莫高窟壁画都由画院的画工制作,缺乏新的变化,逐渐流于形式化而走向衰退。西夏占领敦煌后,新开了一些洞窟,如榆林窟第3窟、第2窟等,反映出传自中原的新型水墨山水画风。

中国美术发展到两宋以后,山水花鸟画

authentic basis for us to get acquainted with the works of Li Sixun's school. At Mogao there are a great many landscapes in Caves 217, 103, 148, and 172 from the High Tang period, especially the sutra illustrations based on the "Chapter of the Parable of the Conjured City" from the *Lotus Sutra* in Caves 217 and 103. They are relatively independent stand-alone works with complete landscape compositions, forceful line drawing, and gorgeous but uncommon hues, which reflect the characteristics of Li Sixun's style.

After the Five Dynasties, the regime of the Cao clan in Dunhuang exercised its sovereignty over the area. Communications with the Central Plains were interrupted so frequently that the painting innovations there had little impact on Dunhuang. However, the Cao rulers imitated the dynasties of the Central Plains, and set up an imperial art academy. All the murals at Mogao from that period were made by painters from the academy, but no new innovations occurred. Gradually, the wall paintings in the caves became formulaic, exhibiting a trend of decline. After Dunhuang was conquered by the Western Xia, new cave temples were constructed, including Caves 2 and 3 at Yulin, whose murals mirrored the new style of ink wash landscapes from the Central Plains.

After Chinese art progressed into the Northern and the Southern Song (1127-1279) dynasties, landscape painting, as well as bird-and-flower painting rose to prominence, taking the place of figure painting. In particular, the literati participated in painting, adding poetry and calligraphy, so that Chinese painting emphasized scholarly erudition.

兴起，取代了人物画的地位，特别是文人参与了绘画，引诗、书入画，使中国绘画更加强调文学性。人们对于绘画的认识、评价往往是重山水而轻人物，重意境而轻造型，形成了中国绘画的新的时尚。明清以后的中国绘画进一步发展着这种趋势。从这个意义上说，敦煌艺术为我们展示出一个与传统理念上的"中国绘画"完全不同的世界，即以人物造型为主的美术，通过完美的人物形象来表现佛、菩萨等佛教尊像，通过描绘人间现实的宫殿、风景等来表现佛教天国的境界，是宗教的想象力与表现的写实性完美结合的艺术。

Interpretation and evaluation of paintings began to attach more importance to landscapes than figures, and more importance to artistic conception than design, shaping a new fashion in Chinese painting, which was further developed during the Ming and Qing dynasties. In this sense, Dunhuang art presents before our eyes a world completely different from the traditional concept of "Chinese painting". It is a world in which the art is based on design, in which the Buddhas, bodhisattvas, and other Buddhist iconography are represented by idealized figures, and in which the Buddhist heavenly realms are revealed by depicting real palaces and landscapes from the mundane world. This world is a perfect combination of religious imagination and realistic portrayal.

参考文献(原文)
Works Cited

[1] 松本荣一.敦煌画の研究(图像篇)[M].东京:东方文化学院东京研究所,1937.

[2] 姜亮夫.敦煌——伟大的文化宝藏[M].上海:上海古典文学出版社,1956.

[3] 潘絜兹.敦煌莫高窟艺术[M].上海:上海人民出版社,1957.

[4] 敦煌文物研究所编.敦煌研究文集[M].兰州:甘肃人民出版社,1982.

[5] 敦煌文物研究所编.中国石窟·敦煌莫高窟(1~5卷)[M].北京:文物出版社,1982~1987.

[6] 敦煌研究院编.敦煌石窟鉴赏从书(1~3辑)[M].兰州:甘肃人民美术出版社,1991~1995.

[7] 伯希和.敦煌石窟笔记[M].耿升,唐健宾译.兰州:甘肃人民出版社,1993.

[8] 段文杰.段文杰敦煌艺术论文集[M].兰州:甘肃人民出版社,1994.

[9] 赵声良,张艳梅.莫高窟[M].北京:知识出版社,1995.

[10] 东山健吾.敦煌三大石窟[M].东京:讲谈社,1996.

[11] 宿白.中国石窟寺研究[M].北京:文物出版社,1996.

[12] 姜伯勤.敦煌艺术宗教与礼乐文明[M].北京:中国社会科学出版社,1996.

[13] 古丽比亚,赵声良.飞天史话[M].台北:如闻出版社,1998.

[14] 季羡林主编.敦煌学大辞典[M].上海:上海辞书出版社,1998.

[15] 敦煌研究院编.敦煌石窟全集[M].香港:商务印书馆,1999~2005.

[16] 荣新江.敦煌学十八讲[M].北京:北京大学出版社,2001.

[17] 史苇湘.敦煌历史与莫高窟艺术研究[M].兰州:甘肃教育出版社,2002.

[18] 樊锦诗,赵声良.灿烂佛宫–敦煌莫高窟考古大发现[M].杭州:浙江文艺出版社,2004.

[19] 贺世哲.敦煌石窟论稿[M].兰州:甘肃民族出版社,2004.

[20] 施萍亭.敦煌习学集[M].兰州:甘肃民族出版社,2004.

[21] 赵声良.敦煌艺术十讲[M].上海:上海古籍出版社,2007.

参考文献(译文)
Translation References

[1] Buswell, Robert E. and Lopez, Donald S. *The Princeton Dictionary of Buddhism*. Princeton: Princeton University Press. 2014.

[2] 季羡林. 敦煌学大辞典. 上海:上海辞书出版社,1998.

[3] 姜秋霞. 敦煌文化关键词. 北京:外语教学与研究出版社,2019.